The Deck

Stories from a Pandemic

By Taylor Watts and Cody Watts

Paperback ISBN: 9798218530990
First paperback edition: November 2024
Library of Congress Control Number: 2024921693

Edited by Nancy Tupper
Cover Design by Madeline Sweeney
Book Design by Madeline Sweeney
Printed in the USA by Village Books
Chloe Hovind, Sean Kearney, Stephanie Dethlefs, and Carolina Santana
Publishing Team, Village Books

Lost Boys Press Ltd.
Bellingham, WA

We dedicate this book to Mom, Dad, and Wilson

The Deck
Stories of a Pandemic

Foreword

This journal was written by chance and circumstance by our then eleven and thirteen-year-old sons, Taylor and Cody Watts. Julie and I did not envision that the daily exercise we asked of them on March 14, 2020, would become a 200,000-word chronicle of both one of the most unimaginable and challenging years in American history and one of the most wonderful years for this family.

Jimmy & Julie Watts

On Friday, March 13, 2020, I picked up the boys from school to the breaking news that Washington State schools were closing for six weeks to curb the spread of a new virus, COVID-19. Surprised families and teachers went home with no plans or expectations for continuing classes. Initially, it was an early and extended spring break. A week later, Washington State issued stay-at-home orders permitting only essential trips away from the home, with only essential services still open for business. Gatherings were prohibited and social distancing was required.

I was working as a firefighter in downtown Seattle, and my wife Julie as a hospice RN in our hometown of Bellingham, Washington. A month prior, Seattle had the first COVID death in the country and was considered the frontline of what would become a pandemic. By mid-March, Washington had five hundred more COVID deaths and thousands of hospitalizations. So, to us, the fears and unknowns of the virus were already familiar. We had been having conversations about the *what-ifs* for weeks, grappling with masking, personal protective equipment (PPE), transmission, contagion, and decontamination.

Julie and I envisioned how best to manage the near future, with the boys home and us working, to keep us all safe and productive and engaged. The four of us created an at-home school day, came up with a class and activities schedule, and shared our hopes and expectations.

This new school day included thirty to sixty minutes or so of each subject: math, science, arts and crafts, reading, physical education, and writing. The schedule wasn't rigid. Our goal was to get through each subject sometime during the day, and we had *all* day. Between the four of us, we shared one laptop, which required flexibility on everyone's part (including mediating the age-old dispute of whose turn it is). As for writing, we asked the boys to journal approximately one page each day about whatever they wanted.

We felt strongly about limiting the duration of time spent on devices for all of us. Outside of schoolwork, the limit was no more than one hour a day of screen time, unless we settled in to watch a movie together.

Julie and I arranged our work schedules such that one of us was always home. As a firefighter and a nurse, with swing shifts available on nights and weekends, we found the flexibility of our jobs a positive.

It is important to remember that, with each passing day and week, none of us knew what was going to happen next, or for how long next was going to last. Everyone's playbook was being written in real time, with no clock on the game. A sense of disarray existed, but we thought we would be ok. The challenges everyone faced felt surmountable, and we believed that in six weeks' time life would return to normal.

However, we soon realized this wasn't going to be the case. I returned home from the firehouse on March 16 to grocery store shelves completely emptied from panic shopping, as well as a knee injury from work, with surgery scheduled for the next day.

As a nation, the social and political fractures quickly became very real. COVID numbers were getting worse, not better. Businesses were not reopening, and kids were not going back to school for the remaining school year. Even the beaches and parks, pools and playgrounds were closed.
The reality was that these challenges and uncertainties would be with us indefinitely.

As Seattle firefighters, we were responding to over three hundred alarms a day in the city, battling COVID, arson, violence, and social unrest on a scale we had never experienced, as well as a dangerous new street drug: fentanyl. Julie's work as a hospice RN was overwhelming, made challenging by PPE shortages, no-visitors policies, and the politics of corporate medicine. For both of us, work shifts were full and long, and made even more difficult by a workforce becoming increasingly divided by the strain of a viral pandemic and a country sickened by politics.

With the arrival of summer came more unexpected news: public schools would remain closed to in-person learning for the following school year, and stay-at-home orders remained in effect. Schools devised a plan to conduct remote learning via live-stream classes. As parents, our biggest concern was the continued education of the boys, with our limited ability to educate them in knowledge and skillsets that surpassed our own. Our other concern was entire school days spent on devices and screens, and we feared the possibility that schools, as we knew them, may never return.

So, we explored all alternative options available to us for schooling, and we discovered an affordable and reputable online private school based out of Utah, with a track record of educating students via a limited amount of time on the computer. A full-time class schedule involved only ten hours of small and interactive live-stream classes per week, followed by out-of class assignments, independent study, and exams. This was all new to us. The boys were cooperative with this prospect, though not excited about it.

As we had been doing, we told the boys we would be right by their side the whole time and help them in any way they needed. One of us would always be home. Some classes they would even be able to take together, and the boys received an added benefit—my parents gifted them each their own new laptop. The academic pace of this online school was more rigorous and demanding than expected, but they handled themselves with courage and an incredibly good attitude.

The boys continued to journal. In many ways, their days were mundane and redundant; in hindsight, they were also remarkable. Most nights, for fun, we all slept outside on the deck. Every day, we ate three meals together, we took our time, and we became so close. We did everything together. For a year and a half, our home was our whole universe, and in it we were, to borrow the words of Cormac McCarthy, each other's world entire.

This narrative journal is their chronicle of that year. It was edited by the wonderful Nancy Tupper (a former middle school teacher) for spelling, punctuation, and general clarity. Otherwise, most of the phrasing and grammar remain as they wrote it. In no instances were names, dates, or places changed.

In September 2021, eighteen months after closure, Washington State returned to in-person education, and the boys, by then an eighth grader and a high school freshman, rejoined their old friends and classmates in Bellingham Public Schools.

Jimmy Watts

Part I
by Taylor Watts

Introduction

Today is March 16, 2020, the day before Saint Patrick's Day. I am eleven years old and my name is Taylor Watts. I am average height and weight and I have blue eyes and dirty blond, shaggy hair. I have a brother named Cody who is thirteen years old, and he is about a quarter inch taller than me and the same weight. My mom's name is Julie, and she is a nurse. My dad's name is Jimmy, and he is a Seattle firefighter. As you can see, both my parents are in the medical field. Right now it is really special and important to be in the medical field because our world is living during a pandemic and there is a disease that is called coronavirus[1], and both my parents take care of the people who have it. It can be hard right now on a lot of people because their jobs might get taken away because you don't want to spread the disease to other people.

The disease is easy to spread, and there is something called the six-feet rule where you need to stay six feet away from everyone at all times unless they are family or you have been quarantining with them. That's when we get into what quarantining is. It is when you don't interact with anyone and you isolate with others who don't go see anyone, and they also stay in one place.

The coronavirus has been going on for two to three months, and since then 185,067 people in the world have tested positive for having the virus. There have been 7,335 deaths from the coronavirus, and at the rate that

---

1 The disease is also known as coronavirus disease 2019 and has been shortened to COVID-19 or COVID.

it's going, it is worse than the flu. And just in the United States of America there have been 4,661 confirmed cases and 89 deaths. I live in Bellingham, Washington, and it is especially dangerous here because there are fifty states and Washington has 48 out of the 89 deaths. If it was an equal number of deaths in the US, then about each state would have around 2 deaths, but Washington state has 48, so it is really serious if you live in Washington.

What I think about this is that if you are worried, then you should stay in your house. If my family and I go into quarantine, then I would love it because my life is awesome and my family is awesome. But some people wouldn't like to go into quarantine, so I want to respect everyone who does not want to go in quarantine. Right now, all stores are closing, and all places are shutting down, but they are delivering food from Amazon, and you cannot get any toilet paper, and no hand sanitizer either, so we're pretty much going into quarantine, and life might be really hard.

All schools are closed for six full weeks, and it's a high chance it's going to be twelve weeks, so then it would be summer and we would be off for twenty-four more weeks, so that would be thirty-six weeks of no school. That's a long time, but in middle schools we have computers, and that lets us email our teachers, and the teachers give us work. I bet half of the kids won't do the work. I am not one of those kids, and I don't just do the work—I also need to work out for forty-five minutes and read for one hour, and I need to make art projects for twenty minutes and do math for twenty minutes. That is not what the average kid does when you have no school. I bet right now 80 percent of the kids will be playing video games or watching YouTube.

I do things besides playing video games and watching YouTube videos. (I still play video games and watch YouTube, but I am more focused on my education and my academic career.) Instead, I want to write about this hard, difficult time, so if anyone thinks they are having a hard time, then just take a second to think of how people feel in this time. If you are reading this in the future, then I would like you to remember that if you are having a good time, to just think of how others might be thinking the opposite of you and how life can be hard but you just need to fight through it. If you get kicked down, get right back up. Don't let yourself or someone bring you down, but if they do, just get back up. Just to let you know, I am not a motivational speaker; it's just a lot easier if you are trying to motivate yourself instead of talking about depressing things.

Let's talk about what can prevent you from getting the coronavirus. Wash your hands daily. I know I have, because my hands feel like sandpaper because they are so dry. What I'm saying is just don't let anything or anyone bring you down, and if they do—you know what, I'm trying to motivate you again! Let's talk about something else.

How about we talk about how I feel about it. I feel not scared as much as scared for others. I am scared for old people who have not good immune systems, because they can get sick easily. That's how I feel about this virus. Also, if you are wondering what quarantine is, it's when you get really sick or have interacted with or touched people with the virus and then you go somewhere that you can't spread it. Here are the things I've been doing over break.

Taylor Watts

Tuesday, March 17, 2020

My dad just had surgery on his knee to rip out part of his meniscus. When my dad's surgery was over, my mom and I decided that we should go pick him up. My brother Cody stayed home to do work. When we got there, my dad was in the hospital bed, covered up to his neck in a gown. When the doctor came in, he told us that it was his last surgery for a long time because they just shut down all surgeries and my dad was the last one, because of the coronavirus. And he said my dad couldn't go back to work as a firefighter for probably six or seven weeks.

They put him in a wheelchair and rolled him down to the lobby and checked him out. When we got home it was dinnertime. After we ate, I started to read. When I finished, my brother and I went outside and played basketball for a long time, and it was really fun.

Wednesday, March 18, 2020

The next day, my dad, my brother, and I told my mom that no matter what she says we are going to sleep outside tonight. She just sighed and said, "Ok." Cody and I sprinted downstairs to get the futon, and my dad wattled his way downstairs. When we got down there, we decided that we would get an extra blanket because it was below thirty degrees outside. You might think we are crazy, but you need to try it and see how awesome it is. Also, we have a fluffy golden retriever to keep us warm. You might think that is all awesome, but there is one downside to sleeping. I have headgear, and one sidenote: It sucks a lot, and when I say "a lot" I mean it. It's like having a piece of metal in your mouth, but that is really what it is. It's a nightmare. Ha! See what I did there? But besides that, my life is so awesome. Meanwhile as I look outside of the window, I see my dad making a bonfire and s'mores.

Thursday, March 19, 2020

In the morning, my dad had an idea that we could make homemade bread, and I said, "I like that idea." Then he said that we could make it ourselves and l said, "What?!" When we made it, I was super surprised how much I loved it and wanted to do it every day.

Later I was drawing a picture of a Seahawk diving for a catch. Then I heard my mom scream, and I asked her, "What?" and she pointed outside on the deck. I was so shocked to see my dad was climbing the fence around the deck and putting up a hummingbird feeder. My mom said she told him that it was the first day of spring, and he has a crazy idea of what to do, and he had surgery the day before.

Friday, March 20, 2020

I looked at the news about the coronavirus, and the numbers have doubled. In one day it went from 7,000 cases to 14,000 cases in the US. This is serious, and when I say that it is serious, I mean it. Cody and I played basketball, and it was so much fun. It was a really close match, but I bet you can probably guess who won. Correct, I did.

Some things about my dog, Wilson: He is a cream-colored golden retriever, he is completely white, and his tail is always wagging. We call his tail a helicopter because it is always wagging, and he has big, brown eyes and a red collar and two floppy ears. I couldn't ask for a better dog. Wilson, you get the best-and-cutest-dog-in-the-world award.

Later that night, my mom and I were outside playing with Wilson when our neighbor came over. His name is Phil. And he is so funny. After about twenty minutes of talking, he told us that his wife is turning sixty-six tomorrow.

The next day, my mom and I made pumpkin bread. After it was out of the oven it smelled like a bakery. Then my mom went on a hike with some friends, and I ate a lot of the pumpkin bread. And my brother asked if I wanted to play basketball. I said, "As long as you don't cry after I kick your butt. Ha!" Then we went outside and played.

When we got on the court, Cody and I discussed the rules. The way we play is, the first to score 21 needs to win by two points. When we started, I was getting crushed, losing 5–0. Then he shot a three-pointer and it was 8–0. Then when I got the ball again, I shot a deep three and it hit the back rim. "No!" I said, but then he got the rebound and dribbled back when he could have made an easy layup. He tried to shoot a three and it missed, and honestly, I was really confused. After a couple of air balls and missed threes, Cody got the ball back and shot a three and made it. By then, my brother was really confident, winning 13–0.

Then I got the ball and went up for a layup. Cody was sprinting to block me, but I pulled the ball back and stepped back and watched him go flying off the court. Then I shot a simple off-the-backboard shot and made it in, 13–2. After about five more minutes, I was losing 18–6. And I was thinking about quitting, but I said to myself, "It's not over till it's over." Surprisingly, I started to come back. Long shot after long shot, I was back in the game, 18–14. Then I shot a three-pointer and Cody shot an air ball way over the backboard.

When I got the ball back, I was dribbling on the side of the court and Cody in frustration shoved me out of bounds. Then he said he was sorry, that he did not mean to do that. If you were wondering what was going on in my head, I was thinking, "Say what?" After one free throw, I shot two three-pointers and won 21–18. "What a comeback," I said.

Saturday, March 21, 2020
In the US this morning, the coronavirus had 26,000 confirmed cases, and now it is three in the afternoon and there are 30,000 cases. And in the entire world this morning, there were 200,000 cases and now there are 220,000 cases. Also, the country with the most cases is Italy, and the US has the second most. Italy has 46,000 cases, and in the US there are 30,000. That's a difference of 16,000. At the rate that it's going, the US is going to have more cases.

Today I went to my neighbors to do yard work and get paid. The people who live there are Donnett and Terry and they are really nice. My brother and I went to their back yard and threw lots of chopped wood into their truck, and after we finished Donnett drove the truck over and we took the wood out and put it under their patio. And when we were done, she gave us each twenty-five dollars, ten dollars an hour. Then we rode our bikes home and ate some lunch. Then I went on the couch and read my book.

I went downstairs to check on my dad in his shop room, as we call it. The shop room is a small room where my dad makes fly rods. A fly rod is the same thing as a fishing rod, just a different name and it takes about eighty hours to make one. He does not do it all at one time; he spreads it out and maybe spends a couple hours working on it a day. The reason that he is making one right now is because he is a firefighter, one of the firefighters working at his station is leaving, and he decided that he wanted to make him one as a goodbye gift. And all the firefighters pitched in to pay for it. Then Cody and I went outside to play basketball.

Later that day, I was sitting on the couch thinking of what I should do, and I walked over to the table where we have all of our art stuff and decided that I should find all the different types of blue crayons and draw with them, lightest to darkest. When I finished finding all of the different types, I put them in order of lightest to darkest, and I took a piece of paper and split it into thirteen different columns. When I finished that, I started to draw on the paper. Then when I finished, it looked very cool. In the art stores they have colors lightest to darkest, and that is what it looked like.

Sunday, March 22, 2020
My brother and I went outside to play basketball to 21. It was 9–4, I was winning. Then Cody shot a layup and made it, and it was 9–6. Then our neighbor came over on his hoverboard and wanted to play basketball with

us, but we didn't really want to play with him because of quarantine. Then right after he asked us if we could play, my mom walked out and said that she needed to do laundry and needed us to change into cleaner clothes. And I said aloud, "Maybe we could play another time."

Later that day, I went downstairs. My brother was downstairs playing video games and my mom was in the living room and my dad was downstairs making fly rods—and he is almost finished. The steps to make one are, you take a piece of bamboo and cut it into six large pieces, and with a hand plane you scrape off the part of bamboo into a triangle. A hand plane is a small blade that scrapes slivers off the bamboo. After you cut all six pieces into small triangles, you take another piece of bamboo, then repeat the process again, but you make the pieces of bamboo smaller. This might sound crazy, but you repeat it again but smaller—this is not a misspelling, I am serious.

Later that day, a package came in the mail and it had two math books in it, one for me and one for Cody. We opened it and both started to do math. After I did a page or two, I told my dad I was done and he asked if I checked the answers and I shook my head saying no. Then I checked in the back of the book to see if I got it right and I was really frustrated, ha ha, because it was right, even though I had no idea what I was doing, so I decided that I would just go outside and play basketball.

My brother and I were talking upstairs in the living room. I said, "What is that smell?" And I walked into the kitchen and my dad was making homemade granola. Then Cody and I walked back downstairs and stayed down there for a long time.

Monday, March 23, 2020

My great-great-grandma made a famous recipe for cinnamon rolls and they are so good. The recipe is over one hundred years old, and today my dad decided to try and make his first-ever batch of cinnamon rolls. We made the bread and took it out of the oven and then took pieces of the bread out of the bowl and rolled them into, like, snakes and dipped them in melted butter and then rolled them in cinnamon and sugar, then rolled it into many small circles, then put them into a pan. We baked them in the oven for one hour. One hour later, we took them out of the oven and—wait, wait, wait! Why are the cinnamon rolls so big? Oh, my god, the cinnamon rolls are about six inches squared. That is so big. Because they rise.

Cody and I need to do a list of things each day, since we have no school. One of them is that we need to work out, and when I say that I mean lift weights and do planks and push-ups and pull-ups. I went downstairs and lifted weights. When I finished, I came upstairs, and my mom gasped and said that we are on lockdown. Lockdown is where you need to not leave your house or go in public!

Later I tried the cinnamon rolls, and they were the best cinnamon rolls that I have ever had, so good. They melted in my mouth with a hard outside and a soft inside. After I finished, I was already thinking of how hard it will be to not finish eating them. It would be the end of my life if we eat them all, but how could I survive without cinnamon rolls? But the advantage is that we could make more, and now I am thinking about making the next batch of cinnamon rolls. Now I am thinking of finishing the second batch!

Wait! What was that? That was thunder. I looked outside and it was thunder, and it was hailing like crazy. After about an hour or two, the ground was covered in hail and the basketball court was filled with small bits of hail. What a crazy day it has been.

Right now in the US, there are 43,000 people who have tested positive that we know of and 560 deaths, and that is a lot of people. In New York there are 20,000 cases and 160 deaths, and in Washington there are 2,000 cases and 110 deaths. New York has ten times more cases than Washington, which is a big difference. And a fun fact: They think coronavirus comes from bats. I am not sure why, but no animals have gotten the coronavirus, even though it comes from an animal. Is it just me or is that really confusing?

Later that night, my family watched a movie called *JoJo Rabbit*, about kids living during World War II and about the Nazis and Hitler. It was a really good movie and I will not spoil it, but it has lots of action and humor and a good message. Such a good movie.

Tuesday, March 24, 2020

Our neighbor Bryce is nine years old, and he has an older brother named Nathan who is fourteen, and let me tell you something about Nathan. He looks like the tallest kid ever, and not just tall—he looks like he hasn't ever cut his hair and his voice is so deep it sounds like a man's voice.

So, when they came to this neighborhood, I was really happy that I could play with the kids because there are not that many kids in our neighborhood. Then they got a new dog and named it Porter, and he always somehow gets out of their house and comes to our doormat and stays there for a very long time.

Some things that happened today are my mom made bread for the first time, and it was so good, and today it was raining for half of the day, and then the sun came out, and my mom said that we could watch a movie but she wasn't sure what movie. Something almost better is that we are going to sleep outside with Wilson. The reason why I get so happy about that is because Wilson can't go on the carpet or go on the couch or bed, and my room and Cody's rooms have carpet, so we can't sleep next to him in our room.

Wednesday, March 25, 2020

I woke up to the birds chirping and my dog next to me on his back, asleep, and I petted his soft fur. My brother and my dad were still asleep and my mom was inside, also asleep. I walked inside and looked at the news: The Seahawks got a great wide receiver. Then I looked at what was happening with the coronavirus: In the United States there were 65,000 cases, and if you remember, on the first page, I said that there were about 5,000 cases in the US, but now it's thirteen times more than it was eleven days ago. And I thought 5,000 was a lot.

This morning I saw that there were two cinnamon rolls left. I had one and let Cody have the other. My dad made another batch of cinnamon rolls and gave half of it to the neighbors. Last night we watched a great movie called *The Other Guys* and it was one of a kind. Also, it was very interesting and really funny.

My mom has a bike trainer, which is a bike moving in one place. It is so complicated to set up that I don't really understand it, but I rode on it for about an hour or two. I was so tired after I did it, and it was so much fun. I want to do it every day.

Since this break I have made about ten loaves of bread and four pans of cinnamon rolls, and now we are making homemade bagels. When my dad was a kid, he worked at a bakery for two days and then quit because you needed to stay up overnight and make bagels so they were fresh in the morning for customers. After two nights, my dad was like *that was enough.*

Also, my mom and I were gardening today, pulling weeds and cutting branches. After we finished, I came inside and my mom and my dad went on a hike in the woods on Galbraith Mountain, where our house is, and I started drawing. I was drawing parts of the movie we watched the night before.

Thursday, March 26, 2020

It was a nice day. It was pouring down rain, and wherever you stepped you would step in a puddle. I am being sarcastic. But last night we slept outside, and it was really nice. I woke up to birds singing and l looked to both sides of me, and Cody and Jimmy (my dad) were already inside. I looked at my watch and it was 6:20, so I decided to get up, and I walked inside. Julie (my mom) was getting ready to go to work. If you were wondering what my parents' jobs are, my mom is a nurse, and it is stressful because people that have the coronavirus go to her workplace if they are short of breath or can't breathe. That is the main symptom for coronavirus, and cough, and if you have a fever. My dad is a fire fighter, and it can also be stressful because he doesn't just go on calls for fires, he also goes on calls if someone is really sick and can possibly have the coronavirus, and that can spread to the fire fighters, and then they have to go into quarantine. So, both of my parents could get the coronavirus, and it's dangerous if you work to help people. That is called working in the medical field, and some examples of jobs that work in the medical field are nurse, firefighter, doctor, vet, dentist, paramedic, and surgeon.

And today when my mom was at work, my dad and brother and I went on the trail because our neighbor said that they made a big hidden fort out of branches and it is huge. So, we tried to find it, and after about an hour of looking we almost gave up, but I said, "I have a dream that—"

"No! you are not saying a speech," my brother interrupted me. So we looked where we looked before but found nothing, and when we got back it was two o'clock. I looked at my phone and it said that the US has 83,000 cases and China has 81,000. So, the US has the most cases in the whole world, and this isn't good at all.

And before my mom left for work, she asked us to go to the store and get hamburger buns. We all went for a different approach and made homemade bread and the hamburger buns ourselves, and they turned out so great. When she got home, she loved it. Those were the best hamburger buns I have ever had.

My brother and I played a game where we took a hat and threw it at each other, playing tag, and it was so much fun. When we were done, we decided that we should watch a show, so we watched *Little House on the Prairie*, and when we were done we went to bed. Sadly, my mom said that we need to sleep in our own beds tonight, and it was not fun at all compared to sleeping outside. She said that we can another night.

Friday, March 27, 2020

I woke up in my bed upstairs, and I was sad I missed waking up to birds chirping. When I went downstairs, I saw my mom eating breakfast and my dad on the couch relaxing. I heard my brother yelling for me to come downstairs, so I did, and when I got down there he was playing *Madden 20*, a video game, and he was playing as the Broncos and told me to watch him because he made a good catch. I said, "Cool." I walked back upstairs, and as

I was walking I tripped on the stairs and winced in pain. My back has been messed up, and my hips are not leveled right, and that caused really bad back pain, and it has never been as bad as this.

Later that day, I was sitting on the couch, looking at the news on the coronavirus, and in the US we just got 100,000 confirmed cases. I heard my mom say, "Phil is saying hi to Wilson." If you remember, Phil is our neighbor, and also something I did not tell you is that Phil's daughter's name is Katie and she has a two-year-old girl named Avie, and she is so cute. Now Katie is having another girl and they have not picked out a name yet. Another funny thing is that Katie was Cody's fourth grade teacher, and now she is a tech specialist. Then we went outside to say hi and he had Avie. She was so cute, and it was so hard because of the coronavirus. We couldn't get close to her. It was so hard, and it will be even harder when there are two of them.

My mom told me that we have the ingredients to make ranch dressing, so we made it. I asked her if we had pizza, and she said that we don't, so I got an idea that we could make our own pizza bread crust and then use red sauce and then shredded cheese. So we did! And when finished it was great, and we dipped the pizza in the ranch dressing, and it was good. There is a restaurant we love that has pizza. When I was little I got ranch dressing on my plate and dipped my pizza in it and loved it so much that from then on I always said "dippa dip" for more ranch—and that is what we always say to this day when we want ranch with our pizza.

Saturday, March 28, 2020

My brother's room is right across from mine. Like, if I walked straight out of my room and kept walking straight, I would walk right into his room. There's a hallway with doors on the left and right sides, then stairs to the main floor and also a downstairs, and there is a big open space and two different rooms. One room is a guest room and one has a ping pong and pool table, and it is fun to play both of them.

When I woke up, I walked right out of my room, and my brother walked out at the same time I did, and when we got downstairs Wilson was sitting waiting for us, wagging his tail. I looked at the update on coronavirus and there were 105,000 cases. I went downstairs to play *Madden* and played for half an hour and then did some schoolwork, and then my computer died. I went to charge it and then I saw Wilson. I set down the computer and said hi to Wilson, and my mom called my name and told me to eat breakfast and then do my PT (stands for physical therapy) and if you are wondering why I do PT, it is because I have back issues and my back hurts and if I don't do it, over time it will hurt more and more. Then I brushed my teeth, and my dad told me we are going to go on the trail behind our house to hike, so I did that and came down, and my brother and mom and dad were ready.

When we got out of the house, we ran about thirty yards to where the trail started. If you are wondering where we hike, we hike on Galbraith, and it is awesome because it is right behind our house. We don't even need to drive, just walk for thirty yards and we are there.

When we got back, I looked at my Fitbit and it said that I had walked 15,000 steps. Wilson went straight to his bowl of water and drank it for a couple minutes. Then I did some work around the house. I vacuumed all the carpet and that took about forty minutes, and yes, we have lots of carpet—on all of the floors except part of the main floor.

And later that day, I got the idea to rearrange my room, so I did. I took my bookshelf and it fit perfectly in my closet, and then I moved my dresser to the corner of my room. My family and I took a lot of our things that we never touch and gave them to Goodwill. Goodwill is a store that you give your things to for free, and then they give it to the people that could use it for a small amount of money. So basically, we give our things away for people to use.

Then I started reading a great book about two identical brothers. One of the brothers had his arm amputated when we was four. His twin went to the NFL and played cornerback for the Seattle Seahawks, and his brother did not have much hope, because no one would want him in the NFL, because he had only one arm. Somehow the Seahawks drafted him anyway, so he could play with his brother! Read that book. It is called *Inseparable* by both brothers Shaquem and Shaquill Griffin. It's really great.

Sunday, March 29, 2020

This morning when I woke up, I looked around and it looked so weird because the day before I switched my room around. I looked at the clock and it was 7:30, and every morning I wake up at six. I was super surprised that I woke up at that time, and when I got downstairs I could tell my mom and dad were also surprised I woke up that late. I went downstairs to see Cody and he was playing *Madden*. I asked if I could play when he was done, and he said yes.

When Cody was done, I played a very intense game. At half time I was losing 7–0. I kicked a long field goal and missed, and I lost. I was so sad, and when I played my next game I was also losing 7–0 at half time, and it stayed that score until there were thirty seconds left, and I got sacked with no time outs left, so I did a hurry up, and with ten seconds left I got to the ten yard line and got out of bounds with one second left. I threw a touchdown pass and went for two, and Russell Wilson ran it in for the touchdown, and I won the game by one point!

Later I was reading a book called *Inseparable*. If you remember from yesterday, it's the book I read for an hour, and it was so good. I was so sad because I was almost finished with the book and I wanted to reread it, again and again. It has been one of the best books that I have ever read, and also it is cool because I have a brother and we both like football.

And that night, my mom told me that I was going to make dinner for the family once a week, and Cody too, once a week. We would each make dinner for everyone. Later that day my dad made bread and we used it for pizza crust. I made the pizza, and it was funny because it was put on a pan, so the bottom of the pizza was not cooked at all. Whenever you pulled out a pizza, all of the crust would fall right out, and it was super funny and happens every single time.

Later that night, we decided that we were going to watch a movie. We were going to watch a movie about surfers, but it was fifteen dollars if you wanted to watch it, so we did not watch it. I was sad, hoping that the next day we could watch a movie. I crossed my fingers.

Monday, March 30, 2020

That morning, I woke up at five o'clock and heard some rattling. I went to the window. It was raining super hard and the window was hit with rain and looked like a waterfall with water streaming down the window fast. I went back to bed, and when I woke up it was six in the morning, so I went back to bed again. I woke up for the third time and it was seven in the morning, so I walked downstairs and said hi to Wilson and Mom and Dad and Cody. I went to the kitchen and ate some cereal, and my mom got a great idea to go on the trail. I said yes, and Cody said nope and went back downstairs.

When we got on the trail, I went in front. Something interesting is that Wilson is a golden retriever and they are known to go with the hunter, stay in front, and scare a group of birds while the hunter stays behind and shoots the birds, and the dog gets it and retrieves it for its owner. But Wilson does not hunt animals.

When we got back, I was exhausted, so I went downstairs and played some video games and came back up. My mom got an idea to make pancakes, so we did, and they were super good, maybe the best that I have ever had. When I finished my fifth pancake, I did some reading.

My dad's friend told him to play this game with us. This is how it worked. You take three dice and roll them, and with those numbers you need to use addition, subtraction, multiplication and on and on. Then you need to find all ways to use the numbers so you can make from one to ten. And my dad also got two different board games that involved math, and I can't wait to see what games they are.

And just for an update, in the US there are 160,000 cases, and it is going up a lot every day.

Then my brother and dad and I went outside and played Around the World. If you don't know what that is, it is a basketball game that you shoot from multiple places and see who can make all of them first. And it was intense. I was on my last shot, and I missed and went back to the beginning. My brother went all the way to the last shot, and if he missed, he lost. He decided to stay and wait to take his shot and let me go, so I did. I made all eleven shots in a row and won the game, and that is how you play around the world.

Later that night, my mom said that we could sleep outside, and I was so happy I set half of the deck beds up before Cody did anything.

Tuesday, March 31, 2020
When I woke up, I sat up and looked at my watch. It was seven in the morning, so I got up and looked around, and I was in my room. So I walked downstairs and asked my dad how I got into my room. He said he didn't know and was wondering where I went last night. Then I asked Cody and he said the same thing. My mom said she did not know either. Then I thought for a second. I sleepwalk sometimes, and sometimes I kick my feet in my sleep and move a bunch, and I also walk around and into things sometimes, and I make weird sounds sometimes, and my parents and my brother always get annoyed when we sleep outside because sometimes I do weird things. And then we decided that I walked upstairs and slept in my room for whatever reason and I don't even remember it.

Here are a couple things that I did in my sleep in the past that are really funny. When I was three years old, we discovered that in our house there was mold and so we needed to throw all of the things in the house away. Those things included my baby blanket and all of our beds and couches and a lot of other things, and the reason that we had mold is because one of the people that were inspecting the house screwed up and said it was ok. So, for a year we didn't live here while they fixed everything. My parents' friends, who have a boy named Sawyer in my grade and a girl named Natalie a year older than Cody, let us live in their house for a year because they were going to Washington, DC, for that year. I slept in Sawyer's room. Cody slept in Natalie's, but he hated it so slept in the room with me mostly. I was only three years old and a funny thing that happened is that their dad came to see how things were going, and my dad and Cody and Steve (the dad) were sitting at the counter eating hamburgers, and I came in, but I was sleepwalking and went right into the kitchen where they were and pulled down my pants and peed on the floor. And that had never happened before and it never happened again.

Another sleepwalk story is in the middle of one night I walked downstairs and picked up my phone and took a picture of the moon. How I know that is, in the morning, I looked at my photos. There was a picture of a moon from one in the morning, but I don't remember this.

And another one is when I was in Hawaii. It was ten at night, and I walked into my parents' room and got into the bed. My dad told me to go back to my bed, and I said, "This is my bed."

And he said "No, it is not."

Then I said, "Oh, you are right." And I walked back into my room. And in the morning my dad told me this story, but I don't remember.

And another time that we were in Hawaii, I banged on the wall and yelled, "Where is the bathroom?"

And my dad led me to the bathroom and said, "It is right here Taylor." And he went back to bed.

And then I did the same thing and banged on the door and yelled "Where is the bathroom?" Then I went back to bed. In the morning my dad told me what I did in the middle of the night, and I don't remember.

So those are the most extreme things that I have done in my sleep. Also, I have woken up on the couch about five times, and once I woke up and was lying in the middle of the stairway. So those are my sleepwalking stories.

Wednesday, April 1, 2020

I woke up to Cody and my dad talking, and I looked at my watch. It was April 1. You know what that means—April Fool's Day. So I sat in my bed thinking of what pranks I could do that would be harmless, and then I got an idea that I could take Cody's mattress and flip it horizontal. He has a queen bed, so it would be harder to put together.

So that is what I did. I went into his room, right across the hall from mine, and I took his mattress and flipped it, and when I was done, I walked downstairs and said hi to my dad. My mom was at work and Cody was downstairs playing video games. I told my dad what I did, and he just laughed. Then I went to find my phone and picked up Cody's. I got an idea to change his lock screen to poop image for a prank, and I did. You should have seen his face when he saw both of the pranks.

Another prank that I did was not really a prank, just mainly for the person that found it to laugh. I took a carton of eggs and drew a smiley face on all of them, then flipped them over. That was the last prank that I did for the rest of the day.

Then I looked at my phone and went to the news. I saw that there are now 200,000 cases, and that means that in five days 100,000 more people got infected with the coronavirus. On March 27 I said that there were 100,000 people with the coronavirus, and that was five days ago.

Right now the coronavirus is really bad, because in California all of the schools are not going back in till next year, so that might also happen in Washington. I miss my friends at school. You can't even have friends over, because you need to stay six feet away and they might bring germs into the house and that would be really bad. There is one kid that, when I was still at school, had a really bad cough that sounded like a cat on a chalkboard. Everyone was saying that he had the coronavirus. I might be repeating myself, but it sounded super bad, and he was squinting every time he coughed, because it hurt his throat. And I do not want that.

Thursday, April 2, 2020

This morning I walked downstairs and said hi to Cody and Dad, and my mom was leaving for work. Cody and I went downstairs to play *Madden*, and in the middle of our game my dad called our names and yelled to look outside. It was snowing super hard, and I was so happy. I sprinted upstairs and looked at my phone. It said that it would stop snowing in an hour or two. Then I told Dad and Cody, and they were both happy too.

Later that day, I did schoolwork, and then my dad told me that Jason (our neighbor) said that we could all go on the trail together and stay six feet apart. They had made a very big fort, hidden up on a mountain, and they were going to show it to us. It was pouring down rain, so we didn't go, but we decided we could still go on the trail by ourselves, and we did. When we got back, I went on the couch and relaxed for about forty minutes, reading a book that is called *Cristiano Ronaldo*, and he is a soccer player, one of the best. The book is about how he grows up poor and how he learns to play. It's very inspirational.

When I finished my schoolwork, my dad made cinnamon rolls, three batches, and gave one to our neighbors the McGerrs, one to Donnett and Terry, and one for ourselves. They were better than all the other batches we made in the past. I asked my dad why, and he said that it was because he made the icing differently. I told him to always make it that way.

Cody and I started to make these cool photos, and this is what it was like. So, we took a tripod (a tripod is something to holds your phone straight, so it will not move at all) and we set it up and took multiple photos of ourselves and then edited it so it looked like there were multiples of us in one picture. It ended up looking really cool.

Then at the end of the night, Cody and I played *Madden*, and it was close. There was one second left and we were tied, 28–28, and I threw the ball as far as I could. It was incomplete, and the game went into overtime, and I was the Chiefs and Cody was the Seahawks. Cody got the ball with three minutes left, and he threw it to DK Metcalf for a touchdown. He won the game, and I said, "Good game!" and walked upstairs.

My dad told us that Jason came over and brought us fresh homemade pretzels, and they were so good. Then I looked at my phone, and it said that the next day it was supposed to snow for eleven hours. I was super excited, hoping that we could sleep outside even in the snow!

Friday, April 3, 2020

That night, sadly, we did not sleep outside. But my mom is not working for a week and my dad is off for two more weeks, so I hope that maybe we could still sleep out in the snow. I am crossing my fingers.

Cody and I made a funny iMovie. An iMovie is an app where you can put videos together and make a movie. My brother and I made one and this is how the story went. It started with Cody with the camera on him, and he said, "Hello! Today we are going to be interviewing a man who we think has a wife who stole a lot of masks, and we are going to interview him now."

"Hi, are you Taylor?" Cody asked.

"Yes" I said.

"Do you have a wife?"

"Yes," I said, and he asked if she had the coronavirus. I said, "Yes."

Then he ran and grabbed my "wife" and ran away. I tackled him and grabbed my wife, and that is the end. Remember, this is not real. We just made it up.

Then we made a couple of iMovies of hide-and-seek, and that was fun. After a couple of times doing that, we took a break. My dad and Cody and I started playing monopoly. This is how the night went, and we are going to sleep outside.

Saturday, April 4, 2020

When I woke up in the morning, I could not get up. I was so comfortable waking up on the deck, my favorite place to be in the morning, and I looked around me. My mom was inside, and my dad had his blankets over his head, and Cody was fast asleep. I told Wilson to come. And he came and laid next to me, and it was so cute, and after about ten minutes Cody went inside and it was only my dad and me and, of course, Wilson. After twenty minutes, I heard the deck door open and it was Dad. I was so confused. There was a lump next to me, and I looked under the blankets, and it was my mom. I was like, *What the heck?*

I went inside and my mom came inside about fifteen minutes later. I asked her if she slept well, and she said yes. It snowed the night before and was supposed to get under thirty degrees, and she still stayed outside all night. I was really surprised because she usually does not stay out there all night. I'm really hoping that we can sleep outside the next night, because remember, my whole family was not going to work or school for the next week!

Here is an update on the coronavirus. Today it went up to 300,000 cases in the US, and two days ago it was at 200,000 cases in the US. On the news, it said that 630 people died of the coronavirus in New York in one day, which is a lot of people.

Today our family went on a hike. and it was fun. Surprisingly, it didn't rain or snow at all. The other day, when it snowed, I took a little bowl and set it outside when it was hailing, and it filled up with hail. I let it melt, and this might sound weird, but I drank it. To be honest, it was the best water that I have ever had in my whole entire life.

Remember, I am turning twelve on April 25, and my family keeps a chart on our wall in the garage, and every year on each of our birthdays, we mark how tall we are. Cody's and my birthdays fall six months and four days apart, and that is about half of a year, so every half a year we mark how tall we are. It started with my third birthday, when we moved into our house, and it is funny because we also see how tall and how much Wilson weighs. His birthday is on December 12, and that is funny because December is the twelfth month and he is born on the twelfth day and the Seattle Seahawks' number is twelve and the quarterback's name is Russell Wilson and Wilson is my dog's name and I am the one that put that all together a long time ago!

At the end of the night, I made pizza and the dough, and it was super good. I had also made ranch dressing and it was super good— better then all of the other times that I made it—and after I ate that, my dad and I went to Fred Meyer to pick up what we call a ClickList. A ClickList is where you order your food online and go to a parking place and they come out and put the groceries in the back of your car. It was a Saturday night. There was no one anywhere on the streets, and the reason for that is because there are no restaurants open and not many places that you can go for food, and it was super weird.

Sunday, April 5, 2020

This morning I woke up and Wilson was right next to me, outside on the deck. I lifted my covers and told Wilson to come, and he did. He walked over and laid right next to me, and I took the covers and put them over him and went back to sleep. I woke up at seven and no one was there, so I took Wilson out of the covers, and we went inside and said hi to my mom, my dad, and Cody, who was downstairs playing video games. When I went downstairs, I said hi and he said that I could go on and play a game. So that is what I did.

So our neighbor Jason has two kids, named Silas and Luke. Luke is two years younger than me, and Silas is one year younger, and they are nice. Silas and Luke and their dad Jason made a super big fort out of sticks and trees in the woods, and they gave us a map to find it, and we found it after about ten minutes. It was super cool and super big, and in order to be allowed to go in the fort you need to add something to it to make it better. That is the rule and that is what we did. I found two different sticks and one bigger stick, and that stick had a big hole in it, probably the size of a golf ball, and I put them both into the hole of the big stick and made a cross, and I set it on the side of the fort. Cody added some larger sticks to make it more durable and it was cool.

Tuesday, April 7, 2020

This morning I woke up happy, and I wanted to have lots of fun. I did have lots of fun, and here is what I did today. First of all, I walked downstairs. My mom and dad were on the couch talking and I asked if they have been playing Monopoly. They said no. My mom and dad were both winning when the whole family was playing Monopoly yesterday, and Cody and I were both out. My mom had, like, Boardwalk and Park Place, and they are the two best properties in the game, and she had, like, five hundred dollars more. They ended up playing for the next half hour and here is how it went:

It started with my mom. She landed on one of my dad's hotels and had to pay him almost all of her money. After about ten more minutes of going back and forth, my dad did not even have half of the amount of money mom did, and my mom was super happy. Then twice in a row my mom landed on his hotel, and that is how the game ended. My mom lost, even though she should not have, and you should have seen her face when he said how much money she needed to pay him!

19

After I ate breakfast, I set up another game of Monopoly. I had a new strategy, and it was to only buy houses on the expensive side of the board and to spend just a little amount of money on cheaper houses, because if I land on an inexpensive house that someone owns, then I will still be in the game. After about forty minutes of playing this style, my dad got forced out and I was feeling pretty confident on winning, but it was still going to be hard.

Cody and I played hide-and-seek. We both had cameras, and we told the camera recording where we were going and what our strategies were, and after the game of hide-and-seek we would send each other the videos and make an iMovie. The other day we made a video called *Stupid and Stupider*. There is a movie called *Dumb and Dumber*, and it is about two people who prank each other, but they are the stupidest pranks ever. Like, one of them got put into a wheelchair and was in it for life when he was really joking, and he wasted twenty years of his life on a prank. He also could not walk, and it was super funny how it turned out. You might see us making lots of iMovies in the future.

We also slept outside and saw something weird. There were forty satellites going in the same direction, and we counted about sixty more. And we still do not know why, but we did figure out that in November, sixty satellites were exported into the sky in the same direction. And that is what we think we saw, but we are not sure. It was the coolest thing that I have ever seen in the sky, but also crazy.

Wednesday, April 8, 2020
I woke up at 6:20, and Wilson was sitting at my feet and on my blanket, so I did not have that much blanket. Then I looked over, and my mom was the only other person outside. Cody and Dad were already inside. I told Wilson to come over, in between my mom and me, and he came over and got on his back and was kicking his feet in the air and was super happy. Wilson is a really fluffy golden retriever, but his parents are white, so he is called a golden retriever cream, and I think that golden retriever creams are cuter than a golden retriever.

My parents surprised us with Wilson on Christmas day a few years ago. This is how it played out. So, it started after we opened all of our Christmas presents. My parents said ,"Oh, we almost forgot! One more present!" when they really didn't forget. They walked into their room and grabbed a huge box and gave it to Cody and me.

When we opened it, the first thing I said was, "It's a doggy chew toy," and I was clueless that we were getting a dog.

But then my brother said, "Are we getting a dog?" to my parents. And they said, "Yes!"

I ran across the living room, super happy, and I just jumped into the air and hit the ground. It is a hardwood floor, and it was super loud, and my parents were just laughing at me, and my brother was still looking in the box, confused. Now Wilson is two years old and you might be wondering why I remember this word for word. It is because my parents took a video of this on the laptop so I could watch it as many times as I wanted to, and I still wonder why I just jumped into air like the air was going to catch me. Even I know there is no possible way that the air would catch me. And that is the story of when we got Wilson Watts!

Later that day, my dad and I went on the trail. I have a backpack, and I was collecting flat rocks because I was building a tower and seeing how tall I can get it to stack. After the trail hike, our very nice neighbor was finishing her walk too. Her husband is Phil and her name is Sue, and we talked for about thirty minutes.

Thursday, April 9, 2020

That morning, I woke up outside and looked at the clock. It was 6:27. I walked inside and it was really quiet. My brother was on his phone and my dad was reading a book and my mom was in her room asleep. I went outside and said hi to Wilson. We played fetch once and he did not return the ball, even though retriever is in his genes. I walked over to my stack of rocks and put my hand on the top and moved it back and forth. It was rocking and that means that if it was windy, it would fall over, and I did not want that. So, on the trail the day before, I had grabbed about ten super small rocks that are paper thin and about half an inch by half an inch, and it was perfect. When I rocked it back and forth, I stopped at an angle where it was tilted to the side and I slid the rock right in the little crack where it was unstable. After I did that with about five of the rocks, it would not rock back and forth at all. Then I took about three more rocks and put them on top, and it was perfect. After doing that for about ten minutes, I went inside.

You might be wondering what the rock stack looks like. It started with one big rock that is about one foot by one foot, and I took three rocks, two inches by two inches, and I set them side by side on the big rock. They weren't stacked on top of each other. They were all in separate piles, you could say, and on each of those separate piles there were about ten rocks stacked. So it was on the big rock and three piles about four inches tall. Then I took a big flat rock and I set it on all of the three piles, so it was one big pile again. Then I took two long skinny rocks and I put one on each side of the

21

big rock, so there were now two different piles. And I put about five more rocks on top of that, and that is how much I have done so far. Over the break I will be continually putting more and more rocks on it.

Also, here is some crazy news. I heard I am not going back to school for the rest of the year. That means I am not going to school until the end of August, and that is about five more months. I was super shocked when I heard this, and I was happy and I was also sad, because I would miss my friends. I was still happy, but sad.

Friday, April 10, 2020

I woke up on the deck and it was super cold, so I went inside and looked at the clock. It was seven thirty, and I was like, that isn't right at all. I was surprised that I slept in that late. My mom did not sleep outside, because she needed to go to work. She rode her bike to the hospital, and it was six miles and really cold and dark. And she also would come home at eight o'clock, and it would be completely dark and super cold.

Cody and I went behind the house to the back yard. There is a pond, and we skip rocks across the pond, and it is super fun. Cody said that if I can skip a circular rock then I get one dollar. He gave me a circular rock and I skipped it, and he said double or nothing and I said ok. He gave me another rock and I skipped it, and then he said triple or nothing. He gave me a rock and I skipped it. Then he gave up and Cody gave me three dollars.

Cody made a rock stack too, but smaller. He found six rocks and glued all of them together and then there was a stack. It was about half a foot long, and it was cool. I decided that I would make another one the next day.

Today we decided that we would do an Easter egg hunt the next day because my mom will be working on Easter. On Easter, my parents would get eggs, and at eight at night, with flashlights, we would do a second egg hunt. And I could not wait because my grandparents also got us about twenty eggs to also hide, for my parents to find, and we would do a hunt too. I wanted to do it today!

Tonight my brother made ranch and I made pizza, and it was super good. If I did not tell you before, I love this place that has pizza, and it also has this ranch dressing that is super good. My mom somehow got the ingredients, and we started making it ourselves, and it ended up way better than that place, and that is the same ranch Cody made. After we made that, I made ice cream, homemade style, and it ended up great. It was ready right when my mom got home, and she loved it too. I cannot wait till I can make it again.

Saturday, April 11, 2020

I woke up and the blankets were over my head. I was wondering why it was super dark, and then I realized why and took the blankets off my head. But it was super bright, so I put the blankets back over my head. I walked inside about a half hour later, and Cody was still outside. Both my parents were on the couch having coffee. I came over and sat down with them and we talked for ten minutes, and Cody came in from outside, with Wilson. I said hi to Wilson and Cody. Then I sat back on the couch.

Later that day, Cody and I were playing tag. We played tag outside for, I swear, two hours. When we stopped, we went in the basement while my parents hid the eggs. I know it is not Easter, but my mom is working on Easter and Easter Eve, so we did it early. During the egg hunt they hid fourteen different eggs across the property. Our property is really big. After they hid them, the ones I found were under the wheelbarrow that was upside-down, and one on the side of my dad's car, and one inside of a tree trunk, and one in a bush. Also, I found one in between two big rocks. Another one inside of a tree trunk, and the last one was in a fern. Those are all of the places that I found the eggs. My parents said we would do another egg hunt on Easter Day, and I was excited about that too.

That night we had a bonfire and s'mores, and we also went into the hot tub. My birthday is on the twenty-fifth, and that is in about two weeks, and I couldn't wait for my birthday. We decided that we would just do a family birthday, not with friends, because we couldn't, because of the coronavirus. The thing that I want for my birthday is a gift card to my favorite restaurant, and they do delivery because you can't just go in, because of COVID-19, also known as coronavirus. And that is what I did today. Sadly, we didn't sleep outside.

Sunday, April 12, 2020

I woke up and walked downstairs and said hi to my family, and I went to the couch and started to read the news. Now in the US, we have half a million cases and we also have the most deaths of any other country. Something also crazy is that New York has the most cases, more than any other country, and New York is just a state.

Later that morning, Cody, my dad, and I all went to visit my mom. She was at work, and when we got there we aren't allowed to go inside. You need to stay in your car and call them, and then that person would come outside. And that is what we did. When my mom came out, my dad handed her some lunch, and we went and sat down on a bench made by an Eagle Scout. It is funny because my dad was an Eagle Scout, and he made benches and huts and things like that, and he didn't make the bench we were sitting at, but he made things like that about thirty years ago, and that is a long time. And it was fun to see mom.

That day, Cody and my dad and I all played basketball. In the middle of playing H-O-R-S-E, our neighbor walked up with socks in one hand and his shoes in the other. I had the look like, *Why don't you just put your shoes on in the house?* It's not like there is a fire, and we had just gotten here, and I think he wanted to say hi as fast as he could, like he had something to say. I was like, *So, is there anything you're going to say?* in my head.

And he said something, and that thing he said was, "How was your day?" And that was the day that I realized that sometimes it can be super urgent to just ask how your day was. Yup. I wish that I was telling the truth, but I wasn't. It is really not that urgent to run out of your front door with socks and shoes and yell, "How was your day?" Just be patient and put your shoes on first, and then come out. It is not that hard. But maybe he was excited, I guess.

When my mom came home, she ate dinner and went to bed, she was so tired. Cody and my dad and I all went downstairs and watched a show, *Little House on the Prairie*. We were planning on watching a movie, but I think we were going to do that another day. And after the show, we went upstairs and went to bed. That is how my day went.

Monday, April 13, 2020

I woke up and it was a great day. It started off with I said hi to my family and went downstairs and played *Madden* for a half hour. Then I came back upstairs and went to the computer and looked up how long a three-point line is for the NBA, and it was 23.9 feet, and the height is 10 feet. I went outside with a measuring tape and got all of the measurements right, and I took some chalk and wrote all of the things down on the ground, and I shot a couple NBA threes. I went back inside after an hour, and it was lunch.

After lunch, my brother and my dad and I all made bagels, and this is how it turned out. It started with, we made the bread with yeast and then let it rise for about an hour and then made it into the shapes of a bagel. Then we boiled them and put the toppings on, and these are what we put on them: our everything flavor with garlic salt on two, chocolate chips on two, and one plain.

That night, we watched a show called *The Wonder Years*, and this is what it was about. First of all, this kid that just got his license got a speeding ticket, and he got grounded. His dad said that he doesn't want to see his car move one inch, so the kid took his dad's car instead because that is the logical thing to do. His parents were getting picked up by friends, and after they were out of sight, he took his dad's car and picked up his friends and went to a concert and accidentally hit something with the car. A part of the car was hanging off. He went home, and it was obvious they would see it when they got home. He was looking, and it was hopeless. He would be grounded for the rest of his life. Until the car with his parents and their friend driving hit the same spot the kid hit, and then they thought it was their friend's fault, and he knew that it was his fault. He went outside and asked his mom what happened, and he already knew what happened, but he still asked, and she said she felt guilty. He asked why, and she said she hit the car too, the other day. It was funny because it all equaled up at the end of the show, how everyone hit the car in the same spot. So, accidents happen.

Tuesday, April 14, 2020
That morning, I woke up on the deck and it was super sunny. I went inside and said hi to my parents, and Cody was on the computer. Also, you might be wondering what the house looks like, and I will tell you. It starts with the front door. You walk in, to the right, and after about ten feet you can go to the left and there is a staircase to the upstairs. You might also remember what I said it looked like before, and if you do, just skip the rest of the paragraph, but if you don't remember that is what it is like, it is a long narrow hall and it is carpeted. At the end of the hall to the right is my room. At the end of the hall to the left is Cody's room, and the bathroom would be right next to Cody's room. Right next my room, there is the attic door. That is the upstairs.

Also, after you walk in the front door, instead of walking ten feet on the left side, walk fifteen feet and you will also turn left, and there are stairs going downstairs. Right when you get down, to the right there is a big wooden box to keep blankets in that we sleep outside with. If you are looking from the left and keep walking, there is a huge room that is carpeted. There is a big TV and two couches on the left and the right walls. After you walk downstairs, if you keep walking after you get to the bottom of the stairs, there will be a wall. If you walk to the left, there will be another room, but this is cool. There is no door, and when you walk through, there will be a pool table, and you can put a ping pong table on top of it. Right now, on the side of the wall next to the pool table, the ping pong table is resting on the wall.

So, there are two more rooms. One of them is my dad's fly shop room (where he makes fly rods) and where the pool table room is. If you keep going across the wall at the end of the room, there is his fly shop room. Right on the other wall next to the fly shop room is a door that leads to our patio, and on the left there is a hot tub, and on the right there is a table and chairs, and farther to the right there is a bonfire place, and way farther to the right we have a pond, and there are fish and ducks that are always there, and it is really cool. And the second room is, after you walk down the stairs, you go across the wall to your left for about five feet, and then you take another left for about fifteen feet, and then there is the guest room. In the guest room there is a laundry room too, and bed and table and a huge desk with lots of fly rod things and papers, and of course there is a bathroom too, where you can do your business. And that is all of the downstairs, and sorry but we're not done. Still got the main floor to talk to you about.

So, this is the main floor. It started with the upstairs and the downstairs to the left ,and now we are going to go to the right. After about ten feet, you turn right again, and there is the kitchen. If you keep going left, you will find a door that leads to the garage, and after the garage there is a small nook and a table, and after that, to the left, there is another door that leads to the door where we sleep outside on the deck. If you take another left, there is the dining room table. After that, if you keep walking left, you will go to the living room. You might have noticed we went in a full circle, and in the living room there are two big couches that are gray and it looks like half of a square, and in the middle of that there is a another small table that has lots of books. When I say *lots* I mean it, lots. That last room is my parents' room. After you walk in the front door, you go left and then left again for about fifteen feet, and there is my parents' room. That is my whole house, and that might have been the longest that I have written in one day!

Wednesday, April 15, 2020

I woke up on the deck and it was three in the morning. I went back to bed, and a couple hours later I woke up and went inside and looked at the clock. *What?* It was eight thirty in the morning, and I was super confused. I was wondering if the clock was wrong, but it wasn't, I just slept in. I told my mom that's what happens when you sleep outside, and it was a perfect excuse why we should sleep outside every night. There are hundreds of reasons why sleeping outside is good for your health. Like, it can reduce stress, and it is also good for your lungs, and lots of other things. About a month ago I showed my mom all the reasons why you should sleep outside, and there were zero negatives, and no reasons why you should sleep inside and not outside. And I can't even start with how many reasons there are, and it is just mind-blowing how many reasons there are. It's amazing.

This afternoon my brother and I played basketball outside. I was shooting baskets, and if you remember a couple days ago, I set up the three-point line. I was hoping it wouldn't rain, because that would wash away the line and I would need to remeasure all of the lines and that would not be fun. But I just shot threes, and we did a challenge of who can make the most threes in a row, but after a little bit we went inside, and I did some reading. I was thinking that instead of reading in the middle of the day when it was sunny, I would read in the morning the next day because then I would not need to do it later in the afternoon when it is sunny and warm weather.

Tonight we watched a movie called *A Beautiful Day in the Neighborhood* and it was good. It was from a TV show in the 1970s, and it was a kindergartener show about a person who always had a bad attitude and Mr. Rogers helped him to become a better person. I will not spoil it, but it is a really great movie.

Thursday, April 16, 2020

That morning woke up in my bed, and I walked downstairs and said hi to my parents and asked if Cody was asleep. They said yes, so I tiptoed my way to the couch and I went on the computer and looked at the news. There is a really good football player named Von Miller, and he got the coronavirus. I really hope that he fights it. Also, about a month ago, Tom Hanks and his wife got the coronavirus, and they fought it, and that was good news. Here is an update on the state of the coronavirus. The US has 670,000 cases and 33,000 deaths, and in the whole world there are 2,200,000 cases and 150,000 deaths. Something that is also crazy is that the country with the second most cases is Spain, and they have 185,000 cases, and the US has 670,000 cases, and that is 3.62162162 times more, etc.

Later that day, I made another rock stack, but this one is different. So, I found six rocks, and my dad has super glue, and we glued them together. It was a rock stack, and you think that is it and cool, but no. Then I found the smallest and thinnest rocks, and they were about five millimeters squared, and they are so thin they are like paper. I found three of those and stacked them biggest to smallest, and we glued them together too, and then we glued it to the bigger rock stack with six rocks. Then I found a rock that was like a pool ball, and I glued it to that, and it was super cool. Then I got the idea that I should take another rock that was skinny and tall, and I made a T, and it looked cool, and my name starts with a T. I polished and sprayed it with shiny clear paint, and it was super shiny. I showed my parents and Cody, and they all said at the same time that it looks like a cross, and I said, "I like it too," and walked away. I came back and we all laughed.

Cody and I went outside to play basketball, and we played King of the Court. If you don't know how to play, this is how it starts. With one person under the basket and one in the middle of the court, the person under the basket passes the ball to the person in the middle of the court, and you play. If the other person gets possession and/or it goes out of bounds, then you switch possession, and you can play forever. After we played, we went inside and my mom said we could sleep outside. My mom slept outside too, and in the middle of the night I looked and my mom was gone. She told me in the morning that she had a bad dream that she was in the driveway, and she got scared and went inside. I said that it was a bad dream and we laughed.

Friday, April 17, 2020

That morning, I woke up and walked inside. It was six thirty. When it was about nine o'clock, these people came and put this paint stuff on our patio. It smelled like exhaust and was super bad, so Cody and my mom and I all went inside of the car and went for a ride. We had no idea where we were going. My dad went on a bike ride about an hour before, and after about thirty minutes of driving, my dad called and we told him where we were. He said he would meet us at a Starbucks. When we got to Starbucks about ten minutes later, my dad was there too, and we saw a friend, and we all talked outside for about thirty minutes. After that, we went to Bellingham Bay and skipped rocks for about thirty minutes. I skipped ten skips, and that was one of my highest that I have ever done. The most that I ever have done in my life is thirteen.

After that, my dad and I went to a pizza place and picked up some food. When we got home, we ate it, and it was super good. My birthday is coming up on the twenty-fifth, and that is in eight days. For my birthday I want to eat pizza, and I also want to make homemade ice cream. The NFL draft is on my birthday too, and that is going to be fun to watch. The friend that we ran into has a daughter, and she has the same birthday as I do, and we are also the same age, so we were both born on the same day and in the same hospital. The friend that we ran into is Beau, and he is a Bellingham firefighter, and my dad is a Seattle firefighter. Those two places are only about one or two hours apart, which is not really that far apart.

Later that day, Cody and I played King of the Court, and it was fun. It started to rain, so we went inside. I ate the leftover pizza from lunch and took a bite of a carrot, and I screeched, "Ouch!" and went to the mirror and looked at my tooth. It was super wiggly, and I went to another mirror and tried to pull it out. I hurt super bad and kept on trying to wiggle it, and after about ten minutes of trying, I gave up and went back to eating dinner. After dinner I asked my mom if we could sleep outside, and she said yes. I was really happy, and I went outside and told Wilson.

Saturday, April 18, 2020

This morning I was playing *Madden*, and in *Madden* you play football, and there is a play book where all of the plays are and the routes you can run. You pick one, and three or four guys will run the routes you picked. So, after you do that, hovering above each of those players heads there will be either X, Y, B, or A. You decide which guy you want to throw to and then press the letter hovering above their head on the controller. Then the ball will get thrown to the player you wanted to throw to.

And there is another mode, if you want to call it that. This is what you do. So, you pick one of the thirty-two NFL teams and that's the team that you are. Then you do a draft, and it will randomly pick one of thirty-two. Pretend you get one that is a really good pick, because then you get to pick the first player. You can scroll through all of the positions in football and pick one player, and the smart thing to do is to pick either a quarterback or a wide receiver. If you get the first pick, the best player to get is Patrick Mahomes. He is a quarterback. Then after that, all of the other thirty-one teams will pick the next best players, and on and on. After I did that, my team was super good, and I couldn't wait till tomorrow so I could play.

And this is funny, and kind of sad too. Cody made a franchise and forgot to save it. He was done with screen time, and he was mad and got annoyed. One of the things he did is ask my mom a question, and I answered it, and he looked at me with a mad look and said, "I'm not asking you, Taylor!" And I put my hands up and walked backwards. He did lots of extra work so he could earn more screen time, and after that he did another draft, and he forgot to save it again, so his team was erased. I just stayed away from him for the rest of the night.

Also, about twenty minutes later, my family was watching a show, and Cody went and lay down next to me. As kindly as I could, I asked him to sit on the other side, and he said, "Fine." And he scowled and walked to the other side of the bed.

Sunday, April 19, 2020

If you remember, I like to play *Madden Franchise*. This morning, I made a team, and Cody was writing down the players I got and putting them in order and putting the positions on the side, too, so if I want them I knew what players I should get because my team ended up being super good, and I was really happy. Another thing about franchise is that after about four seasons of playing, you will need to sign your players, also known as giving them money to play for your team. Not real money, but you need to do really good in those seasons, and you get money. Remember, not real money. But after about four years or so, that is when you want to redraft and make a new team. So, if I stay with this team and then I'm able to have the same team, it will be the first season again, not the first, second, third, fourth, and on and on. I really cannot wait to play, and this I think is the team that I will be with for a couple seasons, but you never know. And only six days to my birthday, and there will be the real NFL draft on the twenty-third.

Later in the day, Cody and my dad and I all played basketball, H O R S E and it was fun. Cody and I were trash talking the whole time, and it got to the point where I decided to stop because it was getting out of hand. After we went inside, I read and I swept my garage and I vacuumed my mom's car and I also did the dishes, and after that I could play Madden. I wanted to see how my team was, and the team was super good.

Later that night, my mom had some friends over, but they didn't go inside, and they stayed six feet apart, and my dad made pizza for all of us. We also had some ranch, so I was really excited and wanted to eat it all in one big bite, but I didn't. That would be slightly weird if I did. Actually, that would be super weird. After that, my brother and my dad and I all talked my mom into sleeping outside on the deck, and Wilson was going crazy, like he was super happy we were all out there.

Monday, April 20, 2020

When I woke up on the deck, I looked right beside me and Wilson was on his back, asleep. I got up to walk inside, and when I opened the door, he shot up and ran next to me and sat there and looked up to me. I opened the door, and he ran inside and went straight to the front door. I wanted to see what he sees, and he saw a neighbor walking by, and I let him out, and you can probably guess what I heard next—*Ruff!*—in a loud and obnoxious way. After that I went downstairs and started playing *Madden*.

Later, my family went on the trail, and it was fun but also kind of painful because I don't know how but my knee hurts to run and to straighten. I just think that it is growing pains, and you can't really go to the doctors now, anyway, because they are dealing with more important things and helping people that are at risk of death. I would guess that they would pick helping sick patients compared to my knee that is probably just some growing pain, so I am not really that worried.

My math teacher made a small fire pit way up on the top of the Baby Bear Trail. They took a saw and cut parts of dead trees and made them like little stools and surrounded them around the fire, so he can sit there with his friends and maybe with someone else. That is just a guess, and it has a total lookout so you can see so much from there. It looks really good, and I want to go there again.

When we finished the hike, Wilson surprisingly did not get that dirty, but right as I said that, Wilson stepped into a huge mud puddle, and I second guessed myself.

When we got home, I went to the couch and checked the news. There are now 700,000 cases, and that is almost a million.

Tuessday, April 21, 2020

In the morning, I woke up and for some reason had a lot of energy. I ran downstairs and said hi to Wilson and went on the couch and read some news. I was really looking forward to the NFL draft in two more days. It was going from the twenty-third to twenty-fifth, and my birthday is on the twenty-fifth, and it was in Las Vegas, Nevada, and I couldn't wait. I really wanted it to be this day but, it obviously wasn't going to change.

You might be wondering how they are going to do the draft with COVID-19. They are going to do a Zoom-like thing called Microsoft Teams, and it is just like Zoom, just the name is different. It is going to be super cool and really different, compared to the NFL draft last year. Unfortunately, I missed the draft last year because I had to go to this school thing, and I wish I watched the draft instead of going to that thing. It was called the Spring Fling, and all of my friends were going, and I just decided to go, and last year I wasn't really that into football. But this year I am getting more and more interested, and I do not want to miss this upcoming draft.

This afternoon my mom and I made cookies. We took food coloring and mixed it with homemade frosting and decorated the cookies with the frosting and colorful sprinkles. After they were done, we ate them, and they were by far my favorite cookies ever. That is really hard to say, but I said it and I mark my word. After Cody tried them, he said that he didn't like them, and I said, "Thanks." And that means more for me.

My dad and I went on a bike ride. Cody said he didn't want to come, and I thought, *Suit yourself!* We went on a new trail and got lost and used this app to try to help us, but it wasn't updated, so it didn't show the trail we were on. After two hours, when we got on the road, Wilson sat and looked forward. He wasn't on a leash, and there was a deer he wanted to chase, but he stayed. I rode my bike at the deer to scare him away, and that scared him away. I looked farther ahead, and there were about four more deer. I scared them away too, and I went back down the hill and told my dad we could go, the coast was clear. He said ok, and we went home and told my mom and

Cody about what happened. Then I ate one of my delicious cookies, and we ate dinner and went to bed inside (sadly). I wish it was outside.

Wednesday, April 22, 2020
One thing that happened today is my dad made bagels, and they turned out great. I like on the top of my bagels the seasoning that goes on garlic bread, also known as garlic seasoning. It is really good and also has a lot of salt. My brother and my mom and my dad all like a type of bagel, and they call that bagel an everything bagel, and it is what it sounds like. These are the ingredients:

- 2 tablespoons poppy seeds
- 1 tablespoon white sesame seeds
- 1 tablespoon black sesame seeds
- 1 ½ tablespoons dried minced garlic
- 1 ½ tablespoons dried onion flakes

And after that, Cody and I wrestled, and it was fun, and I played some *Madden*. The NFL draft is tomorrow, from five to eight o'clock at night, and I can't wait.

As you probably know, my birthday is in two days. I need to do a hard challenge every year when it is my birthday. I started when I was ten, and the first challenge was to touch the top of the garage, and I did that. Last year, it was to be able to dunk on the hoop outside, and I am not sure how tall it is, but this year my challenge is to touch the ceiling on the top floor. I think I can do it.

Let me tell you what the NFL draft is about. So, it usually has all of the college players sitting in a bunch of chairs, and there is a stage, and there is one person who walks up to the microphone and says, "For the 2020 NFL draft, the Seattle Seahawks have selected _____ (insert player's name)." It will start with one team, and then it will go through the next thirty-one teams, and it does that for a lot of times. When it is done, then it is done. It's that simple.

Thursday, April 23, 2020
When I woke up, I was really excited about the draft, and I wanted the day to go by super fast. This is what I did. I started with playing *Madden*, and I made a new team. I got really good players, and after that I went upstairs and told Cody he could play. After he played, I played again and didn't save

it, so I had to do it again. After I did it again, I saved it multiple times, and it ended up saving. I am happy that it did.

I had to do one project in science today. I needed to take two cups and fill them each halfway with water, and then put ice cubes in one and put the other in the microwave, and then let the ice cubes melt. Then I put one drop of food coloring in each, to see which one dissolves first. After I did it, the cold dissolved first. I was super confused because I thought that the hot would dissolve first, but it didn't. I looked farther into the assignment, and it said, "Explain why you think the hot water dissolved first." Then I reread all of the directions and saw that it also said you need to take a photo during the dissolving process. I needed to redo the project, and then my computer died, and that is the online device to take the photo. I need to let it charge and wait till tomorrow.

My math teacher told me, and all of the other kids too, we needed to do jumping jacks and see how many you can do in ten, twenty, thirty seconds, all the way until two minutes. I ended up doing 500 jumping jacks halfway through, and then I realized that I messed up the count. I redid it, and I ended up doing about 1,500 jumping jacks, total. That is a lot.

Friday, April 24, 2020

When I woke up. I looked at my phone. It said that it is the twenty-fourth, and that is one day before my birthday. For my birthday, I really wanted to have one present before my birthday, and that was to sleep outside. My mom said we could, and I told Wilson. It was still morning and it would happen in about fourteen more hours, but it is never too early to get excited.

Later that day, Cody and I watched the draft. It was starting one hour early, at four o'clock, When we started watching, I went upstairs and grabbed chips and chocolate because it is a celebration and my birthday is tomorrow. After about an hour watching, my mom told us dinner was ready. We put a table in front of us and set our plates there and ate dinner in the basement for the first time. After I ate all of my food, I ran upstairs and grabbed a bag full of strawberries. I ate so many strawberries I couldn't eat one more.

Cody and I played basketball after we watched the draft, and it was fun. My mom said she wanted me to open a present from my dad's mom, and I did. There was yeast, and that is the main ingredient for bread. She gave that to me so we can make cinnamon rolls for the next morning, and she also gave me these candles. I have seen them before, a mix of candles and fireworks. It is super cool, and I could not wait to light one on fire the next day.

Saturday, April 25, 2020

It's my birthday! When I woke up, I walked inside and gathered up my whole family, and I opened one present from Cody. He got me a stuffed animal duck. After that I went downstairs and played *Madden* for a little bit, and when I came up, my dad had made cinnamon rolls. They were super good. Then my whole family FaceTimed my dad's parents. They asked if I opened the card they got me, and I said no. Then I opened it in front of them, and for my birthday I had asked for a La Fiamma Pizza gift card. That is my favorite pizza place, and it has to be to-go orders only, because of COVID-19. They said they couldn't get the gift card, but they just got me cash, and I could spend it on whatever I want. And I thanked them.

That afternoon, I opened a present my parents got me. It was super heavy. I grabbed it and walked my way over to the kitchen and opened it. It was a huge net, and you needed to set it up. There was a net and four paddles, and with that you could play badminton, tennis, and pickleball. There were two pickleballs and two tennis balls. I could not wait to set it up, but it looked really hard to set up. And after that they told me they had one more present, but since COVID-19, it would take another week because it would take super long to get it to our house with Amazon Prime delivery.

Then my parents told me to sit at the table and close my eyes. I assumed it had to do with my birthday, and they walked up to me and set the laptop in front of me and told me to press play. I did, and it showed about fifteen videos recorded, of family and my friends saying happy birthday, and it was five minutes long! And that night we ate ice cream and brownies. They were both really good, and it was a really good quarantine birthday.

Sunday, April 26, 2020

This morning I played *Madden*. After that, my brother and my dad and I all played Monopoly, and after about thirty minutes of playing, I told them I was going to take a break and read. Cody went downstairs and played *Madden*, and my dad started making bread and then went on an hour bike ride and came home and went on another bike ride with my mom for about an hour and a half. And they came home, and they were both super tired, especially my dad because that was his second bike ride of the day. In all, it was three and a half hours. If I did that, I would be super tired.

If you remember, yesterday I got a present, all the supplies to play pickleball, badminton and tennis. My dad and I set it up on our grass, and after about twenty minutes of setting it up, we did it. And we did not even look at the directions. We played badminton, and it was so fun. Cody came out, and I played with him for a little bit. We went inside and had lunch and then came back outside and played some more. My mom came outside and played too, and that was fun.

Later in the afternoon, my dad finished making his bread and we went over and gave the bread to a friend. They were happy to have it. My dad also put big chunks of salt on the top to give it more taste, and he also made another batch, but it was a small one and ended up being really good. About a half hour later, my dad and Cody played Monopoly, and it was going back and forth for about thirty minutes, and Cody ended up winning. It ended on Dad landing on Boardwalk, and Cody owned two houses on it.

Tuesday, April 28, 2020

It's a couple days later. I don't know why I didn't write yesterday. In the morning I went downstairs and played *Madden*, and when I did my other franchise draft, it was a good team. But after about a week of playing it, my players were starting to get older over time. In the game, they get about a year older every week, and they start to get slower and not as good. So, I decided to make a new team. After I made the team, my team was rated 91 overall. That is super good. If you have one player on your team that is 91 overall, then that is really good, but to have an average of all your players 91 is really really good. And I was hoping that I would stay with this team for a very long time.

In the afternoon, I played basketball, and after about one hour of playing, I went inside and my dad was making bagels. I tried them, and they were really good. I wish that there were hundreds of them, because they were so good. My mom told all three of us that we could watch a movie tonight, and my dad was going to be the one to pick it out. I was ok with that (but not really) because sometimes my dad will pick out interesting movies. He picked one out, and I think that this is a really good movie. I have heard about that movie before, and it is called *Forrest Gump*. He said that it is a movie about history and has a really good message.

So, we watched it. I will not give away what happened, but I will tell you about the main parts. The main character's name is Forrest Gump, and he was a little boy at first in the movie, but he has polio. Polio is a disease that makes the muscles not work. He has polio in his legs, and he had a brace on both legs from his knees to his feet. On his first day of school, he went on the bus, and every time he went to sit down, someone would say, "Taken."

And it was really sad, until he got to the back of the bus and a girl his age told him he could sit next to her. In the movie, he said inside of his head, *That is the most beautiful thing that I have ever seen.* After school these bullies were on their bikes, chasing him and throwing something at him. Forrest was trying to run as fast as he could.

The girl behind him was yelling, "Run, Forrest, run," and he kept on running, with special effects that made it look like all of the pieces of metal on his leg were falling off when he ran. He ended up running really fast, and that is the story's message. Multiple times you will see him getting bullied, and he always in his head heard, *Run, Forrest, run*. And he did.

Wednesday, April 29, 2020

In the morning, I woke up and started wondering if I should just do a lot of work in the morning instead of doing my work in the afternoon, and I did that. I took a shower and went downstairs and did about thirty minutes of reading. After that I went downstairs to see Cody, and he was doing screen time. I went back upstairs and ate cereal, and then I went into the bathroom upstairs and washed my face and brushed my teeth. I thought it felt good to start off the day like that and maybe I would do that in the future, and then I thought that, in the afternoon, instead of doing schoolwork, I could play soccer and basketball until dinnertime.

In the afternoon, I played basketball and Monopoly and so many things, when Cody was in his room doing schoolwork. After I played outside for an hour, I went inside and checked on what the news was for coronavirus. The US just hit sixty thousand deaths and one million cases, and that is a lot. I was hoping that the coronavirus could end so the football season would start on time, because I am scared that it will not start on time.

One thing that is different about the day is that my dad went to work for the first time in a month and a half, and that is super long. The good thing is that he will be home for four days after that, and my mom is going to be at work for one day and then I think she will be off for a little bit. At the fire station, he sleeps there, and the firefighters live there like a normal house.

Thursday, April 30, 2020

I woke up at eight in the morning, and that is really late for me. I thought about getting all my work done in the morning, like the day before, and that is what I did. I went and took a shower without even going downstairs. After that I brushed my teeth, went downstairs, said hi to my family, and Cody was downstairs doing screen time. I asked if I could play after him, and he said yes, and I was really looking forward to playing with my new team on *Madden*.

My mom went to work, and she was going to be gone until midnight. Cody and dad and I all went outside and played. We played   H-O-R-S-E and switched it up and called it W-I-L-S-O-N. So, after a couple rounds I had W-I-L-S-O, and my dad had W-I-L-S-O too, and Cody didn't have any letters. My dad got out on the next turn, and it was my turn next. After a couple rounds, Cody and I were tied. We both had W I L S O, and I shot a huge basket from way off the court, and it went in. Then Cody tried that shot and missed.

My mom was still at work and my dad made pasta. After we had dinner, my brother made ice cream, and after it finished, we put it in the freezer and went downstairs to watch a show called *Wonder Years*. After that we ate the ice cream, and it was super good. For some reason it tasted like it had more sugar, and I liked it that way. I put some fruit on top of it, and it was really good.

Friday, May 1, 2020

I got woken up by a very loud screeching noise, and I sat up and looked at the other side of the yard. It was the garbage truck. I went inside and onto the couch. My mom was in her room asleep, and I went downstairs and did some screen time. After twenty minutes I went back upstairs and looked at the coronavirus update. Nothing drastic changed. I really was hoping the numbers would go down, and it is starting to go down a little bit in Washington. I am really hoping that I am going to go to school on time next year, because I have not seen my friends in more than a month and a half. I think that it will start slowing down soon, and I have no idea if I am right or even close to right. I am probably wrong.

Later in the afternoon, I played basketball, and after about ten minutes I decided to do some reading. I was reading *Harry Potter*, and I have read the series so many times. I think I have read the first book, like, five times, and three times with the second book, and one with volumes 3–7. As you can probably tell, I really like that series. If you don't know what it is about, then this is what it is about: a boy named Harry Potter. His parents got killed by a wizard named Lord Voldemort, so he lives with his uncle and aunt and their son, and they are really mean. Their kid's name is Dudley, and he gets really spoiled. One day Harry gets a letter, and it says that he got invited to Hogwarts. That is a wizarding school, and he goes there and makes friends, but Voldemort is determined to kill Harry. When his parents got killed, Voldemort had used his wand to kill them, and he had tried to kill Harry and failed somehow. He used the death curse, and killed his parents with the curse too, and Voldemort is determined to kill Harry. So, each book is one year, and the whole series is all about Harry's full years at Hogwarts. He goes through a lot of obstacles, and if you want to know more, you can read all seven books.

Saturday, May 2, 2020

When I woke up, I was really hoping it was going to be sunny. Outside it was a blue sky and hardly any clouds. I was really happy, and my parents said that there was supposed to be a birthday present coming. My birthday was, like, one week ago, and my present was late. I had no idea what it was going to be.

In the afternoon, my parents told Cody and I that we were going to go on the trail. I was fine with that. When we went, after about five minutes, we ran into one of our neighbors. It was Jason and his wife, and we talked for about ten minutes. Five minutes after that we ran into another neighbor, and her name is Lori. She just got a puppy, and that puppy's name is Stella. There used to be a dog named Stella in the neighborhood, but she died, and that is why she named her dog Stella, and that is nice. We went on the trail for about an hour, and when we got to the end of the trail, we ran into another neighbor, Susan. She was with one of her kids, named Bode, and the other son's name is Hunter. We got off the trail, and those were all of the neighbors we saw, three neighbors in only a one-hour trail run.

During that trail run, I found a sandstone rock and got the idea to carve it into the shape of a person. This is how I did that. I first took another rock and carved the shape, and then I filed it down until it was the perfect shape. After I did that, I was really happy. Then I got the idea to take an electric sanding machine and make it really soft. I did that, and it turned out a lot better than I thought it was going to turn out.

At night we watched a movie called *Anger Management*, about a man who had anger issues. This weird guy helped him fix his problems, and it was really funny. And the funny thing is, the guy didn't really have anger issues at all.

Sunday, May 3, 2020

In the morning, I planned my day out, of what I was going to do. This is what I did. It started with me, and I went downstairs and played video games for a little bit. I went upstairs on my computer to see what schoolwork I needed to do, and there was nothing. I looked at the date, and it was Sunday, and we get no schoolwork until Monday, so I went back downstairs and decided that I was going to see what the COVID-19 update is. In the US there are

1,155,954 cases and 67,296 deaths. Worldwide there are 3,526,117 cases and 24,611 deaths.

This afternoon my dad and I biked the Galbraith, which is the mountain we live on, that we bike on all the time. Cody and my mom went on a different trail and went into town. It was super muddy, there were puddles everywhere, and after about one and a half hours, we got home and I went straight upstairs to take a shower.

Later that night, my mom asked me to clean up the closet upstairs. So, I took out all of the things in the closet, and those were all sheets and pillowcases and things like that. I organized them all into a pile of pillowcases, down comforters, and fitted sheets. After I did that, I organized all of the little piles into smaller piles so I could separate them into queen and twin. After that I put everything onto the shelves, except the pillowcases, and then I took all of the pillowcases and divided them so all of the colors were matching. Then I folded them neatly and put them onto the shelves.

And that is all that I did today. This surprised me, but it took me more than an hour to clean up the shelves. If that doesn't make you think it was messy, then I don't know what does.

Monday, May 4, 2020

I went downstairs and played a little bit of *Madden*. Then I got the idea that I could do a lot a reading in the morning, and that is what I did. I went upstairs and read for thirty minutes. I was reading *Harry Potter*, a great series I have read a million times. Maybe that is not true, but I have read it a lot.

In the afternoon, I played with one of my birthday presents, a remote control car. I made a jump and a landing, and it was super cool. I got the idea because the day before, my dad and I went on a bike ride and saw these people building a big jump track. It was super big, and one of the jumps must have been twenty feet high. I am not exaggerating one bit. It was super big, and in that moment, I looked at my dad and said, "The people that are jumping that are either really good or just stupid."

In the evening, I set up Monopoly. I wanted to play a lot. My dad was at work all day and would be back the next day at noon, so I wanted to finish it. If we didn't finish it, we could just make a new game, but I really wanted to finish it. I got this really good strategy, to get a lot of medium houses and properties that didn't cost too much but do get you a good amount of money. That is what I did, and so far, it is working. I think I am in the lead. I got this really good idea. I took a ziplock bag and measured it out to see what the dimensions are. I put those dimensions on paper and taped it to the ziplock bag. The whole bag is see-through, and I put my money in it, but now no one can see what's in it and how much money there is. In the last game, Cody really wanted to see what I had, but I never told him and he was saying, "I will give you this much money."

And then I said, "Nope."

Then he said, "Please, I am desperate. I will give you fifty. How much money do you have?"

And in the end, he just gave up, and that's what I have been using.

Tuessday, May 5, 2020

I woke up and went downstairs, and my mom told us to only do thirty minutes, and that is what we did. After that we went upstairs and played Monopoly, and I really wanted to finish before my dad was going to be home. He was going to be home in about five hours. After we played for about thirty minutes, I did some schoolwork. My teacher assigned me to do about five experiments, and I really wanted to do all of them fast so I could finish my screen time. After I did all of my screen time, I went downstairs and played some *Madden*, I played one game, and each game is going to be twenty minutes. That is perfect because we do one hour, and that means we can play three games.

In the afternoon, I did some gardening. I wanted to not pull weeds, but that was the only gardening thing that I could do, so I did that and found a lizard. It was a salamander, and they are really slow. I put it on the concrete so I could show my dad after I was done. After about fifteen minutes I was done. I looked at the lizard, and it was on its back. I was thinking That is funny! and the reason why is because Wilson is always on his back, and he is really cute, but then I realized that it is dead. Right at that moment, my dad came, and I said, "It died." I went and put it in dirt, and my dad told me that lizards are not supposed to be on concrete, they dry out, and my dad patted my shoulder and walked away. I went inside, and I was very tired, and when I say it, I mean it.

At night we ate pasta. My mom made a sauce that you put on your pasta, and is was really good. She said that if I eat it, I can have dessert, and I did, and I didn't regret it. There is a place and they have that pasta dressing, and it is really good, and I was surprised that I liked it. I thought I would not, but I did. I hope she will make it again in the future.

Wednesday, May 6, 2020

Last night we slept outside, and it was crazy. There was so much thunder and lightning, and it was lighting up the whole sky. Wilson was surprisingly not scared. The first time, when he was sleeping, he shot up, but that was the only time that he shot up. A couple times he looked at the sky, wondering what the noise was coming from. I ended up sleeping great.

When I woke up in the morning, I went inside, and my dad was the only person that was still outside. Cody was inside and doing work because he got in trouble the night before. It was nine o'clock at night and he still needed to do, like, an hour of reading, and he got in trouble. My dad told him to do all of his reading and work, so that morning he went straight upstairs and did a lot of work from the day before.

Then I grabbed a poop bag for Wilson's poop and went outside. It was really cold and raining, but not that hard. I went back inside, and my dad wasn't outside, and I was really confused. Then right behind me I heard a *thud!* and turned around. It was my dad, and he woke up when I was outside picking up poop and just laughed.

I went on a bike ride with my dad and my brother, and my mom ran behind us for about fifteen minutes and then turned around. After about thirty minutes of bike riding, I stopped for a minute. My legs were totally covered with mud, and there was mud on my hands. We were riding for about one more hour, and I went straight upstairs and took a shower. At the end, there was mud all over the tub.

That night Cody made ice cream. We didn't have the right amount, so we did a half batch. My mom and Cody figured out that the amount of money we spend on ice cream normally at the store is about five dollars, and we spend way less with homemade ice cream.

Thursday, May 7, 2020
I woke up and it was really sunny, not one cloud in the sky. We didn't sleep outside because dad was working, but he is going to be home tomorrow at about ten o'clock, and he is going to be home for four days. The thing is, with my dad's work schedule, he works one day and then he is home for two days, and then he goes to work for one day and then he is home for four days, and then back to work and then home for two days, and then it goes on forever. But he still needs to work overtime shifts, and that means he needs to go to work unpredictably. My mom's work schedule is all unpredictable, but she usually works about two to three times a week, and sometimes it is to midnight, and sometimes it is to noon, and sometimes it is from seven in the morning to seven at night. But one of my parents are always home with us. Cody and I are home alone sometimes, like if my parents need to go to the grocery store or something like that.

In the afternoon, my mom and I made a smoothie, and after about ten minutes of trying to blend it, the things inside of the blender were stuck to the top. My mom hurt her thumb about a month ago, and she doesn't know what happened, but she said that is how long it has been hurting. After about ten minutes of just shaking the smoothie, it finally started to move. I put it in the blender, and after we blended it there was one problem. We couldn't open the container, and that was really annoying. We tried everything, but it still didn't work, no matter what we tried. My mom couldn't twist it, because of her thumb, and I couldn't twist it, because I am who I am and only eleven. Finally, my mom opened it, and we both had no idea how we did it at all, and the smoothie was worth it. Well, not really, but it was good.

My mom had a friend over. Her name is Beth, and she has two kids, named Abby and Channer, and they are both around my age. They talked outside for about two hours, and after that we went on the deck and relaxed, but I knew that there was no chance we would sleep there.

Friday, May 8, 2020

In the morning, I went downstairs and Cody was playing *Madden*. Wilson was eating. I looked at the clock and it was 7:01, and Wilson eats at 7:00. I could hear Cody playing *Madden*. I did some schoolwork, and after that I wanted to play *Madden*, but Cody was on it. We only get to do one hour a day, and Cody ended up coming up at 7:34, and I asked him how much screen time he did. He said he did twenty minutes, and I asked him if he took any breaks when he was playing, and he said no. Then I asked if he fed Wilson, and he said yes. I was really confused, so I asked him if he went downstairs right after he fed Wilson, and he said "No, definitely not. Way after he ate." And I asked him how long he thought Wilson ate, and he said a minute, and I agreed, if not less. I told him that I went downstairs and Wilson was eating, and you should have seen his face. It was like that face of someone when they get caught with their hand in a cookie jar. It was really funny, and after asking him a couple more questions, I figured out that he lied. He did way more than twenty minutes. It seems like Cody stares at screens a lot more than he should. He seems like he reads the news all day, and he reads on his phone and not in like a book or something, and he listens to songs on his phone and on YouTube. He says he is listening, but I always see him looking at his phone the whole time, just watching.

Cody and my dad and I went on a bike ride in the afternoon. I rode Cody's bike and Cody rode our mom's bike. We both really need new bikes. Cody has no tread on his bike, so it slips out, and for some reason when I was going downhill his whole front brake just stopped working. So, I had no tread and my front brake wasn't working and I ended up running into two trees and almost crashing an uncountable amount of times. When we got home, Wilson was super tired, and he went right to the grass and slept. It was almost eighty degrees, and that is really hot for Washington, and also it was just May.

Saturday, May 9, 2020

I woke up on the deck, and it was five forty-five, and I saw Cody was awake too. So we talked for about forty-five minutes and went inside, and remember, we were on the deck. My mom was going to be gone till four at night, and till then I was getting ready for Mother's Day. This is my plan for Mother's Day morning. First of all, we are all going to sleep outside. I am going to take a blanket and set it down, and it is going to be a red one. It will go out from the door like a red carpet, and I am going to take a lot of pieces of paper, and they are going to be like petals, and I will spread them across the blanket and then to the counter. I am going to put a lot of chocolates and candy on the counter, and I will have lots of hearts, and they will be all over. On the counter I will put all of her presents, and don't think that I am going over the top. Well, maybe I am, but my mom likes presents, so I will give her some!

In the afternoon, we went to a friend's house because they had a birthday, but we stayed six feet apart. During that time we played with his kids, and they are, like, five to six years older. We played football, and Cody and I played basketball. When we left, Bret (the one with the birthday) gave me a big rock and Cody a piece of wood, and he also gave us paint and paint brushes, to make things for Mom. And when we got home, I went straight downstairs and Cody and I started to paint the things, and Cody wrote "Mom" on his wood. On my rock, I took the paint and I put rings of colors around to the very center, and it looked really cool. It was like a rainbow but in a circle. Then I looked in our back yard in the woods and found four rocks, and they were all circles. My plan is to take paint them and glue them together and glue all of them to the center of my big rock. So far it is looks like it will work.

My mom came home, and we said hi, and she went upstairs and took a shower. You should have seen how happy Wilson was. I can't wait to see what happens tomorrow morning.

Sunday, May 10, 2020

Last night we ended up not sleeping outside because there were so many bugs. Upstairs, where Cody's and my rooms are, was really hot so we slept downstairs in the guest room. I woke up at six and went upstairs, and my dad was awake, so we started by taking a big sheet, and it was red, and we laid it out in front of Mom's room. Then we put down all of the little pieces of paper (and I was trying to make it look like flower petals). After that I took a chair and put it at the end of the carpet and put out all of the things, like my rock and Cody's wood and all of the cards and chocolates.

When my mom woke up, she was really surprised, and she walked across it, and we all laughed. Cody didn't do really that much. He only wrote a card and painted some wood, so he decided to make my mom breakfast, and he asked her what she wanted.

This afternoon I went downstairs and did some screen time. I was really wanting to go on the trail, and that was what we did. It was really hot, and it was still only springtime but it was eighty degrees. That is really hot, and after almost two hours I went inside and made a smoothie. I took out the old blender because the new one was really hard to close the cap, and to open it was even harder. I put raspberries and peaches and sweet things like that in, and it ended up really good. It was really sweet, and that is what I thought it would be too.

Tonight my brother made dinner, and after dinner we are going to watch Seinfeld stand-up comedy. He played in a show when he was in his twenties, and now he has this show on Netflix called *Comedians in Cars Getting Coffee*, and it is just what it sounds like. He finds a comedian, and they go and get coffee, and it is really funny. I can't wait to watch it, and I am really hoping we can sleep outside too.

Monday, May 11, 2020

In the morning, I went downstairs and I played *Madden*, and after a couple games I came back up and ate some cereal. My dad mowed the lawn, and after about one hour or two he was done and we went on the trail. About five minutes after riding downhill, I told my dad that my back wheel isn't working at all, and that is really bad because if I slam on my brakes and my back wheel doesn't work, then I would fly over my handlebar. So we went back and fixed that, and Wilson was really confused. We went and biked for about ten to fifteen minutes and I looked at my dad and told him, "I have to take a dump."

So we turned around, and when we got out of the trail, we saw one of our neighbors. He is about seventy years old, and he asked us how long did we ride and I said, "My wheel . . . needs fixing." And for about five or ten seconds I said nothing, and he was really confused, and it was really funny.

So my dad and I went home, and after that we went back on the trail and my dad said, "Third time is the charm." We went back on the trail for about one hour and a half.

Right before we got on the trail, I need to cross these logs. You can't go across them, so we fixed that, and we took a lot of rocks and fit them into the cracks and made it smooth. Then we took a lot of dirt, and it looked really good, and it was going to rain all night, and that is good. The rain will pack it down, and it will be great, and it was going really well so far. My dad isn't going to be here to tomorrow, but he will only be gone for one day, we are going to fix the rest of this bridge we're making in two days, and I can't wait.

After dinner we walked over to our bridge to show my whole family, and they liked it, and we walked back, and I ate some food and brushed my teeth and went to bed, and I really wanted to keep on working on the bridge project.

Wednesday, May 13, 2020

Today Cody and I played football, and we ran and made plays like we do in *Madden*. I ran a couple cuts, short slants, and things like that, and it was fun. We did that for about thirty minutes, and I was really tired of sprinting. The reason why is because I was the one running and Cody was the one just throwing. Then my dad came out and we all played a game where my dad throws it and Cody and I both run and see who can get it. If you catch it, then my dad tries to throw it to the other person, and then they try to get to the end zone, and it goes on and on for every play. Well, not forever, because that would be crazy. But we did that for about thirty minutes.

Then Phil (our neighbor) walked down, and his dog just died, and his name was Finn, and he was a black Lab, and he was a great dog, and he had an electric fence, too. Now he is getting a new dog named Banks, and that dog is a yellow Lab, and he is getting that dog on the twenty-third or twenty-fourth. What is also funny is that his daughter taught Cody in fourth grade, so we are friends with them too, and her name is Katie. Katie had a baby two years ago on May 25, 2020, and right now Katie is having another baby, and it is supposed to come around the same time. That will be cool if both of them have the same birthday but two years apart.

Tonight Cody made ice cream, and my mom came home from work, and we had dinner, and after that we watched *Wonder Years*. That is a great show, and it is almost over. There are only I think ten more shows left that are twenty minutes each, and that is sad. But after that we ate ice cream and it was really good, as always, and then everyone went to bed— not outside, sadly, because there is so many annoying bugs right now.

Thursday, May 14, 2020

I woke up and looked out my window, and it was really sunny. I walked downstairs, and my dad was on the couch. Cody was on the couch too, looking at the computer. I sat down and read a book and after a little bit I went downstairs and played *Minecraft*. You might be wondering what that is, and let me tell you. It is a game where you live in the woods alone, and there are trees and grass on the ground and mountains and things like that, and all of those things are blocks, so the whole world is a block with many other blocks. With the trees you can get wood, and then you can build a house.

After you build a house, then you can go and try to find a village. A village is where there are usually five people living, and you can take the things they have. There are also animals, like pigs, cows, horses, fish, squids, chickens, parrots, llamas, and if you blink a certain button on your controller you can hit somethings like to get the meat, but the only animal that will attack you is the wolf, and that is only if you hit them, but if you don't, nothing happens (just like a bee in the real world). At night there are things that come out, like skeletons, and they have a bow and arrow. And there are zombies and creepers (definition of a creeper: they will walk up to you and explode), and there are baby zombies that aren't that common and really small and super fast, and the final one is a witch. They have potions and will throw them at you. And those are all of the animals.

The last thing about the game is that there is another type of village, but no one is there. This is what it is like. When you get there, you go into the village and get to this spot where there is a huge hole in the ground, and it is really deep, and you go into it. But when you get to the bottom, there is a pressure plate, which if you land on it you will explode and die, but if you don't step on it, then you need to try to get the four chests down there, and there are really cool things in them. That is all of the things you need to know about *Minecraft*.

Friday, May 15, 2020

In the morning, when I went downstairs, I said hi to my mom and Cody, but my dad wasn't going to be here today because he had to work. It is Friday and the last day of the week, and I had to still do social studies. I went straight upstairs after I ate, to do all of my work. So I did it, and it took me about twenty to thirty minutes. After that I looked at my computer, and I still needed to do some science, and I did that for about twenty minutes. After that I was done with all of my schoolwork for the rest of the week, so I went downstairs and played *Minecraft*.

This afternoon I was thinking, because in the NFL, before every NFL season, every single player needs to run a forty-yard dash, and the fastest ones run it in about 4.4 seconds, and I was wondering what if I took a measuring tape and I wanted to see how fast I could run a forty yard dash. My mom and Cody and I took a measuring tape and measured it on the side of the road. The good things is that we live in a neighborhood, and not many cars go by during the day, and especially since coronavirus you can't really go anywhere. So we measured, and it was almost the exact amount, but I was not going to get close to getting it inside of four to five seconds. The reasons why are because the players eat certain foods and have certain clothes on and drink the right amount of water and warm up with a professional trainer and things like that. I am not going to do that. I am just going to run for fun (that rhymes). So I ended up running, and the first time I ran a 6.78 and the next time a 6.73. Then we ran with Wilson to see how fast he could run, and he ran a 6.33, but that isn't really right because he didn't go right away and he slowed down at the finish line. But that is still really fast. Then I ran one more forty-yard dash and I got a 6.40, and that is my best. Then we each ate a popsicle and went back inside. After eating dinner and the rest of the night, we were doing nothing except just relaxing.

Saturday, May 16, 2020

I woke up and went downstairs, and my mom told us that we were going to go to Donnett's house and do work, so that is what we did. I really like to work for her. She is our neighbor and she is really nice. I asked my mom what time were we working for her, and she said that we would go at ten o'clock, and that is what we did. At ten o'clock we went to her house, and we got in the back of her truck, and she drove to this certain spot and parked it. We took these pieces of wood, and they were like a normal size piece of wood for a bonfire, and we filled her whole truck with it. We filled the whole truck to the top of a normal truck, and then she asked if we are done, and we said we can do more, and we did. We filled it farther than the top, and after that we told her that we were done, and she said ok. So Cody and I went in the back, and she drove us to this spot under her house where she had another huge stack of wood from all of the other times Cody and I did it, and then we took all of the wood out of the truck and put it all in that spot. After that I texted my mom and asked if she wanted to pick us up, and she asked us if we could walk home because she was cooking, and we started walking. Then Donnett said we could go in the back of her pickup truck, and that is what we did. When we got home my mom was cooking and I changed my clothes and went on the couch and relaxed. And that was fun. When my dad used to have a truck we would ride in the back when we got in the neighborhood after school each day, and it was so much fun.

Later I asked my mom if she wanted me to work, and that is what I did. I worked for one hour, and that is a long time. After working for about an hour and a half, there was going to be a reward. After I worked, I went downstairs and I played *Madden*, and after that I ran about fifteen forty yard dashes. My best was 6.33, and that is my new best.

Sunday, May 17, 2020

In the morning, I went downstairs and did some of my reading. Cody and I need to write a page a day on here, and every day I write about one page, and we need to do our writing before we go to bed each day. I got really annoyed because every time I said I was going to do my writing, Cody wanted to do his too. This has been happening for two months, and I decided that I am going to do my writing in the morning.

Cody looked at me and said that I had to raise my right hand and say, "No matter what, I will not do my writing at night, and I can only do it in the morning, no matter what." So that is what I did, and then I told Cody to do the same thing, and he did, and so that is what I was hoping would happen from now on, and I can write by myself! And we will not have to argue about who gets the computer.

In the afternoon, we went to a place called Civic Field, a football field and a track around it, and we played football for about one hour. The funny things is that there were these two girls, both running track, and during the time we were playing football, Cody about five times would look over, and I would say, "Cody, you spacing out?"

He would say "What?" in a shocked way, and I would just laugh.

After we played, I ran track—and that was the main reason I came. The first time I ran track, I ran a forty-yard dash in 6.36 easily, and after I did that, I was wondering why that was really easy. It was because the track they had is straight, not bumpy. The street at my house is up, then down, and there is moss where I run, so it is more slippery. Then I ran a couple more times at the track, and I got a 6.28 and then a 6.26 and then a 6.24. After that I was really happy, and then I ran my final one, 6.20.

Monday, May 18, 2020

We slept outside and in the morning I went inside and looked at Cody. He was on the computer, and I asked him what he was doing, and he said that he was writing, and remember what happened yesterday, and that got me really annoyed. Cody had never been on time with writing and picking up Wilson poop, and I have always done it when I say I will, and it was really annoying.

Later in the morning, I went outside to run a couple forty-yard dashes, and I did, and then I got my best, and it was 6.13. Then I got 7.04, and I was really confused, and then I realized that I was running against really strong wind and that might have been why I did really bad. I waited for the wind to calm down and then ran one more, and I got 6.23. Then I ran my last one and got a 6.11, and that was my best by far, but it is really not that far because earlier I got only two milliseconds slower, and that is like the same thing. But Cody challenged me that by the end of the month I need to get faster than 6.00, and then I accepted his challenge, and really the things is there isn't any betting or anything, it is just for fun, and that was what I have been trying to do.

Tonight we watched another documentary, the third one we have watched, and there are ten of them, one hour long each, about Michael Jordan. This one was about Dennis Rodman, and it talked about how he had a hard childhood. He got made fun a lot. It showed that everyone was saying that he was different, and the more they said that, the more he got different and the more he wanted to be himself. After that, my mom said that we could sleep outside, and she would sleep outside too.

Tuesday, May 19, 2020

This morning I went downstairs and my dad was home and my mom was home and my brother was home and my dog was home and everyone was here. I went to dad and asked if we could go to the track and if I could run some forty-yard dashes, and he said yes, and I really wanted to, and he said we could go later that afternoon because he needed to mow our lawn, and our lawn is really big. So this is our yard. In the front yard, it is super, super big. If you are looking from sky view, then on the right side of the side of our house there are stairs down to the bottom of our house, and to the left, if you walk down the stairs, is just a lot of bark and plants and bushes, and when you get to the bottom, if you keep walking straight you will get to a bonfire. I'm guessing you didn't guess, but that is our bonfire. From there, it is a big patio with a table and chairs in the middle and a hot tub on the end, and it is a great back yard. There is, like, no one there, just woods. I should be talking about the yard. Well, our side yard going all of the way around the bark area, then it will go around the patio and up a couple of big rocks and then back to the left side of the house and then, in the front side to the left, we have our driveway and obviously on the right side of the front of our house is our front yard, and now we are going in a full circle, and it will go on forever and ever, and that is my whole yard (and patio).

In the afternoon, I went to the Civic track and ran a couple forty-yard dashes, and then I played football with Cody and Dad, and then I started running faster than normal. I ran my best, a 6.06, and then I ran a 6.03, and then I ran 6.00, and then I asked my dad to time me because Cody didn't believe me. Then my dad timed me, and on the first try my dad told me it was 5.97, and you should have seen the shock on Cody's face after that. Then I saw my friends Mason and his mom and sister, and they were going there to play soccer. We all talked for about ten minutes, and then we three went back home.

Thursday, May 21, 2020

I didn't write yesterday. Whoops. My dad is going to come home at ten o'clock, and yesterday I did nothing, no running, didn't really even go outside. I sat on the couch and read a book and looked at the news. The reason why is because I really wanted to do a lot of track the next day and be rested and fast, and that is what I did. When my dad got home, we went to Civic track, and when we got there, I was really surprised because there was so many people running track. There were still a lot of places I could run because I am faster than all of these people! (Don't tell anyone I said that.) Ok, good. Glad we cleared that up.

So we got down there, and we both ran four hundred meters, and after that we did stretches for about fifteen to twenty minutes, and then I was ready. My first one, I went kind of fast but not really fast. I got a 6.13, and after that I got a 6.07, and after that was really happy, so I ran about five or ten more, and then on my tenth on I got 6.07 again. After that I was starting to slow down and then I got a 6.13 and then slower and then slower, until I got a 6.28, and that was my worst for the whole day. Then we made our way toward home and went for coffee and then got home, and my mom and Cody were on a bike ride. That was what I did, and I ended up averaging really good.

Tonight we ate dinner and then started making ice cream, and let me tell you the steps to make ice cream: (Before the whole thing you need to put a huge special bowl into the freezer for about 10 hours, and then it is good.) First you mix sugar and milk for about two or three minutes, and then in the same bowl you mix heavy cream and vanilla to give it a sweet taste, and then you put it in the large special bowl and put the bowl in this machine, and then it will mix it for twenty five minutes, and then you put the large special bowl into the freezer and leave it in there for about twenty minutes, and it will be good to eat.

Friday, May 22, 2020
My dad is going to be here until tomorrow, when he needs to go to the fire station. He is going to leave at four in the morning, and then he will work for one day, and then he will be home for four more days, and that means lots of track, and since my dad is here today, we are going to run track today. That is what I am really hoping to do, and but we are going to wait until this afternoon. This morning I have a dentist appointment.

This is what the appointment was like. I went to go to Dr. Schmidt's office to get parts of my braces off so it will be easier to clean, and that took about ten minutes. It was completely quiet, and then I accidentally kicked over the garbage can, and I picked it up, and everyone in that room looked at me, and I walked over to a seat and sat down. But I had a mask on, and I would wear one until I got to the chair, and then they did what they needed to do in my mouth. Then I put the mask back on and went out.

There is another doctor's office on the other side of the parking lot, and that is Dr. Piper's office. I walked straight over to his office, and when they called me in, Cody was in the chair right next to me. I thought he would at least glance his head over when the person wasn't doing things in his mouth, but when I sat down and they lowered the chair to a flat surface, there was a movie screen and a movie and called *Onward*, and it is a new movie that just came out. After that I went back to Schmidt's office, and they put the braces wire back on, and we went home.

And then I ran track. I didn't do super good. I had watched videos of what to do, and not really any of them helped, but I did beat my best. I got 5.90, and that just keeps motivating me to get faster and faster, and that is really all I did today.

Saturday, May 23, 2020
In the morning, I thought of what I should do, and my idea was that I am not going to go to the track today because then I will be really ready for the next day, and I will hopefully be fresh and ready to run millions of forty-yard dashes.

At ten o'clock we went to go work for Donnett. We worked for her one week ago at ten o'clock on Saturday, and today is ten o'clock. One week ago she asked us if we wanted to just get our money now or get our money next Saturday, and we decided that she will just pay us next Saturday. More like, Cody decided because he didn't even ask me, he just said next Saturday, and I just went with it. So she is going to pay us double, for both days. This is what we did. To start, we took all of this wood from with one spot in the back yard really far back and put it all in the truck, and it took us about 30 minutes. After that she drove the truck and went to the side of her house, and we unloaded it there, and that took us about one hour. That was all we were planning to do, and then she asked us if we wanted to do another hour of work, and that is what we did. We took twigs out of these spots where she wanted to plant some things, and one hour later she paid us forty dollars. Cody and I were both really surprised, and we said thanks, and it was twenty for last week and twenty for this week.

And when we got home, we took off our clothes and put on new ones and cleaned up. When we were done, I felt like eating, and that is what I did. I ate a lot of food, and then Cody and I went downstairs and played for a little bit. My mom told Cody and I that tomorrow we are going to be home alone for a couple hours. There is a movie called *Home Alone*, and that got me scared to be home alone, until I was about nine and I realized that it was just a kid's movie.

At night we watched a movie called *Bruce Almighty*, and it was really funny. I will not say anything to tell you about it, but is really funny, and as you can tell it is funny, and that is all I will say about the movie.

Sunday, May 24, 2020

I woke up at six forty-five, and my mom would have left at six thirty to go to the hospital, so she wasn't here, and my dad was going to get home at ten in the morning, and that was fine with me. I went downstairs, and remember, both of my parents aren't here. Cody was downstairs, and he had headphones on, and he looked like he was asleep. I think Cody overdoes it when it comes to the screen. He is usually on the screen, on his phone, or on the laptop, and on the TV or on the Xbox. I came down and did some schoolwork right next to him, and he didn't even look or say hi. He didn't even wave, and he didn't even look at me. After about forty five minutes of me doing schoolwork, he takes off his headphones and puts them down and still doesn't say anything to me, and he is still looking at his phone. Then after about another fifteen minutes, he looks up from his phone, and I bet you couldn't guess what he said.

"Do you want to watch YouTube?"

I said, "No, I need to go outside and pick up poop." And that is how my morning went, just wonderful.

When my mom came home, we watched another Michael Jordon episode, and it is now the seventh one, and I am going to call Michael Mike, just to let you know. So Mike played for the Chicago Bulls. He started playing in 1984, and in 1990 they won a championship game, and then in 1991 they won another one, and then in 1992, and then his dad got murdered. His dad always wanted for Mike to play baseball, and I bet you couldn't guess what he did for a year and a half. He played pro baseball, and then he went back to basketball for another couple years until 1998, and then he retired for good. That was what Michael Jorden did and what it was about.

Monday, May 25, 2020

This morning I went inside because we slept outside, and I got this idea to make my own bird feeder. I also really want to get squirrels to eat from my feeder too, and this is my idea. I started to put about fifteen walnuts on the side of the deck, and that will make it so birds can get it and squirrels can get it also. My idea is to put up a camera, with a tripod to keep the camera from falling, and I don't think it will be easy to get a squirrel, but I will try. Tomorrow I think that I will try to make another attempt. You could call it to get birds and squirrels, but the thing is that Wilson has been scaring all of the birds and the squirrels away, so I need to put this feeder in a spot where Wilson can't get it, and that will be on the other side of his electric fence. That might be hard to get because I don't know if the squirrels can get to that, but we will see what happens.

After about three hours, I got no footage of squirrels, but I got a lot of birds on the camera, and I got a really good bird called a Steller's jay, and that was cool, but I still am thinking of a way to get a squirrel, and the way I got the idea to do this is from Mark Rober's YouTube channel. He made a whole course of spots where they could get there, and I will just need to keep trying. All day it has been raining, and it is looks like it will rain for the rest of the day, and that means that I need to put a ziplock bag over my camera so it will not get wet and ruined.

At night Phil came over with Banks, the new dog, and he told us that he needed to give him back because he was a rescue dog and he thinks that he was abused and he has nipped, like, six times in forty-eight hours, so he is giving him back. Some good news is that his daughter is in labor right now, and today is Avie's birthday, so they might have the same birthday, and they will be sisters and two years apart. They are really happy, and I can't wait to see if the baby comes out today.

Tuesday, May 26, 2020

A couple months ago, I had surgery on my mouth. The procedure was that they cut open my mouth back in the palate because my canine tooth was going the wrong way and it was going to hit another tooth and mess everything up. After they cut open my palate, surprisingly, they didn't put me to sleep, so I was awake throughout the whole thing. They still numbed my mouth with a really long needle, and it wasn't like a little shot. It hurt like really, really badly, and after they did that, they did it again in a different spot in my mouth. I was thinking *Just put me to sleep!* but they didn't, and in the doctor's glasses I could see everything reflecting that they were doing, and it was really distressing.

Then I heard them say they found the tooth, and then they said they were almost done. About one hour later they were done, and they pulled my tooth down and didn't take it out but attached a bracket onto it. That is what the surgery was, and now the tooth is coming out, and it is just right there in my mouth, and today they attached a rubber band to it and then attached the other side to my braces, and over time it will move all of the way over to where it is supposed to be, and at one point it will just be in the middle of my mouth.

When I got home that afternoon, I was thinking of what I could do with my feeder to get birds and squirrels, and then I got an idea to put some platform on the other side of Wilson's fence, and that is what I did. I put a platform of wood in my backyard, and it was perfect. This time I put bird seeds, carrots (for bunnies maybe, but not hopeful), leaves, walnuts, and finally oranges, and they are all for any animal. It is going to take a long time for all of the animals to realize that it is there. I set my phone up and then clicked play and it was rolling.

After a couple hours, my phone died. I charged it and checked the camera and nothing came, only one or two birds. I charged my phone for about one hour and then put it back out there.

That afternoon my mom and Cody went to Seattle to run and get some things. Seattle is about two hours away from Bellingham. My dad and I didn't do much .We played basketball and things like that in the afternoon.

Wednesday, May 27, 2020

Yesterday I really wanted to try to get more and more animals and things like that on my camera outside, and I put a piece of wood out there and had food on it and a lot of walnuts, and today they are all gone. I am guessing that something went there that didn't go there before, because before, nothing ate it, and that was really confusing. I did not have my camera on it, so that sucks.

In the afternoon, Cody and my dad and I all went to the track and played football. During the game both of my ankles started getting sharp pains, like a hundred needles stabbing in my ankle, so I stopped for a little bit and stretched, and then I started running track. The first time I went really slow just to warm up, and I didn't time myself. Then I did a couple timed ones, and then I full-on sprinted, and halfway through the forty-yard dash I stopped, and then we just all went home.

I got a little bit frustrated, and the reason why is because the last time we went to the track, for some reason the whole time I was gassed and out of breath, and it was really weird, and it was seventy degrees, and I didn't bring a water bottle. Today I told Cody and my dad that this was my water bottle and they can go get their own inside, because I was going to be getting really thirsty. That is what I said, and neither of them brought a water bottle, and it was the same temperature outside, and they wouldn't stop drinking out of my water. I kept on telling them to please stop, and they didn't, and I had an attitude about the hundredth time they did it. That is why I got frustrated. I know you might be laughing that I was getting frustrated at a water bottle, and now I regret doing that, and now I know that it was just really stupid and I should have not done it. That is all we did today, and nothing really exciting happened the rest of the day.

Thursday, May 28, 2020

Today my dad is going to be at the fire station for the whole day, but tomorrow he will be home at ten in the morning. When I woke up I looked at the clock, and it was 6:40. I decided that I would read and that is what I did. After reading for thirty-five minutes, I went downstairs and my mom and Cody were there, and I thought that today I would do a lot of schoolwork and then on Friday I will not need to do as much. I did some schoolwork and then Cody and I went downstairs and played *Minecraft*.

I did a simulation where you can play a certain type, and I am going to tell you what it is and what it is about and the goal of the game. So, first of all, you can't break anything, and there are four and sometimes five chests, and you start right away, right next to each other, and you both try to open as many things as possible of the four chests, and you usually get only two if only two people are playing, but you can get a lot of things. Here are a lot of things that are usually in them: swords, bow and arrows, potions (can throw them at others and cause damage), and lots of things like that. You get, like, fifteen seconds to do that, and then you can fight each other. But before those fifteen seconds, you can hit the other person. After you get the chests, you usually run the opposite direction, and there are other chests hidden around you, and you try to find them. When you feel like you have the better weapon, you try to find the other person and kill them. The game involves violence, but there is very little blood and I don't know if I would even call it violence. Just a game.

That night nothing happened. We just relaxed and did nothing, and I am happy because tomorrow I will have twenty minutes of screen time because I saved it. I wouldn't be surprised if Cody doesn't think I have extra screen time tomorrow.

Friday, May 29, 2020
This morning I was thinking of what I wanted to do, because my dad is going to come home today at ten in the morning. I looked at the clock and it was eight o'clock, and my mom asked me if I wanted to wash her car. I said yes, and that is what I did. However long it takes, I get that much more screen time added to my one hour because every day we get one hour. We usually get two hours on the weekends, because on the weekdays we have school and we do schoolwork and things like that on the weekdays. Then on the weekends, we get two hours of screen time on Friday, Saturday, and Sunday, but we get one hour on Monday, Tuesday, Wednesday, and Thursday. When I washed my mom's car, it took me about thirty-five minutes. When I was done, Cody and I did some screen time for about one hour. Then we went back upstairs and I did the rest of my schoolwork for today, which took me about one hour, and I didn't have as much because I did a lot yesterday.

This afternoon we didn't do anything. My dad came home and mowed the lawn, and that took him a couple hours. When he was done, I went in our backyard to relax, but there was a deer eating the food I put out for the squirrels. Sadly, I didn't have my camera, because I was charging it. I went inside and told Cody and Mom, and they saw it, and it was funny, and we all went back inside for the afternoon.

Tonight we ate dinner and watched an episode from the series about Michael Jordan. It was episode ten and we thought that there was going to be a part two, but there wasn't. After that I made ice cream, and that is all we did for the night. We slept outside and there were so many bugs I was wondering if I could ever fall asleep. I ended up falling asleep and my mom went in early, and that is all we did that whole day.

Saturday, May 30, 2020

It was six thirty in the morning, and I woke up. My brother was on my right and my dad was on my left and my mom wasn't even outside. I was guessing she went in earlier in the night, and that is what she did, and this is what she said about why: "It's because I went in and out, like six times, over and over, and the reason why I did that is because there were so many bugs out there. I had to go inside and change my clothes and cover my whole body, and I needed to have a little hole so I could breathe." But Mom said that is what woke her up, because she was right next to the door outside, and she could really hear it open and close. So I am just going to try to not do that the next time, because I don't want my mom to wake up really early.

Later that morning, I played *Minecraft*, and there is this huge water fountain in the game, in the lobby, and there is a way you can stop the water, and this is how. First of all there is a little stop there, and there is a small hole in the ground, and there is a lever that you can see, and you go in a door that is right next to it, and then you go through another hidden door, and then there is another hidden door. You go in it and down some stairs, and there is a picture of a water bottle, and if you click LT on your controller, it will move it around in a circle, and when you get it facing upside down, you go back up the stairs and out a couple of doors. Then you go to a different stop and open that, and then you go upstairs, and there will be another water bottle picture, and you turn it upside down too, and then you go down the stairs and go through two more doors, and there will be stairs that go down, and you go down those, and there will be a button that will make the water stop, and that is how you can do it. That probably was really confusing, but there are a lot of videos on how to do it, and it will have a screen to show you, and it will be really easy. That is how I figured it out, but after playing for a little bit, the rest of the day was just relaxing.

Sunday, May 31, 2020

Today my dad is going to the fire station to work. A couple days ago a Black man was killed by a white police officer, and there are many people protesting and looting stores in Seattle (looting means stealing and destroying all of the things from the store). My dad works in Seattle, and he is going to have a bulletproof vest, in case there are people shooting and things like that, because there are these huge protests blocking the roads so no one can get through, and people in the protests have assault rifles, and they are, like, threatening people and the police and things like that, and people are breaking windows and setting places on fire, and the fire station isn't supposed to put them out because it is not very safe. And they are dealing with more serious things.

There are photos on the news that show people jumping on police cars and breaking all the windows and dancing on top of the car, and after that it showed the person on the car get down and light the car on fire, and there is smoke everywhere.

People are fighting and there are smoke bombs everywhere, and it is absolutely crazy. My dad needs to be there, and there are so many people tweeting about these things. One of Trump's tweets on Twitter was taken off because it was threatening, and he is saying, like, "Send vicious dogs after the thugs." And he means after the protesters and looters. And before the looting, he said, "After the looting, here come the shooting." And that was taken off Twitter.

At the end of the day, my dad called and said that he is ok. That night we went for just a little bike ride, and I crashed. I was just going uphill, and nothing was in front of me, and it was like my bike got locked in when I turned it to the left, and I fell to my right side, and landed on my arm. I sprained my wrist and cut my fingers, but it will just be sore for a couple of days, and I know that it is not a serious injury.

Monday, June 1, 2020

This morning my dad came home and I told him that I was getting a little big for my bunk beds and that I wanted to switch my bunk beds with the queen-size bed in the basement. He said ok, and that is what we did. That afternoon we went downstairs and took apart the whole queen-size bed and everything. Then my dad and my mom took the top of my bunk bed off and laid it down. It is really—and when I say "really" I mean it—it is really heavy, and my mom and my dad ended up doing it somehow. After that we took apart the top bunk, and then we brought all of things from the top bunk down downstairs. We put the bed back together, and there also was somethings that you might not have realized, that we needed to bring everything that was really heavy up and down the staircases.

It was about two thirty and we had just finished the second bunk bed. I told my dad I needed to take a break because I have only had a slice of pumpkin bread this morning and nothing for lunch. We took a break, I ate four full bowls of cereal, and I was ready to work again. Then we brought all the queen bed parts upstairs, and this was the big bed, so it was the heaviest. After that I needed to vacuum everything, and then we put it all together, and it looked great. The only thing that didn't look good is my dresser, and I told my dad I could do it myself. So I moved it to the place I wanted it, to a different corner, and then I took this bench-like thing that was a bench but the top could open and there would be things inside of it, and I carried

58

that downstairs by myself and switched it with a square table that wasn't rectangular. Then I was finished.

That night we ate dinner outside and had a bonfire (made by Cody), and after that I did some reading because I got a new book, and I really liked it. It is called *Gathering Blue*. It is the second book of *The Giver*, and there will be two more after this book, and they are called *Messenger* and then *Son*.

Tuesday, June 2, 2020

My parents give Cody and me ten dollars a month for allowance, and my parents have not paid us our allowance for four months now, so today they paid Cody and me our forty dollars. I counted my money to see how much I have. My whole life I have saved my money. Like, I have not spent anything. I counted my money and I had seven hundred dollars and ten cents. A couple years ago I grew out of my wallet, you could say, but I could not fit any more money in it, so now I have it just on my dresser and it is somewhat safe. I asked my dad if I could trade in all of my money and get it all in twenties, and that is what we did. Now I have seven hundred dollars in twenties.

This afternoon Cody and I played basketball for about twenty minutes, and then it started to rain. We played for ten more minutes, and by then it was pouring, so we went inside. At night Cody and I watched a movie called *The Giver*, and I am going to give you a little summary of what it is about. If you don't want to hear it because of spoilers, skip this part. Jonas and his two friends Asher and Fiona lived a life that was ruled by rules, and there was a barrier around them, so they couldn't cross it, and Jonas starts to realize things. Like, he starts seeing colors (no one can see colors), and no one in the community knows about the history of animals, weather, war, and lots and lots more, and Jonas starts knowing. He wants to tell everyone the past, and there is one problem. He doesn't know how to tell everyone, because they will not understand. Read the book and watch the movie and see what happens and what Jonas will do and how he will help others see what he sees. So that is all we did for the whole day. Not really anything, now that I read over what I have written, but whatever. That is all I have to say.

Wednesday, June 3, 2020

In the morning, when I went downstairs, I first went to do my schoolwork. After I did about twenty minutes of that, Cody and I did some screen time for about forty minutes, usually longer than what we do in this time frame, so we only had twenty minutes left, and I went upstairs. On Monday and Tuesday I did schoolwork, and I did a lot of it, more than I usually do. Today I looked at my schoolwork again, and I realized that I did so much the last two days that I only needed to do a small thing for language arts and I would be done for the rest of the week. I did that work and now I am done for the whole week, and it is only Wednesday. I did the rest of my screen time, and then my dad came home. He is going to be home for two days and then go back for one day.

In the afternoon, Cody and my mom went to Joe's Garden. They got a lot of strawberries, and when they got home, my mom and I did some gardening. It started with my mom wanting to move this flower, dig it out and move it, but she wanted to not ruin the plant by cutting the root. She said that she was hungry, and she went inside, so I did it myself. When I moved it, I got it to the place she wanted to put it, and then I shoveled a huge really big hole, and after that I put the flower in it, and that ended up taking one hour and twenty minutes.

In the evening, we ate dinner and then watched a show called *Wonder Years*. I mentioned it before, and it was about twenty-five minutes, and it was really funny and really lifelike. After we did that I made myself homemade ice cream, and I have memorized all of the ingredients, and that makes it a lot easier and faster to do. That is really all we did, and my dad will be home for one more day. I think my mom might be going to work tomorrow, but I am not really sure. I will find out tomorrow.

Thursday, June 4, 2020
At four in the morning, I woke up and remembered a dream I had. This is what happened. I was at my school, and everyone was sitting in a circle, and one teacher looked at me and said, "Taylor, you are late." I sat down and said I was sorry. Then for some reason I had a scooter and I asked Cody what my classes for this school year were, and he said to check my locker. I went to my locker and halfway there that teacher that said I'm late told me I got detention. That is when I woke up, and I was really confused when I woke up, but after that I petted Wilson on the head and went back to bed.

Right now during coronavirus, there are still lots of protests about the death of a Black man named George Floyd. He got killed because a white police officer arrested him for no reason and kneeled on his neck for nine minutes until he died, and it was all because of racism. There are books about racism, and one of them is called *How to Be an Antiracist*, and I have heard about it, but I don't know what the details are except that it is about racism. Another reason people are protesting is because of Donald Trump.

Friday, June 5, 2020

This morning I went downstairs and my mom said that her friends are coming over tonight, but outside because of coronavirus, and that we (Cody and I) could watch a movie and the only expectation is that we needed to just do a little bit of chores. And that is what we did this afternoon.

We made our mom a bonfire for her friends when they came over, and it was great. It stayed lighted for the rest of the night. But that afternoon I swept and mopped the whole floor, and that took me about thirty minutes. Then I went upstairs and got some socks and went outside, and when I got out there, I wanted to play basketball, but I couldn't. Yesterday Cody and I were playing basketball and I tripped over Cody's feet, and Cody added in a little push, and then I put my hand out to catch myself, and it was gravel right there, and I cut my hand. It got pretty bloody, and I put some bandages on it and played more basketball, and after about five minutes, I told Cody I was going to stop because my hand was hurting, and I went inside.

The other day, Cody and I both made a bench, and this is what we did. Yesterday my dad took a ton of wood and cut it, and then we first made the top part where you sit on it, and then we made the legs and put those two together, and then by myself I painted it and made it a darker shiny color, and it looked really good.

At night we watched a movie called *Central Intelligence*, and it was really funny, and I could watch it again. The two main actors are The Rock (Dwayne Johnson) and Kevin Hart, and they are both in my top ten favorite actors list. The movie had great reviews. That is all we did when my mom's friends went home. We all just relaxed, and after a little bit of food, we all went to bed.

Saturday, June 6, 2020

When I went downstairs, my mom and Cody were there, and my dad would be there at ten in the morning. My dad said that he is going to go to a Bellingham (we live there) protest to support Black Lives Matter. When my dad came home, he showed us some disturbing video. It showed some police shoving innocent people, and they didn't do anything. Like, that is the saddest one, and this one is all over the news. So one old guy was 76 years old, and I think he needed to bring something for the homeless, and he was just watching, and he didn't do anything wrong, and the whole sidewalk filled with police officers. He didn't mean any harm, and the two different policemen shoved him to the ground, and he hit his head, and he was 76, remember. There was blood everywhere from his head, coming out of his ears, and he got knocked out and wasn't moving at all. Something that was almost as bad as shoving the guy to the ground is that no one stopped and helped him. All of the police just walked right over him, and no one did anything, except the protesters. They were trying to help him, but the police were shoving the protesters away, and the guy who fell was really hurt. It ended up being a skull fracture. He will live but he was really hurt.

In the afternoon, Cody and my dad and my mom and I all went to the protest. We cheered and supported, and it was peaceful and nothing happened. After doing that for about one and a half hours, we went home and drank some water. Cody and I played some *Minecraft*, and my parents went into the hot tub. It was just a chill night, and that is all we did.

I am starting to do weightlifting, and I am just starting curls and things like that. It is fun to do on a rainy day so I get some exercise in without going into the pouring rain. We have five-, eight- and twelve-pound weights. I am starting with five, and then over time I will go to eights, and then after probably a while I will go to twelve pounds, and that is all I did today.

Sunday, June 7, 2020

Today I have some things to tell you, and first I am going to tell you some facts, the current things that are happening. First of all, my mom will be going to work at two o'clock and she will come home at midnight, and my dad is home today and then he will go to the fire station tomorrow, and then after that he will be home for four days.

In the afternoon, my mom left and Cody and I played some cards. After that, we didn't know what we could do. Cody got this idea that we each get a little amount of wood, and we ended up deciding that we could each get a piece twelve feet by three inches by one inch, and we had no idea what we could do. I got this idea for mine, that I could make a cornhole board. If you don't know what it is, it's just a game where there is a board and a hole in the middle, and you toss a little bag and try to get it into the hole. I tried to do it first, and we ended up accidentally getting ten feet instead of twelve, but we made it work. I found scraps from when we made the benches, and after that everything was going well and was almost finished, and I put in the last screw, and I was finished. I sandpapered some things, and it was all done. Cody made a wood feeder for a squirrel, and we will see how that turns out.

We FaceTimed my mom and showed her what we made. Tomorrow she will be able to see it in person, and we could maybe play the game that I made—cornhole. We originally didn't have any bags for the game, so when my dad gets back, we will get some. It will be really fun to play this summer. That is all I did today.

Monday, June 8, 2020

Today my dad is going to be at work but my mom will be home. Then tomorrow my dad will be here for four days and my mom will be home for one day after tomorrow, and then everyone will be home again. Right now, with school, it is Monday, and this is the last week of school, and then it will be summer. The thing is, it is like summer but we still get schoolwork.

In the afternoon, Cody and I went outside and played basketball. After that, I went inside and Cody stayed outside and played more basketball. Then I went in the basement, and my mom was down there lifting weights. Cody went downstairs and would not stop following me, so I went outside and he went outside. I told him I wanted to play separately, and right after that he asked me if I wanted to play cards. I looked at him and said, "What?" and he smiled. I walked away and laughed.

In late afternoon, Cody dared me to try to sleep in my closet, and I said, "What?" He said he would give me ten minutes of his screen time tomorrow if I sleep the whole night in my closet, until seven in the morning. I was really confused. He said all I could have was a little blanket and a pillow, and that is what I somehow agreed to. The thing is, if I don't sleep the whole night in there, I will need to give him ten minutes of my screen time, but that is what I am going to do.

At night we watched a *Modern Family* show. It is about a family and goes back and forth between the main family and the mom's brother's family and her dad's family. It is the funniest show that I have ever watched, and it makes me laugh until I can't breathe. I don't know if that is a good thing or a bad thing, but that is all we did the whole day. Tomorrow my dad will come home from work.

Tuesday, June 9, 2020

Right now in Seattle, my dad is working and will be home at ten this morning. In Seattle there are five current police stations, and remember, protesters are protesting against police because a policeman killed George Floyd by kneeling on his head for nine minutes until he died. So, one of the stations is close to the fire station that my dad works at, and it is surrounded by some things so nothing and nobody can get into the police station. Everyone at that station left because they just couldn't do it, with all the protesting against them. They took down the wall around the station, and now there are only four police stations in Seattle. That surprised me, but after a little bit it made sense.

That evening, Cody and I played basketball for about thirty minutes. I stopped because Cody was mad and he was just not that fun after a while. I went downstairs and lifted weights for about thirty minutes, and my parents came home. They had gone on a hike a little bit ago. My mom made dinner, and I helped her clean the counter and mop a part of the floor. Then I did the dishes. I had been helping her for a long time and I asked her if she needed anything else. She said no, so I went out of the kitchen and started going downstairs, and my mom said, "Thanks for helping me! There will be a reward."

I was thinking of what I could do and then decided that I might do some reading, and that is what I did for thirty minutes. I was done and at that same moment my mom called me and said that dinner was done, and I went upstairs. I ate dinner with my family, and I was wondering whether I had dessert last night, but I didn't. We, as a family, eat dessert every other night, so today we could have ice cream, and I was really looking forward to that.

Wednesday, June 10, 2020

The night before, my mom went inside because she didn't think she could sleep the whole night outside. Cody went in too, for whatever reason—I have no idea. My dad and I stayed out there, though, and Wilson was obviously out there too. In the morning my mom went to work at six thirty, and my dad will be home for three more days, including today. My whole family will be home today and tomorrow.

Tomorrow Gavin and Carter, two of Cody's and my best friends, are coming over. They are siblings, just like Cody and me, and because of coronavirus we aren't going inside. We are going to have a bonfire in our back yard. Also, their parents, Aubrey and Rob, are coming over too.

Cody and I each have a box that has a lot of things from when we were younger. I found pictures of me in first grade and second, and it was so much fun to see. We did that for a long time, and when we were done my mom went downstairs. She just got home from work. Cody and I went outside and played basketball, and my dad called us in for dinner. We set up the table, and that is all we did that night.

I want to tell you some things about Gavin and Carter. First of all, Cody and I have known them for, I think, six years. Gavin is Cody's age and Carter is two years older than Cody. Cody became friends with Gavin in first grade, and since then we all have been friends. Cody and I have not seen them in a long time. I think we last saw them a couple months ago, and Carter had knee surgery because he tore his ACL or MCL, not sure which, but I think he is fully recovered, so that is nice. I can't wait to see them tomorrow.

Thursday, June 11, 2020

This morning it was pouring really hard. Like, I didn't know if it would stop. The weather report said that it will stop, but I don't know if we can do this, because all of the chairs by the bonfire will be really wet. But we will see. My mom left this morning for work. She wasn't planning on it, but she did. After she left it was seven in the morning, and it was still pouring down rain. Cody and I went downstairs and did some screen time, and we asked our dad if we could maybe do some extra and clean the house after. He said that was ok, and we did that. We played *Minecraft* and we are still making this really cool thing. This is what it is. So first, there is a stop where people will start, and there are four chests with things in them that Cody and I put in. We get the chests, and then I bet fifteen houses with hidden chests in them, and you need to find them. After you do that for a while, if you find the other person then you fight them, and it is not violent at all. I would say people seven years old and up can play this. I don't know why, but it says ten and up, but whatever.

The afternoon was still pouring down rain, and I was starting to give up on them coming over. At one o'clock it was still raining, and I was starting to think about when can they come over another time. I looked at the weather, and it said rain, and at two it was still raining. At about two forty-five it stopped, and the sun came out. For a couple hours it was sunny, and I was really happy. I looked at the weather, and it said it will be sunny the rest of the night. I told mom and Cody and dad, and they were all excited too. I really wanted it to stay sunny, and it was looking like it would, but I don't know. They are going to come over at five thirty or six, and I can't wait until they come. It is now four, and Cody and I played some basketball, and then we came in and played some poker for fun, and we went outside and played more basketball. By the time we did all of that it, was four forty-five, and I was really waiting, and I couldn't wait and flip the page to see what happens tonight.

Friday, June 12, 2020

I woke up to a bright moon shining in my face and the clicking sound of the rain hitting the gutters. I looked beside me, and to my left was my mom and then Cody, and my dad was to my right, and Wilson was lying at my feet. I pulled the blankets because Wilson was on top of them. I pulled a blanket to me, and Wilson just looked at me and sighed. Then he went back to sleep, and I sighed too and went back to sleep. Then, in what felt like not even a second, the sun was where the moon once was, and to my left Cody and my mom weren't there, and to my right neither was my dad, and my feet were not under a fluffy dog. I lifted my left wrist and looked at my Fitbit watch, and it was 7:59. I walked inside and looked at my watch again, and it was eight.

This morning the weather is still the same. It is pouring down rain, and I am wondering if the clouds might pop, with the amount of rain that they are holding. There aren't really any things to do, but my mom asked Cody and me if we wanted to go on a walk. I didn't know if she hadn't checked the weather outside or hadn't noticed that it had been raining for the last five hours straight, but I somehow agreed to go. When we got home, I was drenched, my whole body, except for my chest because I had a rain jacket.

At night we watched a movie called *The Bourne Identity*, and it was a really great movie. It has a really famous actor named Matt Damon, and he was the main character. Basically, he loses his memory, lots of people are trying to kill him, and he doesn't know why. There are multiple movies and they will all connect. I really want to watch the next couple movies later on. When I got upstairs after watching the movie, it was still pouring down rain and I was still not knowing if it will ever stop, but there is no possible way to know. This Friday is the last day of online school, but maybe next week there will be a little assignment, but who knows. That is all I did today.

Saturday, June 13, 2020

This morning my mom is home and my dad is at work, but he will be home tomorrow. I think that he will be home for two days, but hopefully he will be home for four, but I am not sure which one, but another time I will look at the calendar. Now I need to tell you what happened today. So first, this morning my mom asked Cody and me to go for a car ride. I asked where, and she said nowhere, that we are going on a cruise and just have no designation. After we did for about an hour, we came home and there wasn't really anything to do. I checked my school computer, and there wasn't anything new, so I decided to read. After reading for a long time, I thought of what I was going to do today. It was, like, eleven o'clock, and I went downstairs and looked at my phone, and nothing was new, nothing with coronavirus.

In the afternoon, Cody and I played basketball for about thirty minutes, and I went downstairs and played down there for another thirty minutes. I didn't do anything after that, but I did relax.

Tonight Cody and I watched a movie. My mom was having a friend over, and of course they were social distancing, but the movie we watched is called *Ferris Bueller's Day Off*. It is a really funny movie about a kid who skips school and tells his parents that he doesn't feel good, and they both leave for work and said that they would be back at six o'clock, and he does some crazy things with his two friends, and they do things that I can't even put into words. I think that this movie would be good for kids twelve to thirteen years old because there is a lot of swearing and there are some parts that some younger kids shouldn't see. If you want to know what happens when he takes the day off, go and watch the movie.

Sunday, June 14, 2020
Today my dad is coming home, and he is going to be home for four days because it said that on the calendar, unless the calendar was lying to me, but I hope it wasn't. This morning I went downstairs and watched thirty minutes of a show called *The Flash*, about a place called Star Labs. It sent a huge wave of some sort around the whole city, and it gave about four-fifths of the city super powers. You might be thinking this is probably a baby show, but it is not. It is rated for ages fourteen and up because of the violence and the swearing, so take that everyone who thought it was a baby show.

Well, there was one person, named Barry Allen, who got hit with that wave, and this is the story of him. There might be some spoilers, so don't read it if you are going to watch the show. Ok, so Barry was about seven, and he went downstairs because he heard something loud in the kitchen when he was asleep and woke up. When he got down there, there were flashing lights of red and yellow, and it was going in circles, and his parents were in the middle of it, and then it went away, and his mom was dead on the floor and his dad was alive. He didn't know what happened, but the police came to the house and arrested Barry's dad for murdering his wife, when he really didn't do it. After that his dad went to jail and his mom was dead, so he went and lived with a family with only a dad. The dad had a daughter who was Barry's age, and he was twenty when the explosion happened. He became a speedster, and that means he can run up to 186 miles per second and can time travel because he can run as fast as light. He ends up going back in time so see what really happened to his mother the night she died, and he figured out that another person got powers from the explosion and was fast, too. For whatever reason (it really isn't important), the other guy killed his mom, and the reason he saw the lights is because when a speedster runs, that light trailed behind him, and that is why he saw the light. I think it is a really good show, and I didn't really do anything today besides that.

Monday, June 15, 2020

Today my dad will be home, but tomorrow he won't. I really wanted to do something with wood, like wood working, and my dad said we could. This morning he went to the hardware store and got some more wood, and I made a squirrel feeder to go up into a tree. This is my design. First I want to get a flat bottom, and then I am going to make a slanted roof for the little house, so when it rains the water will not just go into the little feeder. This is how it turned out. We made a little box but not the roof or the bottom, and after that I was almost finished, but I did all of the measurements for the roof so it will look good, and it ended up looking really good, and I was now thinking to myself, *I am really almost done now.* Just the bottom, and first I am going to make the bottom piece two inches longer so that the squirrels can walk around to get to the hole where the food is.

That afternoon it was pouring down rain. I didn't want to go outside, and I decided today will be my yesterday for exercising, and that is what I did for this afternoon—nothing. And I was just sitting on the couch doing nothing when I got the idea that I will do a ton of homework, and then I will be able to do not that much later this week. Remember, this is the last week of school, and this is really cool, so on Thursday (today is Monday) I will go to my school and I get my yearbook. All the kids will be social distancing, and it will be fun to hopefully see some people that I know. The things is, there isn't really anyone that I know who has the first letter of their last name starting with P through Z. The reason why I say that is because there are only going to be kids with the last name between those two letters at that time frame, and that is kind of sad, but it will still be fun to do. And that is really all I did today, making wood, and tomorrow my dad will be going to the fire station at four in the morning. I hope you read what happens tomorrow.

Tuesday, June 16, 2020

Today it is Tuesday, and I really wanted my dad to be home today. Unfortunately, he is at work today, but tomorrow he will be home and that will be fun. I was thinking what I could do today. I thought it would rain, because it was raining this morning. Later in the morning it started to get a little bit sunny, and then it stayed sunny for an hour or two, until ten o'clock. I went outside and picked some salmonberries, and I got a lot of them, and I went inside after picking for about an hour, because it started to rain again. Today it has been off and on, rain and then no rain, and then before you know it, it will just start raining again.

In the late afternoon, I was thinking of what I could do, because it was pouring down rain now and I could, but I didn't want to, go outside.

Then I went upstairs and did some reading, and after I did almost all of my reading, I went back downstairs. It wasn't raining at all, and I thought I might as well just go outside before it starts raining again, and that is what I did for about thirty minutes, and then it started to rain again.

At night we watched a movie called *Mr. Deeds*, and it is about a man (Adam Sandler) who lives in a really poor town, and no one has ever left that town because they are so poor. Two really rich people come to their town and tell Mr. Deeds that his uncle died climbing Mount Everest and that he was really rich and that all of the money was going to Mr. Deeds. Mr. Deeds laughed and walked away, and then he finally realized that they were telling the truth. He went with them to New York because he needed to sign a couple contracts. When they got to New York, he asked how much money he was getting because of his uncle that he didn't even know had died, and they said that he will be getting forty billion dollars. He was in shock. At the end of the movie it wasn't really Mr. Deeds's money. It was someone's else's money, and the guy that got the money was his butler, and the butler said that he would give Mr. Deeds one billion dollars, and that is what happened. He gave all his money to the people in his hometown, and he gave everyone a really nice Porsche, I think it was. And that is all we did today.

Wednesday, June 17, 2020

This morning I played some *Minecraft* with Cody, and I think that I might play some *Minecraft* in the future (FYI tomorrow). After playing for about thirty to forty minutes with Cody, I watched a show called *The Flash*, and it is a really cool show, and when I say it, I mean it, a great show. It is about a man that gets superpowers, and on and on. You have heard it all a couple of pages ago. But after watching it for a little bit, I came upstairs.

That afternoon I played some basketball with Cody. We didn't play one on one and keep score, but we played a game called King of the Court. It is about one person at half court and one person under the basketball hoop, and you only need one hoop because, well, you will see. So the person under the basketball hoop has the ball and passes it to the person at half court, and you play from there. If the ball goes out of the court, then the person who was under the basketball hoop gets the ball, and it doesn't matter if you hit it out or not. If it goes out or if the person from under the basketball hoop gets possession of the ball, they get the ball and go to half court. But if the person that wasn't under the basketball makes it into the hoop, then they get to keep the ball, and that game just goes on forever. You might be wondering where the basketball hoop is. It is right next to our house, but technically it is our neighbor's, but he lets us use it.

That afternoon my dad spray painted our backyard furniture. It is metal, if you are wondering, and it was my dad's parents who gave it to our family. It is old and just rusted, and my dad spray painted it by himself, and it looks really good. Unfortunately, he got black spray paint all over this part of the yard, even with something under it to protect it from going everywhere. That didn't necessarily go everywhere, but it did go almost everywhere. And that is what my dad did that ended up looking really, really cool, like new.

Tonight nothing happened, but Cody and I played corn hole, and really nothing else happened. Wilson has an electric fence, and it is under ground, and on Wilson's collar it will beep and buzz and shock him if he goes past it. He has it well memorized, where it is, but it will beep if he gets close to it, and then it will vibrate and then shock. It will just shock him, not harm him. He was sitting on the edge of his fence looking in the bushes, and there was a bunny, and that, I can see, would get Wilson annoyed that he can't go across his fence, and he didn't cross the fence.

Thursday, June 18, 2020

My dad is going to be home for three more days, till the end of Saturday, I think. Today you can probable guess is Thursday, and today from nine to three o'clock Cody and I are going to go to school. We need to give the people from school our library books back, books that we needed to give to them a couple months ago, but because of Coronavirus we need to turn them in late. And the other thing is that Cody and I are going to get our yearbooks for 2019–2020, and that will be fun. But that isn't till this afternoon, so there are still some fun things to do before then, like basketball. And that is what Cody and I did until it was eleven o'clock, and we went inside, and my mom was just walking out the door to leave for work. She will be gone for twelve hours, until almost midnight.

This afternoon we went to school, and it is really weird to go there again. I haven't been there since March 13 of this year, I think. I wonder if next fall I am going to be back here, going to school again. Soon they—and by *they* I mean the governor of Washington State—will decide if we are or not. I think they need to decide by next week. I am not sure, but that will be interesting. When Cody and I got there, only a couple teachers were there, and they handed us each a yearbook, and then we gave them the books we needed to return, and then we went home. We played some basketball and looked at the yearbook, and that was fun because there were some kids that I remember from when Cody and I went to school a couple months ago. But of course, we can't go to school now because of COVID-19. You might be wondering why it is called COVID-19. The reason why is because COVID is short for Coronavirus and 19 because this all started in December of 2019. I just learned this a couple weeks ago. And we didn't see any kids from school, really, or talk to anyone.

At night I did some reading. My mom will come home in a couple of hours, and tonight Cody and my dad and I are all going to be sleeping outside, and that is for sure. That is really all we did tonight, but I really didn't do anything. Now my dad is watching a movie, and I forget what it is called but it is about racism. I might go and watch it with him, but I am not sure.

Friday, June 19, 2020

In our driveway there is a huge pile of bark. It is really big, and my dad started to work on moving it, and after about thirty minutes of doing it, I helped him, and we did that for forty-five minutes. It is really hard to fill a wheelbarrow with bark and then bring it down a hill. It is really hard. My mom and Cody said that they wanted to help, and that is what ended up happening. It was then noon, and it was really hot. I think it was like seventy-five degrees outside, and that is hot. In Washington that is really hot, because Washington is known for being a rainy cold place, but not today. It was really hot, and my mom and I and also Cody came up with a plan. Cody would shovel all of the bark into the wheelbarrow, and then my mom would also help him and then take a wheelbarrow and bring it to me, and I would take it and spread it everywhere.

You need to be smart when you spread bark because it all needs to be the same thickness, and I was doing it for about thirty minutes, and this might surprise you, but that part is hard. I thought it would be really easy, but no, it wasn't. After thirty minutes, I went inside and got two cups of water and brought it outside. Cody and Mom said thanks, and I said, "Sorry, but—" and then I dumped the two water cups on my head, and it felt really good. By then it was almost halfway done.

When I went in to get the water cups, my dad was in there, and he said, "It would be easier and faster if you guys let me do it. I will do it way faster, and I think I might be able to do it even by dinner." It was one o'clock.

I said, "We will see." And I walked out and told mom and Cody what he said. That made me even more motivated to do the work. The bark was almost a fourth done, and my dad left to get some fake rocks to cover something. I don't even know what it is, but he left.

My mom said, "Let's finish strong and do it by the time Dad gets home, and he will be super surprised!" I needed to go upstairs and change my shorts because they were filled with splinters and poking my butt. After I did that, I came outside and did the bark spreading as fast as I could. When we finished it was two thirty, and we proved my dad wrong. I was super surprised myself. After we high fived and stretched, I went upstairs and took a shower. I put the water temperature as cold as I could, not kidding. It was really cold, but it felt good. I came back down after the ice-cold shower, and my dad walks through the door and says nothing and just gives me a big high five, and I gave him five. That took up the whole day, so I will just say see you tomorrow.

Saturday, June 20, 2020

Today is the day before Father's Day, and my dad is going to work tomorrow. My family is pretending that today is tomorrow, and that will be fun. Cody and I worked for some screen time, and I vacuumed the downstairs. Cody did the dishes and swept and mopped. You might be thinking that is way harder, what Cody is doing, and the reason why it's not is because the basement is really big, so it takes a lot longer than you would expect. Just trust me. After we did that, my dad let us go downstairs, and we did screen time for a little bit.

My mom left at six thirty this morning for work, and she will be home tonight at eight o'clock, and that will be fun because we will just pretend that today is Father's Day tonight, and I already said that, so let me tell you something interesting. I am going to teach you how to ride a bike. Nope, just kidding! Cody and my dad and I also went into my dad's car and, trust me, it will get interesting. Then we started the car and got ready. We drove on the road. And you might be wondering where we were going. We went to my mom's work at the hospital and said hi to her and went outside and talked, and that was nice. And this is interesting: We went to the car and got in, and then my dad drove the car down the road to a mystery place called the Watts House (aka my family's house), and that is all we did this morning.

In the late afternoon, my dad and I made doughnuts. We did them almost the same way as how to make bagels, but we added cinnamon and sugar on them, and they were just like doughnuts. They were really good, and we saved some for my mom when she gets home. I can't wait to see what she thinks of it.

That night my mom came home and told us she needs to work tomorrow. My dad is going to work tomorrow, and that means Cody and I are sleeping outside. It was going to be for four hours, and then my mom will come home, and I think she will go there at seven in the morning and come home at around noon. Tomorrow I will tell you what happens and what my mom and Cody and I got my dad for Father's Day. Read the next paragraph, and we will find out what ends up happening.

Sunday, June 21, 2020
Today my dad left at four in the morning for work, and my mom just went to work at six thirty, and she will come home at eleven thirty this morning, and then tomorrow my dad will come home at ten in the morning. Today is officially the first day of summer, and that is really fun because that means no more online school. Online school seemed like it would be fun, but after a couple weeks it kind of got old, so now there is no schoolwork to be done. But there is an academy called Khan Academy, and it is just math. It is divided into eight sections, and in those eight sections there are about five quizzes, and in each section there are about five little math assignments that have about five problems in those five assignments. Not confusing at all. But Cody and I are going to do that this summer.

This afternoon Cody and I played some basketball, and I looked at my Fitbit (a type of watch), and it said that I had done twenty minutes of exercise. After a little bit longer, I looked at my watch and it said I had done forty-five minutes of exercise. I was wondering if that was true because when we started it was about twelve-fifteen and now it is one o'clock. If you haven't guessed, my mom came home about an hour ago, and she took a shower and came outside and said hi to Wilson, and Cody and I and my mom all went inside. My mom told me that her friends are coming over tonight (not inside) and that Cody and I could watch a movie. I was trying to find any good movies, but I couldn't find any.

Tonight Cody and I watched a movie called *Liar Liar*. It was really funny, and of course every great comedy movie needs to have Jim Carrey, and this movie has Jim Carrey in it. If you don't know, he is a really funny actor, and I will not spoil it. He gets in a divorce, and he is a lawyer, and his son's birthday is tomorrow, and he needs to work then, and he doesn't want to work but he does, and he made a promises, and he lies a lot in work, and his son wishes that for only one day he couldn't tell a lic, and it comes true. I can't tell what happens, but all I can tell you is that this movie is definitely comedy.

Monday, June 22, 2020
I woke up and went into the living room. It was seven thirty in the morning, and today it was going to get up to seventy-three degrees. We have this thing—The Thing—and you attach a hose to The Thing, and there are a ton of water balloons connected to The Thing, and then you fill it up. After like

thirty seconds, all of the water balloons are full, and it might be confusing because I am just calling it The Thing, but just trust me. It is really hard to put into words, and the thing is, it will fill thirty-five water balloons in thirty seconds.

This afternoon I pulled out the balloons and filled them up and they were ready to be thrown. My dad went on a trail run, and he will be gone for one hour. I brought it all down and everyone (but my dad) had a water balloon fight. It was fun until Cody started running right to me and practically was slapping me, not even throwing the balloon, just tagging me with a balloon in his hand. I got him back and did the same thing about two or three times, and that made him stop. Finally we all went inside. After I dried off, I went back outside to play basketball. My dad came home, and he was with Wilson. I went in the garage and got my basketball and played for about thirty minutes and came back inside.

In the evening, my dad mowed the lawn and accidentally broke the lawn mower. I don't know what happened, but the motor stopped working. My dad told me that this is the same lawn mower he has been using for the last ten years, and it shocked me that it has been working that long. But its time came, and it stopped working, and my dad went to a store and got a new one. It was five hundred dollars, and I didn't think that it would be that much, but it was.

Later in the evening, my mom made Cody and I pizza. She did it homemade, and it was really good. The crust was really thick and full of air, and it was really weird to bite out of it and there was just air. After Cody and I finished, I ate a bowl of cereal. That was all we really did at night.

Tuesday, June 23, 2020

I woke up on the deck, covered with blankets, with a cloudless sky and a white furry dog at my feet, looking through the fence at the squirrels running by and birds chirping and leaving the bird feeder swinging back and forth and then stopping and going again and again. I said, "Come here, Wilson," in a whisper voice, and Wilson slowly gets up and walks up to me. He collapses next to me and sets his head on my pillow, and as I hug him, both Wilson and I fall asleep again.

When I woke up, it was six thirty. Wilson back again at my feet, I look to my left and see my dad nowhere in sight. and my brother slowly gets up and opens the door and walks inside. I hug Wilson again, and now I am awake for the second time in the night, and I come inside also, followed by Wilson, my mom still fast asleep in her bed and my brother and my dad on the couch both welcoming me. I collapse on the couch, and now I think today will be a relaxing day.

This afternoon Cody and I played basketball, and after playing for about twenty minutes, I go inside for about an hour, and then we both go back outside and play more basketball. I went inside about thirty minutes later, and I look at the weather. It said it was seventy-five degrees.

In the late afternoon, Cody and I did a challenge where we need to find sticks and make a fire (of course in the fire pit), but we each get only one match. I got sticks with lots of pinecones and things like that, and I cut the sticks and set mine up, and mine was twice as tall. Then we each took a match and lit it on fire, and mine went up in flames. Cody's didn't do anything, and I wasn't surprised. Next I want to try to do it when it is raining, with only one match. Let's see next time if I am up for the challenge of lighting a bonfire with only one match, in the rain!

In the early evening Cody and I had a water gun fight and a water balloon fight, and it was really fun until it started to rain. We went inside, and I was really hoping to play more, but unfortunately, that was all we could play. We all ate dinner, and it was six o'clock and my family watched a really good documentary called *13th*. I think that it is for only fifteen years and older, but it was really sad to accept the truth of what slavery was and about the things Black people had to go through. One thing it said was that the chance of a Black person going to jail is one in three, and for a white person it is one in seventeen. That just isn't right. For the United States, they have one fourth of the amount of the prisoners in the world. The United States, one country out of 195 different countries, and we have a fourth of the amount of prisoners. All I need to say: Why is this happening, and what caused this to happen?

Wednesday, June 24, 2020
My dad left at four in the morning, and he will be home tomorrow at ten in the morning, and then he will be home for four days. Today is Wednesday and tomorrow is Thursday, and if you didn't know that, then I have no response. When I woke up, I was in my bed and wearing my swim shorts from when I was a couple years younger. They had sharks on them, and they looked like tight short shorts, and I was really confused. On the floor was a pair of shorts and underwear, and the second-to-last drawer of my dresser was pulled open, so the clothes on the floor I know was from the night before, and I know it was from sleepwalking. If you connect the dots, my clothes are on the floor, and my shorts drawer is open, I am commando with swim shorts, so I think I was sleepwalking. That is just super, super weird.

Later in the morning Cody and my mom and I are all going on a walk on the trail, and of course we are bringing Wilson. Wilson is the best, and he loves to go on walks. When I say love I mean it. He goes crazy every time Cody or my dad or mom or I say, "Wilson, you want to go on the trail?" And we went, and it was fun.

In the afternoon Cody and I were playing basketball and we played for about thirty-five minutes and it was now too hot to play, and it is around seventy-five degrees. Tomorrow it is going to rain (according to the weather man). And the next day it is going to rain (according to the weather man). And then the next day it is going to rain (according to the weather man). Cody and I went to the back yard to say hi to my mom, and she was lying in the sun reading an Oprah magazine, and if you don't know who Oprah is, she is a person that is way too complicated to tell you, but I think that the internet can tell you that better, so go to the search bar and type "Who is Oprah?"

Later in the afternoon, Cody and I played basketball. We only played fifteen minutes, and Cody was seeming to be arguing with every single thing I said. That might be exaggerating. Maybe not every single thing, but one time. That makes more sense. Well, we just went inside, and Cody was just seeming to be mad. He is now thirteen and almost fourteen, so it seems like it might be his hormones, but hopefully it is just a phase. Now I am starting to sound like a person judging my brother even though I am younger than he is and just talking about his actions! Oh, wait. I am the younger brother, and I am talking about his actions (no response).

Thursday, June 25, 2020
Today is the twenty-fifth. When we got Wilson, my parents surprised Cody and me on Christmas (classic), and at the end of unwrapping all of the presents, they said there is one more in their room. They brought it out, and it was huge, and they put it down in front of Cody and me and said, "Wait!" and they grabbed their camera and started the video. We opened it together. Inside was a ton of dog chew toys and treats, and I was busy going through and looking at all of the things they were, and I never even guessed why Cody and I were getting these, until my mom told us that we are getting a puppy. As far as I can remember, actually since I could write a full sentence, I have been asking for a puppy every single year. I never got one because Cody was allergic and I kept trying.

I finally got what I wanted, and my parents told us the dog's name was Sam, and Cody and I were like, "Yay! Wait—Sam? What were the other names you were thinking of." They said that the other name was Wilson.

Cody and I were like, "What? Why wouldn't you name it Wilson?" And we eventually named it Wilson, and that is why Wilson is named Wilson now and will always be named Wilson Watts!

This morning my dad is coming home, and he needs to drop off his car at a place, and he was going to run home, and it isn't that far away, and then he called my mom and told her that he needed her to pick him up. I was wondering why, and when my dad got home, he was in pain and felt sick and said, "Sorry guys, I can't hug you."

I asked why, and my mom said, "He throw up on the way home."

My dad went straight downstairs to sleep, and after about five minutes he came up and asked my mom to take his blood pressure. It was low but not super low.

Cody and my mom and I went on a trail run. It was twelve thirty, my dad was downstairs, and we all went on the trail (not my dad). On the trail my mom told Cody and me to stop running because we will trip. I stopped but Cody didn't, and my mom told him again, and sure enough, after about twenty seconds he tripped and scratched his knee, nothing bad.

He said, "I might have broken it, but I don't think so."

And I said "Cody, you will be fine. It will be better by the end of the hike."

Cody seemed like he thought he got really hurt, but I knew he would be fine in a couple of minutes. He got up and was totally limping, and I just walked away laughing to myself because I bet in a couple minutes he would be running again. Five minutes later, Cody was running again. What did I tell you!

After that we all went into the car and got some pizza. We got Pizza Hut and I haven't ever had that kind of pizza. The reason why we did that is because we were going to get some La Fiamma pizza, my favorite, but they were closed. We ate outside because we didn't want to wake up Jimmy (my dad).

Speaking of my dad, right then he walked through the door to get outside and said that he was starting to feel better. He and my mom both think that it is migraines, and I don't know what it is. He was feeling a five out of a ten, and earlier he was feeling a one out of a ten, so that is great.

A little bit later, my mom went to work, and that is all my family did today.

Friday, June 26, 2020

This morning I was wondering if my dad is going to be 100 percent, because he wasn't feeling good yesterday. When I woke up outside, my dad and Cody were both to my left, and Wilson was there too, of course, right next to me. and I looked at Wilson, and he was asleep at my feet. and I called Wilson to come next to me, and he did. He was really funny because he came and walked past me, went back to my feet, walked back to my head, and lay down with me. I fell back to sleep. When we all woke up, my dad said he was ten out of ten. I went inside, and Cody and I did some screen time. It was really fun but we didn't do that much.

In the afternoon, my dad and Cody came outside with me, and we played a game called Bump. This is how to play: You need three people to play, and more is ok. You have a line, and you go in a line, and the person in the front shoots first, and then the person behind them shoots right after them, and they see who can make it first. After the first shot, you can shoot from wherever you want. Once one person makes it, they pass it to the third person that was in line, and then they try to make it, and then they try to make it first in front of the person that was in second. If the person, at the beginning, is the second person in line and gets the ball in before the person in the first line, then the person that was, that makes it in second, will lose. It is really complicated, and you probably have no idea what I just said, but try to make the best of it. If you want, you can just go on Google and search up what it is, and you will find out. Later in the afternoon we all played again. After about forty-five more minutes, we were all tired and went inside, and that is all I did today.

Saturday, June 27, 2020

Today my dad is home, and he is definitely 100 percent. Hopefully, you remember that my dad got sick a couple days ago, but he is fine now, and today I want to play basketball with Cody. This morning I was thinking what the weather might be today. I hoped it would not rain, but this morning it is really raining right now. I was lying on the couch and looked out the window, and it was pouring, and it rained for two hours, until ten in the morning. I was really happy it stopped, and I went outside and played basketball with Cody. We played for a little bit, and Cody went in, and my dad came out, and we played Bump.

Hopefully, you remember when I talked about how to play the game. There is a game just like it but a little bit different and a lot less complicated, and this is how to play: It is the same way, but you start with two people standing right next to each other, and the person on the right shoots first, and the person on the left shoots, and that doesn't really matter but it works better so it isn't super complicated. Then after each person shoots, you each can shoot from anywhere on the court. When someone scores, they win and the next person in line goes to the right, and then the person who won before goes on the left, and if there isn't any line then you just pretend that the person that lost goes on the right, like they were in the line but obviously they weren't in line.

In the afternoon I played more basketball, and I was just getting a little tired, so I stopped. Nothing happened, but I stopped playing, and that is what I did. I know it wasn't really anything, but it was just one of these days, I guess.

Sunday, June 28, 2020

That morning I was thinking of what today would look like, because I personally like to plan my day out. But instead of me telling you about what I want to do, I will tell you what I did do. The reason why is because you might drool all over this, and another reason is because you might fall asleep.

This morning I went downstairs and played some *Minecraft*, and then I went up two sets of stairs to my room and read a really good book called *The Moth*. It just has like two hundred stories that are each a couple pages long, and there isn't really any genre. I read one and I think it was really funny. It was about a boy and his dad, and every night they have been Instant Messaging each other and just saying how their day went. Even though they are in the same house, they do that. I am not sure why, but every night they message each other. One night the son wrote "LOL" at the end of a message, and the dad thought it meant "lots of love."

After texting each other for about, I think, six or seven months, the son got confused because the dad was saying things and then saying "LOL" at the end, and it made no sense. So the boy asked his dad why he said that, and the dad messaged back, "Because I love you." The son was confused until the dad realized it meant "laughing out loud," and he said to his son that he thought it meant "lots of love."

In the afternoon my mom left for work and all of the boys in the house but Wilson played basketball. Then our neighbor asked all three of us to help him with a ladder, and we did. We went inside after that and found a movie that seems funny called *Anchorman*, and it is the movie we are going to watch tonight. The day went by fast, and then it was dinner. I will tell you what the movie was about, but just wait and you will soon figure it out.

Monday, June 29, 2020

This morning I looked at my phone and it was a minute after seven, and I was sitting on the couch, and Cody was looking at his phone. My mom asked Cody and me the day before to let her sleep until eight o'clock, and that is what I was thinking about doing. The reason is because my mom worked until one in the morning.

My dad left for work at four in the morning, and my dad is going to come home tomorrow at ten in the morning, I think, but I will see. I was also thinking how long my mom will get to be home, but the thing is that she is asleep, so it is kind of hard to read her mind. I can just look at the calendar, but the kitchen is too far away (15 feet away). As you can see, I am tired.

In the afternoon I played basketball for about five minutes. My heel was hurting really badly, so I went inside. The movie that I watched yesterday, I don't want to spoil it, but I will just tell you it is really funny. The main actor in the movie is Will Ferrell.

At night my dad and my brother and I Facetimed my grandpa and grandma. They got us a little hotel place to come see them, and I think it is in Sandpoint, and that is not really far away. By car it is eight hours away, and there is a really nice pool and a huge lake, and I am going to swim a lot. That will be August 10–15, and that is going to be really fun. I don't think I will be writing those couple of days, but we will see what will happen.

Nothing happened the rest of the day, but we all ate dinner and that is all I did that day.

Tuesday, June 30, 2020

Today my dad is coming home at ten o'clock, and my mom is home all day today. Tonight I don't know if I am going to sleep outside on the deck or inside. I want to sleep inside.

My dad came home, and I played some basketball. He had a really good idea to go to my old elementary school and play, and I played basketball for about one hour and thirty minutes and saw two kids from school I know, and we all talked for a surprising one hour. We went home and saw my mom and her friend talking in the driveway, and they went on a bike ride for about one hour, and then they just talked, and that is really what we did all morning.

Later in the afternoon, I played more basketball and then just read for about twenty minutes. Then it started raining, and then I ate dinner, and surprisingly, nothing has happened today but those couple of things.

In the US there are 2.68 million COVID cases, and that is right now. In the whole world there are 10.4 million cases, and that means that more than one fifth of the world's cases are in the US.

Wednesday, July 1, 2020

It is the first day of July, and that means in less than a month and a half, I will be in Idaho. I will be swimming in eighty-degree weather, and then after I swim, I will swim some more, and then maybe I will swim more. But that is more than a month away, so let's not talk about that. Let's talk about what I did today.

In the morning at eleven, my dad and I went to Geneva and played basketball. Unfortunately, Cody didn't come, and the reason why is because sometimes, if not all the time, Cody wants to do absolutely nothing. When my parents make him do it, then he ends up having a lot of fun. The things that he hasn't wanted to do are basketball, football, soccer, track, swimming, biking, hiking, picking berries in the woods, playing outside when it is hotter than seventy-five degrees, water gun fighting when it's seventy-five degrees, water balloons fighting, and the list goes on and on, but you don't want to read a book of all of the things Cody doesn't want to do and then ends up enjoying. And by the way, that book would be really big.

I just realized I was talking about playing basketball. My dad and I played for a long time, and it was pouring down rain the whole time, so we went in the shed. That is outside and there are two basketball hoops. My dad and I wanted to see who can make a basket from full court first. Surprisingly, in about ten minutes my dad ended up making it, and about three shots after that, I shot a swish. That was really fun.

In the late afternoon, my dad took a shower and my mom said that he should have the water as cold as it gets and have it like that for thirty seconds. My mom said that her friends told her that. Speaking of her friends, they went on a bike ride for about two hours and that was really fun, she said. My dad did that, and he said it was really cold, and I definitely believe it. I don't know if I can do that, but I did do something called The Ice Bucket Challenge, and this is what you do: You get a bucket and fill it with water and ice cubes, someone dumps it over your head, and it is really cold, as you can probably imagine.

That night my dad said he wants to watch a movie called *A River Runs Through It*, I think it is called. I don't know if it is good, but it seems good. I will try to tell you what it is about without telling you things that would spoil it for you, but I will think about whether I should tell you some parts or not.

Thursday, July 2, 2020

My mom said that my dad isn't home today but will be home tomorrow. I went outside and said hi to Wilson, and at nine in the morning all three of us went to Bed Bath and Beyond to pick up a couple of things. And the things are, my brother got a pillow thing—I am not really sure what it is, but you can read with it—and my mom got some sheets. And it has been raining all morning and I am hoping it will stop later on.

In the afternoon it was still raining, so I stayed inside and watched a movie called *Pet Detective*. I will not spoil it, but I will only tell you the main character. The character is Jim Carrey, and that is all I need say.

In the late afternoon, all three of us played tennis for about thirty minutes, and it finally stopped raining. That made me really happy. I got a net for my birthday, and I can play pickleball, tennis, and I think one more thing, but I cannot remember.

For dinner we were going to eat pasta, and for whatever reason the pasta has a lot of weird things like black peas in it. It was really, really weird, so I had cereal and corn with peas, and that was a really weird dinner, but that is what happened for dinner.

Friday, July 3, 2020

My mom left work at six forty-five to get there at seven. I was awake and was going to be home alone with Cody until ten o'clock, and then my dad would come home. When he does, I am really hoping that he wants to play basketball at Geneva (my old school) again.

When my dad came home, sure enough, he wanted to play at Geneva. But not until this afternoon. In the time before that, Cody and I did absolutely nothing. When we stopped doing absolutely nothing, it was noon and we all went to my mom's work to see her and bring her a coffee. After that we were all thinking that we could go to Geneva and play because we had all of the balls in the car. That is what we did, but there was a daycare or something like that there, and they were playing where we wanted to, and we decided that we could just go home. That is what we did. I was really hoping that we could play, but unfortunately, we didn't.

In the late afternoon, Cody and I cleaned up the whole house while my dad was on a run, with Wilson of course. He came home at the same time we finished, and that surprised me because I didn't think that would happen, but it did, and my dad said that we all can watch a movie because we did all of that work, and my dad said that we might watch *Pitch Perfect!*

Just for your information, you might be wondering what type of movie that is, and I am still wondering the same question after I watched it. But now I am still wondering why we did. It was about a group of people trying to get into a collage musical, you could say, but it was definitely funny. I just want to tell you that it was a one-of-a-kind movie, and I know I might have said that in the past, but this one is one of many, many movies.

Saturday, July 4, 2020

Today is the Fourth of July and I am going to go to my neighbor's house with my family, and we are going to just talk outside and watch fireworks. Tonight is the lunar eclipse, and it starts at 9:11, I think.

That afternoon my mom and dad went on a bike ride. I was home, along with Cody, and we played some basketball for a little bit. Then we went inside, and my parents came home, and went in the backyard and in the hot tub, and I played more basketball with Cody for a little bit. A dog named Porter came on to the basketball court and peed all over the center of it, so I went inside and got some water and poured it over it, and Cody and I played more basketball. Then Wilson was running around with Porter, and that was just really annoying. When we stopped, I took a shower, and by then I found some sparklers and lit them with Cody, and that was fun. It was almost four thirty, and when it turned five at night we all went to Donnett's house. We had a bonfire with Mark and Pam—they are married—and then also my mom's friend named Kris, and she was with her daughter, and that was all the people.

We all just talked about life and funny things. Kris is a teacher for a high school, and I think Pam also has something to do with school. I don't know what she does, but Kris was just telling stories. In a couple paragraphs I will tell you what I need to say about the eclipse. I might not see it. After going for a couple of hours at the party, until eight thirty, then everyone went home.

Sunday, July 5, 2020

Last night I didn't see the eclipse because it was behind the cloud, but that is okay. Later that night, I saw Phil outside and he told us that he is going to get a new dog. She is four years old and is a black Lab. He isn't going to get the dog until November because the dog is going to have one more litter of puppies. Phil invited us up to his house, outside, to watch the fireworks. It was Fourth of July and really cool to watch, and we even brought Wilson with us. It was about ten at night and we were still watching the fireworks. We stayed up there until eleven thirty last night, and we had two parties tonight. We all went back, and it was really dark, and we all slept outside but my mom, because the fireworks were really loud. For some reason, Wilson didn't mind the fireworks. I think the reason why is because when Wilson was a puppy, the people that took care of him hit pots together to get the dog to use to loud noises. And that, now that I think of it, was really smart. I woke up at eight o'clock, and I think that reason why is because I stayed up until midnight last night. I was the last person to stay outside that long, and when I came in, my mom was still asleep, but my brother and my dad were both wide awake. By then, I was fully awake, but I lay down on the couch. Cody went downstairs and did some screen time.

In the afternoon we all went on a walk, and yes, including Wilson. That was fun, and it was super hot outside, and I was wondering how it could get hotter outside. I am certain that it will, but I will see in a couple of months.

Late afternoon, I played some basketball, and Cody started to twist the rules, but I just stopped playing and went inside and did an hour of math. After I did that, I started watching a new show that I have not watched before, called *The Arrow*, and I don't know enough about the show to tell you, but it seems really good. That is what I did this afternoon. Tonight my dad is going to make pizza, and my family, including me, is going to watch a movie called *Best In Show*. I don't really know what it is about, but I think it is really funny.

Monday, July 6, 2020

My dad left for work at four in the morning again, and he is going to be gone for two days because today he needed to work an extra day so next month when we leave for five days it will not affect his work schedule.

At eleven in the morning, my mom and I went to a little public beach at Lake Whatcom, near where we live. We went into the water, and my mom went swimming a little far out. Wilson wouldn't just stay there and swim. He would follow her, and I even called him, but he still went there. I didn't wear a wetsuit or anything. I just wore swim shorts, and that is it. But now that I think of it, I did wear this thing that you put on your feet, and it is like a sock, and I realized because of that I didn't feel stepping on sharp rocks anymore. Just to let you know, the rocks are really sharp.

Later in the afternoon, Cody and I were playing basketball, and he was arguing so I stopped playing. I started walking to our house and he said, "Are you going to take your ball and go home?" I was thinking I am not going home. For one, I am home, and it is my ball, so I have the right to do what I want to do with it. Also, Cody is just using one of the neighbor's balls, because his ball got flat and was like a frisbee.

I was just thinking, *Think what you say before you say it*. Cody does not do that. I have noticed that in the past and almost definitely in the future. And when I am saying these things, I absolutely don't think I am perfect and pointing out everyone's mistakes. I could go on a list and say what I have done and what a million other people have done that was wrong, but these things I am saying, I do also, but just not as much. I can point out millions of things that I can do, but I will not, because if I do that, then it would just get boring.

I am partly a vegetarian, and the only things I like that are meat are sausage and bacon, and that is it. My mom and I decided that I should try to have no pasta for a week and to have tacos and put whatever I want in it. I don't know when I will start both of those, but I think it will be soon.

Tuesday, July 7, 2020

My dad is coming home tomorrow. My mom and Cody and I all went to Western. That is a college, and my dad happened to go there when he went to college. We played tennis for about an hour There is a sign on the fence, and it says, "For staff and students only." And we weren't sure whether that meant only during school. It is the coronavirus pandemic, and even if the coronavirus wasn't a thing, there would still be no school, because it is summer. Cody and I are hopefully going to go back to school on September 2, 2020, but no one knows what will happen until then.

In the afternoon Cody and I played basketball for about ten minutes, and then I stopped because Cody was just arguing and wasn't making it fun at all. I went inside and now I am not going to play with only the two of us. I will play with my dad and Cody, but not Cody alone, because then my dad could settle the argument, and he could say if it was in or out or if it was a foul. But my dad isn't going to be home today. He will be home tomorrow at ten. I already said that, I think, but just a reminder, if you forgot.

In the late afternoon we all played some tennis. We stayed home and did it in our driveway, and that was fun but super weird. The court is so big at Western, but at my house, in my driveway, it is smaller, but it is still really fun to play.

That night we all had dinner, and I went out of my comfort zone and had tacos. I had lettuce, salsa, avocado slices, red pepper, beans (also out of my comfort zone), and that is all I had and all I did today.

Wednesday, July 8, 2020

Today my dad is coming home at nine thirty in the morning. He is coming home half an hour early from when he usually comes home at ten, but I can't wait until he comes home. At eight thirty my mom left to swim with one of her friends, and they went to the same beach that I went to with my mom two days ago. The reason my mom didn't and doesn't go to the gym is (by the way the gym is open, kind of) because she doesn't want to go there and get anyone sick because she thinks that she has handled COVID patients (also, I agree). There is one person who works at the hospital as an ICUSTAT nurse, and don't even ask me what it means. But his name is also Cody (sounds familiar), and my mom is a friend of his, and they worked at the hospital for ten years. Also, he got COVID-19 and went to ICU. That it is where the sickest patients go, and he is starting to get better, but he is still really sick. My mom wants to respect not getting anyone sick if she is sick from COVID, so she doesn't got to the gym.

Later in the morning, my dad came home and said that later today he is going to go and get chips and salsa, and that he wants us to come so we can play basketball at Geneva. Cody didn't really want to, but we finally convinced him to come with us later that morning.

We all went, except Wilson and my mom, to Geneva, and we had fun and in the covered basketball area. There is a door, and I missed a shot, and it hit the rim and went over and rolled right by the door, and I stood up, and in the door there is a little glass window. There was a kid in it, probably in first grade, and he had a camera in his hand and was taking a video of me. He was laughing, and I told Cody and Dad, and they looked and the kid was still filming, and we didn't stop playing until he opened the door and got closer and didn't stop filming. We just kept playing until it had been another five minutes, and we went out of the shed to another basketball hoop and played. That was very weird, and I hope it never happens again, but it is quite the story.

Later we ate dinner, and my dad made homemade flour tortillas. They were really good, and I can't even put it into words, but we ate, and that is all we did for the night.

Thursday, July 9, 2020

My dad went to work at four in the morning again, and you might be wondering why my dad leaves so early, and he really leaves around four o'clock. He leaves and then gets to the fire station and then will work out and take a shower, and then it is seven, and he does his normal job firefighting, and my mom leaves at either six thirty a.m., eleven a.m., two p.m., and only sometimes she will leave around seven p.m.

That morning, I watched some of my show (*Arrow*) for forty-five minutes and then took a break and ate cereal and then brushed my teeth and watch fifteen more minutes, and then I was done. Cody watched a movie called *Austin Powers 2*, and I think it's inappropriate. I will let you watch the movie yourself, and you will understand why I am warning you right now that kids under ten shouldn't watch this, no matter what. Trust me, somehow and somewhere I watched this movie when I was seven, and my dad didn't think it really was, and now I am always going to remember some parts of it. Just an FYI: The movie Cody watched today is the second one, and you just don't need or want to know what it is called. And if you are wondering, there are three movies, and Cody watched the first one, and they are all interesting movies.

In the afternoon, Cody and my mom went to get something, and I did nothing but relax, and that is all I did. They ended up being gone for two hours, and tomorrow morning I think my mom and I are going to do something like that, but that isn't today, that is tomorrow.

Tonight we watched a *Modern Family* show, and it was really funny. You need to watch it. They make parts of it so funny you will laugh your socks off. Now that I said that, it seems a little like I am turning into a different person. And that is all I did today. Tomorrow my dad is working again, but then he will be home for four days. I don't know what happens after those four days, and on and on, forever and ever.

Friday, July 10, 2020

My dad is coming home tomorrow. My mom is leaving tomorrow morning at six thirty, and my dad is coming at ten. That is tomorrow, but this morning I went with my mom and we picked up five more juggling balls. Cody got three black and white balls, and I got two more blue and white balls, so now I have five blue and white juggling balls. I got the other three from Christmas last year, and I have now learned how to juggle three balls easily for more than a minute. Then usually I accidentally make the balls collide in mid-air, and then it messes me up, but that is almost all of the time, but sometimes I just l lose my focus. Now I am starting to learn some new tricks.

This afternoon I was really tired, and I don't think I am sick, and I sure hope not. I went down and sat on the chair outside, and I didn't really do anything, and then I was just really tired.

Tonight I took a shower, and at the end I put it as cold as it gets, and then I went downstairs. My mom and Cody were listening to a comedian. I forget his name, but he is really funny. We all listened for about ten minutes and then had dinner. Then I did a little bit of reading. Tomorrow I am going to do a little bit extra of my reading.

Saturday, July 11, 2020

My dad is coming home today, ten in the morning, and my mom left at six thirty this morning. Cody and I both did our Khan Academy at the same time, because Cody did it on his computer. We did some screen time until my dad came home at ten.

This afternoon, all three of us went to play football and say hi to my mom at work. We went to see my mom first, and then we all just talked. The thing about Cody is I don't think he understands what warming up means, and stretching, because we all need to do it before we play football. Cody was warming up and stretching at Hospice House, where mom works, and by the time we got to the field and started playing, it had been thirty minutes. I was stretching and thinking *Why did Cody stretch that long ago?* But it is his choice. If he gets hurt it is not my fault.

Tonight Cody and I made dinner together, meaning we made generally the same meal and made sausage. I attempted to make mac and cheese sauce, and I was thinking, *This doesn't look right.* Then at the end, it looked good. My dad started putting the pasta on my plate, and I said it was enough, and he said I need more, and I said ok, and then he put all of the cheese on it, and I was saying it was enough about three times when he was pouring the cheese, and he just kept on doing it. I ended up eating half of that amount until I went in the kitchen and ate normal pasta with butter and parmesan cheese. Cody made a different type of cheese sauce, and I forget what it is called. That is the same thing as mac and cheese but with less cheese and that is all we did today. I am hoping to sleep on the deck tonight.

Sunday, July 12, 2020

We ended up sleeping outside last night, and it was raining when I fell an asleep. I am not sure after that if it was raining, but my mom needs to leave at six thirty again. She needs to work for twelve hours, and yesterday she did the same amount of time. My dad is going to stay home for three more days, and my mom is coming home tonight at eight o'clock, and we will all be home for two days. Then my dad is going to work, and I think my mom is going to be home that day, but I am not sure after that.

I woke up at eight o'clock in the morning. I went to bed at I think ten o'clock, and I usually wake up at seven. Today I asked my dad if I could learn to fly fish, and he said that he would teach me this afternoon. I think that he will teach me, but this morning Cody and I did some screen time while my dad went on a bike ride, and we did more screen time, and he came back.

This afternoon my dad taught Cody and me to fly fish, and we did it on the grass first. We did it for an hour, and then it was really complicated, and we both learned how to do it while he taught us to do it above ground. After we did it and mastered it, I learned more things and we did it a little more. Then I went inside and did my reading.

My dad made pizza for dinner and my mom came home later that night. That is all we did, and my dad said we should go to fly fish the river next! And if we wake up early, we can go super early.

Monday, July 13, 2020
I woke up at seven in the morning, and then I came in from the deck, and everyone was awake. My dad told me that Cody and he had already left and come back from fishing. They said they got no fish. I was wondering if tonight I would catch any fish, but that isn't right now, it is tonight.

This morning Cody and I did some screen time for a little bit, and then I took a break, and then I did some more, and then my mom and my dad went on a bike ride, and I am not sure if it was on the trail or if they went on the road.

There are now 43,167 COVID cases in the United States, and there are 710 cases in Whatcom County. That is where I live right now. Well, not necessarily where I live, but it is where the nearest place is to my house, and it is really only ten minutes away from my house. There are only 41 deaths, and it could be worse, but it still isn't great.

This afternoon I did Legos. There is this box and it has a lot of Legos in it, and there is a little book that tells you directions on how to do it, and I did it. When I finished I wasn't satisfied, and then I kept on adding things, and then I was lost. I took it apart and put it all together the way I wanted to. And after a couple hours, I was finished and it looked really good. And after that, mom left for work for only five hours. That is all I did until tonight. I went fishing with my dad and I will soon tell you what happened!

Tuesday, July 14, 2020
That morning, I came inside from the deck and looked at my watch, and it said it was eight o'clock, and I realized that I have been waking up a lot later than I have in the past. That might just be because I am getting older, but that is just what I think. My dad left at five in the morning to go fishing with his friend Jason. They went up to Mount Baker, and that is about an hour away, and it is all up hill, and they took it by a car. It is a mountain, as you probably have thought, because of what it is called, and you circle up and around the mountain to get to the top. I am not sure if they went all of the way or if they just went up halfway and hiked from there, but my dad told

me after the drive it was about an hour's hike to get to the river, and that he and Jason have been to the place many times before and he wants to take me.

This morning Cody and I did some screen time, and then I ate some food and brushed my teeth. You might be wondering why I have not run track in a while, and the reason why is because I have growing pains in my heel that hurt really bad. You are probably rolling your eyes right now and saying, "Here he goes again, always talking about something hurts," but I am not going to talk about that. I am going to talk about what I did next. I did some juggling for just a little bit, and then I did some more screen time. In the middle of the screen time, my mom told Cody and me to bring up some clean clothes from the other room upstairs. When it was done and when we were finished, we brought the clothes upstairs. Then I just relaxed and looked at the news.

This afternoon my dad came home and said he didn't catch that many fish and that neither did Jason and that it was just not a good day. He said that some days they catch over thirty fish, but that wasn't today.

Later in the afternoon, my dad and I went fishing. We went for about an hour's hike, jumbling over rocks, and I was scared I was going to fall on some rocks, so I just stepped in the water. It was just over my knees, and I just accepted that I would get wet. We didn't catch any thing after two hours, and when we had been gone for almost three hours, we went home. We had no fish, and even if we did catch a fish, we wouldn't have brought it home because it might smell super bad. And that is all we all did today. I am not sure what my mom and Cody did when my dad and I were gone.

Wednesday, July 15, 2020

Today is a Wednesday. In one month my family will be driving home from Sandpoint, Idaho. That is where we will be going on the tenth of August. Last night my mom said that we can sleep outside as a family, and we went out there to sleep, and everyone including Wilson was out there but me, because I still needed to brush my teeth and get my headgear. But what happened was like one of those moments where you are thinking, *Can anything possibly get worse?* And yes, it does, as you soon will see.

So, this is what happened:

First I went in my mom's bathroom to get my toothbrush. I got it and put toothpaste on it and put water on it. Then I realized that I got water all over the counter, and my mom hates when I get water on the counter, so I took some toilet paper and wiped it. As you can probably guess, toilet paper will peel off if you let it get wet, and that is what happened all over the counter. I cleaned that up, but before I cleaned it up, I put my toothbrush on the toilet paper, and my toothbrush was wet, and you know what happens when water and toilet paper get put together.

I walked over to the living room to tell my family the funny mistake I made, and when I got to the deck door, I realized there is nothing on my toothbrush, and then I retrace my steps and find it spread out on the floor—it fell off my toothbrush. Then I went into my mom's bathroom again, and guess what I did. So stupidly, I got it wet and swiped the toothpaste that was on the ground, and now I had smeared it all over the ground, and there were also some little pieces of toilet paper on the ground mixed with that. Then you think it can't get worse. Well, it did. I got it wet again, but carefully, and cleaned it up and realized my mom always gets mad when I get things in the cracks on the floor, so I went to the kitchen and got a butter knife and cleaned that up, but I couldn't really see or remember what cracks it was in, so I just cleaned all of the cracks.

It was dark, so I couldn't see, and the reason I didn't turn on the light is because I was lazy. After I cleaned all of the cracks, I realized it would have been easier if I just did it with the lights on. After that, I finished brushing while sitting on the ground not moving, and then I was wondering if I closed the little cabinet to get the knife, and I went around the room to the kitchen, and Wilson's toy was on the ground, and I stepped on it, and it really hurt my toe because it bent it up like a right angle. Then I was jumping up and down trying to get my toe to stop hurting, and then I looked over and saw that I did close the cabinet.

By then, I wanted to just go to bed, but of course I needed to get my head gear on. I looked all over the main floor for about five minutes, looking because I thought I left it on that floor. Then I went upstairs to look, and it was black because there were no lights on, and what could possibly got wrong—I fall on the stairs.

I eventually found my head gear on the middle floor and went outside. All three of my family members, but not Wilson, were sneezing and sneezing. They all went inside, and I joined them. Sadly, that is all I did that night.

Thursday, July 16, 2020

Today is Thursday, so I need to take out the garbage so the garbageman can get it tomorrow morning. I don't think that tonight any of us are going to sleep outside, because of allergies. Even though I don't have any allergies, my mom will not let me sleep outside alone. I want to, with Wilson so I won't be alone.

This morning my dad came home at eleven instead of ten because he needed to pick something up from a store. It was fresh fruit from, I think, Joe's Garden. That is right next to where my mom works, at Hospice House.

This afternoon I went outside and played some volleyball with myself. Don't ask me why or how I did that, but Cody joined me for a little bit. Cody said that he and Dad were going to fish tonight, and that was okay with me. The thing is that Cody and I go alone because the creeks that we go to, you can't fish with two people at the same time, and my dad wants to help us one on one. Also, I asked my dad if he and I could go to Mount Baker and fish there. It still has snow all over the roads, so we will need to hike, and that is okay with me. But somehow now Cody is coming, and I don't really want him to come. The reason why is because we always go and do something and he wants to leave after just a little bit, but I guess that is what is happening. Tomorrow I think we will leave at nine o'clock, but I am not sure. My mom is just going to stay home, and I think she might go swimming with her wetsuit for exercise.

Tonight we ate dinner, and I had pasta. I know I said that I wouldn't eat pasta, and the reason why is because my goal is only once a week I can eat pasta, when only my mom is home but not when my dad is home. After dinner Cody and my dad went fishing and my mom and I watched a movie called *My Spy*. It was really good, and it was about a spy, and he helps a nine-year-old girl become a spy.

Cody and my dad came home and said that they got a fish. Tomorrow I hope that I will catch a couple fishes, but I am not sure. Cody and I slept in the basement because it was so hot upstairs, and my parents slept in their room.

Saturday, July 18, 2020
This morning Cody and I played *Minecraft*, and I watched part of my show. If you don't know, I am watching a show called *Arrow*, and it is really good and well put together. But later in the morning, Cody and I had done forty minutes of screen time, and then we went fishing.

We went to a river called Clearwater Creek. I grabbed a flyrod from the back, and it is the one Cody and I have been sharing for the past week or two. There was another one, and it wasn't put together. Like, the string wasn't on it, and a couple other things, and I grabbed the one that was ready because I wanted to fish right away. But then my dad said, "No, Taylor, that is for Cody." I didn't know why. He put the fly together, and Cody just watched the creek.

My dad said, "Done," and handed me the rod, and I asked why he gave me this one and not the one Cody had, and he said, "Because look on the side."

I looked, and on the side it said, "This fly rod 7' 4'"" and that means it is seven feet long and four inches, and then right after that it said, "This fly rod is made for Taylor Watts," and then it all made sense. The other fly rod says, "To my boys, Cody and Taylor," and what I think is that when I was born he made that for each of us, and the one that I had he made a little bit later in my life, but I am not positive.

When we started, right when I put my fly in the water, Cody was still picking out the fly that he wanted. I looked over my shoulder to see what fly he was picking, and I swear after, like, five seconds a fish jumped out of the water and grabbed my fly, and I pulled him in, and I was really surprised. I was thinking that it is a bad day to be a fish. Then my dad took a picture and we let the fish go. I was still laughing and looking over my shoulder, and I looked at the fly Cody was picking out, because the fish that got my fly a little bit ago startled Cody and my dad. Then I wondered how many fish I would catch, and I was still looking over my shoulder.

About five more seconds went by after I put my fish in the water, and I got a fish again. It was a different fish, and I was feeling really confident, and then Cody got a fish. We left our home before ten in the morning, and we ended up coming home after three in the afternoon. At the end, my dad got a fish and Cody and I each got three. Cody's third one grabbed Cody's fly, and Cody started pulling it up, and he jumped off, and I wouldn't really call it a catch, but he is, and it is his fish, so it is his call. It was a really great day, and I have a fly rod now. My dad wrote my name on it!

We went to Donnett's for a bonfire, but this time Jason and his family came to the bonfire and we went for a couple hours until it was dark, and we went home and said hi to Wilson, and it was nine and we went to bed at around nine thirty. I did some of my reading until around ten thirty, I think. I am not sure, but then I went to bed, and we slept inside.

Sunday, July 19, 2020

I woke up at 6:21 this morning and I was wide awake. For the last week, mostly, Cody and I have been sleeping in the basement. I saw Cody still asleep, and I was wide awake, and I was going to go upstairs after sitting in my bed for about five minutes. Then I decided I will just go back to sleep, and that is what I did. I slept until eight this morning.

Later Cody and I did some screen time. I played some *Minecraft* and also watched some of my show, not at the same time because that would just be really weird. And after Cody and I did some screen time, Cody went with my mom to the grocery store. While they were gone, I did a little bit of screen time and then went downstairs and did some reading for about twenty minutes and then came up stairs.

This afternoon I did some more reading for about twenty minutes, and then I did Legos, and then I did more reading for a while, and I did a little bit for tomorrow. And that is all I did, but my brother went in his room and did reading and then went outside and played. I went out there also, into the back yard where my dad was in the hot tub and my mom was just relaxing, and that is all I did that afternoon.

This evening my brother and my dad went to Olive Garden and got takeout dinner, and then we ate. and After dinner my mom was doing the dishes, and my neighbor Phil invited us up to see their new dog because my dad didn't see the dog yesterday. But the dog's name is Ru or Rue, and I think that is how you spell her name, but I am not sure. Something funny is that her real name is Rumor Has It, and that is funny. But Phil calls her Shadow because she follows him everywhere. We all just talked up there for about an hour, and that is it. We did nothing else that day.

Monday, July 20, 2020

This morning I woke up on the deck, and it was seven thirty in the morning. When I walked inside, my brother was sitting on the couch with my dad, and he was on his phone and my dad was reading one of about five of his magazines that he has been in. Most, if not all, have been about fly fishing. If you think I am serious, I am. And my mom was still sleeping, but she woke up shortly after I woke up, I think a little bit before eight.

My dad left at seven thirty to go fishing with one of the firefighters (Mike), and he came back about thirty minutes later because Mike forgot his shoes. (Classic.) My dad made a fly rod for Mike because he retired from the Seattle fire department. My dad left about an hour after that and said they would be gone for this afternoon, fishing. Cody and I played *Minecraft*, and I watched my show for a little more than an hour.

This afternoon I went in the backyard and did nothing. After that I just did my reading and Legos and then about fifteen minutes of watching my show. Then I was done with screen time. I started doing my math for tomorrow. A couple days ago I did an hour extra, and then I did it for about forty-five minutes, and then a little later I did more.

This evening my dad came home, and he brought chips and salsa and guacamole for dinner. I had a quesadilla, and then after dinner we all watched a movie called *Hamilton*, and it is a really popular movie. It was three hours long, and it was all a play, and it did not stop, and it was one of the best movies that I have ever seen. It was about history and the first couple presidents. Then we slept outside and then went to bed.

Tuesday, July 21, 2020

Today is my parents' nineteenth anniversary, and that means that they have been together, married, for nineteen years. I woke up at six in the morning, and the reason I woke up that early is that I was the last one outside, Wilson was whining at the door, wanting to go outside, and I managed to get up and open the door, and then he went inside. I somehow went back to sleep until a little after seven, and I think if I didn't wake up because of Wilson the first time, I would have slept longer outside.

That morning, I did screen time, and all three—Cody and my mom and I—were going to go swimming in the lake, and I decided to stay and spend time with my dad, and we could play. Cody said that he and Mom were going, and I said I am going to stay, and I said I am just going to come down right after they leave to do a little more screen time, and about ten minutes later I came down, and I couldn't find my dad. After, like, one and a half hours, my brother and then my mom came in, and then I asked, "Where the heck is Dad?' and he came in the door. He ended up swimming with them, and I was thinking, *Just, if I knew.*

This afternoon I did a little reading and Legos for a little bit, and Cody and I helped my mom make the cake (by that I mean eat the frosting and just watch and cheer her on) while my dad was mowing the lawn, and that is really everything that happened this afternoon.

Later this afternoon, Cody and I did water guns for a little bit, and then my parents left to do things for their anniversary, and I am not sure what they did, but Cody and I did some work and then did some of our screen time because of that. I still have some for tomorrow that I saved from this morning, and it is just a little bit, but it is something. Tonight my parents came home from dinner and we ate cake. Then we all went downstairs. It was too hot upstairs, and this might sound funny, but I think it is too hot to sleep outside.

Wednesday, July 22, 2020

This morning I woke up a little after six. Cody and I brought the mattress downstairs the night before, and my parents slept in the twin beds, and Cody and I slept on the floor on the mattress. When I woke up, no one was there and it was six in the morning. Confused, I came upstairs, and only Cody was awake, on his phone (not a huge surprise). Right when I came up, he took his phone and turned it off and put it behind him, and I don't think he was looking at something he shouldn't have, but he just didn't want to me know that he was on his phone. I sat on the couch, and he said I should read the news, and he grabbed the phone. The funny thing is that he didn't know or hope that I knew he was on his phone. And my parents told me, when they woke up, that Wilson was walking around a lot, so they came up and slept in their room at four in the morning. Then everything started to make sense, because when Wilson walks around you can hear his paws below in the basement.

Later in the morning I did screen time, and then my parents needed to do a call to talk to a new private school district, and we are all looking to go there or just do it online like a Zoom with a lot of kids and a teacher or more. And my parents just asked questions, and after that I learned that there will be an hour a day, Monday to Thursday, and on Monday and Wednesday I will be doing the other classes in the afternoon, so that will be nice. My grandparents are also talking about getting Cody and me an Apple laptop, and then it is not just school but a normal laptop and we can use it for school. My grandparents are going to pay for everything, which is really nice of them.

This afternoon we went fishing, and it was fun, and at the end I got six fish and Cody got four, and that is ten in all, and that is four more, in all, from last time. We got back at dinner and didn't do anything for the rest of the night. I think I am going to sleep downstairs tonight.

Thursday, July 23, 2020
There are only two and a half weeks until I go to Sandpoint, Idaho, and when I am there, I am not going to be writing about what my day was about, because it is kind of like a break/vacation. When I get back, I will write about what I did, but not all of the details because that would be hard to remember. And speaking of remembering things, we are going on the tenth of August. If you remember that, you probably remember that we will be going until the fifteenth, and as you probably thought, we are just driving because of coronavirus. It is usually six to eight hours to get there, but because of coronavirus, not many people are driving. So that means less traffic, and that means that the drive will be faster, and that means that we will get there faster, so that means that I get to play and see my grandparents faster. And yes, I am done.

Late this morning, after I did screen time, I went outside to play with Wilson and play some volleyball. Later that day, I went on the trail with my mom and Cody. My dad is working, so he didn't come. When we got back it had been about forty-five minutes we were gone, and my mom said that we can each have twenty minutes of screen time for going with her, and that was surprising.

Tonight we ate dinner and my mom's friend came over. They went in the back yard and just talked, and Cody and I did screen time while they were gone. Then my mom came in, and her friend left because it was too cold for both of them, and by then it was nine o'clock. Cody and I did Legos until about ten, and I was awake for about ten minutes, thinking about things that I can't remember, and then I fell asleep.

Friday, July 24, 2020
This morning I woke up at nine, and I don't know why that late, but it happened. I did screen time for a little bit, and then I ate food and brushed my teeth, and then I did more screen time, and then I came up stairs, and then just realized the rest of the day.

This afternoon I went on a walk with my mom. Cody stayed home, and he was on his phone doing something, no idea. We went for about fifteen minutes, and then my mom said, "Let's walk to the pile of wood over there and then turn around and go home," and it was about a hundred feet away.

I said, "How about you turn around and walk that way, and then I will run to it and back, and we can get home faster."

My mom was like, "Okay?"

Then I did it and came back, and then right before we went into the dark woods, I was like, "Hey, is that dad?" and it was. He was running and had come home a couple hours ago at ten and then went on a walk. We went on a walk about thirty minutes after he left, and then he got over to us, and we all went home, my mom, my dad, me, Wilson, and sadly, not Cody. But it was still really nice to be separated from him.

Tonight I ate dinner and then had some bacon, and then I thought I could also just save it for tomorrow instead of having it all tonight. and that is what I am planning on doing. After dinner I we watched a little show for about half an hour, and then we talked to my dad's parents and thanked them for getting us the computers. We haven't got them yet, but we will tomorrow. And then I will start writing on a new computer, and I will transfer this document onto my new computer tomorrow!

Saturday, July 25, 2020
There are officially sixteen days until my family is going to Sandpoint, Idaho, and that is exciting. Then in two days, it will be two weeks, and I think we are going to start packing two days before we go, and then we will leave early in

the morning at, like, eight to nine in the morning would be my guess. That will get us there at about two in the afternoon, if we left at eight or nine, but I am not the boss. My parents are, so I have no clue what time I am going to be going.

This morning I did screen time and watched my show and played some *Minecraft* with Cody. Then I came upstairs and did some reading, and then my mom was at work, so my dad and Cody and I thought it would be a nice time to get our computers, and we did. We left at ten-ish, and it took us, I think, almost two, but three hours to get there, to Seattle, where the Apple store is. That was unexpected, because there was a huge accident. A big semi-truck had an oversize load and hit the sign that is above the freeway, and it was closed because it fell in the middle of I-5 on a Saturday afternoon. But we got the computers, and then we got bagels from this really good place nearby, I forget the name, but then I got a smoothie. As you probably didn't know, we brought Wilson on this adventure too. I don't really have anything to say now, but we got home, and then we didn't do anything after that.

The only thing that happened is, my mom came home and we ate dinner, and at about seven my dad needed to leave for the fire station right away, unexpectedly, because of protesters and things like that, and that only happens, like, I wouldn't even say ever, but he left right away, and then the rest of the night I did nothing, and nothing happened.

Sunday, July 26, 2020
My dad isn't home today, but he will be home tomorrow morning around ten. I woke up at eight, and Cody was on his computer and my mom was still sleep. She woke up fifteen minutes later, and then I did some screen time and ate and brushed my teeth. My mom left on a hike with her friends, and then after that she went to the lake with one of those friends, because all of the other friends had something else to do, and they jumped in.

This afternoon I did my midday brush and then I did some reading. I tried tying more knots, and I learned a new one called figure eight, and it isn't that hard to learn. I also learned one called a square knot, and another name for it is reef, but I just like to call it square.

Later in the afternoon my mom and Cody went and got the newspaper, and then we all went in the back yard and read it for about forty-five minutes or so. Then I went inside and tied more knots from my book for about five minutes and went back outside and read some more. Then I said hi to Wilson for a little bit and also took the bench from outside and put it in the back yard, and it looked better instead of having it in someone else's yard.

Later I did some work, and then we ate dinner. I am not sure if we are, but I think we might watch a movie, even though it is really hot outside (it got up to eighty-five today). If we do watch one, it will be later tonight.

Monday, July 27, 2020

Today is the first day I am writing on my new computer, and it types really fast, and I don't even need to touch or push down on my keyboard because it is just so new. This morning I did some screen time, and today my dad is coming home, and he is going to pick up groceries from Fred Meyer. If you didn't know, he does this thing we call ClickList. You click a button on the computer, and then you go to a certain parking spot, and you pay earlier from the computer. For my dad's case it was a computer, I am guessing, and the reason I don't know is because he did it from the fire station. It is ordered to be picked up at, I think, ten or eleven. And they put the groceries in the back of your car (or front, I guess), and then you just sign something and you are good to go. My dad came home at about eleven thirty. At the grocery store, it was really busy for some reason. I am not sure, but I think he said he was there for over an hour. That would be really annoying, to be in the car for so long. But then, you don't have to go in the store and maybe get COVID, so I guess that is that.

This morning I did screen time for a little bit. Then I came upstairs and did reading with the knots book, and then I read the newspaper, and then I went back downstairs and did a lot more reading down there.

Something that's always been confusing is when people are sarcastic. It's when you say something where you are exaggerating, and that means if you say like, "It will take me years to finish this," when obviously it will not, but you are saying that to show that is going to take a long time. So that is sarcasm, or you can say exaggeration. And it is really weird because you make people either really confused, or not confused, but it is just a really weird thing.

We did nothing this afternoon, but tonight we had dinner and then just talked, mostly. We slept outside, and my mom slept outside with us. I don't know if she will sleep all night, but I hope so.

Tuesday, July 28, 2020

Cody and I are going to get haircuts today, at eleven to twelve, I think, but it depends how long it will take. This morning Cody and I did some screen time, and we all slept outside the day before, but my mom came inside and slept inside for the second half of the night because she couldn't go back to sleep after she woke up.

Later this morning we all three left (Cody, my mom, and I) and got haircuts, but my mom didn't, just Cody and I. All three of us realized that my mom forgot her wallet, and she texted my dad and asked him to bring his or her wallet. And after we all figured that out, I got my hair cut first, and I just got a little trim. When it was Cody's turn, he went and got his, and my mom and I needed to stand outside because the people that own it wanted the littlest possible amount of people in the place because of coronavirus. When Cody was done, we went and got some bread and some other things, and then we went home. That is all that happened in the early afternoon.

Late this afternoon my dad and I went to Lake Padden (a swimming beach), and we did the same thing as the day before, but we weren't with Cody and my mom. About thirty minutes after we got there, Cody and my mom came too, and we all just floated out there in the middle of the lake. When we got home, we relaxed. That is all we did, but my dad accidentally somehow popped some of the floaty things, but it was because something sharp hit or bumped into them and popped them.

We just ate dinner, and I think that tonight we are going to sleep outside, but we might sleep inside because everyone but me has allergies. I really want to sleep outside.

Wednesday, July 29, 2020
This morning I did some screen time for a little bit, and then I was having some waffles and took a bite and had a lot of pain in my canine tooth. I wiggled it, and it was loose. I finished my waffles really carefully and then put my dishes in the sink. After that I did more screen time, and then I was almost done with my screen time.

This afternoon Cody and my dad and I went swimming. My dad said that every time we swim to the pillars and back we will get twenty minutes of screen time. The pillars are in a certain spot in the lake, and it is about fifty yards away, and we did it six times, there and back, so in all was about six hundred yards of swimming!

Tonight I continued to try to pull my tooth out, and after more than an hour of trying I got it out. I am going to play a prank, but before I tell you what it is, I want you know that if you are under ten years old, don't read past the line that you will see soon.

If you do, then you will be confused, concerned, and you will turn on your parents, and I am telling you please not to read the next paragraph.

Since the tooth fairy isn't real, and if you are wondering, my whole family knows that she just isn't real. So, my family gives Cody and me a dollar or two when we lose a tooth and put it under our pillow, and that is what I am going to do when we sleep outside. I will tell my family that, and my parents aren't going to know that I put a camera showing that they take the tooth from under my pillow, and the best part is that it will just be a bag with a little piece of toilet paper, and it will look like a tooth.

We did nothing the rest of the night, but my mom came home from work a little after seven, and she left at 6:40 a.m. Now we are all going to sleep outside. And by all of us, I am not sure about my mom, but all of the boys are, and by boys, I mean Cody, my dad, myself, and Wilson.

Thursday, July 30, 2020

My dad and my mom are both home today, but tomorrow my dad needs to go to work at four thirty. This morning I did some screen time and then ate my first meal of the day and then did more screen time, until I only had about ten minutes left. I brushed my teeth and then did some reading for about twenty-five minutes. Then Cody and my mom left and went swimming for a little bit.

That whole tooth thing didn't work out at all. I set my tooth down, and then I looked at the clock and it was past nine, and I couldn't find the thing to keep my phone up, and I realized how much that the toilet paper doesn't look like a tooth because it would just flatten out and look like a deformed tooth, and I just gave up. But my dad asked me if he could look in my mouth to see it, and he did, and then he pulled out of my mouth three dollars, and I knew it was not really in my mouth because it would be all wet, but it was still a funny trick.

This afternoon my dad and I went to Lake Padden. I was swimming and swimming until I remembered a movie. I think it was *Dory and Nemo*, and at one part Dory got lost and was singing, "Keep on swimming, keep on swimming," and that was stuck in my head the rest of the afternoon.

Tonight we ate dinner and then Cody and I went outside and made a bonfire. You might be asking why, and that is because there is only about a week left for people allowed to have bonfires, because it is summer, so we are having one tonight. Phil and his wife, Sue, are coming over and we will all sit by the fire.

Friday, July 31, 2020

Tomorrow is going to be the first day of August, and that means that in a week and a half we will be going on the trip. I will give you a little recap on what I am going to bring and some things about it. It will be about seven hours of driving, and what I will bring on the drive are my wireless headphones, my phone, not sure if I am going to bring my computer, and I want to bring a couple swimming things and just, like, all of the obvious stuff.

I want to bring my fly rod there so I can fish. There is a lake to fish at, and that lake is twenty times bigger than Padden, and that is huge. Padden is about a half mile by a half mile, so that means it would be, like, ten miles by ten miles, and that is really big. And that is the main thing I am going to bring, and I will remember many more things but not right this second. The day before I pack, I will write a list of all the things I want to bring, and that will be helpful to put in my writing.

This morning I went swimming with my mom for about an hour, and then we came home and I did some screen time and a lot of reading, and then I did more reading. And then I was almost done with my reading.

This afternoon we went to Sudden Valley and went swimming at a place that I haven't ever been swimming at. Gavin and Carter are the two people we went with, and Carter texted two other friends, and they came over, and then we all played for a couple hours at the lake, swimming, until we all went home.

Tonight I did the rest of my reading and then we watched a movie called *Dinner for Schmucks*, and it was really funny but almost really weird. That is all that we did today. Tomorrow my dad is coming home and we are going to sleep outside, hopefully. And last night I learned I fell asleep outside in the chair by the fire and my dad carried me in, but I don't remember. It was really fun, and when it was about nine forty-five, Phil and Sue were still here and I was starting to get tired. Then it was about ten fifteen, and I don't remember anything after that. So, that is a little weird and I have no response.

Saturday, August 1, 2020

Today is the first day of the month, and that means only ten days until we go to Sandpoint, Idaho. This morning I did my screen time for a little bit and watched my show (*Arrow*). I was thinking, since I have Netflix on my phone, I can watch it with my headphones on the way to our trip and the way back in the car!

This morning I ate cereal for breakfast and then brushed my teeth. My dad came home around ten and he told me that one of the fire chiefs at Seattle (not his, but just one of many, they have different fire chiefs) went outside during a protest, and it was just a normal protest, nothing bad about it, and he went out there and said, "Kids, let's get out guns and show all of them." They didn't do it, but it was just a threat, and now that firefighter is going to probably have some type of fine. My dad said he should get fired.

My mom said that she needed to go pick up some things, and I said that I would come with her. She said that Cody was going to come with her, and I said no, no, and we had an argument, and I think it started going my way. I told her I had a list of the candy we are going to get for the long drive in a little more than a week, and she said no. I meant candy as in chocolate, because we are out of chocolate. I asked if next time she and I could go on a drive and get candy, and she said ok. Then they left.

About an hour later I looked at my phone, and there was a text, and it said, "Can you send us the list of the candy." And I was so mad, but I sent it. I told my dad the whole story and said it was really mean. Then I asked him if he wanted to go to swim later today, and he said yes, and let's just time travel to then . . . Now it is twelve in the afternoon, and my dad and I went, and it looked really windy, and we swam way out to a certain far spot and back, and it was really choppy, and we both had something to float on, so it was safe. Then we drove home, and on the way, we got some candy for ourselves! Yum. Then we got home and showed them our candy, and they had a lot of candy, and they were all the ones I asked for.

Tonight we watched a movie called *Ground Hog Day*, about a person who hated Ground Hog Day, and it kept repeating itself. One funny part is that there was a homeless man who asked the person for some money and he said no. Later the next day the man asked again, and then he gave the homeless man all of his money. The reason why is because he will just wake up again and everything would be the exact same thing. One part is he went in to a store and stole a toaster, and then he filled up his bathtub and put toast in the toaster and toasted the bread and then put the toaster in the bath and electrocuted himself. Then he was back in the morning, and He jumped off a building and went in front of a bus and drove a stolen car off a cliff. The car lit on fire, and that is all I will tell you. But it was funny because it was *Ground Hog Day*. It was really good, and we had chocolate fondue. Then we went to sleep outside. That is everything that we did, and tomorrow there will be only nine days until we can go to Idaho.

Sunday, August 2, 2020

I woke up and came in from outside, and my dad told me that I was sleep talking, and this is what my dad told me I did. I shot up out of bed, and then I was talking loudly, saying, "Wilson, Wilson, where are you?" over and over while sitting up, and my dad asked what was wrong, and I said I wanted to tell Wilson I loved him. I have done more interesting things, but it is still one to put on the list. By list, I just mean all the things that I have done in my sleep, or just weird things I have done in the night when I'm sleeping.

This morning I did my screen time and then ate breakfast and did more screen time and then some reading. Now there are eight days. Then I brushed my teeth. Speaking of teeth, I have an overbite, which means my upper jaw is farther in front of the lower jaw. My brother had a minor underbite, and that is the opposite of an overbite, which is what I have. When I go to the dentist, I have always heard them say, "He has a hundred-plus overbite," and that doesn't sound good at all. I think that means I have a really bad overbite. When I bite down, you can't even see my bottom front teeth. Also, in the top gum area behind my top teeth, my bottom teeth hit the back gums, and over time now it is totally cut because my teeth hit the gums. In almost a week I will have worn my headgear for a year, and there is going to be a lot more years until I can take it off, and when I say a lot, I mean it.

This afternoon I played basketball, then I gardened with my mom for a little bit, and then I vacuumed her car, and from that I got screen time. I did that screen time and saved some so I can do it a little later tonight.

Tonight we ate dinner and watched *Little House*, a show that is about forty to forty-five minutes long most of the time. We are going to sleep inside because my dad needs to go to work tomorrow and my mom doesn't like us on the deck by ourselves after he leaves, but it would be fine, and Wilson is still there to protect us.

Monday, August 3, 2020

One week until we are going to Idaho, and I think in less than three or four days I will start packing. My dad talked to his parents a couple days ago, and they said that there is a basketball court and we should bring all of the other normal things. They also said that they are going to go to Idaho a day or two early because they are going to fill our place with food and things like that, and they also are going to just set up the place!

This morning Cody went swimming with my mom, and I did some screen time, and Cody did some too, and then I did my reading and went downstairs and played some *Madden*. The *2020 Madden* is coming out in a couple of weeks, and Cody and I are going to buy it. It is around forty to fifty dollars.

This afternoon I did extra work around the house, and I got an hour of screen time, and I had ten minutes left from the morning. Then I went swimming with my mom and got another hour of screen time. Then I did some of it and later went outside and then did more screen time, and then I had one hour.

Tonight I did about twenty minutes of screen time and then we ate dinner. After that Cody and my mom left and brought something to Susan, who is one of our neighbors. That is all we did. Tomorrow my dad comes home from the fire station.

Tuesday, August 4, 2020
Last night when my mom and Cody came home, my mom tripped and hurt her arm really badly. She iced it and called my dad's sister (Katie) because she is an ER doctor. Another neighbor of ours, Donnett, came to our house and brought a sling, and my mom kept it on through the night. My mom had a bad night because it hurt so bad. This morning when my dad came home, he went with my mom to get an X-ray. Then they called back and told my mom that she had a small fracture in the radial neck, which is by her right elbow. So, she has a broken arm now.

I went swimming with my brother and my dad this afternoon. We floated out to the middle of the lake and swam some laps, and my brother and I each did four laps back and forth to the pillar, then we each treaded water for four and a half minutes, and then we swam back from the middle of the lake. My dad said we got one hour of screen time for that.

My dad's mom heard about my mom's arm, and she had pizza delivered to our front door at five this evening, and that was very, very nice of her. We ate dinner, and then I did some more screen time, and then I did my reading, and then I was done for the day. For the rest of the night, I am going to chill. I still have screen time, but I think I will just save it for tomorrow.

Wednesday, August 5, 2020
Today I would like to go swimming, but that is kind of hard because my mom can't go because of her arm. Speaking of her arm, at ten this morning she went to an appointment to talk about her arm, and when she got back she had a new sling. It was a nicer one, and you might be wondering if it is the one with the bandages or the one you just put around your shoulder and rest your hand in. It is the second one and it is black. Before she left with my dad, I did some screen time with Cody for a little bit, and then we played downstairs for a little bit, and then a little bit longer, and then Mom and Dad came home.

This afternoon, as I hoped, I went swimming with my dad and Cody. And when we got there, it was pretty busy, so we found a different spot. It happened to be the spot we went to the first time we came to Lake Padden this summer. After we got to the middle of the lake, I started swimming, with Cody by my side, and we went the same distance it is from the beach to the pillars, if not a little bit longer. I went there and back five times without stopping, and my dad timed how long it took me, and it took me about fifteen minutes of nonstop swimming. When I finished lap five, I saw Cody coming back from the other side of the lake, and I asked my dad if we could do extra and if I could just start swimming now and do extra, and he said no. I asked why and he said because we need to discuss it with Cody, and when Cody got back we talked and decided we will do a little bit extra but not a lot, and then Cody started swimming again. I asked him if I could go, and Dad said no because Cody still had two more left to get to five like I did, and I didn't know that. When we finished, Cody and I both treaded water for five minutes, as another challenge, and then we went home.

After dinner Cody and I did screen time. I saved the rest of mine for tomorrow, and then I ate dessert, and then everyone but my mom slept outside. The reason why my mom didn't is because of her arm.

Thursday, August 6, 2020
This morning I did some screen time. Cody did some too, and he went to get a tooth checked out because there was a grownup tooth behind it. He came back with one tooth out—they pulled the tooth out. That is what we did this morning.

This afternoon I did some more screen time with Cody, and my mom took a nap, and Cody and I did our screen time. When we finished, I calculated what I had done. Before we started, I had twenty minutes more than Cody, and we did the same amount of screen time, so that means that I have twenty minutes left. I think I will save that for later.

Later this afternoon I played outside and my dad went on a bike ride. Then Cody and I played football and went and explored the woods and played basketball and soccer, so pretty much everything. Then my dad came home from his bike ride and we played Flyers Up with him. If you don't know what that is, it is a game with one person as the flyer, and they throw the ball into the middle of as many people as you want (except one), and you see who catches it. When one person catches it (might take more than one try for someone to catch it), the person that catches it becomes the flyer (the person that throws the ball). Next, I will tell you, we had dinner, and yes, you are right. We are sleeping on the deck. (Four days until Idaho.)

Friday, August 7, 2020
This morning I woke up on the deck, and it was raining just like the night before when we slept outside. I went inside to go to the bathroom, and I

started the coffee for my parents, and then I came outside and tried to go back to bed, but I couldn't. It was six in the morning, so I just stayed awake and relaxed. Then I came inside about seven thirty and Cody and I did some screen time.

Later in the morning I had some food and took a shower and brushed my teeth. I said hi to Wilson, and then it stopped raining. Later Gavin and Carter (the two who came for a bonfire a couple weeks ago and we swam with) came over. We played hide-and-seek for about two hours, and then it was three and we played some football, and we went in the back yard. Earlier my dad got some small, individual, chip snack bags, and we had some of that. Then we played with the four water guns that we have, and we also used the hose and sprayed each other. I got an umbrella to block the water, and it took me some time to realize it was raining, I was so wet. I didn't notice it, and after a little bit I realized it had been raining for the past hour. When it turned almost seven they went home for the night. It was so much fun.

Then we had dinner, and I did some extra work for some screen time. We are going to sleep inside because my dad needs to go the fire station tomorrow morning, and we are going to Idaho in three days.

Saturday, August 8, 2020

Today is going to be the second-to-last full day until we leave. The way it is going to look is, today we will start packing and tomorrow we will finish packing, for sure before the tenth. We will wake up tomorrow and take Wilson to a place called Rover Stay Over, and that is where he will stay for the five nights. We come home after that, and we pick Wilson up from his place, and then life is all back to normal. The place in Idaho does not let dogs go there. This morning I did some screen time, and I started thinking of all of the things that I want to bring. Then Cody went to the mailbox to get the newspaper from Donnett, who is on a camping trip, so she lets us read hers when they are gone. I don't know what got us interested in doing it, but it's fun to read the paper and the puzzles.

This afternoon I played outside with Cody for a little bit, and we ate lunch, and we did really nothing in the afternoon but play outside. One thing happened that was unpleasant. We have new neighbors, just moved in about a week ago, and they have a girl one year younger then I am, and one boy and one girl that are both, I think, in first grade. The oldest girl was walking their dog, and Wilson hasn't met that dog yet, and the dog was on a leash, but the dog was too strong and pulled and pulled until he was on Wilson's side of the line, and then Wilson started humping the dog, and I noticed that is just absolutely disturbing, and then he got down and started licking all areas. I just went inside and tried to get the disturbing thought out of my mind, and it was super embarrassing.

Tonight we ate dinner and then started packing. I got all of my clothes but a couple shorts, and then I got a basketball because my grandma told me that there is a basketball court a couple minutes away, walking distance. And then I deflated all of the floaties and we all went to bed. Tomorrow we will finish packing and be on our way!

* * *

A note from Taylor and Cody's parents: After a week at Sandpoint, Idaho, the boys came home and the next day started an online private school called Williamsburg Academy. It was a time-intensive transition with a substantial academic workload, way more than we expected, so we told the boys to take a break from daily journaling until they got their feet back under them.

* * *

Tuesday, September 15, 2020

No, it isn't a typo. It has really been a month, and the reason I stopped journaling for a month is because there was surprisingly a lot more schoolwork than I thought, so I decided to take a break, and now I am back.

Let me tell you about Williamsburg Academy. I just started week five at Williamsburg and I am starting to really like it. My classes are leadership, humanities, math, photography, writing and STEM. I have really enjoyed it at Williamsburg. For my old school, they just started school, so Williamsburg started more than a month before my old school. Besides Williamsburg, this is what has been up:

Cody and I started a Fantasy Football league with my dad's firefighter friends at his station. Cody and I played this league together last year for the regular season, and last year Cody did really everything and I did nothing, and then at the end of the season we lost in the playoffs. I said, "Next time we do Fantasy Football, I am going on my own team and I will crush you." So, we did that. For the post season league, we did our own teams, and you remember how that turned out? I won three hundred dollars and Cody got second to last. We started again this year, and he thinks he will beat me. It is with ten people, including Cody and me. We did the draft a little under two weeks ago, and I got the best player possible, and then Cody got the ninth best player. At the end of the draft, I personally think I had the better team. We played the first week not against each other, but we both won. Cody won by around twenty points and I won by fifty. If we played each other that game, I would have crushed him. Now I am currently in first place.

The last thing I need to say is that my family has started this thing, and it is that every day of September we all need to jump in the lake together. The temperature is at about sixty to seventy degrees, and just to let you know, this isn't normal. It is cold but it feels good after. That is about all that happened today.

Thursday, September 17, 2020

As you can see, I skipped a day from writing. The reason why is because I need to be journaling for one of my classes at Williamsburg, and in the future I don't think I will be writing every day because I might have so much extra schoolwork.

Today I started the day off and Zoomed until twelve in the afternoon. In Williamsburg there are kids from all different places, like there is one kid from Israel and most of the kids are in California and Alaska.

During my Zoom, I started and did math, STEM, leadership, and photography. This afternoon I did Drill Sergeant with my mom and Cody. If you don't know what that is, well it is basically just a workout together. Today I didn't go swimming because I needed to do some schoolwork and I already worked out. You will soon notice I am going to start writing less because half of the day I do just Zoom and schoolwork, and that fills most of my day. My parents said to focus on school.

Friday, September 18, 2020

This morning my mom went to work. I did some homework and screen time with Cody. There is this one assignment I am doing, and I am in a group of seven people including me, and each person has their own assignment and makes a slide, and then they send me their slides. That means I will have six slides, and I will organize and adjust all of their slides and work for our presentation. The assignment that my group is working on is called Freedom of Speech, and I will tell you how it goes when I finish.

This afternoon Cody and my dad and I all went swimming in the lake. We swam for a little bit with Wilson and then dried off and went home and went in the hot tub. That is really everything we did this afternoon. Tonight I had pizza for dinner and then my mom came home and I did my PT, and then we all went to bed.

Saturday, September 19, 2020

I woke up this morning wide awake and ready to start the day. I came upstairs and said hi to Cody and my dad. My mom went to work again this morning. A little later, I checked my schoolwork and still no one has emailed me their slides, so I decided to just wait and do more schoolwork, and that is what I did, more schoolwork. Then I took a break and did screen time with Cody. We played some *Minecraft* and did things like that.

When it was afternoon, I found myself still doing schoolwork, so I decided to take a break and that is what I did. I went outside and said hi and played with Wilson for a little bit, and then I came back inside and did more schoolwork. My dad asked me if I wanted to go swimming, and I said that I needed to do homework.

My dad came home and I had some toast. Then I did some reading, and I am currently reading a book called *Johnny Tremain* that the teacher assigned me to read, and it is a really great book about the life of a boy named Johnny Tremain. He is fourteen years old, and in the book it is 1776, and that is when the Declaration of Independence war happened. I won't spoil the book even though I can't really spoil it because I haven't even finished it, but it is just a really good book, and you should read it some time.

Tonight I had breakfast. Yes, it was my first meal of the day, and I was starving and tired of doing schoolwork. I ate dinner and then my mom came home at about seven forty-five. You might be wondering why I haven't been sleeping outside, and the reason why is because outside it's really smoky right now. It happens every year because of forest fires. You might be wondering why there is smoke in Washington, and the reason why is something I don't know. I really don't know, but that is all that I did today.

Sunday, September 20, 2020

That morning I came upstairs and took a shower, and because it was Sunday, I have no schoolwork. After I took my shower, I went in the car with Cody and my mom to the store (Dad at work). Because we were out of food, we went and got some, and we got some candy for the football games that day.

Then we went back home and started watching some football, and then we went outside and took a break. We exercised and did some Drill Sergeant for a little bit and went back inside and watched more football.

This afternoon my mom and Cody and I went to the lake and went swimming, and it was really cold. It was okay, but it was still fun. I went and swam out into the lake for a little bit, and then we got out of the water and dried off and went home.

Tonight we watched another football game, the Seahawks game, and it was versus the Patriots. On one of the first plays of the game, Russell Wilson threw a pick-six. The game went on, and there was a crazy ending in the last three seconds. The Seahawks stopped Cam Newton from running into the end zone, and that was really breathtaking.

Monday, September 21, 2020
I woke up and it was seven in the morning, and I have a Zoom at eight, so I got ready and then went downstairs to start my Zoom, and I started it. The Zoom went on until noon and then I played outside with Wilson and my dad came home. And you are thinking that is a long Zoom, for four hours, and you are right!

Later this afternoon we all went swimming, and it was really cold. It was around sixty-five degrees, and Wilson was off chasing ducks, and I just went swimming around, and then I swam in an aimless direction, and then we all went home. Wilson was super sad because he wanted to swim more after ducks, but when we got home he just slept for the next three hours until dinner was over and the dishes were getting put in the dishwasher, and that woke Wilson up. He started getting really happy and wouldn't stop licking the dishes until we closed the dishwasher, and he got really sad again. Then we ate dessert and watched a football game, the Raiders versus Saints. Surprisingly, the Raiders won.

Tuesday, September 22, 2020
I woke up and did some screen time and then went back downstairs and did my Zoom until noon. Then my mom had an appointment at two thirty, but the lady at the place said it was at eleven. It turns out that wasn't true, and it was two thirty, but by the time she told us that it was too late to go, and then the lady at the desk said that maybe she could move it to three forty-five, and that was okay with us. We got to in the car to go to the appointment (everyone including Wilson). It took us about two hours to get there, and then my mom had her appointment, and it took less than five minutes to get it done. Then my mom went shopping for about two hours, and we all had dinner outside at a pizza place, and then we all started making our way to the car. It took us about an hour to get to the car because my mom couldn't stop saying, "I wonder what is in that store." We got home, and it was, like, eight thirty, and then I went to bed. If you're thinking that wasn't that fun, it wasn't that fun.

Wednesday, September 23, 2020

When I woke up, I came upstairs, and it was really windy outside. I took a shower and then started my first Zoom and it was STEM. Then I had math, and about thirty minutes into my Zoom, my power went out and I was kicked out of the Zoom. Then I just needed to wait for it to come back on.

The power came back on, and I looked at the time. My next Zoom was starting in thirty seconds, and I ran downstairs and then got in, and everything went great. When it turned noon, I was done with Zoom. Then I did some schoolwork and some screen time, and then I got a call from my mom. She said that she was coming home at five o'clock, and that was in about an hour, so I got all of my things done and went and played outside. Then my mom came home, we all had dinner, and I went in the basement and did some PT.

Thursday, September 24, 2020

I woke up and did some screen time and then ate breakfast and did some schoolwork, and then it was time for my first Zoom. My first Zoom was math. When I finished math, I had to do leadership, and that took about an hour. Now I have all of the slides for my Liberty Pulse project.

This afternoon it was raining, and my mom and Cody and I went on a thirty-minute hike (without Wilson), and we saw some neighbors on the way back. After talking to them, we got home and my parents went to get a new sink for one of our bathrooms. My dad painted the whole bathroom, and the paint will be dry in a couple of hours. Later we all ate dinner, and then the paint was dry and looked really good. The last thing I did is my PT, and that took about a half an hour. That is about everything that happened today.

Friday, September 25, 2020

This morning I did some screen time and then some schoolwork, and I ate cereal and brushed my teeth. I didn't have really any work to do after that. Before I knew it, it was ten and my dad came home. After saying hi to him, Cody and my mom went on a drive to get some things from the grocery store. When they got back, I did some more screen time and schoolwork, and I finished my schoolwork for the day.

This afternoon I went outside and played with Wilson, and then I was done outside because it started raining and it started not being fun playing outside. So, I went in the basement and played for a little bit until I checked my schoolwork and did some more. My dad started making pizza, and it looks like it will be really good. I can't wait.

Saturday, September 26, 2020

Today is Saturday and I woke up with very little energy. For Fantasy Football this week, I am almost positive I won't win because all of my guys are now injured. This week I am just going to see how they play and hope I can win next week.

This morning I did a lot of schoolwork so I don't need to do as much later, and then I did my reading, and I am ahead on my reading for school, and that is great. Then I did some screen time and started watching this really funny show called *The Office*. It has a really funny actor named Steve Carell, and it is about a lot of funny actors that all work in this office. There is one character named Jim, and he plays a lot of pranks, and it is funny to see the anger on the people's faces when he pranks them.

This afternoon I played some basketball and played with Wilson, and that was fun. I went inside and looked at my Fantasy Football roster, and so many of my guys weren't going to play, and it is kind of disappointing. From the last couple games, tons of people have been injured, and I think it is because everyone was limited at practice because of coronavirus. I think that there would be at least a fourth of those guys not getting injured if it wasn't for coronavirus. So, I think coronavirus is to blame for them not practicing as much in preseason.

Tonight my family ate dinner and did something we haven't done in a long time. We all get to sleep outside now because the smoke outside finally cleared out, and that might not be really exciting to you, but it sure is exciting for me.

Sunday, September 27, 2020

I woke up and came inside, and I was really excited to watch football. The Seahawks play at one thirty in the afternoon, and they are playing the Cowboys. It is going to be a close game.

Later this morning, Cody and my dad and I all went to the store because we need chips for the game, and we got some candy for the game. It is going to be great, and when we got home, my mom was still asleep at, like, eight thirty. I guess she was just tired.

This afternoon we started watching the game. The Seahawks started off not doing super good, and then they started getting better and better, and near the end of the game Dak Prescott (Cowboys' quarterback) was almost sacked and then got out of the pocket with six seconds left and losing by seven points, and he launched the ball into the air and the Seahawks intercepted it and got the ball and ended up winning the game. It was really exciting, and the Seahawks have now won three games in a row and lost zero. The last time Seahawks got three straight games in the beginning of the season was six years ago, and they won the Super Bowl, so who knows, this might be the year the Seahawks win the Super Bowl again.

Tonight my mom and dad talked and decided they are going to do a challenge. My mom is going to try to lay off being in charge and let my dad manage all of the rules, and my dad will do that for a month, and my mom will rate him on how he does. My dad is working tomorrow, so I think we will start it in two days.

Tonight we are going to sleep outside, but at four thirty we are going to all go inside because my dad needs to work then and my mom doesn't want us to be outside alone, but that's ok. Cody and I will go inside and fall asleep when he leaves.

Monday, September 28, 2020

I woke up and it was seven o'clock, and I was in my bed upstairs, and I don't remember how I got there, and I am not that surprised. I talked to my mom later, and she said that she woke me up at six thirty. Well, I woke at seven, and there is just a bunch of confusion, but I don't remember my dad bringing me inside at four.

My mom went to work at six forty-five, earlier this morning. She isn't going to be back until one, and my dad is at work, so my brother and I are home alone until my mom gets home. But it's fine because we just did Zoom and schoolwork.

My mom came home, and then Cody and I talked about Fantasy Football, and then I ate lunch and went outside and played basketball for about forty minutes and came back inside and did more schoolwork.

Tonight we all ate dinner and I ate corn, avocado, and cheese eggs. Not a very exciting dinner, but I just ate a big lunch, so I wasn't that hungry. Later my mom left to drop something off at her friend's house and tell her happy birthday, and then Cody did screen time and I did some schoolwork, and then I did some screen time. My mom came home so I couldn't do all of my screen time, but that is okay. Then I went to bed in my bed upstairs, and that is about it.

Tuesday, September 29, 2020

When I woke up this morning, I found myself in the basement. While I started off sleeping upstairs, I ended up in the basement. So, apparently, I sleepwalked again, and I had a blanket that was from downstairs, which would make sense. It would be weird if I brought all of my blankets from upstairs downstairs. But I also didn't have my headgear on, and for the last couple nights I have woken up without my headgear, and I don't remember taking it off, so that is also kind of weird. But I went upstairs, and my mom was still asleep and my brother was looking at his computer, and I came up and did my reading and took a shower. Then I ate breakfast and brushed my teeth.

Later that morning I did my Zoom, and then my dad came home at ten, and I finished my Zoom at noon, and then I did some schoolwork, and I did the dishes, and my mom left to get groceries. Tonight we all ate dinner, and we were going to have ice cream but it turns out there isn't any left, so my dad did a ClickList and got some ice cream, so tomorrow he will get the groceries, and that will be great. Tonight we get to sleep outside, just the boys. My mom isn't going to because she needs to go to work tomorrow.

Wednesday, September 30, 2020
Today is the last day of the month, and tomorrow I get my allowance for the month. My parents forgot to give me allowance this month, so they will need to pay me twice as much money as they usually give me. They give Cody and me ten dollars a month, and that means that we will get twenty dollars this month.

This morning I did my Zoom. I started at eight o'clock and did Zoom until nine, and then I had an hour off to do schoolwork, and before I knew, it was already ten. Then I did two more Zooms, and then I was done for the day with Zooms. But later tonight I might do some more schoolwork.

This afternoon we all went to play football, except Wilson and my mom. My mom was working and they don't allow pets on the field where we go to play football. We went and played football, and my heel and my toe hurt but not bad enough to make me stop playing football. We played for a little more than one hour and then started making our way home. And to tell you, when we play football, usually my dad plays quarterback and Cody and I take turns being the receiver and the other defense.

Then the three of us had dinner, and my dad made pizza for dinner. My mom came home at seven thirty, and then we all ate dessert, and then we all set up for sleeping outside. My mom is working again tomorrow, and that means that she needs to wake up at six and get ready for work. And my mouth was super painful because of some reason that will take too long to explain from my braces, but I took a Tylenol. That didn't help, so I just went to bed and didn't wear headgear because it hurt too bad. It would just make the pain worse, and that wouldn't be good.

Thursday, October 1, 2020

Today is the first day of the month. When I came inside from the deck, I took a shower and ate breakfast and brushed my teeth. Then I had a couple school Zooms until noon, and then Cody and my dad and I all went and played football again.

By the time we finished playing football, my toe was really hurting, so we decided to go home, and that is what we did. But besides that, it was a lot of fun to play. Then we went to check on my mom, who is at the hospital working, and she said hi but it was a quick hi because she needed to get back to work. Then we drove home.

Later this afternoon I made cinnamon rolls, and it was for school. They asked me to make a dessert and show one way for each contraction, convection, and radiation. When my dad and I finished making the cinnamon rolls, they came out great. I made half cinnamon rolls and half cinnamon sticks, and it is that same thing except it's just a stick instead of a swirl.

Tonight Cody and my dad and I had dinner, and I wasn't that hungry because I already ate a ton of other food, but I sat at the table with them while they ate. Then at seven forty-five my mom came home, and she took a shower, and my dad called his mom because they sent over a present full of Halloween candy for Cody and me. Even though it is not even close to Halloween, she still sent it over, and we thanked them and then got ready for bed. Sadly, it was inside, but hopefully, tomorrow we can sleep outside.

Friday, October 2, 2020

This morning I did some reading, and it was Friday, so I didn't need to do any Zooms. I finished my reading, and then on the news it said that Donald Trump got coronavirus and he went to the hospital, and that was really shocking news.

This morning my mom didn't need to go to work, and my dad is home today, but tomorrow he needs to go to the fire station. I had a cinnamon roll, and it was really good, and then I brushed my teeth and did my homework for about two hours. Then I did my midday brush, and then I did my PT, and then I went outside and played basketball, and that was fun.

Later this afternoon I did more homework and then some screen time. And before I knew it, dinner was ready. I came home and had pasta and then finished my screen time. Then we all had ice cream, and it was really good.

Saturday, October 3, 2020

When I woke up, I looked at the clock and it was seven in the morning, so I went downstairs and said hi to Cody and my mom, but my dad isn't here because he left to go to the fire station earlier this morning. My Fantasy team is doing really good. I think Cody and I will win this week.

This morning I had no Zooms, so I just got all of my work done early. I took a shower, brushed my teeth, and did my PT, and then I did homework for a couple of hours.

This afternoon I did my exercises. My mom said that today can be my off day from exercising, but I decided that I want my day off to be tomorrow, because tomorrow is football.

In the late afternoon, I took a bath because I didn't really have anything else to do. I realized one of my teeth was wiggly, and I wiggled it, and it fell out, and I jumped out of the bath and dried off really fast and put some toilet paper on my mouth because it was totally bleeding. Then I had dinner, and then we all just relaxed the rest of the night, talking about stuff.

Sunday, October 4, 2020

Today the Seahawks are playing, and my mom left this morning to go to work, and my dad is coming home at ten, and the Seahawks play at ten, also. So Cody and I are home alone until then.

The whole morning, I did schoolwork and reading. Then before I knew it, I was sitting on the couch watching the game. The other team started with the ball, and then the Seahawks got an interception, and then the Seahawks got a touchdown.

By the end of the game the Seahawks were clearly going to win, and I was really excited. In Fantasy I was doing really well, and I was really happy, so the day was going perfectly.

This afternoon I did more schoolwork and reading. Tonight there was one game on, and the team I was playing in Fantasy was up by a lot, but then one person that was playing that night did amazing and caused the other team to get super far ahead, so it looks like I am going to lose, but there is still a chance. At night we all ate dinner and then ate dessert, and I did more schoolwork, and that is about everything we did today.

Monday, October 5, 2020

Today is Monday. It is going to be a long day because today is my homework day, and that means that today I am going to do a lot of homework so I don't need to do as much in the week. I had breakfast and took a shower and then did my reading and my PT. Then I did Zoom and homework until noon.

This afternoon I did my exercise right away and then had lunch and said hi to Wilson. Then I did my chores and writing. I do my writing for the day before, sometimes. Like today, I did my writing about the day before, so I can just do my writing whenever throughout the day instead of having to do it at the end of the day. So, that is probably confusing.

Now it is dinnertime, and tonight we can't sleep outside, and tonight isn't a dessert night, but that is okay. Cody and I ended up losing Fantasy Football tonight. Hopefully, next week I win. Tomorrow my dad is working, but at least he will be home for four days after that.

Tuesday, October 6, 2020

Today is Tuesday. I am going to try to get a lot of homework done so I don't need to do as much later in the week. I did a lot yesterday, so if I do a lot today, I will only need to do very little, later. This morning I did schoolwork and Zoom until noon, and my dad left for work, so Cody and my mom and I are the only ones home today.

This afternoon we all did Drill Sergeant. I had five cheese slices for lunch, and some apple. My mom got some food, and that included caramel and green apples, and you know what that makes. Yes, caramel apples, and that is what we are going to have for dessert tonight, and that is going to be great. But this is the twist. My mom got caramel that is already made, so all we need to do is put some in a bowl and cut up the apples and we are set.

Tonight we all had dinner and then I cut up two apples and put some caramel in a bowl and put it in the microwave for about thirty seconds, and then it was all ready to eat. We started eating some, and the first bit was really good, and so was the second and the third and every other bite. Then Cody and I and Wilson and my mom all went to bed. Sadly, we went to sleep inside. After today we get to sleep outside because my dad is coming home. He has to come home at noon because he has an extra appointment, but that is okay.

Wednesday, October 7, 2020

Today is Wednesday. This morning I woke up at seven to my alarm clock, and then I took a shower and brushed my teeth, and then I started my Zooms. During my math Zoom, we needed to start our midterm tests, and I will do half of it today and the other half tomorrow. Basically, for the rest of my other classes, they are just doing things like a month-long project, and one of my classes isn't even doing any test at all.

The Zooms went on until noon, and at noon I ate lunch and went and played outside for about forty minutes. We all played catch. Cody and my dad and I played, and I accidentally bent my thumb back and kind of twisted it, and then we went inside, and my thumb will be okay. But it will still take some time to heal. Then I needed to go get acupuncture, and that is when they put about five needles in my left foot and a couple in my right foot. This is from all of my many soccer injuries. When I got home I did some screen time. I looked at the clock, and my acupuncture took forty minutes, and the drive is a long drive, so it was already dinner when I got home, but my mom is coming home tonight at eight. And if you are wondering why I get acupuncture, it is because I am tight from sports injuries.

The rest of the night I did some screen time and homework, and then my mom came home and we all had some caramel apples, and those were really good. There was another debate tonight for the president. I am not sure really who was in it. Tonight we are going to sleep outside, and tomorrow I am going to do some Zooms, and it is going to be great.

Thursday, October 8, 2020

Today is Thursday. I woke up and did schoolwork, and then I ate breakfast and brushed my teeth and took a shower, and then I did Zooms until the afternoon. Today is garbage day, so I will need to take that out tonight, but that isn't for a while, and it isn't going to be that hard, so it will be great.

This afternoon I went in the back yard and did some squats and push-ups and lunges and things like that, and my finger is starting to actually feel worse, but again, it will take time to heal. I did that for about forty minutes and then came inside and ate lunch.

Tonight I didn't take the garbage out, because my dad said not to. It is super windy and he will do it in the morning, because otherwise they will blow over. Later Cody and my parents and I played some board games, which we don't do enough. We played Chutes and Ladders twice, and I won both of them, and I am guessing they got tired of losing to their youngest family member. They decided to stop playing, we had dessert, and then we all went to bed outside. I hope the garbage man doesn't wake me up in the morning.

Friday, October 9, 2020

Today is Friday and only two days until the Seahawks play. Their bye week is next week. There are seventeen games each season, and each team randomly will have one week that they don't play at all, and the Seahawks will not play next week, and that is sad, but at least it will just get it out of the way so they don't need to do it again this season. Basically, each team will play at least sixteen games, and then it is the playoffs, and it is just like a pyramid.

It will start with a lot of teams, and then one by one each team will be eliminated until there is one team left standing, and that team is the Super Bowl Champion.

This morning I didn't have any Zooms, and I basically did homework the whole morning and then had a late breakfast and went outside and exercised for thirty minutes and then did my writing. I have a very little amount of schoolwork left now, and my goal is to leave the smallest amount of schoolwork for Sunday. That is when the Seahawks play, but they don't play until five at night.

This afternoon my whole family watched a documentary about nature. I can't really describe it, but it is just facts and cool things that happen in nature. Then I did my midday brush, and then I did screen time until dinnertime.

Then we all had dinner and played board games until it was time to go to bed. We played one long board game, and Cody and I tied, but technically he won. Then we all slept inside, sadly.

Saturday, October 10, 2020

Tomorrow the Seahawks are playing, and I am really excited for that, but they don't play until five at night on Sunday. I will just have to wait, but today is Saturday, so let's talk about what I did. This morning I ate breakfast and did most of my homework, and then Cody and my mom and I all went on a drive to get groceries. The drive was nice, and after we went to get groceries we went for a walk up this hill called Taylor Hill. It is funny because that is my name. It took us about forty minutes to do that walk, and then we started making our way home.

When we got home, I did more homework, and then before I knew, it was the afternoon, and then I had lunch. I had to do this writing assignment, and it took me forty-five minutes to do, and then for some reason it didn't save, so I needed to redo it, and that took me another forty-five minutes. In all, the project was supposed to take me only twenty minutes, so that was kind of frustrating.

Later this afternoon, Cody and I played outside. It started off by my mom just kicking us outside, and on the drive from earlier that day Cody and I got pumpkins, and I started cleaning mine. I thought it looks really nice, but Cody said something that hurt my feelings. He said that my pumpkin looked really bad and that it looked better when I didn't even touch it. I just took a leaf and put it in Wilson's water bowl and started wiping all of the dirt off it, and when Cody said that, it kind of hurt my feelings. Then I was playing fetch with Wilson, and Cody grabbed my shoulder and turned me around and ripped the balls out from my hands, and I don't know what had got into him, but he was acting like a total jerk.

Then later in the afternoon/evening, we were playing this game and I asked Cody if he wanted what is in my left hand or right hand or my pocket from my sweatshirt, and he said left hand. I asked if he was sure, and he said yes, and I set my gum next to him. My gum was completely dry because it fell out of my mouth and into this dirt from earlier that hour, and he grabbed the gum and tried the throw it at my face, and he was really close to getting it in my hair, and that would have been super bad. He missed and it went right into the grass and dirt behind us. By the way, this whole time we were in my back yard, and then I went to the front yard wanting to go inside, because he wasn't making it fun anymore and he was kind of being a jerk. I was about to step in the front door, and Cody grabbed my shoulder and ripped me around just like earlier and tried to put the gum in my mouth, and he was successfully getting it in my mouth, and I kind of spit it out and ran inside, and that is when I called my dad, and Cody got in big trouble.

I am not really sure what trouble Cody is in yet, but all I know is he lost his phone. Then we all ate dinner, and then I watched this Halloween movie, and it was really funny, and then we all just went to bed. My dad is working overtime, so he will not be home tomorrow for the football game, which is really sad. Cody, I am not sure if he loses his Fantasy Football team, but we will see tomorrow.

Sunday, October 11, 2020

Today is Sunday and football is here. This morning I did the rest of my schoolwork, and then I went on a walk in the woods with my mom. Tomorrow my dad is coming home, and when I say my dad worked for a forty-eight, that just means he has stayed and worked at the fire station for two straight days. A twenty-four is just one day, and he has worked a forty-eight, so he will be coming home tomorrow morning at ten.

This morning we walked, and it was nice. It was all three of us, and for some reason my Achilles tendon was starting to hurt really bad. I didn't know why, but I just went on with it. If you don't know what your Achilles is, it is the big, thick tendon in the back of your heel, and it goes up your leg about half a foot until you can't feel it anymore. I looked it up, and it said that a common side effect for an Achilles tendonitis is when you can't bend your foot down. I can't do that, but I am not that worried. I will just talk to my dad when he gets home.

The Seahawks game started off really bad. At half time, we were losing 13–0, and then after the third quarter we were tied 21–21, and then they got a touchdown and went for two and missed, and then we were losing 21–26, and then Russell Wilson threw an interception, and then the other team was in our red zone, and then it turned into a fourth and inches, and then they could have kicked a field goal and been in the lead by eight points, but they went for it, and the Seahawks stopped them, and there were two minutes left, and after a couple plays the Seahawks were at midfield and it was forth and ten, and Russell Wilson threw it for a first, and then it ended up being fourth and goal at the nine-yard line, and there were ten seconds left, and Russell Wilson threw the game-winning touchdown to DK Metcalf. That is how the night ended. That is a good night.

Monday, October 12, 2020
Tonight there is going to be one football game, and sadly, I am probable going to lose Fantasy Football again. I am currently winning by four points, but the guy I am playing has two really good guys playing tonight, and they are both running backs, and one of them is the best currently in the NFL, and the other is the starter for the other team, so they will be guaranteed to get over thirty-five points, and then I will be losing by, like, three. Surprisingly, there is a game tomorrow on Tuesday, and that game is at four o'clock, and I have my kicker playing that night. Kickers get, like, five to ten points, so I have a very small chance of winning, but that is still a chance.

This morning I did schoolwork and chores until nine, and then I did some more schoolwork and ate breakfast and brushed my teeth. That is about everything I did, except I did look at Fantasy Football, and as I said in the last paragraph, I have a small chance of winning.

Early afternoon my dad came home, and then I did more schoolwork. Then we all made a gingerbread house. We did it and glued it and all, but it just fell off. Then we decided that we would just stop and do more, later.

Then later this afternoon, we decided that we will each just put frosting on one piece and decorate it ourselves. I decorated mine for about one hour and then was done. Cody started getting upset because I used most of the frosting. That was very unnecessary, I thought, but I didn't really care.

Then we all went on a hike, and my Achilles started really hurting, but I just ignored it. I talked to my dad when we got home, and he told me that there is probably just a little tear but it will be fine, and I looked it up. A rupture is when the whole tendon snaps, and that would be a lot more painful than just a little tear.

The rest of the afternoon until dinner, Cody, my dad, my mom, and I all had a couple-hour family meeting about what Cody has been doing wrong with his attitude the last couple days. And they said that they will discuss his punishment later, and that is okay with me because I am not the parent.

Tonight I did my PT and some schoolwork, and then the football game was on. I didn't want to use my screen time on that, so I did separate screen time. My dad ordered takeout food from my favorite place, and that was great. The Saints were playing the Chargers, and the Saints ended up winning. I saved forty minutes of my screen time for tomorrow, and that is great. I might watch some of tomorrow's game.

Tuesday, October 13, 2020

Today is Tuesday. There is going to be one game on tonight, and it is at four o'clock. When I woke up, I looked out my bedroom window. It was super windy and the trees were blowing back and forth and it was super crazy. That is kind of fun, but also kind of annoying because the wind is really loud.

The rest of the morning I just did my reading, writing, workout, and my schoolwork. Tomorrow is when my midterms are due, and that means that I will need to do a lot of studying today, and tomorrow is when I do the test. I have done all my other midterms already, but I only have to do my STEM tomorrow. That one will be super easy because it is only twenty questions and it is just multiple choice.

This afternoon the power went out, and that wasn't a surprise because it was so windy and it was predicted by the weather people to go out. Before the power went out, I put my favorite foods in the mini fridge because that is the fridge that we can open when we lose power. But we are still going to try to open that one less than we usually would so it stays cold.

The weather people said the power would go back on by, like, two. Well, it was still out, and I was eating dinner. We went out to this place and got this good Italian food to go and it was really good. When we got home, the power was still out, and it was, like, seven. I was starting to get annoyed because I really needed to study for my midterms, and I couldn't do it because of no Wi-Fi. But it is okay, and we all just put flashlights and headlamps on and played games until we were so bored we brushed our teeth and were going to bed. It was, like, eight thirty. Then right before I was walking upstairs to go to bed, the power came back on, and I immediately went in the basement and checked my email and did about fifteen minutes of studying, and then I came upstairs and went to bed.

Wednesday, October 14, 2020

Today is Wednesday and this morning I woke up at eight. I did a lot of studying for my midterm, and I did everything on my list of what to do, and

I did my chores and everything, and then it was almost noon. Then I did my exercise in the basement for about thirty minutes with Cody and my mom. Then I was done with work for the day, so I did my screen time.

After screen time I did more studying, and before I knew, it was already two. Cody did the rest of his midterms, and I have one midterm left to do. I will do that after dinner. I did more studying, and then I was in the car with my mom because I needed to go get acupuncture. My mom had to stay outside because of COVID. When I got there, I told the acupuncturist that I have been having a lot of pain in my Achilles, and then I went inside her office and I laid down on the table and she stuck like ten needles in my hands and legs. After that she left me in the room alone for about forty-five minutes, and then I went home.

Tonight I did more screen time and had dinner and did my midterm studying and test. I did really good on my test, and my STEM score for my entire class is 99/100. That is really good and I am really happy. That is all we did. We had dessert and then went to bed.

Thursday, October 15, 2020

Today is Thursday and my chores are to sweep the floors. That will be easy. I got an email this morning from my STEM teacher, and he said that I can have an extra try on my test because I didn't get that much time to study, and that was fine with me. I did it again and then I got 95% on my test. That is saying something because before I got 85.3.

I did some more homework and then swept the floor and was done with almost all of my work. I did my exercise in the basement with Cody and got, like, one hour. Then I did more homework and answered some email, and then I was done for work for the day, besides more homework and writing. Then at ten my dad came home.

My dad told Cody he needed to have a serious talk with him, and he did. Basically, he doesn't get any phone privileges, and that means texting, no Fantasy Football, and some more things. Then we went to my mom, while she was working at the hospital, and we dropped off some food for her and just said hello. That is how the whole afternoon went.

Tonight Donnett, our neighbor, said she will bring dinner to everyone's house, and she did. She brought meat sauce, bread, pasta, and vegetables. We all ate dinner, and then my mom came home. She was tired, so she just ate her food. Then we had some dessert and then to bed on the deck. We are going to sleep outside.

Friday, October 16, 2020

Today is Friday and Gavin and Carter are going to come over. We aren't going to play inside, we are going to play outside, and they are either going to come tomorrow or the next day, depending on the weather. I think they are going to come tomorrow because in two days the weather says it will rain really hard. We will see.

This morning I did all of my homework for the rest of the day. I had breakfast kind of late, and when I finished breakfast, I brushed my teeth and then took a shower and did my reading and washed my face and did my chores, and then before I knew it, it was already two in the afternoon. Then Cody and my mom and dad all went on the trail. I stayed to do more schoolwork, and I finished, like, right when everyone walked in the door.

Later I finished all of my work and then did my schoolwork and then my screen time. Before I knew it again, it was dinner. For some reason this day has been going by really fast, I was thinking. But then we ate dinner, and after that we all four had a talk. It was about screen time, and we all decided, after a long time of talking, that every day we won't be allowed to look at any screen (besides schoolwork) all day until it was two, and then we would be allowed to do screen time until four, and we would be done for the day. Except for Sunday, because with football that all will change. So basically, we are doing too much screen time, and just from two until four is our break to do screen time, and the rest of the day we can play games or go outside or just chill, but no screens.

Saturday, October 17, 2020

Today is Saturday and my mom left for work at seven. She will not be home until four. My dad texted Gavin and Carter's parents, and they said that they will come over today at two o'clock, and that is great.

This morning I finished all of my work by nine o'clock, and that was amazing. Cody told my dad and me that for one of his midterms he needs to watch a movie and take notes. And we all watched the movie. It is called *Mr. Smith* and I don't really know what happened. I was playing football, and my dad took out this huge box of Legos, and I just played with those. The movie was really long, so we finished it, like, when it was noon.

Two hours later Gavin and Carter came over. We all just played hide-and-seek for, like, three hours. Then we started playing this really fun game, and it is the opposite of hide-and-seek. Three people count and one person hides, and then all three people try to find the person. The last person to find the person that hides loses. Then we all played ultimate football until my parents made everyone two pizzas. We ate them and then started burning wood in the bonfire my dad helped us build. One thing that is really crazy is that Gavin is now taller than Carter, like a couple inches. I think Gavin had another growth spurt.

Sunday, October 18, 2020

Three days until Cody's birthday, and that is great. So far, my parents have told me that Cody is going to get a basketball, air pods, a pull-up bar, and more that I don't know of. Today is Sunday and the Seahawks aren't going to play because they are on the bye week, so that is great.

Cody's birthday is on the twenty-first, in three days. My grandparents are coming on Tuesday, and they will surprise Cody on Wednesday, and Cody doesn't know that they are coming. This is the first time for either Cody or my birthday that my grandparents have come and surprised us, and they have come plenty of times but never when we didn't know.

In the morning, I did the rest of my homework and chores and everything, and then I did some of my screen time and watched part of a couple football games. In the afternoon, my dad went on a run and my mom is at work. Also, my dad is going to work tomorrow, so we will not be able to sleep outside. I can't wait until my grandparents are here.

Tonight we all had dinner and then watched these home videos that we have in, like, five discs, and they are of Cody and me from when I was born until I was about five. They are really funny to watch and make us laugh every single time. Then we all went to bed, and Wilson was super sad that we needed to sleep inside. He eventually gave up and just went to bed, and so did I. When we sleep inside, he sleeps on the floor by my parents' bed.

Monday, October 19, 2020

Cody's birthday is in two days now, and my grandparents are now going to surprise Cody tomorrow. It is so funny because he still doesn't know that they are coming. I probable already said this, but I got Cody a Seahawks football.

This morning I did Zoom and schoolwork until noon. Today my dad left for work, so he will not be here today, but he will be here tomorrow, and that is great. This afternoon I went to a dentist appointment, and it took a really long time and hurt super bad.

When I got home, I did screen time. Before I knew it, I was eating dinner. This day went by really fast for me. After dinner I ate dessert and finished my screen time and, sadly, we went to bed inside. But tomorrow I think we are going to sleep outside.

Tuesday, October 20, 2020

Tomorrow is Cody's birthday, but today my grandparents are coming, and this is our plan. We are going to go to eat dinner outside at La Fiamma, and we are going to walk up the stairs to the front doors. We told Cody we made reservations, and after we walk up the stairs, we will walk around the building and go to the outdoor seating, and there will be my grandparents, and he will hopefully be surprised.

This morning I did my Zoom and homework until noon, and then I came upstairs and had my very late breakfast. I did have some bacon during my Zoom, but very little. I had cereal and then did some more schoolwork.

Tonight we went to La Fiamma and did the plan. He was super surprised, and it was really fun, and we sat down and ordered our food. Cody and I got a large cheese pizza to share, and I got a large salad, and then my parents and my grandparents got a type of pizza that I have never heard of before. We all just talked until it was, like, seven thirty, and we went to their car and said bye. They handed Cody a present to take home, and I think they are air pods, but I am not sure. Then they handed me a ziplock bag of cinnamon rolls, and we went home and slept outside.

Wednesday, October 21, 2020

Today is Cody's birthday, and for the whole morning until it was the afternoon, I was doing Zooms and schoolwork. When we finished our Zooms, I let Cody open my present. I got him a Seattle Seahawks football, and it is just a normal football. Cody and I grew out of our other footballs, so I thought it would be a good idea. I was planning on getting Cody football gloves, but then I found this football, and I told my parents it would be a good idea to get him gloves because it would go with the football.

Later, at two, Cody and I did some screen time and then opened the rest of the presents. It turns out my parents did get Cody football gloves. Cody and I did the rest of our screen time until three, and then we went to see my grandparents at the place they were staying.

When we got there, we just talked about school and life for a couple hours, and then we drove separate cars to the place Cody wanted to go to. The place is called Anthony's, and it is an amazing restaurant. We went there and ate dessert. I saw this dessert that looked really good, and it is raspberry and strawberry ice cream with blackberries melted over it, and I had it, and it was super good. When we got home, we just went to bed inside.

Thursday, October 22, 2020

Cody and I both started the day off with homework. One thing that is kind of funny is that in one of my Zooms, we needed to share with the class about one time when someone made you feel left out or different, and I shared when in first grade a girl wouldn't stop making fun of my hearing aids. But that isn't the funny thing. The funny thing is that one kid who is kind of really annoying, but that is just my perspective, but getting to the point, he said one time he felt left out is when he had a wart on his finger and needed to get it fixed, and in quotes he said, "Oh my god, you wouldn't imagine! It hurt, like, super bad and I am not kidding! It was the worst thing ever." I kept quiet about this, but I have had warts, and I had to have them all treated, and to get them treated you need to put this extremely cold thing on your wart and keep it on there for, like, three minutes, for a couple weeks. That might not seem funny, but to me it doesn't hurt that bad.

Later in the afternoon I went on a walk with my mom. Cody didn't want to come, but that is okay with me. Then I grabbed a little bag my mom wanted to give to one of our neighbors, and my mom texted them and then walked up to their house and gave them the basket. It was just a couple of baby things and baby presents, because they just had a baby. Tonight we all had dinner, and then I went downstairs and watched some of the football game that was on, and then I did my PT. Before I knew, it was time to go to bed.

Friday, October 23, 2020

Today I don't have any Zooms, but I do have a lot of homework. My mom left for work at seven, and my dad will come home but not until eleven. The reason why is because he needed to finish up just a little bit more work. This morning I started off with a shower and then brushed my teeth and then went downstairs and did my chores and then my reading and my writing, and then I ate a late breakfast.

This morning at ten, Cody and I did our first hour of screen time. When we finished that, we came up because my dad was home, and we just talked to my dad until noon. Then my dad left to get something from the store for Cody because he needed something for school. When he got back we started carving our pumpkins. I cut the top part off first, and got all of the pumpkin seeds and everything out into a bowl, and then I started looking for ideas for carving. I came up this weird idea to take a drill and put a ton of holes in it. My dad got the drill, and then I took a pen and put all of the dots where I wanted the holes to be, and then I was done with the first part. Then Cody did his pumpkin, and it was just a normal face with two eyes, one nose, and a mouth. Then I drilled all the holes, and I swear there was, like, more the a hundred holes, and I filled the whole pumpkin, and that got me shocked. When we finished it was almost dinner.

Cody and I did our last hour of screen time, and then we had pizza for dinner. My dad said he wanted to watch a movie, so I looked for movies and found a really good one called *Stranger Than Fiction*. It was really good, and it also had Will Ferrell. It is always a good movie when he is in it. I will not spoil it, but it is just a really good movie.

Saturday, October 24, 2020

Today is Saturday. Tomorrow the Seattle Seahawks are playing at five-twenty, and I can't wait. This week in Fantasy Football I think I am going to win, and my injured guys are starting to get better, which is really exciting. I really want to win, because I have only won one game and if I start winning now, I might be able to get to the playoffs. I think I can, but I just would like to be safe.

This morning I did my reading and writing and ate breakfast. Since it is Saturday, I have no Zooms, so that is great. Then I did a lot of homework, and I did so much I am done for the next week. I was so bored, I did homework that is due in two weeks.

This afternoon I did a lot more homework, and then I had lunch. My dad left because he needed to do some work for another article that he will be in. Tomorrow the Seattle Times paper is coming out and he will be in it, and this time he is in the paper, not the online paper, which is a big deal.

Tonight my dad came back, and we all ate dinner. I had an avocado for my vegetable, and then I had pasta. Then I did the rest of my screen time, and my mom and I did this cool thing. I forget what it is called, but it has, like, lots of marbles. It's like a whirlpool, where you make a track and the marbles loop on the track. It is cool. Then we went to bed outside.

Sunday, October 25, 2020

Today I woke up and it's Sunday, so the Seahawks are playing. and they are playing a good team, so it might be hard to win. I woke up late and brushed my teeth, ate breakfast, and took a shower. Before I knew it, the first football game of the day started, and it will go on until around one, and it is ten. I watched a little bit of the game and did my schoolwork, and then the game ended at one. The day before, I worked for hours of screen time, so it is kind of nice.

Later I watched more football, and then my dad's friend came over and they had a bonfire. Then I did more schoolwork and ate lunch and did more screen time, and then it was four. Cody and I and my dad played football until the Seahawks game started. Tonight was great because the Seahawks WON by fifty points! I wish. Actually, we lost, and it was in overtime, so it got really intense until the last minute and Russell Wilson threw an interception. That was sad. But we're sleeping outside and having dessert tonight, and that is great.

Monday, October 26, 2020
Today is Monday and I need to do a Zoom at eight, so it is going to be hard to wake up. I woke up and right away took a shower and then did my reading and then ate and brushed and started my Zooms until noon.

This afternoon Cody and my dad and I all went outside to play football. Tomorrow Dad is going to be at the fire station, so I want to play with him today. We played outside until it was two, and then Cody and I did our first hour of screen time, and then I did homework until four thirty. Then I started getting ready for dinner.

Tonight we all had dinner, and I had vegetables and pasta. When we finished, Cody and I finished our screen time. At night we all had dessert. We have to sleep inside because my dad is going to work tomorrow.

Tuesday, October 27, 2020
Today is Tuesday. When I woke up, I went downstairs and said hi to Wilson and then did some schoolwork. Then my mom and I decided to go on a walk, and we did and it was really fun. But when I got back it was time to do my Zooms, and I did a couple hours of that until noon.

This afternoon I went outside and played a little and said hi Wilson. Cody and I did some screen time, and I made a *Madden* team and I played that and *Minecraft*. Then I did my chores and Cody and my mom went on a drive, and that gave me time to do more homework.

Later this afternoon when my mom and Cody came home, Cody and I did the rest of our screen time until it was dinnertime. Then we ate dinner and went in the basement and played this game called Twister, and it is really fun. We played that and a couple other games for an hour or two. Then we all went on a walk. My mom said I can use that as my exercise for tomorrow, and that is great. Then we all went to bed.

Wednesday, October 28, 2020
Today it is Wednesday and just another day of Zooming. I did Zooms from eight to nine and then my reading and journaling until ten. Then I had two

more Zooms until noon. This afternoon we all played football, Cody and my dad and I. Then we all went inside, and I did my chores.

Later this afternoon I played with this thing, and I think it is called Whirlpool, and it was fun. Then my mom came home from work and we all just talked about our day. Then we played more football, Cody and Dad and I—and mom played for a little bit as quarterback.

Tonight we all had dinner, and I had a smoothie and pasta and red peppers and spinach and then, finally, I had a full avocado. Then I finished my screen time, set up the deck, and went to bed out there.

Thursday, October 29, 2020

Today is Thursday and I only needed to do two Zooms and then I am done. I did those two Zooms, and I did homework—did so much I only need to do, like, ten more minutes and I am done for the rest of the week.

This afternoon Cody and my dad and I played football for about two hours, and then I did more homework, and then I did my chores and reading, and then I did my writing.

Before I knew it, dinner was here. I just made my own dinner because I was really hungry. After I ate, I watched a football game that was on. It was the Falcons versus Panthers. I saw Cody watching a movie, and I watched part of that movie too, and then we all went to bed, inside because tomorrow my dad needs to go to work.

Friday, October 30, 2020

Today is the day before Halloween, and tomorrow we can't do much because of coronavirus, but we will still just buy some candy from the store. When I woke up, I was happy because it is Friday and I don't have any school Zooms.

This morning I did my reading right away and my journaling, and then I did my chores with my mom and put my laundry away. My dad isn't here today because he is at work, but tomorrow he will be here.

This afternoon I had lunch and did a ton of schoolwork and more reading, and then I went outside and played. Tonight we all had dinner and then watched two *Modern Family* shows, and those were really funny. Then we finished the night with dinner and made caramel apples!

Saturday, October 31, 2020

Today is Halloween and I am really happy because that means lots of candy, and that means I will get hyper, and it is going to be a lot of fun. My dad made this really fun treasure hunt map, and it is going to be awesome. We will go do that and try to find the treasure in the woods. He hid a bag of candy way up on Galbraith and wrote a riddle telling us how to find it, and my dad invited a couple other families in our neighborhood to come hunt too, and we all are going to be six feet apart, and we all are going to be wearing masks, and it will be fun!

This morning at ten o'clock, my mom and Cody went on a hike and found a couple of hidden colored Halloween rocks and returned them to this house that hid them, and she gave us candy in return for finding them. It was, like, find the hidden Halloween rocks and exchange them for candy. My neighbor who painted the rocks and hid them is an artist named Lori, and we have one of her paintings. That was a lot of fun, and then we got home, and my dad was home. I gave him a big hug, and that is what we did this afternoon.

Then in the afternoon, we all went on the treasure map hunt. At the end I found the bags of candy way up on the mountain trail, and there were six bags, and everyone got one bag. There was Cody and Silas and Luke and Hunter and Bode and I. Later that afternoon, I sorted my candy and went to two other neighbors who said they will give us individual bags of candy for trick-or-treat.

Tonight we all ate dinner and watched a fun Halloween movie. Then we all went to bed, and I will sleep inside because I want a good night's sleep before the Seahawks, and it looks like it will be cold.

Sunday, November 1, 2020

Today is the first of November. I can't wait for the election in two days, but I am still worried. I am going to try not to talk about it that much, because that might get me excited, and I don't think it would be a good thing if I am too excited.

Today the Seahawks play, and I can't wait. Also, today is my dad's birthday. This morning we opened a couple of presents and I did homework and everything else I needed to do.

This afternoon it was time for the Seahawks. We watched that game until dinner, and it was exciting. The Seahawks played the Forty-Niners, and that team is good, but we ended up winning. The score ended up 37–27, and it was a great afternoon. Tonight we all had dinner and cupcakes for my dad's birthday. It ended up being a great day.

Monday, November 2, 2020

Today is Monday and I need to do school, and that is really sad. I did schoolwork and Zooms until twelve in the afternoon, and lots of people were talking about politics in the chat box. It was funny watching people argue about it, and then my teacher ended up shutting it down because it was getting a little out of hand.

This afternoon Cody and my dad and I played football for a couple hours, and it was a lot of fun. We didn't keep score and we never had fouls, and we figured out that is the most fun way to play, after many, many arguments. When we came in, I took a shower and did more homework and did my midday brush, and then I did my screen time.

Then it was dinner, and I had pasta and red peppers and carrots. I tried eating carrots, but it hurt my teeth to eat it. The reason why is because not so long ago, I got a teeth cleaning and a couple tightens on my braces, and that makes my teeth hurt and sore. But it was okay to have red peppers and pasta. When we all finished, I did the rest of my screen time and went to bed.

Tuesday, November 3, 2020

Today is election day. It starts late tonight, and my guess is my family will stay up until ten or eleven to see what happens. Tomorrow I have an early Zoom, so I might be tired, but it will definitely be worth it. This morning I did all my Zooms until noon.

This afternoon I did my exercises and my midday brush, and then I went outside and said hi to Wilson. Wilson seemed really tired, so I left him alone. My dad was supposed to work today, but he took it off.

Tonight we all had dinner and started watching the election at seven, and that is when it generally started for the results. We all watched it to about ten.

Wednesday, November 4, 2020

Today is Wednesday. Tomorrow there is going to be a football game, and I have three people playing for my Fantasy Football team, and that is out of nine players. This week is a special week in Fantasy Football because I am playing against my brother. Just letting you know, there is going to be a lot of trash talk. This is the only week this year Cody and I will play against each other, so it is kind of going to be a big deal when I win, because Cody is going to hate it. Just warning you.

This morning my dad left for work, and I looked at the news. There's not much different about the election night thing, but it turned out not to be one night. It will be more than one night till they know who wins, and I am not surprised. Donald Trump is going to make all the states recount their votes, but that is only if he is losing, and that is just my guess. Pretty much that whole rest of the morning, I looked and watched the election with my mom and Cody, and then I did my Zooms and homework until it was the afternoon.

Then this afternoon I did some exercise and then my chores and midday brush, and then I did my reading. Pretty much the rest of the afternoon I just did screen time. Tonight we all had dinner. I had avocado and pasta. Yesterday my dad went to the store and got this really good and fresh pasta, and it only takes two minutes to make it, that is how fresh it is. Then tonight we just watched the election more. Before bed I read some of *Calvin and Hobbes*, but just for fun because my mom wouldn't let me do that as my actual reading. It doesn't count.

Tomorrow my dad is coming home from the fire station, but it should be really rainy, so we probably will not play football. I think the day after that we will, because it should be really sunny and nice then, but that is all according to the weather man.

Thursday, November 5, 2020

Today is the last day that I have Zooms. I definitely have homework I need to do on the weekend, but today I only needed to do a couple hours of homework. This morning I did my Zooms until noon and then went outside and played fetch with Wilson and came back in and did homework.

This afternoon I started doing my screen time. I did that until three and then did my reading and journaling. Then I did my chore, which was to sweep. As I did that, the day started going by fast, so I was just relaxing and thinking about my life. I did that for about thirty minutes, and before I knew it, I was sitting in the kitchen eating dinner.

After dinner we all watched the election. Surprisingly, it is still going on, and I think it will be completely done in three or four days at the most. Right now, Joe Biden has 253 electoral votes and Donald Trump has only 214, and the race is the first person to 270. There is only Georgia (16), Pennsylvania (20), North Carolina (15), Nevada (6), and finally Arizona (11) left to count. The number right next to each of those states is how many points they are worth, and you can do the math and the little bit he needs to win. And Biden is winning in Georgia, Pennsylvania, Nevada, and Arizona. The chances of Trump winning are really small.

Friday, November 6, 2020

Today is Friday, so I don't have any Zooms that I need to do. My plan is to just do a lot of schoolwork, and that is what I did most of the morning. Then at ten I did my reading and writing. When I finished both of those, I went outside to say hi to cute fluffy Wilson, and I came back in and started more schoolwork.

This afternoon Cody and my dad and I all played football. We went to this high school called Sehome High School, and they have a brand new football field with awesome turf. Since there isn't any public school going on, we have been going there for the last seven or whatever months, 'cause it is awesome. When we finished, it was already three o'clock, and time really went by fast. I guess that is why they say time flies when you're having fun.

That night we all had dinner, except my mom because she is working. I had homemade pizza, and vegetables. Then my mom came home, and we all watched the election. Then I did my PT, and we all went to bed. Tomorrow my dad is going to the fire station, so sadly, we won't sleep outside.

Saturday, November 7, 2020

Today Biden is now the President of the United States of America, and that is exciting. The funny thing is, while Trump was playing golf, he got the news he wasn't the president any more. There are plenty of funny memes on that.

This morning I did my reading and writing and a lot of homework. When I finished a little bit of homework, I did chores and then took a shower and washed my face. Then I went outside and played with Wilson for a little bit.

This afternoon my mom and Cody and I made a bonfire and celebrated—with candy. Then we all came in and I did my PT and then my midday brush. Then I went outside and played with Wilson for a little bit and came back inside for dinner.

Tonight I had pasta, pizza, sausage, avocado, and more vegetables. After dinner we didn't have dessert because we didn't have any ice cream. We watched the Biden winning speech, which was good. After all of that, we went to bed to get ready for the Seahawks game! What a good day.

Sunday, November 8, 2020

Today is Sunday and the Seahawks are going to play at ten in the morning. It is kind of early, but I can't wait. This morning the Seahawks got off on a bad foot. They started losing by a lot and kept getting crushed. Near the end they were down by a lot, with only five minutes left, but they started catching up. Then the time ran out and the Seahawks lost. It is sad, but they are still one of the best teams in the NFL.

Then late afternoon one of our neighbors came over, and we all went outside and played for a couple hours until dinner, and then my brother and I came inside to eat dinner. And yes, we were wearing masks the whole time.

And yes, we were keeping our distance. But it was still fun to play outside with friends.

Tonight we all had dinner and then started getting ready for bed. I did my writing and reading. When I finished those I just went to bed.

Monday, November 9, 2020

Today is Monday and I need to do school. I woke up early and took a shower and got ready for my Zooms. I wasn't able to eat, so after my Zooms I was starving. And when my Zooms finished, I had a couple bowls of cereal and then did some screen time.

This afternoon I did all my screen time and then my reading and writing and then some schoolwork. Then my mom and I left for a drive, and we just drove around and talked and had no idea where we were going. It was fun, just my mom and I, and then we came home. It was almost dinner.

Tonight I had pizza my dad made, and it was amazing. My dad made homemade ranch, and that was amazing also. We all had an idea for next year to go away for a whole month (if coronavirus is still going on, which it probably will be). My dad gets a month off from the fire station every summer, but next summer we think we will go with Wilson to a beach somewhere to play and stay there for a whole month. I really hope we do 'cause that will be so great.

Tuesday, November 10, 2020

Today my dad came home from the fire station. He needed to work overtime, so he was gone for a couple days, which is forty-eight hours, but he is back now, so that is great! The whole morning I did Zooms and things like that. I lost Fantasy Football against Cody this week, but the score was 142–147, so it was really close. Yes, there was a lot of trash talking, but fair is fair, and Cody won. But there is always a rematch!

This afternoon my mom and I went for a drive. My dad's mom's birthday is coming up on the seventeenth of this month, and my mom's birthday is that same day, and that is funny. But my mom and I went shopping for a couple hours for birthday things. That night we all had dinner and went to bed extra early because my dad was up all night working the night before. He was tired from fires at night, so we went to bed at, like, nine. It's funny because my dad always says, "I'm not tired," but then he says, "OK, yeah, I am tired."

Wednesday, November 11, 2020

Today is Wednesday and this week in Fantasy Football. I am playing against Dynamite. His real name is Ray Simon, and he is my dad's friend, but I am playing him this week, and I played him a couple weeks ago and crushed him, so it will hopefully be another easy win. I think I will win.

This morning I did homework and Zooms until noon and then some screen time for a couple hours. Then I called my dad at the fire station, and I FaceTimed with Ray because he was working with my dad. They work together every shift, and it was fun trash talking with him. After I did that I had lunch.

Later I did more screen time and then ate dinner. I had pasta and avocado, and that was really good. After that I had dessert, which was really good. Then I went to bed. Since my dad is working, I can't sleep outside, and that is sad. Hopefully, we can sleep outside when he comes home.

Thursday, November 12, 2020

Today is Thursday. This morning before my Zooms, I went to the new dentist. This guy was at a different office, because we needed another appointment. It went well, and then I got home, and now I am going to get my braces off this month. I will get a ton of new mouth things, and it is going to be cool. I don't have to have headgear, and this new dentist is way better than the one I have had. After that I did all of my Zooms, and those were all the Zooms I needed to do this week!

This afternoon I did my screen time and homework and then went outside and exercised for hours. Then I had lunch and did my next hour of screen time. By then it was almost dinner, so I started setting up the table and helping my mom.

That night we all had dinner, and we didn't have dessert because we did that the day before. After that I just chilled, and since it was Thursday, there was one football game on. I couldn't watch it because I already did my screen time, but I just went to bed pretty early anyway.

Friday, November 13, 2020

Today I did my screen time early and had breakfast and watched a documentary for an hour or two for school. After that I went outside and brought Wilson inside, and then my dad came home and we talked with him for a little bit, and Wilson couldn't stop wagging his tail.

This afternoon I did some more screen time and then went outside and played and then did my chores, and then I did more schoolwork and my reading and writing, and after that I had lunch.

Then at night we all had dinner. It was really good, but for some reason I had pasta, milk, cereal, avocado, corn, and other vegetables with ranch. Later my dad and I did the dishes, and that is about it. We have a rule: Whoever does the dishes gets to pick out what music is playing. So I played my music.

Saturday, November 14, 2020
Today is Saturday. The Seahawks are playing tomorrow and I can't wait, but they are playing the Rams, and they are really good, so I am crossing my fingers that the Seahawks win.

Then late morning I did my reading and chores and my writing. After that I went upstairs and brushed my teeth and took a shower. Then I did my homework until noon. This afternoon I did mostly homework, but then I did some of my screen time, and then I did more homework and had lunch.

This afternoon and on Monday, there is going to be a guy coming. He is going to be redoing our garage floor, so my family and I need to take everything out of the garage and take it to the dump if we don't use it or can't give it to a family that needs it. We also are going to take everything from the basement that we don't want and can't give away and take that to the dump, too. And that is what we just did, pretty much, all afternoon and after dinner. We had a fast dinner and went back to work. One place we give it away is called Goodwill, and some things friends might want. The rest we take to the dump.

Sunday, November 15, 2020
Today the Seahawks play, and I can't wait. This whole morning I did all of my work, and that included schoolwork, which I did for most of the morning. Then I did my reading and writing, and after that I took my shower.

Before I knew it, the Seahawks game was on, and we watched that game until dinner. This is what happened. Basically, the Seahawks got off to a bad start and continued to play badly until they lost, simple as that. I am really mad because Russell Wilson didn't even throw any touchdowns, and to make it even worse, my Fantasy Football team lost. Now there is, like, a 1 percent chance I can even make it into the top six, and if I don't get in the top six, I don't even get into the playoffs. To make it even worse, I lost 101–102, and I couldn't believe it.

Tonight my mom and Cody and Wilson and I all had dinner. My dad is at work, so he wasn't eating with us. Tonight I am just relaxing and going to bed.

Monday, November 16, 2020

Today is Monday and that means I need to do schoolwork and Zoom all day, but I started it off with reading and writing and then took a shower and started my Zooms.

Then this afternoon my dad came home, and I had lunch, and Wilson wasn't allowed outside because the people are painting in the garage and he would run around wagging his tail on the wet paint. And I will tell you this, and maybe I told you before, but Wilson has an electric fence, so he doesn't have a leash. It goes around our whole house and he loves running around all day wagging his tail, so I know he is sad he has to stay inside this day. This late afternoon I started getting ready for my mom's birthday, which is tomorrow, and I got everything set up. I can't wait to give her my present!

At night we all had dinner, and there was one football game on. I didn't watch it, because I didn't think it was worth my screen time. So, I just played *Madden* instead. Later I had dinner with my dad, my mom, Cody, and Wilson. After we all ate, I went upstairs and went to bed surprisingly early. You might be wondering why we haven't been sleeping outside. The reason why is because everything that was in the garage we moved to the deck, so we can't sleep out there because there is no room this week out there.

Tuesday, November 17, 2020

This morning my mom woke up and I gave her part of my present, which was a card with many little gift cards I made her. They had, like, free coffee service, twenty minutes of massage, free breakfast service, and things like that, and she liked it! And if you didn't know this, I can make coffee and breakfast. When I was little, I used to say, "all by myself" because I just want to do things by myself. So, I can make my mom coffee and breakfast!

But then I needed to do my Zooms, and I just did those until noon. At noon we opened more presents, and most of them were magazines and candles and things like that. Now I think I know what type of candle my mom wants for Christmas.

At night we all had dinner, and my dad made my mom twice-baked mashed potatoes and three steaks, and she loved it. Then a couple of her friends came over and surprised her, and they relaxed in the garage and just talked until it was time to go to bed. They couldn't come in the house, so they stayed six feet apart in the garage.

Wednesday, November 18, 2020

Today is Wednesday and today is my long Zoom day, so I will Zoom from eight to nine, and then I have a one hour break, and then I need to do Zooms for two more hours until noon. I woke up at seven and ate, showered, brushed my teeth, and started my Zooms. After my first Zoom I had one hour off, so I did my thirty minutes of reading and my journaling. After that it was time for my next Zoom.

This afternoon I checked my Fantasy Football, and this week I am playing Makowichuk, who is funny. He is the funniest firefighter, and I am projected to win 140–118, and that is good. But after this week I play Mellein, and after that I am playing Mahnke, and if I don't win all of those three weeks, then I lose. I am hopeful, but it is close. The rest of the afternoon, I did schoolwork and then my chores and screen time.

Then when we all had dinner. I had pasta and vegetables. After dinner we watched a movie called *Star Girl*. My dad made us watch it, and I didn't really like it, but it wasn't really my choice. I went to bed at ten because I stayed up reading for the next day, and then I fell asleep waiting patiently for tomorrow's Seahawks game.

Thursday, November 19, 2020

Today is Thursday. This morning I woke up and went downstairs and then had a fast breakfast and brushed my teeth and took a shower. Then I went straight downstairs to do my Zooms. The first one I had was math, and then I had leadership, and that was all the Zooms I needed to do for the week.

This afternoon I went outside and did my exercise. I came back in, did my chores and one hour of screen time, and then I did my reading and writing. When I finished, I went downstairs and did the rest of my screen time.

Tonight the Seahawks played the Cardinals, and it got really intense. It came down to the last play of the game. The Seahawks were winning 28–21, it was the last play on fourth and long, and then Kyler Murray went back to throw it long, but then Carlos Dunlap came in and got the game-winning sack, and the Seahawks won. Then we all just went to bed with smiles!

Friday, November 20, 2020

This morning the painters came and painted our garage floor some more, and after they did that, the house heater went on and spread the smell of paint everywhere inside, and Wilson was barking because it smelled so bad. We opened all the windows, I put Wilson in the car, and we left for a couple hours. We just drove in an aimless direction, and then at about three, we came home and walked inside, and suddenly there were bugs flying everywhere. They were all in our faces, and on the wall to the front door there were at least a thousand little gnats, and we were so confused.

We learned that the gnats can fit through the little screens, and they were flying everywhere. I immediately went upstairs to see if they were there too, and the windows were all open, and they were everywhere. Then I went downstairs and there was an uncountable number down there. Confused, my mom called my dad at the fire station, and he didn't answer because he was at work. Then my mom called Bio Bug, and it went to voicemail and said, "Sorry, since it is the weekend we can't help you until Monday," and it was Friday.

That is when I needed to get Wilson outside to go to the bathroom. I had to take him on a leash because the garage needed to be open to let the paint dry. I took Wilson outside, and he went pee. I started walking back to the front door, and then Wilson suddenly lunged the other way to the yard because the two dogs across the street got out of their fence. Wilson pulled me at least ten yards, no joke, and I couldn't let go because he didn't have his electric collar on because I needed to put a leash on, and I fell on the ground three times getting pulled by Wilson until both my shoes came off. Then Wilson ran inside because my mom called him, and I went inside thinking this day couldn't get worse.

Then I came inside, with bugs everywhere, and then my mom called her sister. They tried to figure out something to get the bugs away. I just had a cold piece of pizza for dinner because I couldn't eat with the bugs, and my mom was, like, this is the worst. So, that night we all watched a movie, swatting the bugs from our face, until we all went to bed very uncomfortable. And that is what we did all day, nothing much.

Saturday, November 21, 2020

Today is Saturday. The Seahawks aren't playing tomorrow because they already played on Thursday, so that is sad. They will play in nine days, next Monday, so it is a long week. I can't wait for tomorrow, because Fantasy Football games are on, and I think I am going to win. But remember, if I lose this next game or the next game after, I can't possibly win.

This morning I started the day off with reading and writing, and then I did a lot of schoolwork, and then I showered and brushed my teeth and did more schoolwork. This afternoon I did my chores, and after that I did my couple hours of screen time. And that is what I did.

Tonight we all had dinner and I finished up my screen time, and then we all relaxed until it was time to go to bed. Tomorrow I am going to, hopefully, win Fantasy Football, and I am playing someone who has a record of 4–7, and I am 3–8. So, if I win, I will go up to seventh place, but that is only if I win. And finally, the bugs are gone, and the paint smell, so the windows are closed, but jeez.

Sunday, November 22, 2020
Today is Sunday and the Seahawks aren't playing. There are still a lot of other games on, and if I don't win Fantasy Football this week, I can't get into the playoffs. This morning I started off with reading and writing, and then I did my chores, and then I looked at Fantasy Football. It was looking like I am going to win, but I am not sure.

This early afternoon, Fantasy Football started off well, with a win. My third wide receiver got a fifty-yard touchdown reception, and he got twelve points, and that is really helpful to my team. And later that afternoon I started my screen time.

Later that night I finished my screen time and did my exercises. After that I came inside and ate dinner, and then I checked Fantasy Football. I was winning. I checked an hour or so later, and I looked again, and then we all watched the last part of a real football game. Then I checked Fantasy Football after that, and I won Fantasy Football for this week. Then I went to bed with a smile on my face!

Monday, November 23, 2020
This morning I started off the day with my reading and writing, and then I did my Zooms until the afternoon. With Fantasy Football, if I win my next two games, I will definitely go into the playoffs. But next week I am playing Mellein, and that is going to be a hard team to beat because he is really good. My dad said he has won the championship before, in the fire station league.

This afternoon I played in the basement with Cody for a little bit, and then I did my screen time, and then I checked Fantasy Football. I am just really wanting to win, but it is going to be hard, and I know I am talking about Fantasy Football a lot, but it is just because it is exciting. I probably said this before, but the winner in the playoffs gets five hundred dollars, so that is why I am so hyped up!

Tonight we all ate dinner, except my dad because he was at work. Then we watched this movie called *Mr. Popper's Penguins*. It has Jim Carrey, and it was really funny. Then we all went to bed, and we have finally taken care of the bug problem. Sadly, Cody lost Fantasy Football. But I went to bed with a smile on my face again because I am competitive.

Tuesday, November 24, 2020

Today is Tuesday and right now in Fantasy Football I am in seventh place. I need to get in sixth place, and then I can go into the playoffs. Even if I win both weeks, I will be the last team to make the playoffs, so I would need to play the best teams, and that would be really hard. I am just crossing my fingers.

This morning I did my chores and my reading and then all of my Zooms until the afternoon. This afternoon I played *Madden* and watched some YouTube for an hour and then went outside and did my exercise. Then I came back in, did my writing, and then just finished up my screen time.

This evening we all had dinner, and Cody and I played some football in the basement. Then Cody hurt his thumb, so we stopped. My dad went to go check on his finger because it was bent really weird, and they went to the doctor. Cody dislocated his finger, and the doctor popped it back to where it needed to be. Cody just got, like, a little cast on his hand and finger. I am just glad it wasn't broken, because that would be bad.

But I hope he gets better soon. He is being really strong and tough, and he is having a great attitude about it, and attitude is everything. And when it happened, he was, like, "Um, that's not how my finger is supposed to look." We walked upstairs, and he wasn't crying or anything, and he was, like, "Um, Dad, look at my thumb," kind of funny.

My dad said, "Well, it's time to go to the emergency room!"

Wednesday, November 25, 2020

Today is Wednesday. I don't have any Zooms, because it's the day before Thanksgiving. I can't wait, because we are going to have lots of pie, and it is going to be lots of fun. Last year, I tried pie for the first time, and it was pumpkin pie, and I didn't like it, but I really like berry pie.

This morning I did lots of schoolwork and reading and then had breakfast. After I finished, I went in the basement and did more schoolwork and then my writing. Later in the morning I did some exercise for a little bit, and then I did more homework, and then I came inside and had some more food.

This afternoon I did the rest of my exercise and then my screen time for a couple of hours. Cody and I watched this movie called *The Game Plan*. It has The Rock in it, and it is really funny, about a football player. A little girl shows up at his door and tells him that she is his daughter, and it is really funny. We finished it and then I did more homework and got ready for dinner.

After dinner I finished the book *A Christmas Carol*, and then we all watched the movie. Last year we watched the movie, but this year we decided to watch a different version because there are hundreds of different movies based on the same story. After we watched that, I had some ice cream and went to bed. That is what we did all day.

Thursday, November 26, 2020
Today is Thanksgiving. This morning I did my schoolwork for a couple of hours and then my chores and writing, and all of that made my morning go by fast. After that I had breakfast and took a shower and brushed my teeth, and then I did my reading.

This afternoon my parents said that we didn't need to worry about screen time, and so this afternoon I just watched football with Cody and then went outside and did my forty-yard sprints for school, and then I just came in and did more schoolwork and more screen time.

Tonight my dad made these really good things. They are called croutons, which are when you take bread and rip it apart into little pieces, like one inch by one inch, and then my dad pours melted butter on them and then warms them in the oven. They are really kind of crunchy and soft and good. Then I had milk, an apple, those melted butter croutons, and lots of sausages, and I tried a little bit of ham. Then after dinner we all had pie. I had about half a blueberry pie and then went to bed satisfied and thankful.

Friday, November 27, 2020
Today is Friday. This morning I did my schoolwork for a couple of hours, and then I did my chores and writing, and all of that made my morning go by fast. After that I had breakfast and then relaxed and then took a long morning bath. Then I got out and did some more schoolwork.

This afternoon I did my screen time. I made a great *Madden* team, and I played *Madden* for an hour. Then I went outside and did my sprints for school and came back in and relaxed. Then Cody and my dad and I all went to get a Christmas tree. We got one, and my dad and I carried it back to the car. When we got home, we put it up.

Tonight I finished up my last hour of screen time and then had dinner. My dad made pizza, and it was good. We still have ranch, so we all had that. Then my mom came home from work, and she had dinner, and we decided we would decorate the tree another day because it was getting too late, but we played Christmas music all day.

Saturday, November 28, 2020

This morning my dad went to work and I started the day off with my reading and writing. Then I went outside and said hi to Wilson and came back in and relaxed. Then I did my sprints and then came back in again and did schoolwork for a couple hours. Later in the morning I did my chores and then ate breakfast and then took a shower and brushed my teeth and washed my face.

This afternoon I did more sprints, and then I came back inside and did more schoolwork for two hours, and then I brought Wilson inside and dried him off because it was raining, and I played with him. Then I did my screen time for a couple hours. I will warn you: When it snows, I will be outside all day, and then I will come back inside and lay in a blanket and read.

That night we all had dinner and watched my all-time favorite Christmas movie called *A Christmas Vacation*. It is so funny and definitely inappropriate, but I have watched it every year for, like, lots of years, and it never stops getting funny. Then we all went to bed. I went to bed laughing so hard remembering some of the funny parts. You just have to go watch it, and you will think is it funny.

Sunday, November 29, 2020

Today is Sunday and the Seahawks aren't playing until tomorrow. I think they will win because they are playing the Eagles, but we will see. I started the morning by waking up a little before nine, and then I did my reading for thirty minutes, and then I did my writing until ten, and that is when the football games start. It started off really bad, and I did some of my screen time and then asked my dad if I could go a little over so I could finish my *Madden* game, and he said that today screen time doesn't matter if I take care of my responsibilities. So I said, "Great with me," and I finished my *Madden* game and started doing school for a couple hours.

This afternoon I did more schoolwork, and then I went outside and did sprints for about fifteen minutes, and then I came back in and worked out downstairs for another thirty minutes, and then I checked Fantasy Football. It looked like Fantasy Football is over for me, but it is still possible and anything could happen.

Tonight I finished my screen time, and my dad took everything off the deck and put it in the garage. The paint is finally dry, so we are all ready to sleep outside. But we still have those bugs outside, and they are on the deck, so we need to take care of that before we sleep outside. My dad doesn't know why flies are outside right now, but he said that if only we could go fly fishing here, that would be great. That night we all had dinner, and then I watched some football and went to bed inside.

Monday, November 30, 2020
This morning I started the day off with taking a shower, and then I ate and brushed and did my Zooms until noon. Also, Fantasy Football is over for me. There isn't any possible way I could win, but that is okay because you can't win all of them.

This afternoon I worked out in the basement for forty-five minutes. I did lunges, squats, short sprints, box jumps, and a couple other things, and then I looked at my list of things to do. All I needed to do was homework and writing and reading and chores, so I just did those the rest of the afternoon.

At night we all watched the Seahawks game, and they played the Eagles, so it looked like it would be an easy one. We started off the game with a 14–0 lead, and then it was back and forth for the rest of the half. At halftime I had diner. I had pasta, an apple, red peppers, and a couple other vegetables. The Seahawks ended up winning 23–17 with, like, thirty seconds left. The Eagles threw a Hail Mary pass and got it, but they were still down by eight. Confusedly, they went for two and got it, and they went for the onside kick and didn't get it, and the Seahawks won. It was a great game, and I went to bed with a big smile on my face.

Tuesday, December 1, 2020
Today it is Tuesday. It is now December, and I can't wait until Christmas. Whenever people ask what your favorite part of Christmas is, everyone stutters and says, "Spending time with family," when you are really thinking *What the heck? I want the presents!* And your parents tell you to wait because they want to take a video when you open the presents, and they ask what you think the present is, and you are thinking, like, *I have waited a year for this day! Now just let me open this present!* And you open the present, and they finish the video, and then they take another video asking you to say thank you, and you're thinking *When does it stop?* But that's just funny. Yea for presents!

This morning I did my schoolwork and Zooms until noon, and then it was noon, and Cody and I played the new game we got. It was really fun. We did that for a little more than an hour, and then I did my reading and my writing for an hour. Then I went in the basement and did my workout and came back up, and everyone played Clue for a little bit. Then Cody and I did the rest of our screen time until it was time for dinner.

Tonight we all had dinner and then watched a Christmas movie to end the night. It was about Santa dying, and the son of Santa needed to take over, and he was doing really bad, so then the new Santa's sister told him to take the weekend off. He went for the weekend and didn't come back, and they needed to find him. It was a really funny movie, but I don't remember what it was called.

Wednesday, December 2, 2020
This morning my dad went to work and I started the day off with taking a shower and eating breakfast for a little bit. Then at eight I started my first Zoom, and then I just relaxed and had lunch.

This afternoon I did my exercise in the basement. Then I went upstairs and played a game of Clue with Mom and Cody. Then Cody and Mom went to the doctors, and they came back, and Cody had a cast on his hand. The doctor said he will have the cast for two weeks. Later I just relaxed and did some screen time until dinner, and then I set the table. Tonight I had pasta and carrots, and then I did my reading and writing and then screen time for a couple hours. That is how my day went.

Thursday, December 3, 2020
This morning I did my Zooms until noon, and during the Zooms it was really funny because I had a sub in math and we played a game called Skunk. It goes like this. First I went in a group with three people, and then we would roll two dice, and with five different columns. If you got a one on either one of your people, you get zero for that round, out of the five rounds. If you get double ones in, let's say, the third round, then you would get zero for that round and all of the rounds before. So, you want to roll, but go as long as you can without a zero. I ended up winning, and that was really fun.

This afternoon I went with my dad to get my braces off. They took them off and it hurt really bad. My dad was sitting next to me, and he said that there was a lot of blood. I wouldn't think that there should be blood when you are taking my braces off, but they did that, and my dad said I could have some extra screen time. But I couldn't do extra because it was so late and I needed to eat dinner. Still, I did screen time until dinner, and then we all just chilled and played Clue. I guess tomorrow I will just get extra screen time, but we will see.

Friday, December 4, 2020
Today is Friday and I don't have any Zooms, so I am really excited. This morning I woke up at eight thirty and went downstairs and did some

reading, and then I went upstairs and took a shower, and then I brushed my teeth and washed my face, and then I flossed, and the last thing I did was use mouthwash.

Later this morning I did some screen time with Cody, and we played a video game called *Gang Beasts*. We figured out that Cody can play with his cast, so that is nice. Basically, the game has, like, twenty different animated people that you can be, and you choose one. There needs to be two people; there can't be one. Then you pick how many rounds there will be, and you go to a random map. For one example, there is a blimp and you appear on the blimp and try to push the other person off while staying on. If you do that, you win round one. Cody and I usually just do five rounds, and the first one to five wins, and if you both fall off, then it is a draw and no one wins that round. There is another part of the game were you appear on a Ferris wheel, and we played that the whole morning, and then we relaxed.

This afternoon we all played Clue, and then we all went on a trail walk, and after that we just went inside. Cody and I finished our screen time, and after that I just did my homework for about two hours. Then it was almost dinner, so I just came up and did my chores and my reading and writing. Then we all had dinner, and I had pasta and a smoothie because my mouth was still in pain. After we finished dinner, we all played Clue. Then I went upstairs and brushed my teeth and washed my face and went to bed.

Saturday, December 5, 2020
This morning I started the day off with writing and then did some chores. Since today is Saturday, I decided that I am going to just relax. I took a shower and brushed my teeth and washed my face, and then I just relaxed. This morning I did my reading and writing for about an hour, and then Cody and I played some Clue. That is what we did all morning, and we relaxed.

This afternoon I started my screen time with Cody, and then I played some *Madden*, and then I just played *Gang Beasts*. Later my mom and Cody and I all went on a trail walk, and then we all came inside because it was cold. I think it got to, like, thirty-five degrees.

Tonight we all had dinner, and it was really good. I had two smoothies because my mouth was still sore, and then I had pasta. That is what I had the other day, but it was still good. That night we all played Clue, and I ended up winning. After that we all just went to bed.

Sunday, December 6, 2020

Today is Sunday, and the Seahawks are playing at one and I can't wait. They are playing a really easy team, the Giants, and their quarterback is out with an injury. Hopefully, that is all they need for the win.

This morning I did my reading and my writing, and then I had a lot of homework to do, so I did about three hours of that. Then I went upstairs, and my dad is not going to work overtime today, so that is great. We can all watch the game. This afternoon we all went on the trails, all five of us, Cody, my dad, my mom, Wilson, and I.

When we got back, the Seahawks game was just about to be on. We watched that, and when the game was over, the Seahawks had lost. They just didn't really play well, and I hope they win next week against an even worse team, but we will see.

Tonight we all had dinner, and my mouth was feeling a little better. We all played some card games for one to two hours, then my dad and I played football catch in the basement, and then we all went to bed.

Monday, December 7, 2020

Today is Monday, so I have a long Zoom day. Today I don't need to do homework, because I try to do a lot of homework on the Zoom days that I have few classes, which will be tomorrow and two days after that, so on Tuesday and Thursday, and then I only have Zooms from ten until twelve. On Monday and Wednesday I have it from eight to nine, and then I have an hour off, and then I have to do two more hours. Those are my Zoom classes, and that will not change every week.

This morning I did all of my Zooms and then went outside and played with Wilson. I came inside and did screen time with Cody, and we played that game called *Gang Beasts*.

Tonight we didn't do much. We just ate dinner and then relaxed and did our reading, and then we just went to bed. I slept on the floor with Wilson, on the main floor. You should have seen his face—it was filled with joy! I put the mattress from the deck on the floor, and his tail wagged so much.

Tuesday, December 8, 2020

Today is Tuesday. I woke up in the morning and looked at the clock and it was almost nine, so I ran upstairs and turned the shower on and jumped in and took a long warm bath. Then I came back downstairs, looked, and it was about quarter to ten. I went downstairs, did some schoolwork, started Zooms until noon, and then I came upstairs and had an afternoon snack.

This afternoon I had some food and then went outside and turned on the Christmas lights and played with Wilson. I came inside and played *Gang Beasts* with Cody. As you remember, it is just a game where the floor is lava and you try to get the other person on the floor.

Tonight we all had dinner, and I had pasta with carrots and corn. After I finished that, I relaxed on the couch and did some reading and then went downstairs, checked my schoolwork, and did that for about an hour. Then I came upstairs and had a little snack and went to bed.

Wednesday, December 9, 2020

Today is Wednesday. I woke up and looked, and it was seven on the dot. I watched some funny video with my mom and Cody, and it is really hard to explain, but it was funny. Then I looked at the clock and it was thirty minutes until eight. I went upstairs, took a shower, brushed my teeth and flossed, and then finally I did mouthwash. I went down two floors and did my first Zoom, and I don't know if I told you this, but I mostly do my Zooms in the basement. I put my laptop on the ping pong table, and that is my desk.

Later this morning at nine, I got up out of my chair and played football with myself for about ten minutes and then did homework for about forty-five minutes. Then I started my second-to-last Zooms. After I finished one of two Zooms, I came upstairs, had some food for about ten minutes, and jumped back to my next Zoom.

This afternoon we all played in the basement, and then Cody and I did some screen time for a couple hours, and then I played catch in the basement with Cody. We both came upstairs, and then I did my reading and writing, and then I did dusting as my chore, and then I went upstairs and did more reading.

Tonight we all had dinner, and I had corn and pasta. Then we all just relaxed, and I did more screen time and reading. I read some *Calvin and Hobbes,* and after I did that, we all had ice cream. It was really good. Then I went to bed on the main floor, with Wilson rubbing his belly. I don't know if I told you this, but I'm mostly sleeping in the living room on the mattress by the Christmas tree, and it is great.

Thursday, December 10, 2020

Thursday morning, I woke on the floor with Wilson. I got up and looked. It was almost nine, so I took a fast shower and brushed my teeth, washed my face, and came back downstairs. I looked at school for about thirty minutes and then did my Zooms until lunch time.

This afternoon I did my reading for thirty minutes and then about one hour of schoolwork. Then for a couple hours, Cody and I played *Gang Beasts*, and then we played *Madden* for about forty-five minutes, and then I did some YouTube for the rest of my screen time that afternoon.

Tonight we all had dinner, and I had pasta and some corn. After I ate that, I was still hungry, so I had some avocado, and that is what I had for dinner. Then I went downstairs and played more video games with Cody because my mom and dad said Cody and I could have some extra screen time.

Friday, December 11, 2020

Today is Friday. I can't wait until Sunday because the Seahawks play. They are playing the worst team in the NFL. The team has lost twelve games and won not even one, so I like the Seahawk's chances.

This morning I needed to do a lot of studying for my finals, and I did that for a couple hours. Then I just went outside for a trail hike with my mom and Cody for an hour, and after that I went back downstairs and did more schoolwork.

This afternoon I did screen time for a couple hours until dinnertime, and after my two hours of screen time, it was time to have dinner. I had corn and a smoothie, and my smoothie had strawberries, mangos, pineapple, oranges, and a banana and a couple other things. After I had that, I set up my bed to sleep with Wilson in the living room because my parents said I have to put the mattress away during the day and then can put it back for bedtime with Wilson. We watched a Christmas movie, and it was funny, about a kid who ran away for Christmas.

Saturday, December 12, 2020

Today is Saturday and I am officially out of the Fantasy Football chances of winning the five hundred dollars, but it is okay. Cody still has a chance to win, so that is great. This morning I did my reading and chores right away, and then I went to the basement and exercised for about an hour.

This afternoon my dad and Cody and I all took Wilson to his happy place, to go swimming. We did that because today is a very special day! It is Wilson's birthday. After we played in the water and skipped rocks, we went to a dog store and got Wilson some treats and bones. He was so excited. And you're thinking we swam too, but we didn't. Just Wilson swam, and we skipped rocks.

Tonight my mom came home at four, and then we all had dinner. I had pasta and a couple different vegetables and a smoothie. Then Cody and

I did all of our screen time and watched the Sounders play. They played in the finals and ended up losing. It was sad, but hopefully, the Seahawks win tomorrow.

Sunday, December 13, 2020

Today the Seahawks play. They don't play until one in the afternoon, so I can't wait. This morning I woke up at nine and cleaned up my bed and checked my schoolwork and saw that I needed to do a lot, so that is was I was doing most of the morning.

Then at about noon, my family and I went on a hike all the way to the top of Baby Bear Trail. We got home right before the Seahawks game. The Jets are the team the Seahawks played, and the Seahawks started off winning by fourteen pints, and then the Jets' kicker missed three or four straight field goals. I think it was three, but maybe four. But the Seahawks ended up winning 40–3, and it was a great game.

Tonight we all had dinner, and I had a smoothie with strawberries, mangos, pineapple, oranges, and a banana and a couple other things in it, and it was really good. Then I played a game called Sorry with my mom, Cody, and my dad, for a little bit. After that I set up my bed, to sleep with Wilson and the Christmas lights.

Monday, December 14, 2020

The morning started off with Zooms. In my first Zoom I had STEM, and I took my final for that class and got a 97 percent. That means that for that class I earned an A+. Then after that class, I took my math final, and it was a completion grade, and I got 100 percent.

This afternoon, for my first hour of screen time, I played *Madden* and then *Rocket League*, which is basically soccer with cars, and it is fun. Then I had lunch and finished up my screen time playing with Cody.

At dinner I had pasta and corn and a smoothie, and I had the usual in my smoothie. I had strawberries, mangos, pineapple, oranges, and a banana. Tonight Cody watched a movie called *Napoleon Dynamite*. My dad said he didn't like it, but Cody still watched it, and he didn't like it either. Then again, I set up my bed with Wilson, and we went to bed.

Tuesday, December 15, 2020

This morning I did my Zooms until noon, and I looked at the coronavirus cases. There are now almost 75 million cases and 1.6 million deaths. Now there is a vaccine coming out, and it is arriving today. In about three days, my dad will get the vaccine because he is a firefighter, and first responders are going to get the vaccine first.

That afternoon I went on a hike with my mom and dad and Cody and Wilson for about one hour. Then I looked at my watch and it was almost two, so I went inside and did screen time for about an hour until a little past three, and then I did my chores for about thirty minutes, and then I did some reading for another thirty minutes, and then I did my last hour of screen time until dinner, and then I set the dinner table. Then we all had dinner, and I had pasta and sausage and a smoothie. After dinner we all went to bed a little early.

Wednesday, December 16, 2020

This morning I did my schoolwork and finals for the rest of the semester. They will, hopefully, all be graded before the end of the week. I now have no more Zooms, so this morning Cody and I played *Madden* and did some screen time, and then I put away my bed in the living room.

This afternoon I went on another hike with my mom and Cody and my dad, and after about an hour of walking, we went inside. Cody and I did some screen time for the afternoon. After we go on walks, Wilson is so funny because he rubs his head all over the grass and rolls his back on the grass, and it is so funny.

Tonight we all had dinner, and my dad made pasta for me. I had pasta and a smoothie, and then we all relaxed and watched a Christmas movie called *Jingle All the Way*, and it was funny. It was about Christmas and an adventure of someone to get this one Christmas toy for his son, and it is really funny.

Thursday, December 17, 2020

This morning Cody and I did some screen time, and then I did my reading and writing, and then I did my chores, and that is what I did this morning, until I went on my computer and looked at my finals. Still nothing has been graded, but I think most of them will be graded tomorrow, because it is technically the last day of school until winter break, but maybe one or two will not be graded until the end of the week.

This afternoon my family went on an hour hike, and then Cody and I finished up our screen time, and then Cody and I played a fun game called Sorry. It is hard to explain how to play, but it is just a fun board game. You draw a card and go that many spaces, and if you land on the other player, you say, "Sorry," and they have to go back to the start.

Tonight we all had dinner, and then my mom showed us this funny prank video with this person named Jimmy Kimmel. He played a prank on his cousin, and it was really long but funny, and he pranks his sister, and he got a friend's email and started emailing really weird and funny things. Jimmy Kimmel is a funny person who has a show and makes funny things. Tonight I went to bed, with Wilson again, and I had a great sleep.

Friday, December 18, 2020
Today it is Friday. The Seahawks are playing in two days, and they are playing against a team that changed their name to the Washington Football Team. It was originally the Washington Redskins, and then people were saying that it's a racist and inappropriate name, so they changed it.

This morning I did some screen time, and in the afternoon we all went on a family hike. Tomorrow my mom is going to work, and she is going to give out the coronavirus vaccine to first responders and nurses and doctors. Hopefully, she will get the vaccine soon.

Tonight we all had dinner, and I had a bowl of corn and a pizza that my dad made, and it was good. I ate it really fast, then I made a smoothie, and then we all had dessert and watched a movie called *Christmas Break-In*. It was about a kid who was left at school, and a couple people came and robbed a bank, and then they hid out in that school, and the kid was protecting the place. It was really just like the movie *Home Alone*.

Saturday, December 19, 2020
This morning we all had a family breakfast and then went on an early hike at eight, and when we got back, my mom left for work to give out the vaccines to nurses and doctors. Then we all relaxed and Cody and I played some *Rocket League*. It is just a game of soccer with no out of bounds, and it is indoor. Instead of with people, it is with cars, so you drive and try to get the ball into the goal, and it is really fun.

This afternoon we all finished up our screen time and then I just relaxed and went in the basement and checked Fantasy Football. Then I looked at Cody's team, and it didn't look like he was doing so good, but we just need to see.

Tonight we all relaxed, and I had pasta and corn for dinner. Then we all played Clue. The game is basically a murder mystery game. There is a board with five people and eight places and six weapons, and you shuffle the cards and put out one person and one place and one thing, and you ask people questions and try to figure out who is the murderer. Then I put my bed out and slept with Wilson.

Sunday, December 20, 2020

Today the Seahawks play. They play early in the morning at ten, and I woke up at eight thirty and went in the basement and did some exercise for thirty minutes and took a shower. Then I had breakfast and brushed my teeth and got ready for the Seahawks game.

This morning the Seahawks started off with a 6–0 lead because they got two field goals, and then the other team had two three-and-outs in a row, and then the Seahawks got a touchdown, and then the other team got a touchdown, and then it was half time. The next half nothing really happened. Each team got one more touchdown, and then the Seahawks won. Then we all had a fun afternoon playing board games.

Tonight we all had dinner, and I had pasta and a bowl of corn. Now it is five days until Christmas, and I can't wait until Christmas because I want to have a great dinner. Most of all, I want to open presents, and when people ask you what you like most about Christmas, you usually always say spending time with family, but what you really like is the food and the presents!

Monday, December 21, 2020

Today is Monday. Sadly, it is a school day, not, "I am on Christmas Break— Yay!" This morning Cody and I just chilled and did lots of screen time, and then my mom left for work. At noon my dad is going to Seattle and getting his coronavirus vaccine. It should only take about three hours. So, Cody and I will stay home alone with Wilson, and that's ok.

This afternoon my dad left, and then it started snowing a lot, and it kept on snowing the rest of the day, and then it started getting really windy. My dad said that it might take a little longer than three hours because of the traffic driving from Seattle, and he told us that we could do screen time while he was gone but to remember that Wilson may want to come inside and go outside, because he loves the snow, and to just make sure he doesn't stay outside too long.

Tonight Cody and I had to make our dinner because my dad was still gone, and it was almost six that night. I made pasta for Cody and me, and it was good. Then at about seven o'clock my mom and dad came home at the exact same time, and it was really weird. We ended up playing a lot of board games and things like that, and by then it had stopped snowing. It snowed about four inches. Then my dad and Cody and I went in the hot tub, and my mom didn't want to because she was too tired. It was fun. We play where you have to go lay down in the snow for, like, challenges and then get back in the hot tub. We do challenges like make snow angels or run laps around the house and jump back in, and it is so fun. Then we all ended up going to sleep on the early side, at about nine.

Tuesday, December 22, 2020
It didn't really snow during the night, but all of the snow turned into ice and froze. That makes all the snow really slippery. Our neighbor Rich fell, and he is pretty old, but he is ok. This morning I woke up about eight and went downstairs with lots of energy. My dad had left to get groceries, and he came back, and I found in one of the bags a puzzle when I was unloading the food. He said it was a Christmas present but it is okay, and we pulled it out. There are a thousand pieces, and we started. It is going to take a long time to make, but I like puzzles.

This afternoon I did my screen time for about an hour, and then did my exercise in the basement. Christmas is in only three days, and I am so excited and can't wait to open my presents. Then I worked on the puzzle, and Cody and my dad and I all did the outside rim of it. My mom was at work, so she couldn't do it with us. Then we all just relaxed and did some screen time.

Tonight we all had dinner, and I had a bowl of corn and half of an avocado, and then I had pasta, and that is all I did until I looked at the clock, and it was about eight and I wasn't even close to going to bed, so I worked on the puzzle for about an hour. Then we all went to bed.

Wednesday, December 23, 2020
Today is Wednesday, and I can't wait until Christmas in only two days. This morning I woke up at a little past eight. I got up, had waffles for breakfast, and then had an apple. And I should tell you how I make waffles, my favorite. I mix water and batter, about one cup. When the waffle maker is hot enough, it goes beep and the light is green, and I spray this stuff in it and then pour batter in and close it, and the light turns red. Then it goes beep again when it is ready and the light is green. Later that morning, at about ten, I played with the puzzle for a little bit. It is coming together but still a long way to go.

In the early afternoon I went in the basement for about half an hour and did my journaling. Then I came upstairs and did my reading. Then I had to do dusting, and there was this one spot in the shower, and it had so much dust, and I have really never looked there.

Then later that afternoon, I did my screen time got this game called *FIFA*. It is just like *Madden*, but instead of football it is soccer. I played that for most of my screen time, and then I played *Madden* with Cody.

That night I had pasta, and my mom got these new noodles, and they are so good, even though they taste the same. They are just bigger, and I love them. After dinner we watched my all-time favorite movie and Christmas movie, called *Elf*. The main character is Will Ferrell, and it is about a kid who is in an orphanage, crawled into Santa's bag full of presents, and got taken to the North Pole. He was raised as an elf, even though he is, like, a six-foot-five guy. He is so much taller than all the elves. Then Santa tells Buddy (who is Will Ferrell) that he isn't his real father, that his real dad lives in New York City. It is, like, a journey, and he finds his dad. That guy doesn't believe that Buddy is his son, and it is just all comedy and makes me laugh every time I watch it. Also, I watch it every single Christmas, and it has a good message.

Thursday, December 24, 2020

This morning I woke up and went downstairs, and my dad made a great breakfast. It was eggs and bacon and sausage, and it was good. Then Cody and I went in the basement to play video games. And it is Christmas Eve!

Then this afternoon my dad and I went on a hike in the snow with Wilson. Cody didn't come, and my mom didn't either, because she is working, but only until two this afternoon. When we got back, Cody and I went in the basement to do more screen time.

Then my mom came home at two and we worked on the puzzle. I would say we are a fourth done with it, so a lot to go. Then we all went and played in the snow, and it was surprisingly still there. Then we all just came inside and did more of the puzzle and screen time.

And then I walked into my mom's room to go to the bathroom, and there was a present in there I probably shouldn't have seen. I told my parents I saw it, and they weren't mad. They just said that it could be our Christmas Eve present, and we always open one present on Christmas Eve. You might be wondering what it was. It was the biggest present there ever was, and it was a big TV! I felt bad, but they said that the guys are coming on Monday, and it is Thursday. They will put the new TV in, and the older one was, like, twenty years old and permanent on the wall when we moved in, from the people that lived here before us. But this new TV is bigger and will be so fun for movies and video games and for Seahawks!

Tonight we all chilled and had a great dinner. I had a special pasta with sausage and bacon and corn and avocado and my dad's croutons, which is the same thing we had on Thanksgiving and it's my favorite. Then we watched a Christmas movie called *A Christmas Story*.

Friday, December 25, 2020

This morning I woke up at four, and for some reason I couldn't go back to sleep. My dad told me to wake him up at five, so when it was five, I woke him up. He said to just wait another hour, and that is what I did. But Cody and I looked at our stockings, which had so many fun things. So at six o'clock we all woke up and opened the presents. I will give you the summary of what I got. So, first a TV, Xbox controllers, a sled, Uggs, lots of great clothes, and lots of candy and gum in my stocking. Cody got me this hat that had speakers inside of it that you can listen to music with, and a big fuzzy blanket.

This afternoon Cody and I did screen time most of the time, and my dad found a movie we could watch. It is called *Soul*. I don't really know what it is about, but we are going to watch it after dinner.

Tonight we all had dinner, and I had the same things as last night, which was pasta with sausage and bacon and corn and avocado and croutons, which was good. Then after dinner we watched the movie. It was a good movie, not the best. It was about finding out what you like and what is your purpose in life, so it was a good message. And that was the best Christmas.

Saturday, December 26, 2020

Today is the day after Christmas, and tonight for dinner I am going to have some pizza from La Fiamma because I got a gift card for Christmas. This morning Cody and I did our screen time. Today is Saturday and tomorrow the Seahawks are playing. They are playing against the LA Rams, a good team, and we lost to them last time we played them, but I think we can beat them.

This afternoon I played in the basement with Cody. We played *Madden* and then some *FIFA*. Later I needed to do my exercise, so I did my workout in the basement with Cody and my mom, and then we all relaxed and did more screen time until dinner.

Tonight we got La Fiamma for dinner, and I had pizza and salad and a smoothie and corn and oranges. It was really good. Tonight we didn't do much. There was a Raiders game on, and they played against the Dolphins, who have turned out to be pretty good. The game ended, and it was really exciting. I didn't care who won, but I was hoping the Raiders would win. It was a last-second throw, and it ended up being a catch, and then the Dolphins kicked a field goal and won.

Sunday, December 27, 2020

This morning we all just relaxed. I woke up at eight forty-five and did my reading until a little after nine, and then I did my chores and journaling. Then I checked my schoolwork, and we still don't have any, but I checked just to be safe and see. After that, Cody and I relaxed and did some screen time and my dad went on a bike ride and my mom left for work.

This afternoon we took down the Christmas tree and ornaments, and then the lights. The lights were a struggle, but we did it, and then we had to sweep the floor to get all the pine needles and things like that. Then it was the Seahawks game, and they played the Rams, and they are good but not great. The Seahawks started just winning, and then it was 20–6, with the Seahawks winning at the fourth quarter, and then the other team's quarterback threw a pass, and then with this throw he went down after the throw and was hit by one of his teammates, and then you could see the thumb get dislocated inwards, and then he popped it back in by himself, and then he continued playing but in pain. The Seahawks ended up winning 20–9, and the other team's quarterback ended up dislocating and breaking his thumb, and it looked like he is going to be out for a while, but he is really tough for playing the rest of the game.

Tonight we all had dinner, and I had corn and pasta and a smoothie. After dinner we all relaxed. My mom came home, and then something really exciting happened. We finished the thousand-piece puzzle, except there ended up being one missing piece. I happened to look for that one piece a lot when we were making the puzzle, and oh my gosh, it was not even there. Then that night we all went to bed at nine thirty.

Monday, December 28, 2020

Today is Monday and today someone is coming to put the TV up. When I woke up, I was really excited, and it was almost eight when I woke up. I went straight downstairs and had a big breakfast because I was really hungry. Later I did my reading and writing. Then I took a long shower and brushed my teeth, and then I felt that I was ready to start the day.

Later that morning, at about nine, the guy came to get the TV set up. He started setting it up for a couple hours, and then I went down to look at what he was doing. He took down the old TV, and apparently it was super heavy, and I would guess because it is, like, twenty years old and had a speaker attached to the screen that is, like, a little more than half a foot, and the TV is about fifty inches, and I think that includes the long speaker. When I play *Minecraft* or *Madden* or watch football on the old TV, the bottom of the screen is cut off, so it is annoying. But once we get a new one, it will all be different and so better.

Then he put up the new TV, and it was, like, really small. It was fifty-five inches, but it didn't really fit the spot right, so we ended up going to Costco and replacing it and getting a sixty-five, and it ended up taking a while, but when we got back, the guy waited and put it up. It looked perfect. Then he told us how to work it and the new controls, and it looks really good. Then he left, and that ended up taking up almost our whole day. And I know what you are thinking. Yes, we all wore a mask, and we kept a window open downstairs, and he was nice, though, and waited, and the new TV is worth the wait.

Then at night we all had dinner, and I had a bowl of corn and a big smoothie. Then later we watched part of a football game on the new big TV, and that was fun. Then we didn't have dessert and just relaxed, and I did my chores a little too late, but I did them, and we all went to bed.

Tuesday, December 29, 2020

It is only three days until the new year, and I can't wait until 2021. It has been a long and hard year, but for the end of the year, I will say how many people have, sadly, died from the coronavirus and how many got coronavirus. So far, 82.6 million people have gotten COVID and 1.8 million people have died.

This morning I did my reading and chores right when I woke up, at a little before eight, and then I did my writing. Later I took a shower upstairs, and after I dried off, I went to a doctor's appointment.

When the appointment was over, I went on a hike with my mom and brother. My dad is working overtime today, but tomorrow he will be home. When we finished a walk, we all went to our house and just relaxed.

This afternoon I did more screen time with Cody, and then I did more reading and more screen time. Right now the Seahawks have one more game until the playoffs, and the only way for them to get a bye week is for them to win and for the Saints and Packers to lose, and that is a really small chance but still possible. The LA Rams and the Arizona Cardinals are going to play on Sunday, and whoever wins that will probably play the Seahawks in the first week of playoffs, if the Saints or the Packers lose.

Tonight we all relaxed, and I had a smoothie and this good pasta and corn, and that was my vegetable for the night. Then we watched a movie called *Wonder*. I have watched it before, and it is a funny but sad movie. I have also read the book a couple times.

Wednesday, December 30, 2020

Today is Wednesday. I woke up at eight and went downstairs and did my journaling. Then I dusted, and then I did my reading for about half an hour. Later this morning Cody and I did our screen time. We played some *Madden* and *Gang Beasts* for a little bit, and then I came upstairs and had cereal, and then I went back in the basement and did more screen time with Cody.

Then at about ten, my dad came home from the fire station and Mellein ended up winning the five hundred dollars and the Fantasy Football championship. Then my dad went and got the groceries, and I put them away for him and did more screen time with Cody, and then I just relaxed the rest of the morning.

This afternoon I made a smoothie with strawberries, a couple oranges, a banana, mango, blueberries, and finally protein powder. Then I had a bowl of cereal and brushed my teeth and went in the basement and looked at the news.

Tonight we all relaxed and had dinner. I made a homemade pizza and later we all went to bed, and I can't wait until next year. Also, tomorrow at nine o'clock the apple will drop. In New York their time is three hours ahead, so the apple will drop at nine our time. That is midnight in New York, and I can't wait until 2021.

Thursday, December 31, 2020

Today is the last day of the year, and it has been a long hard year. I can't wait until next year! This morning I did my journaling early and then took a long bath and did some screen time with Cody for about twenty minutes. Then I went upstairs and had a big breakfast, and then at about eleven we all went in the car to Mount Baker. That is about one hour away, and we are going to sled there.

This afternoon it was about twelve thirty, and we were going up this long road that circles the mountain to get to the top, where we will sled. About halfway up the big mountain there were a lot of cars stopped, and my dad went to see what was going on. There was a big truck blocking the road, and my dad asked why he was blocking it, and he said that there was a big avalanche ahead and that it would be about half an hour to get it cleaned up. We just waited.

About forty-five minutes later we could go up, and when we got up there, it was so crowded there wasn't any place to sled. It was crazy, so we just found our own little trail, and we found a spot, and the snow was, like, three feet deep. You couldn't sled because it was too deep, so we just played in the snow. I made a big snowman, and then my dad took a Slo-mo video of me tackling it, and it was really funny. And it was so much snow that Wilson could barely walk in it, but he was loving it, and it was all the way up to his head. Then after an hour or two we went home. And Wilson was like a giant snowman dog!

When we got home my mom ordered dinner from a good place, and I got pizza, and it was really good. Then after dinner the whole family watched a movie and called *War With Grandpa*, about this kid who gets in a prank war with his grandpa because the grandpa moved in their house and into his bedroom, and the kid needed to go in the attic. It is a really funny movie. So, we couldn't watch the apple drop at nine because nothing was live, so I tried to stay up to midnight, but I got too tired and went to bed a little before eleven with Cody. And my mom and dad were already asleep.

Friday, January 1, 2021
Today is the first day of the year! Before I woke up, my mom went to work, so it was just Cody and my dad and me. I woke up at about seven thirty and went downstairs. I relaxed and did my journaling in the morning, and then I did my reading. After I finished my reading, I had my breakfast. I had a piece of toast and some fruit and cereal and brushed my teeth.

Later this morning I went back upstairs and took a long bath, and then when I got out, I did more reading. Then I went in the basement and played *Minecraft* with Cody. Cody and I made up this thing called *A Day and Night*, and basically you have a day and a night to collect materials and build things, and then when the sun rises, we fight to see who the winner is. But it's not real fighting. It's just game fighting and not serious.

This afternoon my brother and my dad and I started a Monopoly game, and it was really fun. I started off on the wrong foot and ended on the wrong foot, so basically Cody started dominating me and my dad, and kept doing that until we were both completely out of money. Later this afternoon I finished up my last ten minutes of screen time and then did my chores and relaxed.

Tonight my mom came home, and she and my dad both left to go to Donnett's house. They just went in their back yard and talked, and Cody and I were home alone, and they said we could do extra screen time but we had to do it together, and we did. We played *Minecraft* and watched YouTube until they came home at about six, and we all had dinner and relaxed. Then I put the bed out with Wilson, and we slept in the living room.

Saturday, January 2, 2021
Today is the second day of the year. I can't wait until the Seahawks play tomorrow, and they are playing against the Forty-Niners, and then that will be the last day of the season until the playoffs. And then if you lose you are out, so I hope the Seahawks do good.

This morning my dad left for work at about five that morning, but I wasn't awake until eight. I went downstairs and did my journaling early and then had some cereal and toast. When I finished my great breakfast, I brushed my teeth and then did some reading. Cody and I played *A Day and Night Minecraft*, and I explained what that is the other day.

Later this morning, at about eleven thirty, I did my chores, which was sweeping. Cody mopped. Then my mom left to just get out of the house, and Cody and I did the rest of our screen time.

This afternoon my mom came home after about an hour or two, and then my mom gave Cody and me some extra chores to do so maybe we could watch a show tonight. That afternoon we all played Monopoly, and my mom ended up losing, and then it was just Cody and me. I ended up winning, and it was fun. Later that afternoon, I did my exercise for about forty minutes with my mom, and then the rest of the afternoon I relaxed and played more Monopoly with Cody and my mom.

Tonight my mom made pasta, and I had some, and it was really good. Then at about seven we all went in the basement to look for a show, and there was only really one show that we all liked, and it's called *Shark Tank*. Basically, one person comes on the show with an invention, and there are five investors, and then the person tries to make a deal with an investor. It is a really fun and intense show. Later, at about eight thirty, we stopped watching the show and had dessert, and I had some vanilla ice cream. Then we all went to bed.

Sunday, January 3, 2021

This morning I did my journaling at about eight thirty, and then I did some of my screen time with Cody for about ten minutes, and then Cody and I started a Monopoly game. Cody started off getting lots of houses, and I started saving my mom because she was going broke, and then we just took a break and had breakfast. See what I did there?

When I finished breakfast, I brushed my teeth and took a shower and washed my face, and when I got out of the shower I went downstairs and relaxed and did some reading. When I finished my reading, it was almost noon, so I decided to do some screen time. When I finished my screen time, it was about one. Cody and I started playing more Monopoly until the Seahawks started playing.

This afternoon the Seahawks started playing, and first the Seahawks got a field goal, and then the Seahawks forced a three-and-out and got the ball back and got another field goal. The game ended, and the Seahawks won by three points. It was 26–23, and it was a great game. Now they are in the playoffs next week. We are going to play the LA Rams, who we played a couple weeks ago.

That night we all had dinner, and I had pasta and corn and avocado, and when we all finished dinner, I went in the basement and did some schoolwork for about half an hour. Then I came upstairs and played Monopoly with Cody the rest of the night until I went to bed upstairs.

Monday, January 4, 2021

This morning my mom left at about seven, and today is Monday. That means the first day of online school again after winter break. This morning I looked at my class times, and only one time changed. Instead of having leadership from eleven to twelve on Tuesday and Thursday, I have it from seven to eight, so I need to get up early, but that isn't until tomorrow.

I did my journaling at about seven thirty, and then at eight I started my first Zoom, and I did that until nine. Then I had an hour off, so I did my chores and went on a hike with my mom for about half an hour. When we got back, I started my last two Zooms for the day.

This afternoon I did my reading and then Cody and I did our screen time until about one, and then I relaxed and played Monopoly and Clue with my dad and Cody for a couple hours. Then Cody and I finished up our screen time until dinner, and then we set the table and started eating.

I had pasta and avocado tonight, and then at about six I had a smoothie. Cody and I did some extra work for my dad for some screen time, and we did screen time for about an hour. Then Cody and my dad and I played Clue until my mom came home, and when she did, she had dinner and then I had some ice cream, and then I went to bed with Wilson and had a great sleep. At almost midnight, I couldn't sleep, and I realized it was because Wilson was growling. He was so cute, and I realized he was having a nightmare. He was on his back, and so I rubbed his belly and he woke up and looked so confused but so cute, and then I hugged him and we went back to sleep.

Tuesday, January 5, 2021

This morning I needed to wake up around six thirty, and it was really annoying because when I woke up, I still needed to have breakfast, brush my teeth, take a shower, and get my things ready for school. So, first I started off with taking a five-minute shower, and then I went downstairs and brushed my teeth, and then I went downstairs and got my school stuff ready, and then I sprinted upstairs and made a smoothie and drank it all and then looked at the clock, and there were still almost twenty minutes until class. Then I just did my chores, and that was just to sweep. I did that, and there were five minutes until class, so I went downstairs and checked the news.

Then I started my first Zoom, and since my time changed, I didn't know anyone in my class, but my teacher was the same. So, I did my things in my Zoom and then had an hour off. I came upstairs and had a bigger breakfast and asked my dad where my mom was. He said that she left for Seattle and probably will be there the rest of the day. Then at ten I had my next Zoom, and that was math, which was really boring because I knew everything that they were saying already. Then my Zoom ended, and I did my journaling and reading and had lunch and then relaxed.

Later this afternoon, Cody and I played *A Day and Night*, and if you don't remember how we played, we both have a day and a night in *Minecraft* that is really just twenty minutes, and we gather materials and then just fight at sunrise and see who wins. Then I played some *Madden* with my Franchise team, and after a while Cody and I were done with screen time. Then we played more Monopoly.

At about three o'clock I made a really good pie. I should tell you I have gotten pretty good at making blueberry pie. And after an hour, the pie was done and I had the pie in my hand, and my mom walked in, and I dropped the hot pie, and it burned my foot really bad! Just kidding! I really got you there, didn't I? Well, I just put the pie down and hugged my mom and then we all relaxed and played games until dinner.

Tonight for dinner I had a quesadilla and almost one and a half avocados, and that was super good, and then I had some bread. Later we all relaxed, and my dad had an idea for all of us to watch a movie called *Mulan*. It is a classic movie I have seen a couple times but not in this new version. We watched it, and it was fun but not the best because I knew almost everything that would happen. But later I had pie and ice cream, and it was really good. My dad said he was pretty tired, so we all just went to bed a little early.

Wednesday, January 6, 2021

Today is Wednesday and the Seahawks play on Saturday against the Rams. We have played the Rams before and won one and lost the other. Now if you lose, you're out for good, so it is pretty dangerous. And I can't wait.

This morning I started my Zooms at eight. My first one is STEM, and I did that one for an hour, and when I finished, I had a hour off, so I decided to just do some homework and screen time. Also, I asked my teacher and changed my class from seven to eleven, so now I don't need to get up really early anymore. Then at ten I started my math Zoom, and I had a smoothie during my Zoom, which was good. Then I had my humanities Zoom right after that, at eleven. Then I did my reading and journaling and chores, and then Cody and I did some screen time, and then I had lunch. I made a mini pizza. Basically, I took a tortilla, put pizza sauce and cheese on it, put it in the oven for five minutes, and it was great.

At about three, Cody and I did the rest of our screen time, and I looked at the news. Jamal Adams, a safety on the Seahawks, is good to go. He had a shoulder injury but is okay, and the quarterback Jared Goff is the guy that dislocated and broke his thumb and had surgery on the thumb. Hopefully, he won't play because that would be good for the Seahawks, but we will see what happens.

Then I made a blueberry pie, and there was this crazy thing that happened at the US Capitol. A group of what looked to be thousands and thousands of people broke into the building and destroyed the whole entire place, and that was during the final count for the election. It was all over the news, and it was really crazy! And my parents said we need to watch the TV. My dad called while he was running errands and said, "Taylor, turn the TV on and tell me what it is showing," and I told him. He said it came on the car radio and he didn't believe it.

That night I had a smoothie and a small pizza and carrot and more vegetables, and when we all finished dinner that night, we all played some games. Tomorrow my dad needs to go to the fire station for overtime. Later we all had pie I made and watched the news on our TV, and then we all went to bed, and I did the rest of my reading. And it was really sad about what was happening.

Thursday, January 7, 2021

This morning I woke up around eight. My dad left for work in the morning, and my mom left for work also, so Cody and I were home alone. My dad isn't coming home until tomorrow and my mom isn't coming until two.

This morning I started my Zooms. I first had math at about ten, and then I had leadership, and then I was done with all of my Zooms. I did some of my screen time, and then I did my chores and took a long bath and came back downstairs and had a great big breakfast, and then I brushed my teeth and did some of my reading and journaling and played with Wilson.

At two my mom came home. She said she got the second COVID vaccine, and tomorrow my dad will get his second vaccine when he comes home. I made a really good pizza and then had a smoothie, and Cody and I finished up the rest of our screen time and got ready for dinner.

Tonight I had a smoothie, and it was great. I didn't eat much because I had a big late lunch. After dinner I finished my reading and did some schoolwork for about an hour, and then I came upstairs and had a late snack and went to bed.

Friday, January 8, 2021

Today is Friday and no school. This morning I did some reading and journaling and some screen time and things like that. Then at about ten, my dad came home and I hugged him and then went back to my screen time, and later I had some breakfast. I had cereal and toast, and that was really good.

This afternoon I finished my screen time and then just relaxed and played games with Cody. Later I did my chores, which was to vacuum the stairs and upstairs. My mom wasn't feeling good, because of the vaccine, so she relaxed a lot.

Tonight I had some pizza for dinner. I learned to make my own with a quesadilla crust, and I put pizza sauce and cheese on it, and it was really good. After dinner I played Connect Four with Cody, and it was really fun, and then we all went to bed and relaxed.

Saturday, January 9, 2021

Today is Saturday and the Seahawks are playing. My dad said that the firefighters are now doing a Fantasy Football for the post season and he wanted Cody and me to be in it. I wasn't expecting it, but I am happy.

First thing this morning, I did some journaling and then some screen time, and then at about ten my dad told me that we are going to the store to get new shoes for me. We got there, and he said that they aren't open till eleven, and we had a little less than an hour to kill. First we went to the grocery store and got some food, and then we decided to get some La Fiamma. They weren't open until eleven, so we just sat in the car and waited. At eleven we went in the shoe place, and it said that they were open from ten o'clock until six at night, so my dad was wrong. We sat in the car for an hour, and we could have just got our shoes. So, we got some shoes, size 9.5 in women's because they didn't have any kid sizes, so that worked out. Then we got La Fiamma and went home at about eleven forty-five. Then I watched some of the Bills versus Colts game, and the Bills won in a close game. Then I relaxed and took a shower.

This afternoon I went on a hike with my mom, and then the Seahawks played. They started off losing really badly, and then at the end of the game they sadly lost 30–20, and the season is over for them. It is okay but a little sad, but there is still football to watch, and it is okay that it isn't the Seahawks.

Tonight there was another game on. It was the Buccaneers and Washington, and the Bucs won. Then we had a late dinner, and I had pizza and a great salad. Later I finished up some schoolwork and did my reading and played games, and then I went to bed.

Sunday, January 10, 2021

Today is Sunday and there are going to be a couple games on today, and not any tomorrow. I started off with reading and journaling and then took a shower and had breakfast, and then I brushed my teeth.

Then, at about ten, the first game was on. It was the Titans and the Ravens, and I watched part of that game and then did some schoolwork for a couple hours until about noon. Then I relaxed and checked Fantasy Football, and I was in first place!

Later that day, at about two, Cody and I watched part of the Saints game and then played Monopoly and a couple of other games, like Connect Four. Then I checked Fantasy Football again, and I bumped down to second. That is okay because in this league there are eleven people playing and fifty dollars to put in, each, and the top two players split the money.

Tonight there was one more game on, and I didn't watch that, but in the first quarter the Browns were beating the Steelers 28–0. That is the most points in one quarter post game, and that is cool. Then I had pasta for dinner, and after dinner we all played more Monopoly and I did some extra work for my mom. Then we all went to bed.

Monday, January 11, 2021

Today it is Monday and I have school. This morning I woke up at seven fifteen. I first did my journaling, and then I had breakfast. After I finished my great cereal, I took a shower and brushed my teeth, and then it was about eight. I had my first Zoom and then one hour off, so I did my reading. Then I exercised and swept, and after that it was time for my final two Zooms.

I finished my Zooms at twelve and then did schoolwork for about forty-five minutes and then Cody and I did some screen time. At two this afternoon my dad came home. He came home late because he had to do a fire department physical at the doctor, and he does it once a year for the last twelve years. In those twelve years he has not gained or lost more than four pounds, which was really surprising to me. He says firefighters have to be healthy and strong, and he is super strong.

Later, at about four that night, Cody and I played Monopoly and Connect Four and then it was dinnertime. I had a smoothie and I put in a banana and a couple oranges and ten pieces of lettuce and lots of fruit mix and two cups of milk. Then I had it, and it was great.

Tonight Cody started being mad at me, which surprised me because it is usually me that gets mad. He was mad at me because he found a piece of paper of mine, and I was keeping track of how many times he was whistling, because I was curious. He hid it from me and wouldn't give it back. I was reading, and he started getting frustrated with me because I accused him of hiding my piece of paper, but that isn't important to me at all, and whatever. After that event I went to bed and had a really good sleep.

Tuesday, January 12, 2021
Today is Tuesday, my short Zoom day, so I only have class from ten until noon. I woke up at eight and did my reading and journaling for about forty-five minutes. Then I had a big breakfast and later took a shower and brushed my teeth and finished up some things. Then finally I did my chores and there were about twenty-five minutes until class, so I did some screen time.

At ten I started my first Zoom, which is math, and then I had humanities. Right now in Fantasy Football, for the playoffs I am in second place, but I have one more person playing, and there will be two Saturday games and then a couple on Sunday.

Later this afternoon I did my chores and Cody and I played *Minecraft* and *Madden*, and then I watched some screen time. I watched a thing on YouTube called *Things That Were Caught on Camera*, and if they weren't on camera, no one would believe them. It was a cool and funny video. Then a little after two, I had lunch and relaxed and played Connect Four with Cody, and then we played Connect Five, which is a little game that we made up, You can probably guess how to play.

Tonight at five my dad started making a pizza, and then around six we had it, and it was really good. I had ranch with it from a couple days ago, and when I finished my half of the pizza, we all played a game called Chameleon, and it is a fun game. Then around nine thirty we all went to bed.

Wednesday, January 13, 2021
Today is Wednesday. There are going to be two football games on Saturday and two on Sunday, and my Fantasy Football team is going great. This morning I did my reading and journaling early, and then I took a shower and brushed my teeth and did one hour of Zooms, and then I did my chores and screen time until my next Zooms, and then I had another. Then before I knew it, I was one day away from being done with Zooms for the week.

Then Cody and I did some screen time. I started by playing *Madden*, and then Cody and I played *Minecraft* for about forty-five minutes, and then I had one hour of screen time left. I had lunch and relaxed and checked my schoolwork and did that for an hour or two, and when I finished, I did the rest of my screen time until dinner.

Tonight I had pasta and one avocado. After I finished dinner, Cody and I played Connect Four, and Cody won two and I lost two. At about eight

I had dessert, and I made a milkshake by putting milk and ice cream into a blender. It was really good. At about nine thirty I went to bed.

Thursday, January 14, 2021

Today is Thursday, last day of Zooms. This morning about seven thirty, I went to a doctor and took some X-rays because my toe was really hurting. Basically, he said that there are these three little bones, and they should be one, but it will just take a lot of growing to get them to connect, and I just need to wait, and it's probably from playing so much soccer.

Later this morning, about nine, I did my chores and reading and journaling. At about nine forty-five I had a little breakfast, and then I took a shower and brushed my teeth. At about ten I had my first Zoom, and it was math. and I started that. I finished that Zoom after an hour, and then I had my last Zoom of the week.

At twelve this afternoon I did some screen time and played Madden. On my *Madden* team I have Patrick Mahomes, Henry Ruggs, and my last good player is Fletcher Cox, and he is a DT (defensive tackle).

At about four I did some extra reading, and then I did some schoolwork for about an hour, and then I made a smoothie with milk and a couple different types of berries and finally some lettuce. Later tonight we had a bonfire, and it was fun. Then I went inside because I was tired, and I just did some reading and went to bed.

Friday, January 15, 2021

It's Friday and I can't wait until tomorrow because there are two games going on. There is the Packers versus Rams, and then later at night there is going to be the Bills versus Ravens. I want the Packers and the Bills to win. And in two days the Chiefs are playing the Browns, and the Saints and Bucks, and I want the Chiefs and Saints.

This morning I did some reading and chores, and then I did some journaling and took a bath and washed my face. Later I had some Wheat Chex with soy milk. Soy milk, if you don't know, is my favorite milk. Later I did screen time and played *Madden* and watched YouTube.

At about twelve this afternoon I went on a hike with my mom, and Wilson was mad that we went on a walk without him. We ended up seeing a lot of neighbors, and that was fun. If you are wondering why we didn't take Wilson, it is because we didn't go on the trail, we walked on the street to see if any neighbors were outside. When we got back, I did more screen time for about forty-five minutes, and then I was done with screen time. Then I checked my school and I needed to do a lot, and so I did most of it. Before I knew it, I was having dinner! I ended up having a smoothie and pasta, and after dinner we all relaxed, and I did some more reading for the next day. Then I played a game with my family and we all went to bed.

Saturday, January 16, 2021

Today is Saturday and there are two games on. First there is a game at about one, and that is the Packers and the Rams. I want the Packers to win. There is a game at five, and that is the Ravens and the Bills, and I want the Bills to win. With Fantasy Football, Cody and I are doing really well, both in the top three, and I think there is a chance one or both of us will win, because remember, first and second get the money, but each splits.

This morning I did reading and my chores, which was sweep, and then I played some *Madden*. On my team I have Kyler Murry and Keenan Allen and many more good guys. Then I had a smoothie with raspberries and a banana and two oranges, and my mom and I shared it. Then I relaxed and checked my schoolwork.

This afternoon I did some journaling, and didn't do that much but relaxed, and went on a hike. Later I did more screen time and played a game called *Avalanche*. It is just a game where you start on a ground with blocks falling, and you need to not get hit, and climb up and onto other blocks, and you can only go up one block. But then, after about a minute, red and blue blocks fall, and if you touch red blocks, you lose. Blue blocks make you bounce really high, and maybe onto other blocks, and then bottom levels start disappearing. Then you just need to stay as long as you can, and it moves really fast.

Later I watched part of the Packers game with Cody, and Fantasy Football went great. After our screen time, we all had some dinner. I had pasta and some bread my dad made and another smoothie and some avocado, and that was good. Then we all played games. I looked, and next Sunday, Monday, Tuesday, Wednesday, and Thursday it is supposed to snow, and I am really excited for that.

Sunday, January 17, 2021

Today is Sunday and there are two games that are going to be on, and that is great. The first one is at noon, and it is the Chiefs and the Browns, and I am almost positive the Chiefs will win, but I am not sure. Later the Saints will play the Bucs, and the winner goes to the conference game to decide who goes to the Super Bowl.

This morning at about eight, I woke up and went downstairs. Today is my chores day off, so I don't need to do any. One day a week we all don't do chores, and to tell you, we all four change each week who does what, but some things just my mom and dad do. First, I took a shower and had a big breakfast and brushed my teeth and washed my face. Later, about a little after nine, I started some screen time, and I played *Madden*. I only played two games, and then I went upstairs and made a smoothie, and it was good. Then I did my reading. At ten my dad came home, and since he was on overtime yesterday, he needs to go to work tomorrow, and that is okay because after that he will be home for four days.

This afternoon at about eleven, I started my screen time again, and my dad and I played a game of Ping-Pong, and after that we all played a game of relax, which means reading and journaling and generally just doing our own thing.

Later, at about twelve, I started watching the game, and it went on for about three hours. I watched part of it but not all of it, and the Chiefs' quarterback Patrick Mahomes got injured, and he got a concussion. He got really dizzy and fell over, and he seemed really hurt and ended up being out for the game. That is sad because he is only, like, twenty-four, but he is also the best player in the NFL.

Tonight the Saints game came on at about four, and I just relaxed. I didn't watch any because I was done with my screen time, so I just went downstairs and did some schoolwork for about an hour. Then we all had an early dinner at five thirty, and my dad made pizza. That was great. Later we all played a game as a family for a little bit, and I made blueberry pie, and I that was really good. Then we all relaxed, and I did some reading, and then we all just hung out talking, and slowly, all went to bed.

Monday, January 18, 2021

Today I have no Zooms even though it is Monday, because it is Martin Luther King Day and that is great. This morning I played *Madden* and my *Madden* player became 99 overall, which is really good. My team, I think, is a really good team. I think I can survive a couple years and make some Super Bowls.

Later this morning I did some chores, which was just sweep, and after that I relaxed and Cody and I played some *Avalanche*, and that was fun. If you didn't know, you can play two players on one laptop, but one person uses the arrow keys and the other uses A and W and D keys, so that was fun. Then I did some reading on the couch upstairs. After I finished my reading, I made a smoothie, and that was really good, and I had the same thing as always.

This afternoon at one, I did some journaling for about fifteen minutes. My dad is working overtime, but tomorrow he will be home, but not until two because he needed to do extra things. Later Cody and I played more Avalanche. Then I had a doctor's appointment for checking on my eye, because when I was in third grade I hurt my eye, and that was five years ago, and I got hit in the face with a soccer ball, and I have had a little red spot on my eye, and it is still there, and we have got it checked out, and there isn't really anything to do, and it doesn't affect my sight at all. So, we went there, and a woman walked in and didn't say anything but hi, and she put the eye drops in my eye, and I asked what they were for, and she said, "I am just dilating your eyes, and that is when your pupils suddenly will get really big, and light will turn super bight, and everything gets really blurry," and that confused me. She left, and I was confused, and my mom said it only lasts a couple hours. Then the next doctor came in, and my mom asked why the other lady put drops in my eye, and then that lady left and came back in. Basically, they just were not supposed to give that to me. Then they just put numbing drops in my eye. And I was like *WHAT THE HECK! You don't numb an eye!* And they poked around and the doctor just picked some things out of my eye, and then I was totally confused, and I was so confused, and then my mom and I left, and we connected the dots. Basically, they did an eye exam and were just checking my eye probably, that I have had for many years, and then we went home, and I am just confused.

Tonight we all had some dinner, and I had a smoothie and some pasta and avocado, and that was really good. So basically, I have the same thing for dinner every night. It is either pasta, pizza, smoothie, lots of corn and avocado and lettuce and red peppers and carrots, or the final thing is quesadilla. So, some things you might have realized is I don't have meat, but sometimes bacon or sausage is all, and I could call myself a vegetarian, but I still have those things maybe once every two months, but it is pretty close. That is how I have always been. So, everything was so blurry I couldn't see at all. I just turned the lights off and closed my eyes at eight that night, and then I brushed my teeth and then just went to bed really early.

Tuesday, January 19, 2021
Today is Tuesday and I have Zooms again. I woke up a little after eight and first did my chores and reading and journaling and had some cereal, and my mom went to swim, and I took a long bath. When I got out of the bath, I brushed my teeth and did some screen time until my Zooms.

At ten I had my first Zoom. I finished my Zoom a little before eleven and then went upstairs and had a bite of food and came back downstairs and did one more Zoom. I finished that Zoom at about noon, and I had a big smoothie with a banana, two oranges, two cups of raspberries, two cups of milk, and ten pieces of lettuce.

Later I did some screen time and played *Madden*, and I ended up going to the Super Bowl. I played against the Falcons and ended up winning and then having a bowl of cereal. Later Cody played the Super Bowl and ended played the Falcons also, and he crushed them also. Later that afternoon I went outside and played some soccer with Cody.

Tonight I had dinner and got a letter from Gammy and Paw-Paw, my grandparents, and they sent me a hundred dollars to La Fiamma because I made the honor roll at my school, and I thanked them. Later we all played a board game until about nine, and we all went to bed after having dessert.

Wednesday, January 20, 2021

Today is Wednesday and I can't wait until Sunday because then it is football. Fantasy Football is looking good for me, but I am in second, so I don't want to second guess myself. That morning we all relaxed until I had some Zooms. I had my first one at eight, and I did that until nine, and then I did some reading and journaling, and then I took a shower, ate, brushed my teeth, and did my chores. Then I did two more hours of Zooms until a little before noon, and then I looked at the weather. It says it will maybe snow next week!

That afternoon Cody and I played some games, and I then had a big lunch—I had bread and some avocado—until about two, and I did more screen time. Later I did some more reading for the next day, and then I did schoolwork for two hours, until four thirty. Then I set up for dinner.

Then I had pasta and some more avocado, and after dinner we all relaxed. Cody and I did some screen time because my mom and dad had given us extra. Later we watched the inauguration, and it is basically just a celebration for the Biden presidential win. Trump didn't even go when always the other president goes. So, we watched that, and my dad said that this is important. Then we all played Chameleon until eight, and then we all had dessert. I did some more reading until nine, and then we all went to bed.

Thursday, January 21, 2021

Today it is Thursday and it's the last day of school Zooms. This morning I did my journaling and chores. Later I had a big breakfast and took a shower and brushed my teeth until about nine, and then I did screen time. Then at about ten, I did my Zooms until that afternoon at about noon.

This afternoon I checked playoff Fantasy Football, and I am still in second place. Then I did some exercise in the basement, and then I did schoolwork for a couple hours. Then I did some screen time with Cody.

Tonight we all played Chameleon, and that was fun. Then we had dinner. I had pasta and a smoothie, and we ran out of 2 percent milk, so I used soy in my smoothie, which I liked better. Later we played more Chameleon, and then at about eight we had dessert. I did some reading and journaling, and then we all went to bed. And if you don't know, Chameleon is a game where one person is the chameleon and doesn't know the secret word, and you have to try to guess who it is, and if it is you, then you try to pretend like you aren't it, and it is really fun.

Friday, January 22, 2021

Today it is Friday and I have no Zooms. Sadly there aren't any games tomorrow, when we will just relax. There will be only two games, the Packers and the Bucks, and the Chiefs and the Bills.

This morning I did some journaling and reading until about ten, and then I did my chores and played *Madden*. I ended up winning the Super Bowl in the Franchise mode on *Madden*, and I did the draft and then took a long bath.

Then I ate a big breakfast and brushed my teeth. Later Cody and I watched YouTube and I just relaxed, and later Cody and I played Chameleon. Then we all had a big lunch until about two. Basically, the rest of the afternoon Cody and I did screen time until about three, and I did schoolwork for a couple hours.

Tonight we all relaxed and my dad made pizza. I had it, and it was really fluffy and—I will say it again—really good. When I finished, we all just relaxed and then had dessert at about seven. Then we all played Chameleon until eight, and I did some more reading until nine, and then we all went to bed.

Saturday, January 23, 2021

Today is Saturday. This morning I did reading and writing until about nine, and then I did my chores, which was sweep, and then screen time for about an hour, until ten thirty. Later I had a big breakfast and brushed my teeth, and then I took a long bath.

This afternoon I did some schoolwork for about three hours, and then I did more screen time for a little bit, and then I only had thirty minutes left. I did more reading, and then we all relaxed and played Chameleon.

Tonight we all relaxed, and I had pasta and a smoothie and one whole avocado. We finished dinner at six, and then Cody and I finished up our screen time. Then we all played Chameleon until eight. I did some more reading until nine, and then we all had dessert and went to bed.

Sunday, January 24, 2021

Today is going to be a different day when I am journaling because I am going to reflect on what I did this long, hard COVID year, because this will be my last day of journaling. I might start writing again and show the COVID numbers to see the difference. In my country, the US, 26,337,958 people have had COVID. There are almost 415,520 deaths in the US. The world just hit 100 million cases in the world and 2.2 million deaths in the world.

Last year I went through quarantining, lots of smoke from wildfires, and online school. I have not seen anyone from my grade in the last ten months, and that is crazy. At the beginning of the school year of last year, they said there will only be six weeks away from school. Six weeks is a month and a half, and now it's been ten long months.

Also, I for sure will not start public school until next August or September, and it is January, and I might not even start then. It has been really hard this long time. My mom is still giving vaccines, my dad is still jumping into fires in the middle of the night, and my brother and I are sitting in our rooms looking at little square faces talking on a computer, and we will be doing this for a long time. But I am lucky for my family and my brother. Thanks for reading this far. It's been fun.

***

Tuesday, March 16, 2021

Well, hello again. It has been one year since my first journal, and it is the day before Saint Patrick's Day. Today I am reaching out to say hi, just to give an update on what's been going on. This month, where I live, we will go to Phase 3. This has been a long, hard year, and I can't wait for it to be over. They tell us what phase we are in, and that tells us what is open, what we can go do, and the rules and stuff for going to do things. I am currently on spring break, and it will be one week or ten days off. So, I might peek in a couple times later on and say hi, and maybe when I go back to school, or something like that.

***

Sunday, April 25, 2021

Today is my birthday and just a little check-in. My dad made beignets this morning, and then later our neighbor's grandson came over and we played basketball for a couple hours. Then we got La Fiamma, my favorite, for dinner and had cake and ice cream for dessert. We finished the day by watching the Oscars and then went to bed outside with the whole family on the deck. Also, I am exactly five feet and five inches tall and exactly 100.6 pounds, right on my birthday, and it just ended perfectly. Also, about one month until school ends for Williamsburg Academy!

***

Monday, May 20, 2021
It is about a month later and today is a huge day, because first . . . today was the last day of school! This will be probably my last online Zoom. Second thing, which is one hundred times bigger, I got my COVID vaccine! It's so crazy. I got my first today, and I will get my second on the tenth of June, and that is really exciting. A couple extra things: On the twelfth of May, I made Rangers 08 Gold team, and that is really exciting. I just think it's cool I got my vaccine on my last day of online school. This is a picture of me getting my first vaccine! I just want to say thanks to God and all the first responders and doctors and nurses for always being there and helping everyone at all costs during this whole year. It has been a really hard fourteen months for everyone, and we are getting through it, and we can only do it together.

Taylor Watts

Seattle Times
(March 15, 2020)

Taylor riding a stationary bike
(March 25, 2020)

The Watts family attending a peaceful BLM protest
(June 6, 2020)

Cody and Jimmy building benches in the garage
(June 20, 2020)

Cody fly fishing early in the morning at Whatcom Creek
(July 13, 2020)

Taylor holding up a Whatcom Creek trout
(July 13, 2020)

Taylor going all in to catch a fish at Whatcom Creek
(July 14, 2020)

Cody and Taylor reading the Seattle Times
(July 26, 2020)

Hanging out with Gammy and Paw-Paw in Sandpoint, Idaho
(August 13, 2020)

Cody and Taylor
(August 13, 2020)

The church where Julie and Jimmy were married in Sandpoint, Idaho
(August 15, 2020)

Cody and Taylor enjoying pizza in the back of the car
(September 6, 2020)

Cody celebrating his birthday outside with Taylor, Gavin and Carter
(October 17, 2020)

Wilson on the deck relaxing
(November 1, 2020)

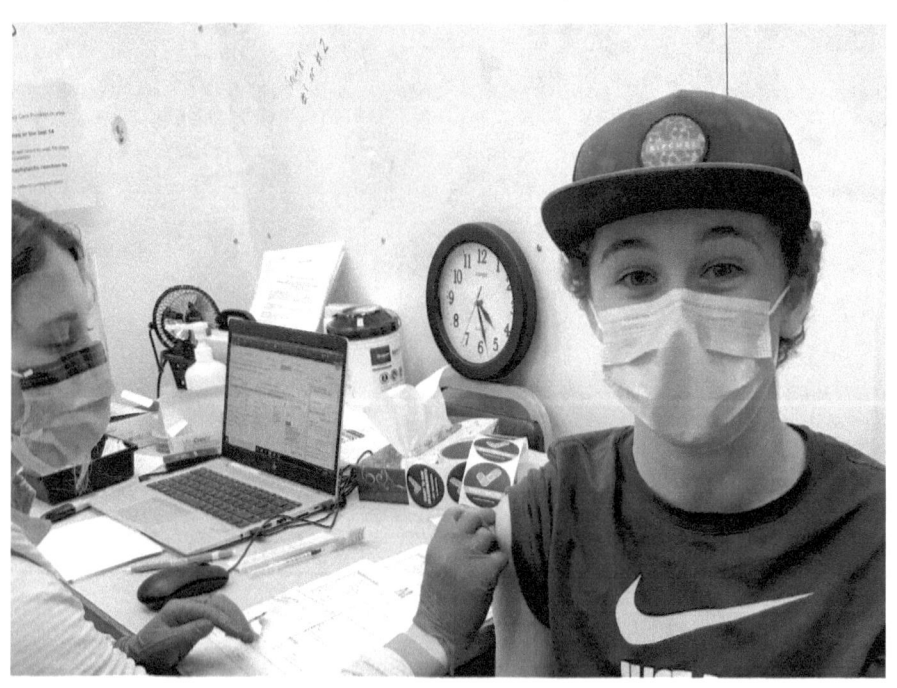

Cody getting his first Covid vaccine at Saint Joseph Hospital
(May 20, 2021)

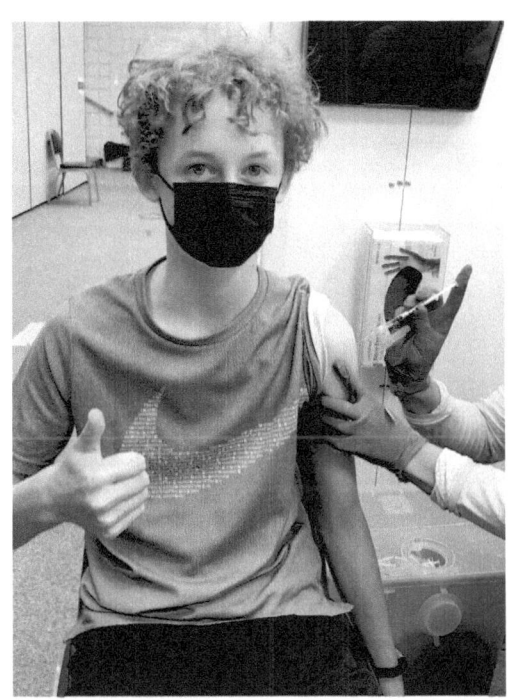

Taylor getting his first Covid vaccine at Saint Joseph Hospital
(May 20, 2021)

Cody and Taylor at Priest Lake with Wilson
(July 2, 2021)

The Watts family watching Sandlot on the beach at Priest Lake
(July 5, 2021)

Priest Lake sunset
(July 17, 2021)

Part II
by Cody Watts

Introduction

I first found out about COVID-19 in social studies in December, while doing a school assignment on the news of the week. It was just a virus in China. I was more focused on finishing the school assignment, and I wasn't even thinking that the virus would affect me. I went throughout the day, and the next day. Fast forward a few months, and it definitely affects me, along with everyone else.

As it spread past the China borders, bleeding into the US, COVID made its way to California and Washington. Making its way to Europe, and other parts of the world, it was labeled an epidemic. Then it was a pandemic. I had never even heard the word pandemic, though I had read it in a book before.

The first true change occurred on Friday the thirteenth, March 2020. We stopped going to school. Some schools had made this decision earlier in the week. In fifth period, it was a rumor. In sixth period, a reality. In seventh period, a celebration. I bet every person who was excited about not going to school for six weeks would have reacted differently if they knew what would proceed. After school got out, I met with Tay, and we both walked to meet my dad at the pickup. We informed Dad of what happened. Taylor and I were excited to be off school for six weeks.

The reason they said that school was out was to stop the spread of COVID. The teachers said they would miss all their students, though I bet a few were excited for a break too. It was odd that they stopped school for COVID-19 spreading, and worried about the wide public, instead of canceling school for the students' safety.

As the weekend went by, it was a time that was used to think about what we would do for a month and a half. I still believe this may have been one of the most crucial times of lockdown, where we used the weekend to reflect on ideas and create goals for ourselves.

One goal, focused by Mom and Dad, was how we were going to continue learning without school. For math, we would solve handwritten problems; they got us some math books. For PE, we would exercise every day. As for science and social studies, they said we'd figure it out later, but we could google some science experiments and we could read the news for social studies. The one that stuck with me, however, and had the longest lifespan, was our plan for language arts, where we would journal every day. Taylor and I were quite enthusiastic to begin this, and I don't have a great reason why. Maybe we were excited to remember each day, and to share it with family later. Mom planned it to also be a form of meditation. So, here is my journal! As you see, it lasted a lot more than six weeks!

Cody Watts

Monday, March 16, 2020

I woke up at 5:11 in the morning today. Wilson got a dirty sock that was left on the floor and said good morning. This ritual he never forgets about and is also a routine he created on his own. Wilson has his fair share of stuffed toys, and sometimes he steals our dirty socks, his favorite thing to carry in his mouth. When I take my socks off after playing outside, I just throw them on the floor. If Mom asks, I tell her it's for Wilson.

Taylor's and my beds are located on the top floor of the house. After seeing me come downstairs from the balcony, Wilson goes to gather his toys and greets me on the last step of the stairs. He breathes heavily through his nose, because his mouth is stuffed with socks and a toy otter. When waking up, I try to be as quiet as possible because frequently I'm the first to wake up.

Since I was two, I've always gotten up around five thirty. I don't know why. My best guess is that I got used to Dad waking up early when I was little, and I woke up with him. We made coffee, and I would do the scoops. I learned to count scooping coffee . . . one . . . two . . . three . . . and to this day I don't drink coffee, but I love the smell. Waking up early has its benefits. For example, because my day starts early, I have plenty of hours to catch up on any schoolwork.

However, today we all woke up early. Mom, Tay, and I all went to Safeway early in the morning, at six o'clock. We went early, assuming that the grocery store would quickly run out of food and toilet paper. My dad called from the fire station last night and said the stores shelves in Seattle were empty.

We read about panic shopping on the news and decided that we should do it. People are preparing themselves for the next while, and stores were getting out of stock. When we got to Safeway, there weren't as many people there as I expected. We got lots of rice and beans. We got Taylor pasta and cereal, both things that he eats almost every day. We also got enchiladas, and dog food for Wilson. We ended up filling two carts full. Dad said that we would most likely be set for food for a little more than a month.

Also, we made sure to get plenty of toilet paper and paper towels. I don't understand why people are so focused on collecting toilet paper because of the pandemic. What about other important things? Why toilet paper? But, because of the toilet paper hoarding, we decided to follow suit.

Mom and Dad told us that because of all the uncertainty going on, and the possibility that there will be shortages of some things, we needed to only use paper towels and toilet paper when we needed it. I did have to catch myself a few times, almost using a paper towel to clean up water.

Tuesday, March 17, 2020
Dad got surgery on his leg today. My Dad tore his meniscus at work. He's a Seattle firefighter, and during training he hurt it. The orthopedic surgeon said that he should have surgery on it. The surgery was done at an office instead of the hospital. Because of COVID, the hospital canceled all elective surgeries so they could use the hospital beds for people that were sick. Dad was the last patient before the surgery center closed temporarily for COVID today.

Dad needs to be on crutches for a little while. Also, he won't go to work for a little over a month. I think it is great because he won't need to respond to coronavirus calls at the fire station. Also, Tay and I are off of school for six weeks, so we will all get a break. Except for Mom, but she only works one or two times a week.

If Dad did catch COVID from work, he would have to get quarantined. If he did get quarantined, it would require him to miss work. Quarantine lasts two weeks and they make the firefighters stay in a hotel room all by themselves. More importantly, he could have gotten sick from responding to someone who's COVID positive. However, the fire department in Seattle has some protective gear for COVID, so that made Mom less worried. Now that Dad won't be working for the time being, she can kind of take a sigh of relief. And plus, we get to be home together.

I doubt that the virus will go away in only a month. The number of coronavirus cases spiked, and six more people died in Washington today. I wonder if I have ever talked to or walked past or even known one of the people that died today, or anyone that has died in the last few days because of COVID.

It is also St. Patrick's Day. We didn't really celebrate it, now that Tay also knows there aren't any leprechauns. I think there aren't many celebrations going on today because everyone is in shock. Sometimes my dad plays the bagpipes with the firefighters on St. Patrick's Day, but they cancelled playing because of COVID.

Tay, Dad, and I slept on the deck last night. We usually sleep outside a couple of times each week. The only reason that Mom doesn't sleep out with us is because it is too cold for her most of the time, though she sleeps with us about once a month. The deck is covered, so the rain doesn't hit us often unless it's windy.

We use two fold-out mattresses that we usually use only when friends of family come over. I slept on my own mattress on the end of the deck with Wilson next to me, while Taylor and Dad slept on the other end closest to the house. The usual clothing for sleeping outside is warm socks, adidas pants, and a hoodie over a tee shirt.

Oh, and Wilson is infamous for lying on our legs in the middle of the night, pulling the blankets off in the process. Wilson did just that to me.

I went up to go to the bathroom and saw that it was a clear night, and there were more stars than you could keep track of. Around the dark figures of the trees, I saw the constellation Orion and what looked like it could be the Big Dipper, though I wasn't sure. Once, all of us were coming home late at night and Taylor forgot the name of the Big Dipper and called it the Big Shopping Cart. So now my family calls it the Big Shopping Cart any time we see it.

This was the first time that we slept outside since Dad's surgery, so we made sure that Wilson stayed far away from lying on Dad's legs the whole night.

We don't have air conditioning. Mostly because nine months of the year it wouldn't be necessary. However, in the summer it gets really hot on the top floor, where Tay and I sleep. So, we started sleeping in the basement when it's hot. One night, years ago, Dad came up with the idea of us three camping outside instead. It was fun. The tent was small but protected us. But because there really isn't any rain in the summer, we didn't need the tent. We had more room, and it worked perfectly. We only camped out two or three times that summer, but we continued to sleep in the back yard a few times each summer.

Once we got Wilson, we slept outside with him. He liked sleeping outside more than all of us. We moved sleeping outside to the deck because Wilson couldn't go into the front yard in the middle of the night, and we didn't want him wandering. The deck is railed and has a small gate, so Wilson can stay with us the whole night.

The next year, we would sleep outside any time of the year. Wilson protests at the door to the deck most nights now, 'cause that's his favorite place to sleep. We don't sleep outside every day, but he says *Why not?* Tay and I figured out the best spots to be, but at this point we would sleep outside at least once a week. Sunny, rainy, snowing, it didn't matter, we would sleep outside.

Dad camped a lot when growing up. Mom is only comfortable with Tay and me sleeping outside with Dad. So, on nights that Dad is at the firehouse, we sleep inside.

Wednesday, March 18, 2020

Today was a lazy day. Dad says his leg is okay, and he said he doesn't even need crutches like he thought. Today Mom went on a bike ride, and a walk with Donnett. Tay and I frequently do yard work and shovel snow for Donnett.

Besides that, COVID numbers jumped. Washington and New York both have over one thousand cases and, in the US, over one hundred people died.

Tay and I also did more schoolwork today. We still have our school computers, even though we aren't at school. Our teachers are sending assignments to us through OneNote. The amount of schoolwork is very minimal so far. Mom and Dad said today that they think that the school will be online for the rest of the year, with COVID cases getting so big and people still dying.

With so much time now, Tay and I are starting to come up with fun games to play. Today we played hide-and-seek. It was just Tay and me playing, so basically the goal is to find the other person the fastest. I hid in the trees next to the septic tank and got a lot of splinters in my hand and back, but Tay ended up finding me. Tay hid on the deck without me noticing until the second time, when I saw the blankets slowly rise and fall; it was Taylor breathing. Wilson was a good help for me when we were playing hide-and-seek tag because he would run and sniff right next to the hider and give them away to everyone else.

This is totally random and has no significance to my day, but it seems like a good idea to write about: Blankets are the single best invention that is not necessary to life. Kind of like paper towels and microwaves (and honorable mention to footballs). Blankets are an amazing thing to have when you wake up in the morning early (like I do, often) and keep you warm when the heater is not up yet.

Literally all my favorite things to do inside include a blanket. Blankets are so good, they don't have to be even that soft or warm. And an upgrade from a blanket is a hoodie; a hoodie is practically a blanket that you can wear.

Thursday, March 19, 2020

Today Dad said that his leg hurt more. In the later part of the morning and the early afternoon, he did a lot of cutting bamboo, for a flyrod that got ordered. His leg is hurting more today than yesterday.

COVID numbers continue to rise. Today I read in the news that scientists are thinking COVID could increase with summer and people being more social, and other scientists said it would decrease because when people did socialize, they would be outside, where it's more difficult for COVID to spread.

I think COVID is just nature being natural, and I think some people are going to falsely accuse people (when regarding coronavirus), and their power about what they could have done will be overestimated. Sure, people could do their job better, and ordinary humans could be more careful about getting the virus and/or spreading it. Truthfully, there is no one to point a finger at and say, "This is your fault." This probably frustrates some people.

Today is the first day of spring. Not that this is significant, as official changes of season are never in alignment with what is the mark of a season change. Seasons change by events, or natural events (I feel like summer is marked by the end of school, fall by the beginning of school, and winter by the first snowfall).

Mom was the one that told me that it's spring; otherwise I wouldn't have known. We were sitting on the patio, and I said that it felt like summer. And it really does, with no school for the near future and sun that we haven't had in such a long time. Except for the one week we went to Hawaii in February.

I feel like the coronavirus will have an impact on the next foreseeable years. My prediction is that there won't be many big technological advancements with the economy being affected. I also think that life will be a little more basic for the remainder of the year.

Today we had what is probably my favorite dinner, tacos. We have tacos two or three times a week. Today we put yam fries, beans, chipotle dip, and cheese in the tacos. Tay didn't have tacos because he doesn't like them. Which is unbelievable, but anyway, he had a ranch salad. I also had a ranch salad. Earlier in the day Tay and I made ranch dressing. Tay doesn't have many foods that he likes for dinner. He likes to keep it basic and mostly has pasta for every dinner.

Friday, March 20, 2020

Today coronavirus cases in the United States doubled. Mostly there is a big increase in New York. New York cases went to more than eight thousand cases. Also, Washington has thirteen hundred cases and is the state with the most deaths. Over seventy people.

Today Tay and I played half-court basketball to twenty-one points. I got out to an early lead and shot multiple threes for a 10–2 lead. Then Taylor caught up to me and it was 8–10. Then I quickly hit a layup as well as a three that hit nothing but net, for it to be 15–8. At this point, Tay turned on the jets to catch up to 14–15. Then I hit another three, 18–14. All I had to do was make a three for it to be ball game, but then Tay scored two layups and then swished a three to finish out the game.

Tay and I are very competitive, especially with each other. Somehow, I think that we are competitive in different ways. I don't know what winning means to him, but I know that for me it's somewhat like this: Losing means not winning, and winning means success. I guess that no matter what, being competitive can help in life and for achieving goals.

Today we made two different types of bread. Dad, being off work for a while, has started a new project. He made a sourdough loaf. The two types of bread that he made today were rosemary bread and focaccia bread, which I had never heard of before.

I'm probably biased, but both of the loaves turned out really good. Tay came up with the idea of a time-lapse video of the bread rising. That video turned out very good as well.

Saturday, March 21, 2020

We got a package on the front door today, and it was addressed to me, Tay, and Wilson. It was an Easter basket from Gammy and Paw-Paw! We love gifts from them, and more recently they have gotten stuff for Wilson as well. In the package there was a dog toy for Wilson. Wilson really loves the toy so far. They also gave us frosted cookies, and Mom and Dad got frosted almond candy. There were Easter-style candy corns for us to share.

Gammy and Paw-Paw are Dad's parents, our grandparents. They live on the other side of the state, and they used to have a house in Spokane, but they moved into an assisted living home. Before they moved into Rockwood, they had a small lake place on Pend Oreille. I hope I never forget the lake place; we went there each summer, and it was always perfect.

Dad says that his leg is getting better. A few times last week, because Dad has less to do for the time being, he spends time in the shop, making bamboo fly rods. "The shop" is in the basement and is a small room that Dad occupied for making bamboo fly rods and for storage. Tay and I sometimes use it for making art projects.

Dad makes fly rods for friends, and sometimes he gets orders to make some. Dad does most of the beginning work in the shop. Making bamboo fly rods takes a lot of time. Dad says that they take about eighty hours. But that doesn't account for waiting for glue to dry or other things that go into it. Dad really enjoys making fly rods.

Sunday, March 22, 2020

I did some art today, and I traced a picture of Odell Beckham Jr.'s catch versus the Cowboys a few years ago. It is definitely the biggest catch of his career. At that point he was with the New York Giants, and he made the catch during a game against the Dallas Cowboys. He made the catch in the Giants' stadium, MetLife Stadium. MetLife Stadium was also the stadium where the Seahawks won the Super Bowl.

Tay and I played basketball outside, and it was kind of a boring game, and no one was getting any points. Then Bryce came over. He's young, so we were nice to him. Bryce is nine and his brother is a little older than I am.

Today Dad continued making a fly rod. I let Wilson into the shop. Wilson quickly decided that it was claustrophobic for him, and then I let him outside of the shop.

I feel like I should formally introduce Wilson. Wilson is an English cream golden retriever, and he spends every day outside. All day. Before we got Wilson, Dad installed an electric fence around the yard, and then he taught Wilson to stay inside the electric fence. Wilson has only gone outside his fence one or two times, so we trust him alone outside. Also, if Wilson is inside, he starts whining to go outside. He loves it outside. This also makes sense why he loves sleeping outside.

Wilson sleeps a lot outside during the day, and when he's awake he's looking at the squirrels in trees around the yard. He also likes to chase birds and bunnies, but he never leaves his fence.

Wilson is also the happiest dog in the world. His tail is always wagging. The whole family loves him so much. Mom and Dad got Wilson as a Christmas present for Tay and me.

Today Dad brought Wilson to Phil's house. Phil is our neighbor, and his dog, Finn, recently passed away. Finn was also an amazing dog. Phil really likes dogs. He had an electric fence for Finn, and Dad and Phil are trying to train Wilson to Phil's electric fence so that he can spend time with Phil every once in a while.

Monday, March 23, 2020

Mom went to work today. Mom works one or two days a week. She has been a nurse for fifteen years, and she has worked at the PeaceHealth Hospital here in Bellingham. She switched floors that she was at every once in a while, but about two years ago she found herself getting exhausted from the stress at the hospital, so she was looking for a new place to go. She got a job at Whatcom Hospice House and has been working there. She says that there is a lot less stress, not that it's easy, but it isn't so overwhelming.

Tay and Dad and I played outside most of the day. We played Around the World. This was fun, and I think we will play it a lot in the near future. In the middle of the game, Bryce came over. We went in after that.

One week in and things have already escalated. On Monday, the first day I wrote in my journal, there were 3,500 cases in the United States. Now there are over 40,000 cases. In California there is a stay-at-home order, meaning you can only go out if it's important, so you stay at home unless going to work for an essential job or shopping for important things, like food or water. Washington had 42 deaths at the start of the week, and at the end of the week it had 111, the deaths more than doubled.

Another thing Tay and I did was make cinnamon rolls, with help from Dad. The recipe is from our great-grandmother. They were the biggest I've seen them, and even though it was the first time we made it, the yeast really outdid itself. They were delicious, even though the first try didn't work out.

Tuesday, March 24, 2020

Today was rainy. We had gotten used to good weather the past few days, so this automatically was a slow, calm day. In the middle of the day, Taylor and I played Ping-Pong, another game we planned on playing a lot for however long we would be out of school.

After Ping-Pong, we played a game that we have never played before: sumo wrestling with bean bags. We have two bean bags that are partially deflated. This is not a game that someone intelligent would make up. With games like this, we'll probably play it a lot, and then when someone gets hurt, we will stop playing and forget. The key is to not be the one that gets hurt, so you can savor the game for as long as possible without getting hurt. It was more fun than Ping-Pong, and no one got hurt.

Mom also made her first bread today. She made a bread that is the same as the one that our neighbors gave us a few days ago, focaccia bread. It came out really good, and it didn't take long until the bread was gone.

Wednesday, March 25, 2020

Today Dad and I decided to make bagels. We started by getting the materials for it and then I filled up and heated a cup of hot water. Then we put that in the bowl. Next, we put the sugar in and followed by putting the yeast into the bowl. I almost put the yeast into the sugar container; that wouldn't be good. There were a few more steps and then we put them in the oven. For the first time ever making them, they were great. The one thing that Dad self-critiqued was that the bottom was chewy because we used a cookie sheet. So, the next time that we make it we are going to put it on a different surface that will make it better.

Dad has gotten more and more creative with bread. A few days ago, he tried to make cinnamon rolls, and they came out good. We helped him. We got the cinnamon sugar and butter, and we rolled the dough in it. They were really huge!

Tay and I also played some basketball, and Tay went on Mom's bike trainer, and now his legs are super sore because he did around two and a half hours on it. Also, Mom and Dad went on the trail with Wilson while I did pushups, sit-ups, squats, curls (and more that I can't think of) in the basement while listening to eighties music.

We watched *The Other Guys*. We had never seen it before. It was a pretty funny movie (with Will Ferrell) about two cops determined to become the cool guys at the police station.

On this rainy day, we told Wilson that we were going to sleep outside. He was very happy about this and was impatient to go outside. I slept on the left side of the deck, and I've decided that right now it's the best spot to sleep outside because (1) I get to be next to Wilson, and (2) I don't hear Dad and Tay snore. Mom and I don't snore, but Dad and Tay definitely do.

Thursday, March 26, 2020

When I woke up, I looked through the window and I saw Dad pouring some coffee. But Dad was also right next to me, asleep. There was a second of me questioning my whole reality before I realized that it was Taylor next to me. All I could see was the back of the head, and he was in Dad's spot. They must have switched places. How confusing, though, for that one second. When I woke up, I saw Mom just before she went to work, and she was going to work for thirteen hours, so I was glad I got to say good morning.

I listened to some eighties music today. I got through phases of entirely different music. I think this is a good thing, because listening to the same type of music for years could get old. Every time that I have a new music genre, I think that it's the best genre ever. Right now, music of the eighties is the greatest music ever.

Then I played *Madden* on the Xbox. After I played *Madden*, I helped take the mattresses and blankets from the deck downstairs because the weather is going to be windy and rainy soon.

Jason, one of our neighbors, told Dad today that he made a fort with Silas and Luke, his kids. He said that it was very well hidden and established. We went up on the trails to try and find it. We were unsuccessful.

I think Dad mostly went on the main trail because of his knee and helping it rehab. Also, Wilson really loves going on walks. When we were looking, I went off-trail a lot because if it's hidden well, it probably isn't visible from the trail.

Friday, March 27, 2020

I woke up really early today, even for my standards. I woke up at 4:55, bright eyed and bushy tailed. I went downstairs and Dad and Wilson were already awake. Wilson, Dad, and I made sure not to wake up Mom or Tay.

Tay slept in, so we did a good job at being quiet. Mom woke up over an hour after Tay. When she woke up, we all went into her room and said good morning. Dad poured some coffee for Mom. Wilson kind of looked queasy earlier, and Dad saw him throw up. We aren't sure why he threw up, but he was fine for the rest of the day.

A little after Mom got up, she thought that we should go on a drive to the Chuckanut Mountains, part of the Cascades. The Chuckanuts are a beautiful, quiet side of Bellingham. On the drive over there are small waterfalls on one side of the road and the Salish Sea on the other side. We took the drive out and back. We talked about whatever came up in conversation, processing what was going on with COVID, ideas on what the pandemic could be like and what we would do in the event of the hypothetical. Past the Chuckanuts, there was farmland. This transition from mountain to flat land is beautiful. We took Wilson out of the car to go pee, and we almost got lost but then found our way home.

Also on the drive, Mom and Dad went to Starbucks and each got some coffee. To our surprise, the order was already paid for. People were giving money to Starbucks so that first responders could get free orders, in appreciation for COVID response. Mom being a nurse and Dad being a firefighter, the whole thing was free. Things like this give me faith in humanity. One day I want to pay for someone else's coffee order; if I did, it would make my day.

When we got home, Dad made pizza dough and we had pizza night. The pizza was very good. The recipe required dough for two pizzas, so I think that we'll have pizza again soon.

Saturday, March 28, 2020

Today, unlike yesterday, I woke up later than usual. Today I woke up at 7:08 a.m. So, I went downstairs and said good morning to Mom and Dad. Tay, I think, was still asleep and Mom was just waking up. I usually wake up from 5:45 to 6:40.

Tay and I decided that we should do spring cleaning, because we had nothing to do. We did so much, I swear we have half of the stuff in our rooms to what we had yesterday. We also rearranged our rooms. In Taylor's room, he put a bookshelf in his closet and moved his dresser to a different wall.

Tay's room looks like we are about to move out. There is nothing on the dressers or on the side-of-the-bed table. I took a lot of stuff out of my room too, no doubt, but most of it was the stuff that I had inside my table and in my dresser and above it. I moved my dresser to an angle and Dad moved my bed all the way to the side wall. Before, there was a small gap between the bed and the window. With the bed against the wall, I feel like I have more space in my room.

Then we went on the trail and looped around and went on a few of the Galbraith trails. There wasn't anyone there. We also kept looking for Jason's fort that he made with his kids, Silas and Lucas.

We still couldn't find it, and we even asked for a clue (via text), but he said that his kids wanted to show us themselves. When we came back from the trail, I did chores to earn extra screen time. Then after dinner I went outside in the hot tub with Mom and Dad while Taylor did the dishes and wrote stuff down in his journaling Word document. I love my family.

Sunday, March 29, 2020

Today started with me laughing. I don't even understand why I was laughing. But I was. I woke up, and it was kind of early, and then I fell back asleep and woke up. I don't know if I was delirious or what. I think it was a great way to start off a day.

I went downstairs and once again only Dad and Wilson and I were awake. Mom and Tay were still asleep. At nine Mom went to the store to get some stuff. She went to Whole Foods, which is right across the street from Fred Meyer, the store that we also frequently get our food from. When she got back, Mom said that there weren't many people there. I was surprised by that. She said that there weren't any sesame seeds, what Dad and I wanted to make hamburger buns and bagels. I guess we'll have to try to get it later.

Later Tay pulled out a board game for us to play, Risk. It is a fun game that I don't think we have played for a few months. I personally really like Risk because it takes some thinking and I happen to always win. Every time. We didn't finish a game today. It looks promising for me to win again because I have more land overtaken than Tay and Dad.

Monday, March 30, 2020
Today was another chill day. There wasn't really any rain besides a little bit in the middle of the day, but not like marble-sized droplets or anything like that. When I woke up, I was confused when I turned to my left and saw my dresser not where I thought it was. I thought it might have been a dream, but it was just the result of spring cleaning.

I went downstairs at six thirty. I am absolutely not confident about it, though, because the memory is foggy. I don't know if I am thinking about yesterday or not, but it was definitely somewhere around six to seven o'clock. Then I did some screen time and went up. I then worked on some schoolwork that is on my school computer. It is optional work, but I do it anyway. Mom and Dad are also strongly saying that we need to do the schoolwork because we aren't going to go to school for a while and it is important to keep our brains active.

In the US the numbers have gone above all others. The US was the first country to surpass 100,000 cases. It's now at 159,184, and the death number is 2,945. Italy, which was in front for some time, has 101,739 cases and has a lot more deaths than anyone else, at 11,591. Spain is third and has 85,195 cases and 7,340 deaths.

At the very beginning of COVID, when people started dying, I wondered if I knew anyone who had died. As time went on, with the numbers so big, I didn't think about it anymore. The deaths were a lot more magnified in the beginning. Now it feels like there is a numbness to the deaths; with the numbers so big, it's difficult to think of that many people dying.

Tuesday, March 31, 2020
Tay and I played H-O-R-S-E today, but we changed it a little. Instead of using the letters h-o-r-s-e we changed it to w-i-l-l-y, in honor of Wilson. Wilson watched us from his electric fence line, and he appreciated us changing it. It started to rain, so we went in early.

Wilson is named after a few things. The first being the volleyball in *Cast Away*, though Wilson doesn't have a handprint on him. He is also named after Russell Wilson, the Seahawks player. If Wilson ever leaves the Seahawks, the ball is a good backup plan, because you can't trade away a volleyball.

We used to have a neighbor who also had a dog named Wilson, and on Sundays during football season she would put a Russell Wilson Seahawks jersey on her dog. Wilson would never let us do that to him. He isn't trying to be a human. He's a dog and is proud of it.

We started another game of Risk, and Mom is playing this time. We explained the rules to her. I'm less confident that I am going to win this time, the reason being that Taylor stole my strategy and messed up my momentum.

Then we started a movie, and Mom is going to make pasta with a great red sauce recipe which is always delicious. Last night I made garden burgers (vegetarian patties) and put vegetables in the oven and cooked them. I also made a sauce that's just mayo and mustard mixed together. It's weird because I don't like either mustard or mayo separately but together it's great. We also made guacamole today. Mom says that it's called avocado spread, but truly it's just guacamole, but Mom wanted to give it a fancy name.

Wednesday, April 1, 2020

So, I'll write about this in a few paragraphs, but I broke my arm today. I'm going to be okay, but I'll write about how it happened.

Every year it snows a couple of times in December, but January and February are better snow months. When it snows everyone goes sledding on the best hill. Until today, I had never seen snow in April. Soon after we woke up, it started to rain, but then it turned to snow. I was hoping it would continue and stick onto the ground and maybe we would go sledding. I didn't have such luck, because it didn't stay once it hit the ground, and the snow stopped just as quickly as it began.

Mom was working at Hospice House, and Wilson, Dad, and I gave her a smoothie and had lunch with her on her break. When we got back, we saw the snow. In town there wasn't snow, but we live on Galbraith Mountain, so at our house there was snow even though there wasn't any snow in sight at Hospice House.

We took Wilson on a walk on the trails, and we went on a new trail this time. Technically Dad had already gone, but we had never explored it. A tiny bit of the snow had not melted, because the trails were even higher up than our house. It's sunny and exciting to explore. When we got to the end of the trail, there was a tractor. Inside: Two beer cans and a fire extinguisher. There was also a pile of burned wood. We don't know if the wood was burned on purpose or not. I wonder if they used the fire extinguisher on the wood. I guess it will forever be a mystery.

After we got back, we finished Risk. I was the last one standing. This was our second game; the first one I lost. Tay wants to play a new game, so we will probably play Monopoly soon.

Taylor and I spent the afternoon taking and editing photos. We used an app called Snapseed. A few days ago, I watched a video on tricks you can use Snapseed for, and we implemented them. The main photo we did was combining a few different photos together, making it look like there were clones of us peeking out of the doors in the hallway.

I actually didn't break my arm. That was a joke. Happy April Fool's Day!

Thursday, April 2, 2020

We slept outside again; I was on the end (to avoid the snoring). On my way back inside, I said good morning to Wilson, and he stayed outside with Tay and Mom, who were still asleep. Mom woke up last. Tay looked up the health benefits of sleeping outside and showed them to Mom. Hopefully this convinces Mom to sleep outside more. Wilson would be thankful.

Then we went on a family hike back to the tractor. This time, Tay and I found rocks that looked like good skipping rocks, and we planned on bringing a few home to skip on the pond. Then Tay found a pretty long puddle, deep enough for us to skip in, and to my surprise it worked. I tried next, and we alternated, sometimes trying to find the same rocks. By the end we got the rocks to go super far. We went past it, and you could see very far from so far up. We even saw mountains in Canada. There was also a tractor that was labeled Bobcat.

We finished our second game of Risk. I won, but I think that Taylor is ready to play a new game, so we might play Monopoly in the next few days.

After we were done hiking, we took pictures together, and that was fun. We did the same thing where we use a photo editing app that makes it look like there is more than one of us in the photo. The first one that we did today was in a hallway, and Taylor was peeking out of the doors, and Tay did some in the photo like in cartoons where multiple people peek out with their heads over one another.

Friday, April 3, 2020

This morning I woke up and went downstairs and hugged Wilson, Dad, and Mom. Tay was still asleep when I woke up and he came down later. Wilson has this thing on the top part of his nose that is a pinkish color. We don't know if it's a scratch. Later Dad called the vet to get him an appointment, to find out what it is. They said it just changes color, pink or black, because of the sun. Wilson doesn't seem to mind if we touch his nose, however.

Taylor and I played *Madden NFL* on the Xbox today. He was the Rams and I was the Vikings. I won 37–29. Tay and I usually do different things for screen time, but it's fun to play with him (winning helps, also).

Maybe I was motivated to win more. After the *Madden* game I started a game of family Monopoly. We didn't finish it yet, but I quickly became broke. The rules we have for Monopoly are a little different, because when we were young the rules were made less complex. After we played the real way, we were both used to the simpler way and liked the other rules better. So, most of the time we play, we play it the simple way. At one point, I had thirty-five dollars. Now I am not homeless, which is good. Tay got so many houses we had to go find green Legos because there were no more houses for Taylor to use.

I guess that Jason ended up just texting Dad where the fort was. We went on the trail with Dad, and he gave us a clue to the general direction of where the fort was. Tay found it first, and it was really far off the trail, a lot farther than I had guessed when we were looking for it before. It was on a hill. There was a blue tarp over the top of vertical sticks. We added sticks to the side, because it wasn't completely done yet. They had a bow, and some other things around, so we left behind two squirt guns for them. Hopefully, they like them. Being that far from the trail made me really feel how much woods are behind our house, because we can only see so much from the trails.

Saturday, April 4, 2020

We went on a long walk on the trail, the whole family. Taylor and I were trying to find rocks that we thought were cool to skip. So, if you have never skipped a rock, the best skipping rocks are ones that have a comfortable curve to go along your finger, are thin, and have a maximum width of your pointer finger. The rock also has to be not easy to break. So, we were collecting the rocks and also skipping the rocks in puddles that were misty with mud. We actually skipped the rocks pretty far. The puddles were small enough that we could only skip it once. So, we went back to the Bobcat tractor, and the view was great. We could see a lot of the city and the country area, and also some mountains of Canada. We then went down the fire road. The fire road is if someone is hurt or there is a fire, then they can have the firefighters and paramedics get to where they need to be. We went far and ended up accidently going to a place where we realized that we had been on our bikes with some of our neighbors.

When we were done with our walk, we finished the game. I wasn't enthusiastic to start playing again, because I was basically broke. But I didn't get out, and eventually Taylor started to lose money, and eventually he got out of the game because of a series of bad luck.

Sunday, April 5, 2020
When I woke up, I was in the blankets outside. I saw Wilson, and I pet him and he licked my hand. That night I had a runny nose and had to blow my nose multiple times. After that Dad and I just decided that we should go inside because we both were not going to go back to bed. Spring allergies must be in full effect. Taylor doesn't get any spring allergies, but Mom, Dad, and I all do. At least I am glad that I don't have spring allergies that are bad, because I know some people get it really bad.

Later Tay and I made a small video, pretending to be a radio show, in the middle of a segment called Knucklehead of the Year. We got the inspiration from listening to a radio show when going to school, where they would review and vote for a Knucklehead of the Week. Tay acted it out, and I was the narrator and held the phone. The person who ended up winning Knucklehead of the Year was a man that thought that he had super powers but failed miserably when trying to show that he had powers.

Monday, April 6, 2020
Mom was on the phone for a little bit, and then she came to tell us the news. States, including Washington, had planned to close school for six weeks and then come back. But the other day, California changed it so that schools wouldn't go back to finish the school year. The news was that Washington's schools would be doing the same thing, and we would finish the year online. Part of me thought that this would eventually happen if things didn't magically get better. I am excited that we get an extra long summer. I'm glad that I am not in high school for this COVID shutdown, because that would be really difficult, considering that it counts for college. I wonder if I can use this extended summer break to my advantage. I plan on enjoying it.

This will be fun because there won't be any meaningful schoolwork for six months! I do feel bad for high schoolers because schoolwork may just get more stressful when not going back to school.

Wednesday, April 8, 2020
We slept outside again today. Wilson slept in between Tay and me. Dad went inside in the morning, and I took his spot in the middle of the night. I

was still tired, so I went back to sleep. I pet Wilson's ears, he moved towards Mom's spot, and I fell back asleep.

I don't really dream often, and if I do, I don't really remember much. Today, after I went back to sleep, I had a bizarre dream. I was at the Super Bowl; I must have been on a field trip, because there were kids from school who were also there. They said that anyone with respiratory problems would have to leave. I must have been thinking about coronavirus, because that is the only plausible explanation. The whole time that we were in the stadium, I never saw the field or the score. Then I woke up. Mom and Dad were drinking coffee at the table. When I went inside, I asked them to not tell me the score of the Super Bowl, and to not say if the Chiefs or Forty-Niners had won. They looked at me weirdly, and I went to get a drink of water. Then I remembered that the Super Bowl was over two months ago.

Then, I woke up again. I was in the same spot as before. I looked out the window and Mom and Dad were in the same spot I had dreamt of them being, and they were drinking coffee. I must have woken up from a dream, in my dream. I've never had a dream inside of a dream before. Weird.

Later, Tay and I played hide-and-seek. We had created some good new spots. The deck was still set up from sleeping out there earlier. I went under the covers, and Taylor thought that could be one of the spots where I would hide, so he jumped onto the covers I was under, but he didn't notice that I was there, so he left, and I maintained my hiding spot.

Near the deck, there is a wheelbarrow that Dad must have left one day, upside down. I didn't think that I would be able to fit inside it, so I never really checked under it. Tay found a way to hide. He stayed there for forty minutes. Neither of us found the other person.

Thursday, April 9, 2020
When I was falling asleep, I imagined a time traveler going back a couple of years and talking about 2020. I bet if that dude said anything about the year, it would be something like this:

"So, yeah, 2020 was a weird year. The president of the United States was a guy from a TV show. The borders of Australia caught fire, leaving a lot of people surrounded on a flaming hot island. Then Kobe dies in a helicopter crash. The world is devastated. Then there is a deadly virus in China. It spreads out of China, despite efforts to contain it. Now the world is really devastated. It spreads so much it's called a global pandemic by the World Health Organization. Quickly after that, a lot more people learn what pandemic means, after quick Google searches. Schools shut down for the rest of the year, so COVID doesn't spread as quickly. There are then barely any TV channels, sports, or talk shows. Their last resort is to play reruns in order to not shut down themselves."

I guess I'll have a lot of stories to tell future kids, and grandkids. I hope this doesn't mean that I'm going to be one of those grandparents that starts every story with, "Back in my day . . ." My poor future grandkids, they're going to have to deal with the grandpa version of Cody. I apologize in advance.

Friday, April 10, 2020
After waking up, we went on a hike with Wilson, on the trails. Today we decided to explore again, and we went on a trail we had never gone to before. After going up the normal connector trail, we went on the trail directly opposite of where we usually go. It was a little overgrown in some parts, and then we found some frisbees, or discs, on the ground. We went even farther, and it connected to a trail behind a house in our neighborhood. We figured out that the trail went to their house when we heard the German Shepherd, who we wouldn't assume was a nice dog, from the bark. We turned around, because we didn't feel like staying around for any longer than we had to.

As we speed walked, we passed the disc again. It had small holes in it, actually the size of bullets. Mom figured it out first. The discs weren't frisbees, they were targets. We walked a little faster. After getting back to the trail fork, we went the other way.

We don't know the people that live in the house. We don't know how many people live there, but they have old trucks, don't wave, and are secretive. They live in the very corner of the neighborhood, and no one else knows who they are to any extent.

I do think there are one or two people up there who are nice. Wilson is the ultimate judge on who is trustworthy or not, and if Wilson doesn't get up to the edge of his fence to bark, they are at least okay. Wilson does bark at them. Sometimes they go by on a horse.

After exploring to the left, we went farther away from the trail. We found a network of creeks, and to cross there were a few bridges. Then we found a great carving of a bear from a stump. The bear was big, it had a bike chain as a necklace, and it held up a sign. The sign said, "Fricker."

Every Easter, when we were little, Mom and Dad would hide Easter eggs in the yard, and for the sake of tradition, we have continued it. Tay and I have made it into a competition, and this time there were fourteen eggs, three being big eggs. Gammy and Paw-Paw had sent the eggs in their basket, and each had a little bit of money and sometimes candy in it. I found all three of the big eggs, but we made a rule before we started playing that you could only take two of the big eggs, maximum, to keep it a little fair.

I didn't know that one of the big eggs was a big egg, so I kept it and kept going. Tay got mad at me for not leaving it. Unfortunately, my brain was in find-all-eggs-you-see mode, and it was a little immature of him to get mad.

He eventually calmed down, and later we roasted marshmallows and went in the hot tub. Mom wanted me to roast a few for her, so I did, and tried to make them the best possible.

Saturday, April 11, 2020
We had not slept inside for a couple of days, so I was surprised when I woke up and I was inside. I remembered that I had something due soon, and I finished that quickly. I just had to do a little writing on what I had last read that week, and to make a goal on reading for the next week. We already read an hour a day, so it wasn't difficult to make a goal and to go through with it.

The last book that I read, just finished a day or two ago, was *Born a Crime* by Trevor Noah. This book is one of my favorites that I have read in the past year. Trevor Noah was really good at telling stories in his book. I laughed and learned while reading it.

We played basketball later in the day. I didn't think that we were going to be able to, because it was raining pretty hard at the beginning of the day, but it cleared up, and the water on the concrete was gone. By the time we played, there wasn't a cloud in the sky.

In the middle of playing, my knee buckled and continued to feel frail, so I only played 50 percent from there on out because I didn't want to hurt my knee anymore. If I didn't hurt it anymore, it would probably be better in the morning. Dad and Tay continued and played W-I-L-S-O-N.

Rich came outside to let Roxy go to the bathroom. Roxy is a nice dog, the same type of dog as Rufus, who was Rich's old dog that died a few years back. He said Ashaan and Corrina, his grandkids, would be coming over tomorrow. We would have usually been excited; however, with COVID, it didn't make sense to play with them.

Ashaan is one year older than I am, and Corrina is a year younger than Taylor. They live fifteen minutes away and used to come over every couple of days. As they got older, they must have had other things to do. Last summer they probably came over only twice, and I can tell Rich misses them coming over often. I don't blame him. When they stopped coming over, he became a little different when talking about them. It was a look I recognize in older adults, when they were nostalgic of the times when they were young and things were different.

Sunday, April 12, 2020

Dad said that he woke up early today to make his bread. He wanted to make a loaf for Hospice House and needed to finish it early if he wanted Mom to bring it there. It came out really good, and he thinks the bread was softer and the crust was better. He cut a big H in the middle of the loaf, for Hospice. I thought it looked like a helicopter landing pad. Later we found out that Hospice House couldn't receive homemade food, but that they enjoyed that loaf that Dad made.

Dad and I are going to make homemade bagels for the first time in the next few days. I think they will turn out good. We are going to eventually put sesame seeds on it, so that we have different types of bagels.

I got some grades back on assignments, and I got a better grade than I hoped for. I don't think that it will eventually matter, because with school being closed so long, I have a feeling that grades will be canceled. I woke up five minutes after Mom left, but later I called her to say good morning. She told me that she'd come home earlier than she originally thought.

COVID numbers are still growing everywhere. In the US, New York has one third of the country's cases. It's not too surprising, considering it's such a big place, and in those busy streets, I'm not surprised the virus would spread a lot.

In Washington, COVID numbers are not as bad as before. Washington used to have the most cases of any state, but now it's thirteenth. Not much has changed, and grocery stores, and any other places, really, require masks to go inside. There are people who overreact about wearing a mask, but for the time being, it's not that bad. I don't like wearing a mask, but to stay safe, it's a small price to pay.

We watched a movie before Mom came home from work. The movie was a comedy about a group of kids that made a fake college. I laughed pretty hard when watching it.

However, we paused in the middle of the movie to do a Zoom with Dad's side of the family from New Orleans. Mom got home while we were Zooming, and she joined in the Zoom. So, we finished the movie with her. Then we got ready to sleep outside, but I couldn't fall asleep, so I just went inside and slept. I didn't get a good night's sleep either way, and I only slept a little.

Monday, April 13, 2020

I barely slept at all last night; I was quite tired in the morning. I started by sleeping outside, but I just came in after a while in search of a better sleep. I also woke up early, because I wondered what the point was of trying to sleep if I hadn't gotten a good sleep, and I probably wasn't even going to fall asleep. Mom went inside too, in the middle of the night; she woke up first after me. Dad woke and got Wilson to follow. Tay spent a little while more outside before waking up.

Later Mom and Dad and Tay and Wilson decided to get some exercise outside. I stayed at home because (1) I had already exercised, (2) I was really tired, (3) I didn't feel like going on a walk, and (4) because I wanted to play basketball later when they came back. So, I listened to sports analysis on the radio. There weren't any real sports on, obviously because of the coronavirus. However, the sports radio people still found things to talk about.

Dad ordered a bike a few days ago. He has wanted a road bike for a while and hasn't had one in a while. He went to Bellevue to get it and came back. While Dad was getting the bike, Tay and I played tag and basketball.

When we slept outside next, Taylor fell asleep in mid-conversation, which took us a few minutes to figure out why Tay was so quiet. Two dogs were barking for a while, before we fell asleep. We don't know whose dogs they were. Also, before I fell asleep, I realized that a light that was coming from another neighbor's house, on a timer. The light turned off at ten o'clock precisely. It took me a while to figure this out, and frequently the light would shine directly into my eyes as I tried to fall asleep, and then turn off seemingly randomly (until I figured out the timer). The triumph that comes from my new discovery is mixed with some sort of disappointment for not figuring it out earlier.

Thursday, April 16, 2020

I woke up slowly today, at around six thirty. I was tired even though I had just woken up, and I didn't feel the need to jump out of bed because . . . there wasn't any school. I mean, there won't be any school tomorrow, and there wasn't any yesterday, but today is one of those days when you wake up and you say, I have no need to get out of bed because I don't feel like it. I also know that there is a Dr. Seuss book on not getting out of bed. It's very inspiring. Well, I decided that I was going to just try to fall back asleep or stay there looking at the wall, until at 7:20 I decided to wake up.

Later we made rock formations and used instant glue to get them together quickly so they will stick and won't fall over. Tay made one that

215

built up, and then he glued a longer one on the top, so it looked like a *T* For Taylor. I wanted to make a rock cave, but it didn't turn out how I thought it was going to, so maybe I will make a basic rock stack later. But for now, the rock stack will do.

Friday, April 17, 2020
The following day we went to a familiar, rocky beach that we went to often when we lived in Fairhaven. Earlier Mom got a coffee at Starbucks, which was free. I hope none of us will take the free coffee for granted or become greedy. I think it would be highly unlikely, but that doesn't change my hope that we don't forget why we are getting the gift. I'll make sure I don't. We went down the road, crossed the train tracks, and got to the beach. Mom and Dad would take us here, and we would have a picnic, or maybe just throw rocks into the water. I don't ever remember swimming at this beach. Tay and I skipped rocks. Tay's pretty good at skipping rocks, and he even got seven once. At this rock-strewn beach, there were many skipping rocks to find.

In these times, I think that I need to remember all the things in the world, because the most basic things are the things that are so easily forgotten. For this, I have to say: The sky was blue and the clouds were gray; the water was blue and the rocks were gray.

Sunday, April 19, 2020
After waking, I picked up Wilson poop. We decided that we should pick up poop before we do screen time because it makes us remember it a little better. Well, I picked up Wilson's poop. I decided to put on my own shoes, but I didn't tie them because I knew it would only be a minute. I couldn't find any Wilson poops, and I was walking down, and then I looked at my shoe. I almost stepped in Wilson's morning poop. If you have a dog, you would be very familiar with the poop I am talking about because you are the one picking it up. After a big sigh of relief, I picked up the poop because I didn't want any poop on my shoe. This is why I should pick up poop in Dad's boots more often, because if I get poop on them, I will probably have to clean it off, but at least it isn't my shoe. I later realized that my shoes were covered in grass because of the mix of condensation and freshly mowed grass.

Taylor and I will alternate picking up poop, so I do it on odd days, and on even days Taylor will. This might be difficult on months that end on a thirty-first day, because I'll do it two days in a row. I won't worry about it. It only takes five minutes anyway.

Monday, April 20, 2020

Today I woke up with Wilson lying next to me. I got up and checked my schoolwork. Today was the first Monday since the news that we wouldn't be going back to school. I was confused why we were getting more schoolwork than usual, but then it hit me. The reason that we were getting more schoolwork, is that the district couldn't plan on teaching only a little; they couldn't fall back on going back to school.

The school changed their way of giving us schoolwork with a new app. We hadn't been taught this, so I would have to find schoolwork, and it was a maze to just get to it. The tabs they gave us had weird names, like SCI-P1S2/CLA28087/20, and I had to figure out the abbreviations. I don't think many of the teachers know how to use it either, so until we all figure it out, which may be a while, it's a mess.

The school assignments that were previously named "Optional" are now called "Expected," but still not "Required" assignments.

Wednesday, April 22, 2020

Today we did not do anything. This is something that I will not be doing a lot, but it happens every once in a while. I woke up and got out of bed. We didn't sleep outside today either, so I hope that we do in the next few days.

Well, Tay and I worked for a lot of screen time, and it was also raining, so it made it hard to go outside. We didn't play basketball; I guess I could have, but that would not be too fun. Wilson was inside a lot, and he was just taking naps. We didn't get to exercise that much today either, so maybe I will do a little bit extra tomorrow.

One more thing that is happening tomorrow is the NFL draft. I think I have talked about it once or twice, writing about it, but it's happening tomorrow. I watched last year's draft. Taylor did not. This year is going to be a weird draft for everyone because it probably won't work out as smoothly, because there are going to be all different types of ways that it's going to be different than any other. I also have my prediction of who will go.

In the US, COVID cases are plateauing. Each day is averaging 30,000 cases. However, with the deaths in the US they are increasing, and the average is about 2,000 per day. In Washington, the deaths today were 24, and the cases were almost 400. I guess it's good that the COVID cases aren't going up as much as they were before. The worldwide cases are 81,000, and the US is accounting for more than two thirds.

Thursday, April 23, 2020

Before the NFL Draft had happened, I made a list of who I thought would get drafted and in what order. My guesses were rarely correct, but it was still fun. I thought that the Seahawks were going to get a defensive lineman, but they got a linebacker who I didn't predict to go in the first round, and I didn't really know anyway. They already have KJ Wright and Bobby Wagner at linebacker, but I'll trust that Jordan Brooks will be good.

The NFL draft was online this year, the first time that they didn't have the people together for a draft before. The coach and staff for each team would be on their own video meetings, using Zoom. They had to submit their picks online too, and I read an article the other day that they did a test of how it worked, and there were technical difficulties on the first pick, but it was okay for the real draft.

Tomorrow is Taylor's last day of him being eleven years old. Then he turns twelve. I didn't know what I should get him for his birthday, because we don't really want much, or need anything. In the end, I decided I would give him a stuffed animal duck. I think he'll like it. He's talked about ducks a few times in the last few months.

I remember when I turned twelve years old, but a lot of birthdays are the same and they sort of blend together. My memory just has one big mashed-up birthday that has some people in some and others in other memories. One birthday that I remember is when my friends and I went in the hot tub in the dark and two neighbor dogs (Mushu and Farley) came over and said hi to us. We said hi to them, and they left and came back again. We have a picture of us with Mushu on the step that gets you to the hot tub. Photos are nice, because they can trigger your memory to remember something you hadn't previously.

Friday, April 24, 2020

Today is Taylor's last day of him being eleven years old. Tomorrow, he turns twelve. I got him something that I think he will like. I remember when I turned twelve years old; well actually, I don't.

Day two of the draft continued, and Taylor's birthday is tomorrow. He's extra excited about having his birthday, because I think celebration in a rising global pandemic would be nice for everyone.

The Seahawks got an edge rusher and an offensive lineman with the second and third draft pick.

Saturday, April 25, 2020

Today, April 25, is Taylor's birthday. Tay got a few things for his birthday; I think he was most excited with my gift. On top of it being Taylor's birthday, it was the last day of the NFL draft. I mostly paid attention to Taylor today, but I checked on the draft every once in a while.

I woke up outside. Wilson clearly wanted to go inside, so I petted his fur for a little and then I let him inside. Dad was inside but Mom and Tay were still outside, so I closed the door slowly and got on the ground and kept petting Wilson and got a sock or two and said good morning to Dad. I got a piece of bread to eat, and I pet Wilson one last time. Then a little bit later, Tay came in and we said happy birthday to him, but quietly, because Mom was still asleep. Mom (again) stayed out there the longest, but we let Wilson go to Mom as she started to wake up.

Later I showed Tay the duck. I put it with a little card and put it in a blue bag. I think he liked it a lot, and personally, I think it's his favorite gift. Taylor got a gift from Mom and Dad; it was a three-in-one tennis/pickleball/badminton set. I am very excited to play badminton with him. As I said, I think he liked the duck better than this, because he may have gotten overwhelmed by how big the set is, even though it's a great thing that we will use all the time. I think for the short-term he will like the duck, but in the long term he will like the net.

Then later we FaceTimed our grandparents Gammy and Paw-Paw. They got to say happy birthday to Tay. It's probably weird to have a COVID birthday, but I guess it's possible that I will have my own COVID birthday, in October, but probability is against it. My half birthday was the other day, on the twenty-first. It was such a busy day that I barely thought about it. Taylor and I are almost exactly eighteen months apart and are frequently mistaken as twins.

Another thing that Mom did for Tay is she got all of his friends to send a short happy birthday message. Mom put it all together in one video and then showed Tay. He appreciated it, I think.

Later that day we FaceTimed some friends for a few minutes. It was good to talk to other people again, because it's been a while.

On Taylor's and my birthdays, ever since we moved into this house, Dad measures us on the wall right outside the door that leads to the garage. Because our birthdays are almost exactly six months from each other, and eighteen months apart, we also include our half birthdays. Taylor is a little over five feet tall, and I am almost five foot two.

Sunday, April 26, 2020

I woke up at around 4:40 in the night. At first, I wasn't tired enough to fall back asleep, but I looked out my window for a little bit and eventually fell asleep. Afterwards I woke up around 5:30 and I couldn't fall asleep, so I looked out my window and eventually fell asleep. This happened a few more times until I woke up for good at 7:20. I went downstairs to write, and I said good morning to the family as they woke up, one by one.

We played another game of Monopoly. It had been considerably rainy, as it usually is in Pacific Northwest springtime. We started to play again a few days ago, but we never finished it. I got all of the railroads, which helped a lot. I lost around three thousand dollars in ten minutes, but I still won.

Later Mom and Tay and I went to drop off bread that Dad made for Gavin and Carter. When I was at their door, I knocked, but they didn't answer. I tried calling them, but it went to voicemail. But then I decided to text them that I was there. They came up, and I gave them the bread.

Monday, April 27, 2020

I started off the day by waking up, and then I went downstairs. I said hello to Wilson. Wilson was very excited when I came down. He was half asleep, and then as I came down and he must have woken up. He was lying next to the couch, and then he was wagging his tail. The tail was hitting the couch. Thump, thump, thump.

Later we decided to go to the beach, Marine Park. Because it was going to be windy, we brought sweatshirts. Before we got there, we went to Mom's work because she had to do something there and it only took a minute. At that minute, it started to really rain. Instead of the previous sprinkle, the rain completely blurred the windshield. We could still drive to the beach, but it was decided we wouldn't because it was rainy. We decided to just go and get something that we would have needed to get after. Dad had to get a new filter for the hot tub.

The rain had slowed by the time we were done with getting the filter, so we did go to Marine Park after all. When we got back to Marine Park, it stopped raining, so we got out and skipped rocks. We found some weird junk there. There was a black beanie, and I also found a golf ball just lying around when Tay and I wandered off.

Tuesday, April 28, 2020

Today we played more basketball. We played King of the Court. We changed the rules so you have to dribble at least twice before you shoot. We did this because we would just keep getting the ball passed to us and then shoot it before the other guy got there, and then it became an annoying pattern that took no exercise or competitive feel to it, making one guy feel powerful and the other guy feel helpless.

We also played Follow the Leader for a little while. It was senseless, but that made it much funnier. I think it started because when I stopped playing basketball, Tay followed me around, and then we decided to just play Follow the Leader.

Tonight, we watched *Forrest Gump*. It was the first time I had seen it. It was a great movie; I think it's one of my favorite Tom Hanks movies that I have watched.

Thursday, April 30, 2020

For dessert we had homemade ice cream. When Gammy and Paw-Paw had the lake place, they found a homemade ice cream maker at the store, and we made homemade ice cream with them. We always made vanilla ice cream, because that's the only flavor Tay really likes, but sometimes he likes sherbet ice cream. They gave the ice cream maker to us when they sold the lake place.

The recipes for each flavor are somewhat different, and once again we made vanilla ice cream. It was really good, and I put chocolate sauce on it. It tasted more like frozen yogurt than ice cream because it was softer than ice cream usually is.

We put it in a medium-sized bowl that fits into this machine that turns it. There are only four ingredients. The first is milk, then sugar, and also vanilla extract and heavy cream. The bowl in the ice cream maker spins around for about a half hour. The noise is really loud, so we thought about putting it into a different room. This was only the second time that we had made it since school ended.

We had forgotten about the ice cream maker, and it was just in a box, placed in the corner of a random room. It was forgotten, sitting there not knowing what to do with itself. Perhaps there are some people who don't know what to do right now, only riding the waves of the pandemic.

Friday, May 1, 2020

Today Tay and I created a new game. It was a nice day and it had been raining for quite some time now. The game was a variation of Capture the Flag, adapted for our yard and for only two people playing.

The first rule is that there is no tagging or sides. We each hid a basketball somewhere and then we would make our way to the garage. We would wait there until the other person got there, and then we would go our separate ways until we found the other person's ball. Then you would have to go back with the ball and get the other ball. Then you would have to go to the garage again with both your ball and the other person's ball, and then you would win. Also, you could hide your ball anywhere later in the game, unless the person is really close to the ball or is in sight of the ball. The last rule of the game is there is no following the other person or puppy guarding your ball. It would take the fun out of the game and quickly become annoying.

The game didn't really get off the ground, because we both hid our balls really well. Tay hid his under a piece of bark in the ground. And his was especially hard to find because it was a brown color that blends in with the wood. I hid mine in the barbeque. One other rule was that it had to be visible from one point of view. Tay's had a point of view horizontally, but it didn't really stand out because of its color. For me, there were little holes in the BBQ that you could definitely see orange, the color of my ball. The game still needs some rules to be changed, but I think we will play this more later.

Saturday, May 2, 2020
Today, I woke up outside. It was the second day in a row that we slept outside. I woke up and Mom was gone. She must have gone back to her room because we got the new mattress. The new mattress we got on Amazon yesterday. It was in a really skinny box that was way taller than its base.

Later we went on the trail for a long hike, and right when we started, we saw some neighbor friends and talked with them for around twenty minutes. They were talking about how he had to sign up for school because one of their kids was going into middle school, sixth grade. I was thinking about how it would be super difficult to be going to a new school after the COVID thing.

Then just five minutes after saying goodbye to them, we saw other neighbors, who had a new puppy. It has been a while since Wilson was a puppy, so it was nice to pet the puppy. I forgot how spunky they are.

After that, we walked for a while and saw some new bike jumps they are building, and they are huge. The size of the average jump must have been fifteen or twenty feet. I wonder how quickly it will be until someone gets hurt jumping on it. I won't be jumping that ever, by the way. On our way back, we saw some other neighbors and said hi to them, and Wilson played with the other dog, and Wilson was nice. It was such a social trail walk. Usually we don't see that many people on the trail; sometimes we don't see anyone. Later we watched a movie and made homemade ice cream.

I read on the news recently that one in seven Americans wouldn't go seek help if they were experiencing the basic symptoms of COVID: a fever or dry cough. I'm not very surprised, but it's unfortunate that many people wouldn't worry about it, considering that it's deadly and that other people can get it easily.

Sunday, May 3, 2020

When Wilson hears anyone say trail, he starts getting super excited. So, sometimes Wilson is going to go on the trail with us and we tell him. We ask him, "Wilson, do you want to go on the trail?" Well, after playing some Monopoly we decided to go on a bike ride. So, we asked Wilson, "Wilson, do you want to go on the trail?" and of course, he did.

We decided that we were going to go on different trails. Mom and I were going to ride our bikes around the trail on Lake Padden, which is only a ten-minute drive away. Taylor and Dad decided that they would just go on the trails on Galbraith. Wilson went with Tay and Dad; Mom and I put our bikes on bike racks at the back of her car.

When we got there, I helped Mom unload the bikes from the car. We looked around to see how crowded it was. Compared to before the pandemic, it would be relatively quiet, but maybe a little more people than usual during COVID. COVID numbers have gradually stopped increasing at the speed they were, and some days the numbers are going down. I am hopeful that the pandemic will end by August.

The trail around Lake Padden is two and a half miles. When on our bikes there were a few times where we weaved around people. Sometimes it was difficult to do because there would be four people all in a row, so that they blocked the whole trail. Another time someone was in the middle of the road but had ear plugs, so they couldn't hear us. We were riding and got a lot of mud sprayed on our back. It definitely rained recently. There was also a ton on our calves, and I got many brown dots on my face. We went around the lake twice. Mom got a coffee after, at Starbucks. When we got home, Tay and Dad were already home. Wilson was panting and obviously enjoyed going on the trail.

Monday, May 4, 2020

I woke up in the morning and went downstairs to say good morning to Mom and Tay. Because I woke up so early, I did my writing before screen time. After doing my writing, I went into the kitchen and fed Wilson. I feed Wilson most days now; it has just become a routine.

Wilson's bowls are at the end of the kitchen, where the smaller table is. Wilson's bowls are close to the garage, where there is a dog food bin, a small garbage bin that has a foot lever to open it, which sometimes breaks, and we manually open it. Wilson gets two cups per meal, and he has two meals a day. We keep a measuring cup in the bin, to measure.

Something funny about Wilson is he always knows when it's time to eat. Wilson eats at seven in the morning and five in the afternoon.

When it's seven, Wilson is usually still inside, everyone is still waking up, and he'll start to softly whine. He almost always will whine at 7:00 precisely, not 7:01. Then Wilson is usually outside at five, and he barks once at the door. Wilson will be looking at the doorknob, waiting for it to turn.

I did schoolwork later in the day, though it wasn't that much. Most schoolwork is done on Tuesday. The assignments I did do were a social studies page that I did and returned, a page or two for language arts that I'll complete tomorrow, and the (despised) book tracker. The disgust for the book tracker is because you can't just get it done in one day. You have to go back to it and then remember to turn it in. I prefer to finish my assignments in the same sitting I start it in. But then, it isn't the end of the world.

Tuesday, May 5, 2020

Today I went downstairs and Wilson was wagging his tail as usual. I hugged Mom and petted Wilson. Tay was still asleep, but he came down just a little later. I did my writing right when Tay came down. Tay started to talk about how he should do his writing before me.

Taylor and I both do our writing on the Apple computer. The family computer is the only one that we have. I guess that we could hand write the journal, but it's easy and fast to write on Microsoft Word.

Taylor said it was his idea to start writing in the morning, and I usually wake up before him and am not finished with my journaling by the time he wakes up. This probably bothers him now, because to stay on top of writing, a rule was established to do writing before screen time. I don't really mind. I'll let Tay find a solution to the dilemma.

Later I tried out Mom's bike. My bike is getting too small for me, and Mom said that I could use hers if Dad allows Mom to get a new bike, which she probably would want. Tay also wants the bike and protested why he couldn't use it. Mom said that because I am taller and Taylor still sort of fits his bike, I get first dibs.

Next, Tay and I pulled weeds in the backyard for screen time. I pulled weeds for forty minutes, and Tay pulled for an hour. Taylor found a salamander that was in the ground, covered with dirt but still alive.

Mom decided that it would be cool to make some Alfredo sauce with pasta, so she found a recipe online and made it. We also used the sauce as a dip for Dad's homemade bread.

Thursday, May 7, 2020

Later in the day, I did a Zoom meeting with my language arts class. It was optional, but I just decided to do it. I saw a few of my friends on it, but it didn't include much stuff that actually connected to school. So, I sat there for a little. It lasted one hour, and after that I decided to go outside where Mom and Wilson were sitting. Wilson was tired when I saw him. He wanted to go to sleep, so I went to the back yard to Mom, who was downstairs on the chaise trying to get sun on her back.

I decided that I would enjoy such a nice day and listen to music. I went on the hammock, and it was nice because instead of a plastic hammock that folds in on you or something like that, it's a rope hammock, it's fun to rock back and forth. However, I make sure not to fall over, and in case I do fall, I make sure there isn't any leftover Wilson poop under it. I think it was originally our Gammy and Paw-Paw's, though I don't know for sure. I went inside quickly to get my headphones and put music on from my phone.

This afternoon Mom's friends came over. A little bit before her friends came over, Taylor and I lit a fire in the bonfire in the backyard for Mom. Dad had already set up the fire, and all Tay and I did was light it. Because of COVID guidelines, when Mom's friends came over, they were six feet apart at the bonfire, and always outside.

We decided to sleep inside tonight, and outside tomorrow. Now that it's getting hotter—it was in the high seventies today—we will sleep outside more often. It will get so hot inside, sometimes that is the only bearable option.

It gets really hot on the top story of our house, where both Tay's and my bedrooms are. So, we sometimes sleep on the bottom floor. The bottom floor is colder than our bedrooms in the summer, when it gets hot. If we did sleep downstairs to escape the heat, Wilson would still have to sleep upstairs. When we got Wilson, Mom and Dad thought that we would keep him on the main floor because I was allergic to dogs, though I'm pretty sure I am not anymore. Besides, when we got Wilson, we trained him to only stay on the main floor. This was mostly to avoid massive amounts of dog hair on the carpet.

Friday, May 8, 2020

With the weather getting better recently, in the middle of the day we went on a bike ride on Galbraith. Mom decided that she shouldn't come because her back has hurt recently, so it was Wilson, Tay, Dad and me. I used Mom's bike; with full suspension on it, riding downhill was much more gracious.

It was fun going downhill, but at one point a bug got in my nose. I reached for my nose while racing downhill and lost my balance. I then got off my bike, while it was still rolling. I lost my balance and fell. I was okay, and once I figured that, I blew out my nose, shooting the bug out. Stupid bug.

Saturday, May 9, 2020

Today we went to Bret's house, one of Dad's friends, to say happy birthday to him. He's a lawyer who Dad frequently flyfishes with. Tay played some football passes with one of Bret's kids, Quen, who's a few years older than we are.

After that, Tay and I played basketball on one of their hoops. We borrowed one of the basketballs and played. Tay started off quick and got an early lead. I was determined to stop him, and I tied it at 10–10. Then we got a designated three-point line, it went back and forth for a while, until it was 19–15. After a couple of rebounds, I shot a three and won.

Later, right before we left, Bret gave us a bunch of paint and a piece of driftwood. Mother's Day is tomorrow and he thought that was a good gift for Mom. Taylor painted a rock, which had varying colors in rings going around the rock. The rock was a nice, circular rock, and if it was smaller, it would have made a good skipping rock. The driftwood, which was about the length from my elbow to the tip of my fingers, was very smooth, and I painted "MOM" on it, with a flower next to it. I could have done better if I had redone it or made a plan for it, but I think Mom will like it nonetheless.

Sunday, May 10, 2020

Today I slept in the basement. Dad decided that there were too many bugs for us to sleep outside. We were going to sleep inside, but we couldn't sleep upstairs because it's too hot. So, Taylor and I slept downstairs. I think that in the middle of the night Tay started reading, in the dark. I ended up waking up at five thirty, and Taylor told me what time it was. For Mother's Day, Tay had this idea of putting a sheet out of Mom's bedroom door and having some confetti on the floor. Tay decided to wake up at around six fifteen to get ready. I was going to go up in a little bit to help him with it, but I accidently fell asleep.

When I went upstairs after waking up, the clock read 1:24; I guess it was broken. I went upstairs and saw Tay's red carpet and it looked cool. There was a sign that said Happy Mother's Day. Dad was on his phone, and I said good morning to him and asked about Mom and the carpet. Then I went to get Mom's food order, and she said she didn't need anything. Tay decided to not let Wilson in for the beginning, because he thought that Wilson would eat the confetti. At the end of the red carpet there were all kinds of candy and Taylor's painted rock and my painted wood. She said that she loved it. I was just impressed with Taylor setting it all up. I felt bad that I slept in, but I think Tay enjoyed being the sole owner of the idea, creativity, and production of it, which makes sense.

Then we went on the trail. The loop that we did was the same as we did on our bikes the other day. Sometimes I thought it was too slow, so I would run ahead with Wilson, who is always very insistent to be in the front. He must want to be the leader, or maybe he also thought that everyone walks too slow for him and his four legs. We also made sure today to wish both grandmas a happy Mother's Day and thank them.

Tuesday, May 12, 2020
Schoolwork Tuesday, once again. *Sigh.* I guess I need to remember that this is just one day of the week, and it's a lot less schoolwork than we would usually get. Summer will get here soon enough.

I do social studies on Monday, and I usually just look at language arts and then end up doing it Tuesday. Language arts homework is probably my least favorite. Don't get me wrong. I love reading and writing, but the structure is just painful.

Today I received assignments and announcements from math, science, and physical education. So, I first looked at PE and it's a daily checklist, so I usually just wait every few days and then fill it out with my best memory. Then I did math, which is easy enough. Then I can go to science, which is kind of like math in the sense that it's a lot of assignments to do but is easy to complete. After that I took a break and then went back to language arts, where technology wasn't my friend, and I had to redo it once or twice.

Also, later I played basketball with myself. I didn't do it for very long. It wasn't as fun as playing with someone, so I stopped and went inside. Later Taylor and I played football catch, which was more fun than basketball. Though, at some point playing with just Taylor, every day, is going to be painfully routine, and the games that we played earlier, and created, will cease to exist. Then we will be bored and shoot hoops by ourselves.

Thankfully, I don't think that will happen soon, so I'll enjoy it now, which is probably the best anyone can do right now. If the past is what is envied, maybe when this time has left, where the rush of regular life is gone, people will envy it.

Thursday, May 14, 2020
Today I woke up inside and then went downstairs. I said good morning to Wilson and, as usual, he wagged his tail and grabbed his toy otter, eager to show me, like it was the first time I had ever seen such a thing. I said good morning to Tay and Mom. Dad was coming home from work and would be back around ten. Mom went to work at seven, so I only got to see her for less than an hour.

I did my writing and Tay did his, but I don't know if he did his earlier than I did. I would hope so, considering he wasted a lot of my time talking about why he should do his writing before me. Tay and I were home alone. I didn't want to play *Madden* that much anymore, so I tried to play a different game, but after I came to the home screen it froze. So, I just went upstairs, and Tay was watching the new *Dude Perfect* documentary, so I just decided to watch that with him. Some things about being famous were really eye opening, and I didn't know how much time and stress they put into their career. I never thought being famous was something to be sought out, and the documentary just added to my theory.

After watching the documentary, I looked at the clock, and it was twelve fifteen, so the mailman may have already come. I have been waiting for my hoodie for a while now, and it was going to come today. So, I asked Dad if I could ride to the mailbox to get the mail.

I got my backpack, and it's been a while since I had worn it, last time being school. I grabbed Dad's keys so that I could unlock the mail, and I grabbed my helmet and my bike. I decided to grab my small bike to ride, because I didn't want to ride into any issues with a different bike. Halfway to the mailbox, I decided to change gears, and my chain fell off. I don't remember a time when this happened before. I laughed that I thought I would have more trouble with Mom's bike. I tried to put it back together, unsuccessfully, until I remembered the thing used to loosen the chain. Then I got it back together. I was hesitant to change gears after that.

Also today, Tay, Dad, and I all went outside to play a new type of football game that didn't make it as competitive as usual. Taylor frequently complains about it being too competitive. The new way was still competitive, but I guess it decreased the intensity enough to satisfy Taylor. We would have four downs to complete a pass that was farther than the house, and

Dad was the quarterback the whole time. Obviously, we caught the ball too much to count, but we could count interceptions. I got two interceptions and a few really close, almost interceptions. Tay got more, however.

When we wished Gammy a happy Mother's Day, she told Taylor and me about five-year plans, what they are, why they are important, and gave us an assignment: to write a five-year plan, how we envision the next few years playing out, how we will approach it, and everything else in between. The official assignment was sent as an email to me: "*Cody, looking forward to this fun dialogue on what you would like your life to be in five years. To start things off, I have five questions. Just respond with whatever flies into your mind. This isn't meant to be an English/essay exercise. It's just me getting to know you better.*"

Taylor and I each wrote our five-year plan and emailed her the link to the Word document. I thoroughly enjoyed doing this assignment. I do wonder how the pandemic will change my plan, but anyway, here is my plan:

> *Part of a future is creating it. A future is always ahead. A future is in a minute, an hour, one day, a week, a year. Part of creating a future is engraving it in, making it more likely, and it is in the back of your mind when making everyday decisions and making them on par with what will give you the likeliness of achieving your goal. We don't even know our future, but we can guess and plan accordingly.*
>
> *There are many aspects to one's goal in life. It can be as small as scoring a soccer goal in a big game, and it can be as big as where you will live and where you will get an education, if you decide to get one. The previous sentence shows that the big goals and the small goals will make an impact. Small goals can make a big impact sometimes, and vice versa. Big and small goals are divided by what we believe will make a large or minimal impact. Just deciding to take a middle school class can drastically change your career. Where you go to college most likely will change your future, but not always as big as we think. Small goals most likely will make a small impact, and big goals will mostly make a big impact, but to quote Marshawn Lynch, "Expect the unexpected."*
>
> *But for now, let's just see where I am aiming in five critical areas. So, I am going to cover where I picture and want myself to be in five years, with five aspects. The five aspects include what I want my relationship with my family to be, what kinds of people I want to be in my close circle of friends, what I want my academic standings*

to reflect, what I want my outside activities to be and what they will say about me, and finally what I am planning to do when high school finishes.

When I am almost done with high school is where I will be in five years, at age seventeen and a half. I want my relationship with my family to be good. I want to be able to have my own ideas, but with my personality, I don't want to wreak havoc with topics disagreed on. That means that I can assume that I won't have experienced a big fight or disagreement with my family. Of course, anything can change, so I am hoping and planning for the future that I want, not knowing what will and will not happen. If I stated that I knew exactly where I will be and what I will be thinking, then that would be foolish.

The second magnified aspect is what type of people I want to be in my inner friend group. Well, that is a question that I can't answer in great depth because I won't know a lot about who I will meet. Some things that I do want to see in people in my close group of friends are that I want to look up to these people, I want them to at least think about what they are planning to do, and I want them to have goals in the same categories as my own. I don't need to agree on everything with my friends, but I want them to make good choices to reflect on their goals that they are eager to achieve.

Another question is what I want my academic standing to reflect. Well, I want my academics to show that I work hard to achieve the goals that I have set for myself. I want them to reflect that not everything comes easily and that one value to me is you can always do something better or more challenging. I also want my academics to reflect on my personality. I want my standings to show people that I am not just one other but that I am my own person and that I am ready to do something that will have significance in the world.

The fourth aspect is what I want my outside activities to be and what they will say about me. I want at least one of my outside activities to be something that is an active sport or activity like a trail running club. Another activity that I want is something that shows that I am willing to help my community. I don't know what that could be and what type of impact that it would make.

The final aspect is maybe the most important one of them all: what am I planning to do after high school. Well, that is a question that I have thought about but still am not sure about the smaller things. I see myself going to college, Stanford. I know that it won't be any walk in the park to be prepared to apply to go to Stanford, but

I see myself getting through it and celebrating it, but not for long, because I will realize that that is definitely not where it ends. I will study for a job that I have great interest in. Right now, the job that I see myself pursuing is to be a surgeon. That could change, but writing it down is a big step in the right direction because there are so many great jobs. Engineering would be another choice, along with other jobs that I can't think about off the top of my head.

Part of realizing what you are going to do is what you picture yourself achieving. You can picture yourself doing all types of things, but you can't do that without making it bigger. An idea, or something that is in your mind or something that you want to do, is a great start, but a big leap is putting pen to paper. On one podcast that my mom recently was listening to, she shared with me one part that was talking about how goals can be one-dimensional, two-dimensional, and three-dimensional. My brain made a visual of it, one-dimensional being just an idea; two-dimensional being writing it down, putting pen to paper; and three-dimensional being the idea actually happening, so this is that last step that I can do until I reach my goal.

Friday, May 15, 2020

I went downstairs after waking up, to go say good morning to everyone. No one was awake. Wilson woke up after a minute of me walking around. I don't think that enough has been said about Wilson, being a dog. When jotting down my daily life, Wilson can become lost. This must be because he is consistent, though that doesn't mean he is predictable.

Wilson is a very peaceful dog, and he believes overreacting a disastrous trait, so he considers everything to be relative to the bigger picture. I don't know what Wilson's main goal in life would be, but if I were to guess, it's to observe. His expectations of everyone and everything were shaped by himself. He trust's his judgment and sticks to his beliefs. He also has a string of values, which form his expectations.

The first value is that expectations are set based on observing. He has different expectations for Dad, Mom, Tay, and me. He also knows that we have different expectations for him. So, he will approach us differently, based on independent research.

He listens to Dad better than anyone. Dad gave Wilson his expectations and trained him. Because expectations were shown to him by Dad, Wilson shows his utmost respect to Dad, and will forever and always listen.

231

If Wilson wants to explore, he'll seek out me. Exploring the yard with Wilson is very compelling. He always sees the things that I don't; his ears lift up sharply when he hears something. Usually I can't find it, and I never figure out what it is. Wilson treats his observing as a mission, along with protecting his yard. I hope he can figure out it's just a hobby, but he understands the world's bigger picture way better than I do, so I trust his judgment, maybe more than anyone else's.

Taylor is Wilson's tug-of-war buddy, his fetch buddy, his play-with-toy-otter buddy. I play with Wilson too, but maybe Wilson believes that everyone has a role and Taylor's needs to be playing. Wilson enjoys playing but gets tired quickly. It's with Taylor where I remember Wilson when he was a puppy, and the young mentality that isn't seen as much nowadays.

Wilson admires Mom the most and misses her greatly if she is gone for a while. He follows her the most. He adores being with her, maybe more than anyone else.

Wilson's second value would be friendship. He approaches people based on his split-second judgment, equally so regarding previous interactions. If Wilson doesn't trust someone, he'll bark at them. If he trusts them, when they go by, he'll either walk up, expecting them to pet him, or he'll stay put, just observing. If it's a stranger, he'll bark. If they come over to pet him, he will become the passive dog that he is and eliminate any hostility towards them.

Wilson is more of a human person than a dog person, unfortunately. Maybe it's because his fellow dogs don't have values, like him. Not all two-leggeds do either, but it must be a safer bet; it's possible he can relate to them more. It's too bad that Wilson can't have philosophical conversations, or any real conversation at all, with humans. They would be extremely impressed. I understand him only because of all the time I spend with him.

Wilson has expressed that I should do the same as him, to observe the world around me, because now time has stopped, and I have time to kill. By the time the pandemic ends, I want to be more like Wilson.

So, my goal is to observe the world around me, and in a greater depth than I ever have.

Saturday, May 16, 2020

At ten Tay and I left to go to Donnett's, because we were going to do yard work for her. We walked on the road through the neighborhood, passing half a dozen homes, and went up the driveway that led to the back part of her yard. There was a huge stack of wood next to the pond, which was overridden with tall grass. If I hadn't known previously that there was a pond, I could have walked past never knowing.

Our job was to put the wood in the back of her pickup truck, and after loading a bunch of wood, Tay and I went to her, telling her that we were done, though she told us we could still fit more in the back. We went back, now enlightened. After that, we tried our very best to get as much wood as possible into the truck. We didn't want to appear as slackers.

After loading the wood, Tay and I rode in the back of the truck while Donnett drove to the front of the house. All of the wood that we had just put in the bed of the truck, we put back into a little shelter. This wood would be used as firewood for their fireplace. Something was compelling about taking wood out of the truck, forgetting all of the work that was just put in, to get the wood there.

After we finished unloading the bed of the truck and stacking the wood, Donnett gave us a drive back home, to avoid the weather. The rain started to pour down by the time that we finished.

Tay and I worked for screen time. Taylor dusted and swept and mopped. I pulled weeds in the backyard. I was thinking, if I was already dirty from doing work earlier, then why don't I just continue to do work. After pulling weeds, though, I took a shower.

Sunday, May 17, 2020
Today we had a chill morning, and overall it was a really fun day. A little past eleven we decided to go to the turf football field at Sehome High School. A little while ago, they closed down almost everything, a lot more than previously, but Sehome was still open. With students not going to school, we could go anytime we wanted.

There were a few more people there than usual, maybe because their original place where they went running, playing soccer, or anything else closed under heavier restrictions. But we didn't need a lot of space, and there were about three other families there. This time there was a new sign that read "No Dogs." We hadn't expected this, but after improvising, Mom stretched and did her workout off the field with Wilson. Wilson would have been fine on the field. Sometimes I wonder if Wilson is frustrated by the lack of decency of other dogs, and that their previous actions are what restrict him.

When we played football, both Tay and I made some good plays. The way that we play football, Dad is always quarterback, one of us is a defender, and the other is a wide receiver. If we get a touchdown, we kick the ball over to the other person and go from there. We originally created this way of playing football with Ashaan. He rarely comes over, so we play with Dad instead.

The first play that I made was an interception on the play, and then Tay got an interception on the next drive. We don't keep score with how many touchdowns we get, but there seems to be an unspoken score of who seems to have done better. Momentum is our score. There is no way to measure this, but Tay and I both figured out who won by the end of the game. Interceptions are the biggest momentum mover, so those are usually the biggest plays that we want to make.

Monday, May 18, 2020

Phil Sharpe, who is in his seventies, was a property lawyer before he retired a few years ago. He lives past our house, where a long gravel road leads to his house. The house has the best view I have seen in Bellingham, taking in Mt. Baker, Lake Whatcom, and a mountain range on the other side of the Canadian border. His dog, Finn, was a big, happy black Lab. Tay and I would go up the driveway and play with him, and we would frequently see him looking towards us, right behind his electric fence line.

Today we helped Phil see where his electric fence is, because the flags that were there are lost. The only way to know would be to hear when the collar beeps, and Phil isn't able to hear the beep. A little bit ago, Phil decided that he was ready to get a new dog. He is going to get a yellow Lab that is one year old, and his name is Banks. I think that is a really cool name.

There is a picture that we find every once in a while, of when we had just moved and Finn was sitting down with Taylor, who was only two years old at the time. Finn had wandered over; this was before he got his electric fence. Finn got his electric fence after he and another neighbor dog, Gordon, wandered too far. They had gone over Galbraith Mountain and were found on the other side. They were far, far away from home. Finn never wandered that far, and it was probably because he was with Gordon, who wandered frequently.

Our neighborhood used to have a bunch of dogs that would wander around the neighborhood's two streets. Everyone knew and loved these dogs, and they were all very similar, though I don't think they were ever all together. There aren't many dogs now that were like these dogs, and there may never be another. Many of the dogs aren't in the neighborhood anymore, but I still remember the pack.

Mushu was some variation of a Chihuahua, and he seemed to live forever. He was one of my favorite dogs. He lived a long life and became

234

very fragile. He had a signature snaggle, a single tooth that rested over his bottom lip, I don't know why he had it. He was battered by a big dog, once, and lost his snaggle. This was less than a year before he was put down.

Farley is a black Lab. He followed Mushu everywhere. Farley was trusting and respectful of his companion, who was smaller and slower. I haven't seen him recently.

Gordon was a bloodhound. I didn't know him well. He wasn't always the nicest dog, but I do remember that he was a dog who led his life on his own account and would travel miles on the idea that he wanted to wander aimlessly, like he did with Finn.

Paw-Paw was a medium sized dog. He lived in the middle of the neighborhood. I don't have many memories of him, but I do remember seeing him walk on the side of the road a lot, never in the middle. Smart call.

Rae was younger than most of the dogs. She's a yellow Lab who was hyper when she was young. Now that she's older, she doesn't wander. Now she's more content with staying in one place.

Most of all, Finn was interested in playing fetch. Or finding a stick and then playing fetch. He lived a life that was focused on having fun, and it was a good motto. When we would have friends over, we would go visit Finn, and they loved him too. From what I have learned over all of Phil's stories, he was always outside, and it seemed like that too.

The long gravel road, where he usually was, is bordered by trees and trenches. On one side of this road there's a cliff with stone steps that goes to a small spot where you could look out far, seeing a few houses, including ours. There was a fire pit and some chairs, used for s'mores and camping. However, I don't think it has been visited in some time.

Another house near us has a mini pack of dogs. They have had two or three dogs throughout twenty years or so, and they have golden retrievers. They would wander around and explore the pond in the backyard. One of the girls had puppies on the Fourth of July years ago, so they named the dogs with Fourth-of-July-like names.

Stella lived almost right across the street from us. She was a golden labradoodle who was really intent on checking in on everyone, to see if there was anything that would interest her. She was chill, like most of the dogs in the pack. Stella used to always walk over to the mini pack across the street from us. Scott, her owner, would usually come over to ask where she went.

Rich had a dog named Rufus; he was tranquil and low maintenance and really enjoyed the presence of humans. Rufus and Rich went on a lot of small walks before he got sick. I saw him a lot; Rich was gloomy when Rufus died, which was difficult to see.

Arf was also part of this pack, but I don't have any memory of him. I know of him because of stories. He was a dog that was the size of a Lab and had shaggy, black hair. Unfortunately, because I don't remember him, I don't know much about him, but everyone knew he was a good boy.

This pack of dogs never really got a name, because they never all met, but they were all similar to one another.

Wilson didn't get to meet the majority of these dogs. To his disappointment, many of the dogs passed away or moved before he could meet them. Many of the dogs in the neighborhood now do not explore. Wilson's electric fence is in the best interest for him. Some neighbors have fences, others also have electric fences, like Wilson. The pack was a time that slowly dissipated. I really loved that time.

COVID cases have started to go down, very slowly, but this might end soon. I hope it does. Some states are trying to reopen, peeling back on restrictions. Those states, though, quickly get a spike in COVID cases, which isn't encouraging.

In the meantime, COVID safety is mostly the same. We wear masks everywhere we go. The only time we are out and don't wear masks is when we are out in the yard or taking Wilson for a walk. Or if we are just getting out of the car to get the mail. Anywhere else, we wear a mask.

Even if there isn't anyone in sight we put on a mask, because just because there isn't anyone there, it doesn't mean that the virus isn't in the air. A sneeze without a mask can travel twenty feet, even when small droplets of water come out of our mouth. Masks help catch most of these droplets.

We also keep social distance at all times. Social distancing is just as difficult as masks. We haven't seen any friends since the last Friday at school, in March. Soon it will be June. It's unbelievable. Even though we don't get along all the time, I am very lucky to have Taylor always around.

In the United States, and in other places, a lot of people are losing their jobs. With many businesses struggling after closing, they have to fire people to stay alive financially. The unemployment rate is at the worst since the Great Depression.

Wednesday, May 20, 2020

This afternoon we watched a part of a documentary about the Chicago Bulls and Michael Jordan. Also, Mom and I went on a small walk down the street. Mom's back has been hurting for a little while now, and she thought that going on a walk would help. I went along because with the weather getting better, going outside is exciting. I'm looking forward to summer. Soon school will be out. During our walk, we saw a few neighbors and talked for a while, but we kept our distance.

Tonight I listened to the paces of my music. It was blended in the fading daylight, with the rhythms guiding, where light, which was less and less elsewhere, more than before in the center, through the music. It was beautiful.

Thursday, May 21, 2020
Today Mom and I went near the Chuckanuts and went biking. I was glad to get out of the house because it becomes crowded when we spend every day together, all day. Nothing is better than going on a bike ride. We went for almost an hour. It was almost all flat, which made it even more enjoyable. I hadn't eaten in a while, and I'm glad we brought snacks, because I needed a break in the middle, because the lack of food was depleting my energy. The snacks were new to me, but I learned to like it. I would have eaten anything at that point. Tay and Dad also got out of the house; they went to the track. Tay wanted to start running again. His goal was to get a new personal best, and while he didn't do that, he still was very fast.

I slept well this night, even though we didn't sleep outside. I think sometimes it's important to sleep inside more than outside, just to understand that sleeping outside is a treat, not necessary.

Friday, May 22, 2020
When I went downstairs, I was expecting Dad to be at work, and I was surprised when I saw him on the couch. I also petted Wilson, and at the same time, I saw Mom come out of her room. The light was already on, so she and Dad must have both been awake earlier than usual, which is cool, because when I wake up early there is rarely anyone there, so Wilson and I are left in the barely light living room, and I try to turn on minimal lights so that the brightness doesn't wake anyone up.

Mom wanted to have the house to herself, to clean the house, and Tay and I were motivated to play some football, so we hopped into Dad's car and made our way to Sehome. On our way to the field, we saw a sign that said, "Happy Graduation! 2020," which kind of scared us, because it was possible that they were using the football field. I wonder what it would be like to graduate now. I probably wouldn't like it. It would be so different, and in the future when the students look back, their graduation photos will be different from what they would've been. To our relief, nothing was happening on the field, so we played as usual.

Saturday, May 23, 2020

At ten Tay and I walked down the neighborhood to Donnett's house. On the way, we pet Jason's dogs, which followed us along their electric fence. She gave us our instructions, and we worked for two hours. We got wood from a big pile and stacked that wood into a stack closer to her house, which she uses for her fireplace. Our fireplace is gas and doesn't use firewood. Our wood stack in the backyard is little compared to all the wood she has. We only use the wood for the firepit, to roast s'mores.

We ended up getting forty dollars, because we did work last week and let her keep the money so that she could guarantee us working later and sooner.

Banks, the new dog that Phil got yesterday, got loose from his electric fence, but they got him quickly after. From afar, it's hard to see if it's Wilson or Banks because the only things separating them is that Wilson has longer fur, a different face, and a different colored collar. I think even if Wilson was next to someone identical to him, I would still pick him out as my dog, but both he and Banks are very similar looking.

When we left school for the last time, I didn't think that there would be any possibility I wouldn't come back that year. Some people probably needed a break from their daily routine, but personally, I was in a rhythm, and I'm still sort of thrown off course from the repetitive day. Any new routines could be temporary, so even when every day seems the same day to day, I'm anticipating change. Because when we come out of this, if I learned anything, it's that the unexpected is as likely as what you expect.

Sunday, May 24, 2020

Dad took Wilson on the trail again today. Sometimes I forget that Dad has a bad knee, because most of the time I can't tell the difference. I think he is fully functioning now that time has gone by.

When Wilson was a puppy, we learned that it isn't smart to run dogs a lot their first year. If its forced, they could become stiff later. Wilson, I don't think, will ever have problems that could be blamed for the first year, which he did run some bit. Like everything else, it was on his own account. I don't worry about Wilson being stiff later, because he did it on his own. He does have an obsession with being in front when going on a walk.

Monday, May 25, 2020

It was my turn to pick up Wilson's droppings. Most days that I pick up Wilson's poop, I always find a flaw, most likely exaggerated in my head, that I can use to criticize Taylor's job the day before. I never confront Tay on these, though it keeps my brain occupied, and keeps my head off my undesirable task.

Today, when I went outside, likely in someone else's shoes, I don't remember, I was scanning the ground for a while, and when I lifted my sight upward, I saw Leaf. Not a leaf, though I decided to name him Leaf, but a deer.

He wasn't far away, and I assume he saw me before I saw him. I got closer and he didn't pay much mind to me. I said something in his direction, just to see what would happen, but still he didn't mind me, and I was close enough now that I would expect any animal to be gone. I noticed his right ear was split into thirds. I wondered if it was from a branch that it caught on, and ripped it, or maybe something attacked him. Then I said goodbye and I went along, picking up. I found one dropping, and then when I came around to the front door, I saw that he was still in the same spot. I decided that I was going to name him Leaf then, because of the fact that he was eating leaves, and his ear that is split into what looks like three leaves.

I showed Dad and Tay Leaf. I took my time, because I knew he wouldn't leave so abruptly. When we went back inside, I saw him walking around the backyard with two other deer. He seemed to be the leader, but maybe it was only an imagination.

What did a squirrel ever do to anyone? We have had bird feeders in the past, as have many people, but when someone does have a bird feeder, they are constantly trying to invent a way to stop squirrels from getting in and taking the food. Taylor and I talked about this, and what manifested from this topic being brought up is we created a squirrel feeder exclusively for squirrels, not for birds.

We made the squirrel feeder with a shoe box and an empty Amazon box, and tomorrow we are going to put food into it. We'll put our phones in the box to catch them on camera. Part of the idea to do this was inspired by a YouTube video that we watched, where one guy made a ninja warrior course for the squirrels in his backyard.

***

Tuesday, May 26, 2020

I was the first one to wake up outside, and I quickly did my two days of writing because I forgot the day before. I quickly did this before Tay got up because I felt like avoiding his wrath.

Today Mom had an appointment close to Seattle. I proposed that I go with her. I hadn't thought of it before, but it felt like a good idea. Maybe because nothing changes anymore, or because I was sick of being with Tay all the time, or something in between. The drive there wasn't that bad; usually it's uncomfortable being in the car for a long time.

Mom got the idea on the drive there that we should get some Krispy Kreme doughnuts on the way back, as a treat. Krispy Kreme doughnuts are better than anything we have in Bellingham. Because it's so far away, we rarely get them. But then again, we barely get any doughnuts in general. I told Mom when we get them, we need to get one for Tay.

We eventually got to the appointment. I got out and stretched my legs, but I stayed in the car when Mom went in for the appointment. We didn't want to increase the odds that we would get COVID, because we've been lucky that we haven't yet, and I can't think of a reason I would go in, pandemic or no pandemic.

Mom's appointment wasn't that long, and when she got out, we were both hungry, so we got tacos across the street. The doughnuts were also close to the taco place, but we forgot to get them. The tacos were filling enough.

Wednesday, May 27, 2020

When I woke up, I felt motivated, and I started to quickly do the chores that I needed to do in the day, like reading. I had to read one hour a day, and I went upstairs and did all sixty minutes in one sitting. The rest were awake when I came down. I barely knew they were awake, and usually I hear them come outside.

Then I got ready to go to my appointment with the orthodontist. I had forgotten that we had an appointment. I brushed my teeth and took a shower. I don't really know if I am the only one who brushes really well right before seeing the dentist or orthodontist, because if there was something wrong with my teeth, I don't think one brush, as good as it is, will hide it or fix it, for that matter. Tay and I got the football and football gloves, because we were planning on playing football after the appointment.

Usually, Dad or Mom would come inside the orthodontist office, but they were just there for pickup and drop off. With COVID, they changed it so that just the kid goes into the office. I got out of Dad's car and put on my N-95 mask and went inside. I had to wait for about fifteen minutes until the person came and took my temperature with a thing that pointed to my forehead and showed the number almost immediately. I wonder why I hadn't seen these that often, prior to COVID. Well, my temperature was fine, which was good, I don't know exactly what would have happened if I had a fever.

I got my retainer and it fit great, and then I went out the door in less than one minute. So, fifteen minutes waiting for one minute of productivity, a little counterintuitive. They should've just thrown the retainer at me from outside. They could have asked me if there was anything wrong, which was unlikely anyway.

After I was done with that, I hopped in the car and Tay, Dad, and I all headed to Sehome. Taylor got frustrated with some of the plays that were called against him, but I thought afterward that I *morally* won the battle, because that is really what we are playing for, and neither of us got any interceptions while we were there. Sometimes we need to hush Taylor when we are playing, because he gets loud quickly, and that'd be embarrassing if people were in earshot.

Thursday, May 28, 2020

Today I set up the box for the squirrels and played basketball, and I was having fun. I only needed to do the smallest amount of homework, and then I got to relax the rest of the day. On some of these days that I have most of the day to do anything, I don't do much, and then I think that I may have wasted the day, and I think about how dumb I was to waste these precious days on the days that I have a ton of homework. Other days, though, I think I did too much on days with all the time in the world, and I wonder if I really enjoyed the day being open to relaxing. I'll find a happy medium sometime, but not yet.

Today, Mom set up the net that Taylor got for his birthday, which we haven't really used more than once so far. I played tennis with Mom, and Tay may have also. I don't know for sure, but I think Tay doesn't like the net much. It's not that he resents it or anything, but he's not as enthusiastic as I would've guessed. I'd predict that Mom likes it the best, which is totally okay. I think that it will be exciting to pull it out every summer.

Friday, May 29, 2020

I woke up with Wilson barking at some loud truck. I think Wilson was louder than the truck. I think he was louder than the garbage truck. I vaguely remember being woken up because of this, because a minute later I was back asleep. I woke up again a half hour later.

The garbage truck comes early in the morning every Friday, though if I was asked what day is garbage day for us, I would say Thursday, because that's the day that we put out the garbage, and every other week the recycling, also. The recycling truck comes later than the garbage truck. Taylor and I are in charge of getting the garbage and recycling out, and the method we use to evenly split it changes often.

We also have water bottle day, which at one point was once a week, the same week. But the water company changed owners, and the days that the water guy came was randomly dispersed to different days of the week. Mom and Dad were more annoyed than anything, because they would forget that it was water day, but eventually Mom decided to just put it on the calendar. Sometimes we are reminded that not even that is foolproof.

Saturday, May 30, 2020

Today Dad came home from the fire station, and right after that Dad got an alert on his phone that there was going to be a thunderstorm. So, we got the mattresses from outside right after, because we didn't want them to get soaking wet.

In the afternoon, Dad made bagels with different flavors to put on top. My favorite type of bagel is either sesame seed bagel or everything bagel, but only when I am up for that much flavor, which isn't always.

It rained the whole day. I need to figure out my method of exercising while doing it inside, which is difficult. Rainy days aren't that bad, but when it rains for days in a row, that's just brutal. Today I watched a movie, and I recently read the book it was based on (*Divergent* by Veronica Roth). A long time ago, Dad and Mom decided that to motivate us to read more, if we read a book, we could watch a movie from the book, in addition to our screen time. I never really needed more motivation to read, but Dad told me the rule was more to influence Tay, who didn't read much when he was younger, as much as Mom and Dad had influenced him to.

Sunday, May 31, 2020

Tomorrow we will be halfway through the year. I feel like it was just yesterday that I was on winter break and sledding with neighbors and friends from school. Waiting for school to start again, to see everyone, it all went by too fast.

It reminds me that in another six months it will be January 2021. One year later it will be 2022, then 2023, then fast forward a few years and I am graduating from high school and then college. It just shows that time will fly by if you take your eye off it for a millisecond.

I woke up and then went downstairs after looking at the clock. It was already half past seven, later than I usually sleep. I went downstairs and said good morning to Mom, Wilson, and Taylor. Then I picked up poop. I got three. Sometimes when I only get one or two, I'm worried I missed some, so I guess the more the better.

Dad had to go to work, and it seemed a little stressful with all the protests that have turned violent. On the news we saw videos from Seattle that showed shops with the windows broken off. There were shirts with hangers still on them thrown out onto the street, for no reason, not for the person to take. I talked to Dad on the phone at the end of the day. He said he only had gone on false alarms, no riot attacks, which was lucky. He did say yesterday that he would have to wear bulletproof vests if he went on those calls.

In the middle of the day, Mom and I went to get the mail. There wasn't anything there, which was a little disappointing, but we also had Mom drop some stuff off to a neighbor, Donnett.

Sue (our neighbor) came over when we were back from getting the mail and after Mom dropped off something to Donnett. Sue came over with Avi, her granddaughter. Avi loves playing with Wilson, and Wilson likes seeing them. Wilson used to bark at Sue when she would walk by, but once she started to pet him when she walked by, Wilson quickly stopped barking.

I think this may be the best age to be inside a pandemic. Though no time is a good time, this may be the best worst. It'd be rough to be an adult during this time, because I don't know how many things would change at the same time that life is going so fast.

Being little, like a toddler, would be okay, but I worry about your view of normal if you are young. Everyone older would know that normal means you don't have to wear a mask or stay six feet from people all the time. That'd be awful, to grow up after the pandemic, with that standard of living.

Monday, June 1, 2020

Today Tay decided that he was going to change his bed. Taylor and I used to sleep in twin beds in the same room. At one point, Taylor and I made a deal where I would move into the guest bedroom across the hall, which had a bigger bed, and Taylor's side of the deal is that he would get a bunk bed, all to himself. Well, years went on after this deal and Taylor never got his bunk bed. I think he sort of forgot about it.

A little bit ago, Gammy and Paw-Paw moved out of their house, which had a bunk bed, and they gave it to Taylor. Tay was excited that he finally would get a bunk bed after all the years of not, but he quickly got too big for it. He said a few times that he would wake up and hit his head on the roof of the bed. So, he changed beds, and now the bunk is in the basement. Taylor's room looks different, and when I walk past it now, I do a double take because I was so used to how it was before.

That night we roasted s'mores. I don't think we make s'mores or go into the hot tub often enough. Sometimes I think we all forget how nice it is, and it'll sit there without a use. So, it was suitable that we used it tonight.

Tuesday, June 2, 2020

Dad is at the fire station again. I slept inside. When I woke up, I went downstairs and gave Wilson a belly rub and hugged Mom and said good morning. The first half of the day was dry, but I must've waited too long to spend time outside, because the second half of the day it was raining nonstop.

A painter came over today to paint the garage. He came a week ago, and I guess Mom and Dad gave him the wrong color. I don't know how they made that mistake, but anyway, the color was the wrong one, so today he painted the garage the right color.

As Tuesdays are, once more I had schoolwork, but because I did a lot of the work I got yesterday, it wasn't bad. I did math, and it was about finding square roots. They haven't yet talked about the algorithm for it yet, but I already know it, so that wasn't difficult.

I also did science. Science is my least favorite class. Nothing of the things that we learn about includes anything interesting. This is really disappointing, because last year's science was awesome, when I had Mr. Johnson, who just gave us a bunch of science things that we would have to do in a span of a month or two, and as long as it was done by then, you were free to conduct how you learned. I don't know if any class I have in the future will be as good, or as free as that class, so I should give seventh grade science a break.

Wednesday, June 3, 2020

Today was a very slow day, something we haven't had in a while, even though I've had a few boring days recently, but I can't consider that a slow day. The difference between a slow day and a boring day is that a slow day is appreciated, and a boring day is when the day feels like it's going to last a week, and I don't know what to do in that week.

To pass time Mom and I went on an aimless drive and around to the beach and then to Joe's Garden, where Mom got some strawberries and a flower and a big bag of soil that I later helped her get out of the car because Mom thinks that it would hurt her back a lot.

Mom's had back problems on and off for as long as I can remember. A doctor told her it was because she did so much biking. She tries to figure out ways to fix it, which usually works, but eventually she's thrown off of a routine, and she goes back to square one.

Thursday, June 4, 2020

Wilson was very interested in the wood pile for most of the day. I think that there is a squirrel or mouse down there, because I know Wilson, and the only reason he would have so much determination to stay in the same spot for so long would be if he was hunting. I know it isn't smart to just let Wilson hunt animals in the backyard, but he'll never catch anything, so I don't give a second thought about the matter.

In the morning Dad and I went to the store to get wood, because Tay and I decided that for an art project we should make wood benches. Dad was all for it, so we decided that today was the day. I was going to make one and Taylor was going to make another. Dad was in the store for what felt like forever.

When he finally came back, he had a ton of long pieces of wood, so I helped him tie it to the car. He also got a mirror for the main bathroom because the one before was all melted from a fancy scent maker that leaned on the side of the frame. We kept it there for so long, and it just continued to be something Mom and Dad put off.

When we got home, Taylor and I played *Madden* twice. Tay won both games, and in one of them he crushed me, and the score was 60–16 or something. I'm looking forward to the new *Madden*, coming out sometime in August.

We started the benches in the garage in the middle of the day. Taylor did his first. I was reading while he did his. Dad wanted to do it with us, one at a time, and I didn't have a preference on going first. Taylor's looked really good when he was done with his. I started mine when he was all finished up, and we kept track of what materials we used for the bench so one day in the future we could remake it when the bench gets old and rotten.

I don't understand what Tay's thinking, but Tay decided that he would put his bench in his room, which doesn't make sense because it's an outdoor bench. His room is already crowded, and eventually I think he'll move it outside. I think I'm going to put my bench next to the pond, which I feel I need to start calling a swamp, since it's getting so messy. A better idea might be to put it next to the basketball court, because I think all of us spend most of our time there, in comparison to the pond.

Friday, June 5, 2020

After waking up outside, I said good morning to Wilson, who was next to Mom's door. Mom did a long shift, so Tay and I made sure to be quiet, and after petting Wilson I went back upstairs to read. When I came back, Wilson was in the same spot.

Later I checked on the bench. The paint was still not completely dry, so it was left unmoved all day.

I played basketball by myself. Tay would've played too, but his hands have been cut up from three different things: one from a bike crash, another time he cut his finger while cutting bread, and he fell on the gravel the other day. Mom's friends came over for dinner, and we struck a deal with Mom that if we did a few chores, we could watch an extra movie. It was worth it. Tay swept and mopped while I vacuumed upstairs and downstairs.

Saturday, June 6, 2020

Dad got home at around ten. Dad said a few days ago that he wanted to go to a protest in downtown Bellingham. We all thought that even though it would be standing up for something that matters, Tay, Mom, and I all believed that it would be much safer to not go, with COVID. I thought that he forgot about it, but he told us that he was planning on going.

I've seen the news of how some of these protests become not peaceful, and people become destructive. Dad brought up the point that there's no way that would happen in a small town like Bellingham, which is true, but everything about it seems like it wouldn't be very safe, between COVID and everything else.

I care about the cause of the protest, but as just one other person, I'd rather support it from afar.

And then, a few hours later, we were all in the car on our way to go to the protest. I'm shocked that Dad convinced all of us to go, but even though I didn't feel completely safe going, Dad did a good job reassuring all of us.

We got there almost an hour before the protest was going to start. Combined with already not really wanting to be there, I wasn't delighted with the idea of waiting in the car. Tay needed to pee badly, and the last resort option was for Tay to try and pee in Dad's leftover coffee cup, which he tried to do while I turned away. He was a little paranoid that someone would see from the window, so it took a while until he was sure that no one was around.

We got out of Dad's car once the protest was closer to starting. Mom rarely goes in Dad's car, because it's also a mess all the time, which Mom can't stand, but Dad likes that it isn't all clean. This car is for muddy cleats and wet dogs, Dad usually says. Dad insisted that we took the Subaru instead of the white 4Runner. Maybe because it contradicts logic to bring a white truck to a Black Lives Matter protest.

We got out of the car with our N-95 masks and went to the protest. To be fair, Dad was right, it wasn't crazy, and there was no yelling like I thought there would be. We stayed up around the back, to avoid people being so close to other people. I think I saw two teachers from Kulshan there, from afar. The people still got close to the six feet, so it's still possible that we get COVID, and maybe I will eat some of my words about being glad that I went, but even then, it was empowering. We were only out for forty minutes, and then we went back home. I had never stood up for something before, even if all we did was stand around, but we were there.

Sunday, June 7, 2020

The weather is getting nicer every day. That is something that I look forward to all spring, and sometimes I think that's all that spring is good for. Not really. Spring has its positives, but here it rains all the time like winter does, so summer becomes the only desirable month.

Summer break is coming up, and I think this time more than ever I'm going to focus on living it up. We won't be doing much this summer. We aren't going anywhere, and nothing is a given with COVID, because it's possible it lasts the whole summer. Everything is so unpredictable, so there is no reason in making plans anyway.

The only other thing that happened today was we went on the trail in the middle of the day. Recently we have been looping around when going on the trail, which is better than going out and back. I like exploring more of the trails rather than just seeing the same part of the woods twice. One of our neighbors was also on the trail, and she had a new puppy and let

Wilson play with her dog while she talked with Mom and Dad. Today was another one of those slow days. Hopefully, something interesting happens soon, because every day is seemingly repetitive.

We had leftover wood after we had made the benches. It wasn't enough to make another bench, but Taylor and I split the wood that was leftover, and we made different things. Taylor made a cornhole board. This shouldn't be forgotten, because something like this may just be put in a corner and lost for a while, but this will be fun to use all summer.

Also, we are in Phase 2 now. They are called phases of going back from COVID (Phase 1, 2, 3, etc.). Each higher phase allows more relaxed rules. Mom said that she talked to a doctor that works at the hospital here in Bellingham, and they said there is only one COVID patient there, meaning that it's decreasing. Maybe by the end of the summer COVID will be a distant memory.

Monday, June 8, 2020

I woke up early today. Dad's at the fire station, so when I went downstairs it was only Wilson and me. I started to run out of things to do in the morning, except I was motivated to exercise early in the day. When I get either reading or exercise done early, it's a weight lifted off my shoulders that day, and the rest of the day can go at my desirable pace, which changes between days.

Recently I have started to do weight exercises, and for me it's just a combination of weights and exercises like lunges and squats. Mom said that I should have alternating days of different types of exercises. She says that the muscles are used one day, and then they need to be repaired the next day. She wrote the exercises that I should do on two cards, one for each day. At school, we had A and B days, where we alternated some classes in our schedule. Mom labeled both days, with A and B days.

I wanted to do my weights before anyone woke up, because I liked doing the weights alone. I'm pretty sure Taylor knows that too, because when he's bored, he comes down and tries to mess with me. When I went back upstairs after a half hour, no one was awake still. It was past seven, so I fed Wilson, which he enjoyed.

Tuesday, June 9, 2020

Today was the last Tuesday that we would get a ton of schoolwork, and because it was the last week it was easier than usual. Today was a very chill day. Taylor and I played *Madden* together and Taylor won. He was the Chiefs and I was the Seahawks.

Later Dad and I went to the hot tub. It was fun, and we did some math money without money. Also, Taylor told me that Gavin and Carter will be coming over for a bonfire in two days. So, I am looking forward to that. Also, I think that we are going to sleep outside.

Wednesday, June 10, 2020
I woke up in the morning at 6:50. We were going to sleep outside, but Wilson was sniffing a lot, so I went inside just in case something was going on. Nothing happened, but Mom and I went in. I woke up and said hi to Tay, Dad, and Wilson.

Then Taylor and I played some basketball a few times. We played more King of the Court, and we moved it back so that it is, like, half court, but whoever wins the round gets the ball next, like King of the Court.

Dad and I finally put some stuff in my squirrel feeder. I think I am not going to put a camera there for a few days, until they figure out that it's a safe place to have food, and that it's even there. Then in three days, I will put a camera out and see if they see the stuff I gave them.

Thursday, June 11, 2020
After Mom came home from work recently, she talked about how another nurse at work said something racist, and she didn't know if she should tell someone, because she was concerned about her work environment.
She ended up calling, even though it was hard for her and she was kind of scared, but I told her that it was the right thing to do.

Then after Tay did some woodwork, we played basketball. We played what we have usually played every day. I should do weights, so I might do that after I write this page. We are also one week from the one-hundredth page of writing.

Gavin and Carter came over today, and it was the first time that we had seen friends, excluding times when we crossed paths, like when we saw Carson and Tyler at Geneva. I sort of forgot how fun it is to hang out with other people. I mean, I knew that I liked hanging out with friends, and I knew that I wanted to, but I really forgot how great it really is. We caught up and had a fun time. They stayed until around ten or eleven.

Friday, June 12, 2020
We slept outside, even though it was later when Gavin and Carter left. Mom also slept with us, which was surprising to me. She doesn't sleep outside usually, and it was late at night. Usually, when it's late, she would

sleep inside. She said she would want to say that she slept the whole night outside, something that is pretty rare for Mom.

Mom said that she was going to go on the trail with Wilson, who was whining, eagerly waiting to go. We all went on the trail, except for Tay. The trails were quite slippery and we all put on rain coats. Then we went to a few trails that were overgrown. It was raining hard, so all of the overgrown leaves were wet, so when you touch them a bunch of water ends up on you.

We went on the main trail and then on a steep one that was starting to get overgrown, and then we decided instead of going down the steep, slippery trail that we came up, we would just loop around. That trail was the longer one, but it was a good decision to go that way and avoid the other way.

Dad didn't go on the trail because he was going to edit an article that he recently wrote and is going to submit to a fly fishing magazine. The article is about Jason, a good friend of Dad's, and he's our neighbor. He's a drummer and he fishes with Dad often. Dad came up with the idea of trying this. A little bit ago, he wrote an article about a pipeline explosion in Bellingham, which happened about twenty years ago. Gasoline rolled into Whatcom Creek, which went up in flames and killed three kids, along with the creek itself. Dad's article was about that day, a kid that died, and the recovery after.

Monday, June 15, 2020

Today Mom and I went on a drive. In the middle of the drive she told me that we were going to do a little bit of exercise, so she took me to Taylor Hill, near the south side of the city, and then we walked and jogged up it. I wasn't really excited or in the mood, but I enjoyed going up the hill. The hill is just a street that is really steep. It's on South Hill, and Mom used to run up it for a workout often. The beginning of the street starts near the dock to the water, but Mom told me not to look back until the top of the hill, because when at the top, there is the best view of the bay. She was right, and when I was done the view was great.

While going up the hill, Mom pointed out a little house that we lived in for a little less than a year, during the time when we had to stay out of our house (that we live in now) because of the mold inside. The house had a lot of steep stairs and was just two blocks from the preschool. Sometimes we watch home videos and there are some scenes that show the inside of the house. The house next to the one we lived in looked newer than our house and all of the houses around it. Mom said that when they lived there their neighbor was a hoarder, and the old house was torn down.

We also went to the preschool; I have a lot more memories of the school than the house. We walked to school every day. I still remember some things about the school, but how much of that is the pictures and videos, I don't know. I do remember some of my friends at the preschool, and I still run into some of them. I don't know where most of the kids are now.

The preschool eventually closed, or ended, sometime ago. The one teacher, Teacher Heidi, we called her, eventually worked at a toy store in Old Fairhaven after moving on from the preschool. Taylor figured out that his second-grade teacher was related to Teacher Heidi; if I remember correctly, she's her sister-in-law.

A reoccurring thing that Mom and Dad bring up every summer is how are we going to keep our brains active while out of school, but honestly, I don't think it really matters. I don't think my brain power decreases over the summer, but Mom insists we read a lot of books and do schoolwork, even though not thinking might be the whole point of summer.

This year, Dad and Mom are going to have us do math on a website named Khan Academy, which is a name I recognize from school, over the years. Mom has figured out Taylor's and my opinions on doing schoolwork during summer, so she justified it by saying that there would be a prize if we did it consistently.

Wednesday, June 17, 2020
I woke up at 7:11 the next day, though I wanted to go back to sleep, so I attempted to get more rest because I wasn't ready for the day to start. That's something that I am glad through COVID that I have been able to enjoy: to be able to start your day when you want to, instead of having to go to school or needing to get up in order to be on time for something. There is no rush when getting up, something I haven't fully appreciated until now.

I was looking around in the yard for Wilson's drops today. I didn't find more than one. Though, during my adventures, I found a lump on the ground, which after further inspection was a dead robin. I don't know how the bird died. I observed around it, which was difficult because it was on the rocks next to the house. I was curious if Wilson got it, though I thought that would be unlikely, with Wilson being such an unfortunate predator. There were no teeth marks, thank goodness, or else my perception of Wilson's hunting skills would quickly change.

In order to keep Wilson from getting the bird, I took a shovel and moved the bird across the creek, I was very delicate with the bird. The reason I was so careful, even I don't fully know. Maybe I felt bad for the bird, or maybe I subconsciously worried that the bird would wake up if I wasn't careful.

Later in the day Dad sprayed the chairs outside to clean them up, because they had always been faded. Dad kept the chairs on the grass, the day was nice, and there wasn't any rain, which would have been a bad thing for the spray because the chairs took a day to dry. We were outside a lot today, and throughout the day Wilson was chewing a new bone that Mom or Dad got him. He finished by the end of the day, which I didn't know he could do.

We slept outside again, something we have been doing more and more as the weather keeps getting better as it gets closer to July, maybe as a celebration of summer. The July weather in Bellingham is much different than June. June weather has more rain, whereas in July and August there is rarely any, and the temperature just gets better and better.

Thursday, June 18, 2020

I woke up outside, and I was the only one awake. I went inside and got a dog bag and went back outside, because I just wanted to get it over with, before Wilson takes his morning poop. I have forgotten a couple of times, and Tay will remind me all day if I do. I didn't find any today, so that made my job that much easier. When I was going back inside, I heard the garbage truck. The truck is very loud and usually wakes up whoever is outside. It typically wakes up Taylor and Mom, even though they are the ones that have hearing problems.

Today, we went to Kulshan. This was the first time that I have gone to the school since March 13; it's been over three months. The reason that we went was to pick up things from school, now that the year is officially over for in-person school. They made designated days for people to go to the school, to avoid overcrowding with COVID. Today was for families with their first letter in their last name S through Z. Tay and I got yearbooks, and I got medicine back that the school had just in case I had an allergic reaction. I was hoping that some of my friends would be there at the same time, but there weren't any. There wasn't really anyone in general, just a desk with a few people in charge of getting the yearbooks and medicine to the students. One of my sixth grade teachers was helping out. He reminded me that he said that middle school goes by so quick, and I'm going to be in eighth grade now. This year is going faster than usual because for the last while there hasn't even been school.

Saturday, June 20, 2020

So, this is the first weekend of summer. Feels good to finally be in summer now, but it's still kind of like school at home, like it was before. We have academic work, Khan Academy. We still have an hour of reading to do each day, along with doing our writing. As much as that is, we still have a lot of time for just having summer fun.

We slept outside, and Tay slept later than the rest of us. Taylor, according to Dad, sleepwalked in the middle of the night. He got out and then he went to the railing and then he kind of moved around. Dad woke up and saw him and asked him what he was doing, and Taylor replied in random mumbles, before going back and falling on to the bed. Dad then woke him up just in case he had to go to the bathroom. Taylor is the only person in our family that sleepwalks/talks/yells. I wonder if Tay's sleepwalking will cease as he gets older, or if it'll happen more often. I like Tay's sleepwalking stories, so I'm rooting for it to continue forever.

Tomorrow is Father's Day, but we are going to celebrate it today because Dad has to work tomorrow. Instead of him missing Father's Day, we'll change the day that we celebrate it. Tay and I got him two custom T-shirts. The one that I got him has a mountain on the back, and on Taylor's there is a fish on the shirt. Mom had to work today, though, so we celebrated late in the day, after Mom came home from Hospice House.

Today is the summer solstice. I don't know why the months of the year are not aligned with the summer and winter solstices, but I do know that these things don't get enough attention. Solstices are the shift of a focus; it either increases hope or changes one's thinking to become more thankful for the days that are to come. However, it seems that I only find out about the winter and summer solstices by accident or from a neighbor, and usually I find out too late, or too early to care.

Monday, June 22, 2020

Today is Monday, and a celebratory one at that. The celebration, we don't have any more school to do, we are officially on summer vacation. I still miss my friends, and as much as summer is great, I will do my best to savor every day as much as I can because doing schoolwork makes me wonder if I have wasted my summer. I am already looking forward to seeing my friends again. If I even see them then. If I know one thing, it's that COVID doesn't just go with what our plan is.

I woke up at six thirty in the morning, and I know I went to bed planning on sleeping in, and it would seem nice too, but I don't work that way. And, when I woke up, I was motivated to start the day and check off things that I knew I would need to do today. I did all of my reading and finished *The River Why*. I don't know what I think of it. Not that it wasn't a good book, but it was difficult to follow for me. I'll probably reread it in a few years, and then I will understand it a whole lot better. Then I'll think that it's a really good book and life will go on.

Taylor was sleepwalking today. I don't know what makes a person sleepwalk, but whatever it is, Tay must have a lot of it.

The afternoon was peaceful (besides the water balloon fight) and perfect. We all went to Marine Park—Mom and Dad, Taylor, Wilson, and me. We skipped rocks at the park. Wilson loved observing the birds and we all knew that he wanted to go and get the birds. I skipped a rock ten skips! Tay is a better rock skipper than me, but I still think that ten is the best that I have ever got. When we got home Dad went with Wilson on the trail. While he was gone, Mom, Tay, and I all had a water balloon fight. I think we used a total of seventy balloons. After we all cleaned up, most of the balloons were on the patio, and that made it easy to find them. For dinner, Dad made a homemade pizza for all of us. I swear it gets better and better each time.

Tuesday, June 23, 2020
It's official: Wilson's poop migrates. Today there were three, and I came early. Maybe yesterday Tay was lazy. They were all kind of in a line, like the belt on the constellation Orion. When we are in the hot tub, Orion is one of the first constellations that I find, and it's because of the three stars in a row, I can't make out much more of it. Anyway, they were on the bark, and before this they were more up the hill. He is pretty consistent, and this is new.

Taylor and I did screen time for the next hour or two, and then I quickly began to read a new book. Now, I have diagnosed five things that I need to do in the day, and I can go through my day checking off these things that I need to do. The first thing is to get ready for the day (brush, shower, etc.). This is followed by reading, then Khan Academy, concluded with exercise and then writing, in the afternoon when the day is over. This is easy to do in the course of the day, if I don't procrastinate.

Today was the perfect summer day, and I hope we have more perfect summer days. Taylor and I played Bump today, in flip flops. Then we filled up the water balloons and played pass back and forth with one, and each time someone caught the balloon (without it exploding) we would take a step back, until the balloon pops.

We did this with a couple of water balloons, but eventually Taylor couldn't resist the urge to start a water balloon fight. So, he did so without warning. After a lot of back and forth, I had the last two water balloons. I chased him around, and then I saw the water gun that was also filled up, and I made sure I got that so Tay didn't use it on me later. When I had thrown the last two water balloons and they had exploded, I figured that the water balloon battle was over. I still had the water gun because I didn't want Tay to use it on me while picking up the balloon scraps off the grass and patio.

However, Tay was irritated by this point. He wrestled the gun out of my hands and started squirting me with it. I laughed, even though I don't think that was the response that he was looking for or expecting. So then, when he was done, I continued picking up the balloon scraps from the yard. Taylor said that he was only going to pick up the scraps of the balloons that he had thrown (don't ask me how he figured which were his, he had no clue). According to Taylor's lack of picking up balloon pieces, he must think he only threw about six water balloons. Even though there were about fifty water balloons when we started, I swear I didn't throw forty-six of them.

Taylor continued to be irritated for the rest of the day. I didn't let it stop me from having a good day. This is just who Taylor is, and most of the time he's better.

At the fire pit, Dad was making a bonfire, and he had a challenge for Taylor and me. The challenge was to light the bonfire with one match, using only twigs and moss. Usually, we have paper scraps or cardboard. Tay made a bird nest shaped moss thing, and it worked. Mine did not light. I didn't think that Taylor's bird nest of moss would work, but I was proven wrong.

I had a fun day, but I am still confused that Tay wasn't happy today. I wonder if it's less of a day-to-day thing and more and more of a personality thing. I am not going to guess anything, but I do wonder.

Wednesday, June 24, 2020

I woke up early in the morning. To be precise, I had woken up at 6:11. Then I took a few minutes to just open my eyes and adjust them to the light that shined on the corners slipping through the window, past the border of my navy blue blinds. They have small holes dotted out on the blinds, acting as stars. I picked up *The Moth*, the book that I started yesterday, and continued reading it. I have read it a couple of times before, but there was nothing else to read and it had been quite a while.

The Moth is a book that holds a collection of small true stories that had happened to people who submitted their writing for the book. I did look up if this was something that they continue to do multiple times, half wondering because I wanted to get the other book if there was one, and half wondering because I thought that maybe I could submit my own story. I don't know what I would write about. I don't really have anything that interesting.

After an hour had passed, I finally made my way downstairs and said good morning to Taylor and Mom. I felt like the day was going to be a productive one. Mom was on the computer when I asked her for the computer so I could do my math on the computer. Now that I am writing about it, I feel bad, because it seems rude for me to interrupt whatever Mom was doing on the computer for me. She willingly gave it to me, though, and I was determined to be productive.

I did screen time, and Taylor and I played some basketball, and Taylor didn't seem very happy again today. It was frustrating to be around him, but I tried to deal with it, and I tried, and then at one point I just gave up for the day because it kind of brings you down to be with someone who isn't enjoying what he is doing, and it isn't because he doesn't like basketball. But I don't know, next time I will try to not be quite as competitive, and maybe let him get a few more baskets than usual.

I made sure that Tay didn't ruin my day. Taylor, Mom, Wilson, and I all went on a walk for forty minutes, and when we came back, we had dinner together and watched a show. Tay was bearable after we came back from the walk and for the rest of the day. I also think I should say this, for the future of every future writing entry: Taylor is nice most of the time, and I feel like when I write it should reflect that. With that said, sometimes he is god-awful. And when he is, I won't sugarcoat it just for the sake of him. I am only writing what did happen, and sometimes it doesn't put Taylor in the best light. Because none of us are perfect. And that includes me, and when I am in the wrong, I won't sugarcoat it either.

Thursday, June 25, 2020

I looked at the clock when I woke up and it was six, but then I turned over and my clock said that it was seven. Now, I think there are two possibilities to what happened, and both are equally as likely. I may have just fallen asleep right after I turned over, and when I woke up it happened to be seven. Or maybe I read it wrong the first time, and it was actually seven the whole time. I guess I will never know.

Then I turned the light on in my room and started to read. After a few minutes, Tay popped his head out the door and asked how long I would read. I ended up reading for twenty minutes before going downstairs, and then I saw Mom and she was in her bed. I said good morning and she asked me to make some coffee for her, so I did that, and after it got started, I went and put on dad's boots and picked up after Wilson. Wilson was outside and barking at Sue. I said hi to her because it isn't very exciting to be barked at by any dog, and it isn't easy to stop Wilson from barking.

Dad was going to the car dealership, since his car needed to be fixed. His plan was to run back home when he was done. Mom had to pick him up after he called her saying that he was too tired and sick to run all the way home, which for Dad must be really sick, because he has never (to my knowledge) needed to call Mom to pick him up for being tired. On the drive home he threw up, and when he walked inside he was very pale. He stayed almost the whole day in the basement in bed. Mom doesn't think that it's COVID, because he doesn't have that many of the symptoms besides just being sick.

Mom, Taylor, and I stayed outside for most of the day because we wanted Dad to have peace and quiet while he rested. We went up on the trails and on an overgrown path. I tripped once. It hurt, and I scraped my knee, but I quickly forgot about it after it stopped bugging me. It was a good way to get exercise and leave Dad be.

We got back, but we got in the car quickly after because Mom and Tay wanted to go in the water. They packed up and got ready to go to this small beach. I didn't really feel like going. I didn't say much about it, but I didn't bring my swimsuit. When we looked at the beach it was full, so we didn't go. I was quietly glad.

So, we went to a different beach, but there wasn't a parking spot, so we went to get gelato ice cream in Fairhaven. We all thought it would be fun to pick up La Fiamma, but they wouldn't answer the phone, for some unknown reason. We were in a little traffic jam, and we saw a Pizza Hut on the side. Lucky us! We got that instead, and it was just as great.

Dad came outside when we were eating pizza and said that he was feeling better. When he first came home, he said that he felt like a one, on a scale of one to ten. When he came outside, I asked him how he was. A six or a seven now, he still looks pale, but that is definitely an improvement.

Friday, June 26, 2020

Dad actually felt good enough for us to sleep outside last night. I was surprised, but it was exciting to do. All of us woke up around six thirty because of the garbage truck. I also knew it would wake Mom up, who worked until midnight and was probably already going to be tired, garbage truck or not.

We all sort of reflected and thought about what may have caused Dad to feel like he did yesterday. He's around 100 percent now. There was a big fire that he went to the day before, that he was at for a while, and it could have been carbon dioxide poisoning or it could have been Dad's first migraine, at forty-three years old. I would place my bet on it being smoke poisoning.

After Taylor and I played on the Xbox together, I did my reading. I am getting closer to finishing the book *The Moth*, and it continues to be a really good book like I remember. Instead of a big story it has fifty small stories that are each, like, seven pages. So that is cool, and they are all real and told by real people. There are stories from astronauts, Run-DMC, other people who have done great things, and also just normal, average people. I think that it's great, as a kid, to reread books, because I have found some things become forgotten or they just go over my head when I am young, and then the stories are better when I understand more. The more I live, the more I understand.

Dad, Tay, and I all are playing more Bump outside recently, mostly because it gets us more out of breath, and a good workout is always appreciated. I'm pretty good at it, which is another reason I keep wanting to play it.

We all went in Mom's car, and Dad needed to be dropped off at the car dealer, because he can now get his car all cleaned up. We dropped him off and went home, and then he was just a few minutes behind us. I didn't do weights today, so I'm planning on doing that in the next few days.

Saturday, June 27, 2020

I finished *The Moth* today. I think one of my favorite things about that one is that most of the stories showed that the people who were writing the stories were far from perfect. Most of them were prisoners to depressed people at one point, people with smoking or drug addictions. Most of them said that after they experienced the story, they changed for the better or reflected on something.

I also finished the seventh-grade portion of the Khan Academy math today. It took me only two weeks to finish it, and next I will do eighth grade. If I finish that before summer ends, then I will do a little algebra online. It doesn't count for actual schoolwork, but I do like the feeling of progressing (and I really like progressing faster than Taylor, in anything), so I continue to do it.

Tay and I played more Bump today. With the nice weather, it's hard to stay inside for long. This is really fun, though I do think that later in the summer I'll find that it's less motivating to get outside. Somehow, I take the good weather for granted. I am going to try to maximize this summer because, if I do, it might be the best imperfect summer.

At seven I went with Dad to go pick up the ClickList, just for fun, and to hang out with just Dad, something that doesn't happen often with everyone being home most of the time. Even though seven at night is the time where I'm usually slowing down, with the sun being increasingly in the sky, I feel more awake. The groceries didn't take long to come, so Dad and I were only in the car for a little bit. We talked about books, writing, and other questions we have about life and the universe.

Sunday, June 28, 2020

June is finishing up already, and I think soon enough we will be going back to school, though COVID numbers will have to go down and stay down for a little while so that everyone is good with going back to school.

Today Mom is working until midnight. She doesn't work all the way to midnight that much, but it isn't uncommon. While Taylor and I were playing basketball, she called saying that she forgot her work badge and needed us to find it for her. It took a while for us to find it, but I eventually found it in Mom's closet. An hour later, Dad and I got in his car and went to Starbucks to get Mom a coffee on the way to give her the work badge. Dad also got two croissants, one for me and one for Tay. We brought Wilson with us, but Taylor wanted to stay home, so I would give him the croissant when we came back.

Mom was thankful for the coffee and her badge. When we came home, I gave the croissant to Taylor. He was also thankful. When he was done eating, we went back outside to play more basketball.

We saw Rich on a ladder trying to clean his gutters that are about fifteen to twenty feet up, depending on the side of the house. Dad was already outside because he came outside to play basketball with Tay and I. Dad offered to help Rich. Considering that Rich is around seventy years old, I think that he probably needed it. Even though he was visibly struggling a little bit, he firmly declined.

So, we continued to play basketball and Rich went around the house to continue cleaning his gutters.

When Rich had come back around after only ten-ish minutes, Dad, along with Tay and I, all watched Rich struggle before Dad insisted that we all help. He easily could've fallen off the ladder if we let him and didn't help. Dad did most of the work, and Tay and I helped hold the latter. Dad also let us up on the ladder, but the gutters were pretty clean already, so we didn't do that much to help him besides look around different sides of the house.

I found that Rich was very thankful for the help. I believe that he knew that he needed help, and I think he knew that he would be thankful if we helped. Help is honestly declined too much, usually because of the pride that people hang on to for dear life when they get older. Why is help declined, even when it's needed most?

Monday, June 29, 2020
I woke up right before seven, and when I came down, Wilson was lying on the stairs, half asleep. He and I were the only ones up. I remembered to be quiet. Mom emphasized that she wanted to sleep in, when she called us from work. She didn't even want me to open any doors to go outside, so I kept Wilson inside until she woke up, and I didn't go outside to pick up after Wilson either.

I think recently Mom has been under more stress with the pandemic. A lot has been happening. When Mom comes home (unless she's at work until midnight) she tells us stories from Hospice House. Some are emotional to her about a patient with a sad past, or someone who has just had bad luck. Other stories are about other nurses. Even though we haven't met or remembered most of the people she talks about, we already know them.

Dad tells his stories too, when he comes home from the fire station, but he's said before that most of them he decides he shouldn't tell.

My handwriting isn't great, this is no secret, but when I am doing math, I have noticed that my handwriting is perfectly normal when solving math problems. Maybe I just get math easily, and because it comes easily to my brain, it's represented well in my handwriting. I already think that it's going to be more difficult for me to finish eighth grade online summer math. I am also accumulating quite the stack of math papers from calculations. I am hesitant to throw them away, and for now they just sit on a table, until I find out what to do.

I did that while Mom, Tay, and Wilson went on the trail, and Tay came back with a knee full of stinging nettles. It was pretty bad, and it looked nasty to me. Mom gave Taylor something that is supposed to calm it down for now.

After dinner Mom and I went on a walk down the road. After seeing Taylor's knee, I don't think there was a chance that we would go on the trail. We turned around at the mailbox. We didn't bring a key though, so we didn't get the mail. On our way back we saw two very small deer on the side yard of one of the first houses, with their mother deer. We all see countless deer around, but I think those were the smallest that I have ever seen. I wonder if we'll see them again. I think we usually only see a deer once, and not the same one again. To my disappointment, I haven't seen Leaf since the day I first saw him.

Tuesday, June 30, 2020
Today I woke up around seven. Wilson was the only one awake, like usual. The morning was very uneventful. Taylor and I brought up the possibility of us getting a new TV, because the one that we have right now is so old and we have noticed that it sometimes has problems when we do screen time or when we are all watching TV. Tay and I have brought this up before, but it seems so unnecessary to Mom and Dad that it never gets followed through. We pitched to Mom that we would all split the cost. I hope the deal doesn't fall apart like it usually does.

When we play Bump, if another player bumps your ball at a bad angle it can roll into the woods, which is a pain to get and really makes the game less fun. So, today, instead of playing in Rich's yard, we went to Geneva Elementary to play basketball.

We ran into friends from school while we were there. It was even more fun to see people than it was before COVID, because since March we haven't seen many people at all. We had fun playing. There are many basketball hoops at Geneva, so we went around and played at multiple ones. We talked to Carson and Tyler Fields, who we knew from school, and it was very fun to catch up with them. We kept far away though, even more than six feet. Then we went back to playing. We played more basketball games than just Bump, like H-O-R-S-E.

While we were gone, Mom went on a bike ride with a friend, and she was energetic when we were done, so I think she had fun.

Donnett came over a few hours after we came home. She came to say that we were invited to a bonfire to celebrate the Fourth of July. I definitely think that we are going. I love having bonfires at Donnett's house. The food is always good, and Donnett and Terry are fun to be around. I'm also looking forward to July weather, because summer doesn't really start until the Fourth of July. I'm still on a mission to maximize this summer. I always seem to somehow think that I took summer for granted, but this year it changes.

Wednesday, July 1, 2020

It's finally July. It seemed like at the beginning of the year that it would take a while before we got into summer. The funny thing is the first real day of summer didn't have good weather. It was sixty degrees and raining all day. The weather app says that it will rain more in the next few days but then lighten up and be sunny every day after.

I went downstairs and said good morning to Mom, who was on the computer, and Wilson, who was as great as always. I was getting ready to go outside and pick up after Wilson, but Taylor stopped me because he said he forgot to pick up yesterday. So, he went outside instead. I'm glad that he stopped me; he could've not said a thing and had me pick up yesterday's droppings as well.

I went downstairs and played *Minecraft* in the basement, but it got boring, and I'm going to take a break and play something else. When I finished downstairs, I went up and did forty minutes of reading. Mom said that she is going to get us some new books because we are down to not many that we can read. I'm going to appreciate that because I have been rereading books that I already feel I know word for word.

Then I went and did my Khan Academy. I've recently noticed that it's getting a little harder and more difficult to do. It just kind of takes more brain power to get it done. But I think I will still make my goal of finishing before August. If I reach my goal, I will be able to start algebra.

Taylor and Dad went to Geneva to play basketball, and I stayed back because I was going to do weights instead. Mom and her friend went on a walk on the trails while Tay and Dad were gone, so we all did our individual exercise alone. It was nice to get some quiet time, because sometimes it becomes a lot to be around everyone.

Later today we are going to watch a movie. I think the one we are going to watch is called *A River Runs Through It*. I think that it will be good, by the way Dad is excited to watch it, which he isn't usually about movies.

Today on the news something came out that Antonio Brown was practicing at Russell Wilson's private field, so maybe the Seahawks will sign him. That would be cool. Also, there is a Chief that might hold out for them, so maybe the Seahawks could swoop in and get him. I don't think they will have enough money to have both of them, but if they got one of the two, that would be amazing.

Thursday, July 2, 2020

Wilson was super happy when I said hi to him in the morning, as always. Tay was awake and I said good morning to him as he was going outside to pick up after Wilson. It's an even day, but he has to pick it up today even though he did yesterday. That was because he had forgotten to pick it up two days ago. I do have to pick up tomorrow but that is okay because I haven't had to do it in three days.

I did my reading before I went downstairs. I only did twenty minutes; I was planning to read for a half hour or longer, but it kind of took a while for me to get up and be motivated to go read. I did read early, and I was kind of motivated to do everything kind of quickly, because then I took a shower, brushed my teeth.

After that I went downstairs and asked Mom for the computer so that I could do my Khan Academy. I am really close to finishing my second of seven units. But again, it's more difficult to understand, but after a bit I end up being, like, *Ohhh, that is how you do it!* Then I do that for the whole time, and I move past it. I think I might get to do that with this last spot. These two units are incredibly small, but even that is okay because they seem like concepts that are the hardest to do!

Mom, Tay, and I went to Bed Bath & Beyond in the middle of the day to get a few things that we had been thinking about getting. We could have got it on Amazon, but it was great for us to get out of the house. I got the reading pillow that I was writing about earlier, because of the Taylor regifting dilemma. Mom got new sheets for her bed. Mom was excited to put them on her bed, though she was a little disappointed with the quality. I think we all should take a step back and realize how silly it is to be disappointed with something so small like that.

When we came home Taylor and I used our screen time to watch a good movie that was called *Ace Ventura: Pet Detective*. It was funny and it had Jim Carrey, who is in *Dumb and Dumber*. He has also been in other good movies we have watched.

As the day was ending, Mom and Tay set up the net that Taylor had got for his birthday. We played some tennis and that was fun to play. We played in our driveway and made it horizontal so the ball couldn't be overhit into the woods.

Friday, July 3, 2020

When I was picking up after Wilson early in the morning, I got a bag and was walking out and opening it, and I found that there was a hole in it. I'm glad that I saw it because if I didn't that wouldn't have been awesome, at all.

So, I went back and asked Tay for another one. Once I got to Wilson's droppings, I saw that there were slugs on it, so I guess that slugs eat that sort of thing. I wouldn't have known. That just increases the gross level for slugs.

Mom had to go to work at six thirty, so Tay and I were going to be home alone for around four hours before Dad came home. I did forty minutes of my Khan Academy. It's getting really hard with this one part. I hope I can pass it tomorrow, but it's very confusing to do. I will understand it tomorrow and start another unit.

I don't have a book to read that I really like, but I think Mom and I will find something on Amazon for me.

Another thing to recognize is that the weather hasn't been nice for the past two or three days. So, barely any basketball. It's been hard to exercise. I should have done weights today, but I didn't. I plan on doing weights tomorrow.

Then at around one we got Mom a cup of coffee. Even though it was pretty wet outside, we passed the football around while we were waiting for Mom to come out. We also were juggling with those types of rocks that are medium sized and sharp.

In hindsight, that was really stupid, but nothing happened. But really, I learned to juggle three days earlier, and throwing rocks over your head with your two hands occupied by other sharp rocks doesn't pose for the best-case scenario. Mom appreciated seeing us, and when her break was over, the rest of us headed to Geneva. We were going to go and play basketball in the shed at the elementary school, but there were other people there. We decided it looked like a daycare, and we were all in agreement that that didn't sound like fun.

Tay and I did chores for a movie when we came home. Meanwhile Dad was running the dog. Wilson is so muscular and healthy because of his runs with Dad. Dad really takes care of him more than any of us, and it really pays off. I think that Wilson is so good because he has gotten such good care. Mom and Dad say that it's the same with kids, and that's why they always have at least one parent at home, and they have work schedules that can work around each other.

One of Mom and Dad's most consistent beliefs about parenting is that kids should never be shipped off to a daycare, because then the parents aren't parenting. We never went to a daycare, or afterschool daycare, or anything. I'm thankful for that.

Saturday, July 4, 2020

We slept outside today. Mom was going to try to sleep out there, but later there were a lot of fireworks and Mom just decided that instead of trying to sleep out there with all those *booms!* sounds, she just went inside. So, we slept out there, and when I woke up, Wilson was on his back and all four of his legs were in the air. That was funny. And then I said hi to him, and we went inside after everyone woke up.

Taylor and I did screen time together today, for the most part. We watched some YouTube videos together and we played on the Xbox. We came up with a new *Minecraft* game to play together.

I then did my Khan Academy. If you remember what happened, there was that one part that I couldn't get through, but just about ten minutes into my KA, I passed it. The frustrations of the last couple of days are fine because the feeling of finishing that unit was great! Instead of celebrating and stopping, I went to another, and it isn't half as hard. It isn't very complex and it's more algorithmic and doesn't depend on the type of question but what to do with the equation. I did that for one hour and then I asked Mom what books to read, because I don't have any. She said that Tay and I didn't have to do our hour of reading, because it was the Fourth of July.

It was a really nice day despite it raining lightly all night. Mom and Dad went on a bike ride for one hour, and in that hour I did my weights. While I was doing that, Tay was doing his hour of Khan Academy, and I got to do five for A and five for B. I am almost fully transitioned to twelves, but for one of them I do eights. I did do twelve for it, but then I think I hurt my shoulder for a day, and Mom said that eights was enough to do.

To celebrate the fourth, Donnett and Terry invited us all over to have a bonfire with a few other neighbors. We left Wilson at home because Dad didn't want to deal with Otis and Wilson. I definitely agreed with this decision. I had three s'mores and a hot dog. Tay and I played corn hole most of the time the adults were talking. We were the only kids there, but we still had lots of fun. It wasn't easy to keep six feet apart, but I did my best. It was really fun.

When we came back, I did my writing for the Fourth. When I went outside, Phil was outside with the rest of the family. Wilson was out of his fence and was happily near everyone. I joined them, and Phil talked about how he is going to get another dog, a black Lab that is around four years old. He can't get her right away but is expecting to have her in November, so not for a while. He asked us if we wanted to go up to his house, where we can see the whole lake, to watch fireworks. So, we did. We stopped the ice cream we were making and just saved it for the next day. Then we went up and there was a constant, surprising number of fireworks. We were there until eleven, and then it started to get cold. Wilson was happy up there and was next to the bird feeder for most of the time. Looking for squirrels and birds. We went down and were all really tired and convinced Mom to let us sleep outside, but she stayed in. I believe we all fell asleep when our heads hit the pillow.

Sunday, July 5, 2020
The day went by really fast. After my screen time, we went on a walk. We went to the main trail, and then we popped out and walked on the fire road for a bit, until we went to a trail called Lost Soul. Then there was a fire road, and we turned that way and went back the trail we came from. I didn't do weight today because I did it yesterday. So, I just did that and played a lot of basketball with Dad and Taylor, respectively. So that was my exercise today.

Then I did Khan Academy for eighth grade, and that was good. Now that I am finished with that one hard part, I am not all free. The part that I am doing is new stuff that I am learning, but it makes a ton of sense, unlike the other one. If you look at one corner of the page on the website, you can see how much longer you have until you are finished with the grade. I am at 20 percent done with about five days done. I helped Taylor a little bit.

I think we are going to watch a movie today, and we also just had homemade pizza. Then we are going to have homemade ice cream and watch a movie. We can't sleep outside because Dad is going to the fire station for work for two days, because he traded his work shift with someone so that he could not have work get in the way when we go to Sandpoint in a few weeks.

Monday, July 6, 2020
I didn't sleep that well. I was kind of waking up and then going to bed, waking up again and then finally, at five I just decided that it wouldn't be worth it to go back to bed, because I would just wake up in a half hour. So, then I just kind of relaxed and did all of my reading. I read one of the *Harry Potter* books for an hour and got that out of the way. My head kind of hurt by the time I went downstairs, and by then I also had a runny nose. But I went and saw Mom and said good morning. I also said good morning to Tay. He was heading out the door with a poop bag, going to get and pick it up. Then Mom said that I should have a Tylenol, so I had that and then did my screen time.

I did screen time by myself while Tay just watched *Arrow* the whole time. I think it's going to be *The Flash* all over again. I don't really have anything to do screen time wise, but I think I am going to go back to watching a movie each day, and I think that will end up being super fun. It'll be nice to be able to watch the movie that I want instead of wondering what one Tay wants to watch, because I bet there are a lot of movies that I wanted to watch that Taylor didn't. That will be fun. Yeah, I will do that.

Then I did my Khan Academy and I got to learn some more things and it seems like I am growing mathematically. I feel a lot better about it than I did a few days ago with the other thing, but I am feeling good in that sense. I think I will get to algebra. That'll be my goal, and then my goal after that will be to finish it or get at least halfway done. I think I can do it, and I will do it well.

A record was broken today. In sports. The best player in the NFL, by a great distance, just signed a new contract. Here are the numbers: Patrick Mahomes, after playing out the next two years in his rookie contract, will be on a new ten-year contract, the longest duration of a contract ever in the NFL. And it isn't really close. Over five years is considered a really long contract. But for the next decade, as long as he plays the whole time, he will earn $455 million. And if he gets a career-ending injury, he has $155 million guaranteed. He is only twenty-four years old. That is a lot of money for one person. But if anyone was going to get it, it should be Patrick Mahomes.

That afternoon we played basketball, and then at six thirty we set up the tennis net in the driveway and played tennis. The tennis net is a really fun gift. I think that Tay is liking it more and more.

Tuesday, July 7, 2020

I woke up, inside. It wasn't a night where I woke up early or late, just an average night. That was nice and I had a weird dream, that I was a soldier in war and there was this spiral staircase, and we would go off ziplines and in go-cart-like things to fight the other people. So, then I woke up and was thankful when I realized that my headache, and also my runny nose, was all gone. So, I got out of bed. Tay and I, randomly enough, came out at the exact time. So, we went downstairs and Mom was still asleep. We pet Wilson, who was lying near Mom's bedroom door, and then I fed Wilson and picked up after him.

Afterward I did my reading and that was okay. I read *Harry Potter*, even though I have probably read the book four times, including one earlier in the COVID age. The second book, the one that I read, is probably the worst one out of all seven, but it was still really awesome. That's one of the greatest things about the *Harry Potter* series, all the books are incredibly great.

So, I then did my KA. I am now finished with the actual lessons and I just have to go and do the test. I think I will do fine, so that is what I will be doing. But I did that. Mom gave me a notebook to write the equations and my work in. I thought it would be a good idea instead of using a ton of printer paper, because that wouldn't be good, because we couldn't have anything to print with. The notebook has been in the console of her car for a while, and she rarely used it.

Mom had the fun idea that we should go play tennis at Western Washington University, because now that it's nice enough to play with the net, she realized that we aren't that good. The way that we all figured that out was with the insane amount of time that we spent chasing the tennis balls into the woods or the street. So, even though we passed a sign or two saying that the tennis courts were for students only, we played. We laughed pretty hard and didn't play that well.

Then I read for the next day. I did fifty minutes so that I don't have to do all of it tomorrow. Then I came down to have some ice cream that Mom said Tay had made. I took a big bite, and something was wrong. I was confused, until they told me that he had accidentally added some almond extract instead of vanilla. They wanted to know if I would notice, and I did, and it was definitely something I didn't want to eat. I don't like almonds or anything like that, so that wasn't great, but I think I will have dessert some other way. It wasn't a good idea to take a big bite. Yuck!

Wednesday, July 8, 2020

Well Dad was going to come home today. He has worked for the last two days, and he is here for one day once he comes at around nine thirty. He is then going to go back to work for another forty-eight hours. So that means he is working four of five days so far, and then he will be off for four days. The reason that he went is so that when we go to Sandpoint, Idaho, in a month, he won't have work get in the way. So, the days he did work, he changed and traded with other people at the fire station. So that is okay.

I may have mentioned it before, I don't know, but Sandpoint was a place that we would always go almost every year, mostly before school (August). It is the place that we went where our grandparents, Gammy and Paw-Paw, had a lake place. We would always go there instead of their other house. We had so many memories there. Then they sold it a few years ago. So, for the first time in a few years, we are going back, not to the same exact place, but the same town. That will be really fun. So, in almost an exact month, we are going there for five nights, or that is the plan. COVID could get in the way.

I woke up, and this time when I woke up, I really was ready to get up. It wasn't like some other days where I would wish I could fall asleep, or it would take a while for me to rub my eyes and make it downstairs. But this, again, was different. I went downstairs around two minutes after my eyes opened. Then I went and got the computer. No one was awake because it was, like, five forty-five. I petted Wilson and then got ear plugs and the computer, and then I did my Khan Academy. I did well on the test of one of them, and I am about to finish it. There is no doubt that I will tomorrow. I am also already 31 percent done with it. It has probably been eight or nine days, but I didn't expect to do it as fast as I had done the other, in around two weeks. I didn't have to do my reading, because I did fifty minutes already the day before. I probably will do my reading for the last ten and then maybe I will do some of my reading for tomorrow.

I watched another movie today, an Austin Powers movie. When we watched *Austin Powers* the first time, when Dad showed us, Mom didn't think it was a good idea, because we were too little. But we just told her that she introduced us to all the other National Lampoon movies. So, I watched that, and I started by watching the first one today, followed by the second tomorrow, and the final one the next day.

Then after Dad came home and a little bit of time passed, Dad, Tay, and I all went to Geneva to play basketball. That was fun, though at one point when we were playing there were two young elementary kids and they started videoing us with their little camera. Honestly, I don't really know how to interpret that into my brain.

Then for dinner we ate Mexican food. This is the third time in a row that I have had Mexican tacos for dinner. Probably the main reason that we had them was that Mom made a big amount of salsa. It's pretty good. I love my whole family.

Thursday, July 9, 2020

I woke up at the same time that I woke up the day before. I woke up at five forty-five, but then after a little I fell back asleep, and at six thirty I went to Khan Academy. I finished the unit, so I have done the two shortest units and also the second longest unit. I have four left, and I think I'll finish it by the end of the month. That will be super cool. Then I can advance to algebra, and that'll be nice because that is what I will go to in September, so I'll get a head start on the class before I even show up.

Mom and Taylor woke up right before I had finished, and then I said good morning to them. They were petting Wilson, and I came over to pet him too. Then I gave Wilson the opportunity to go outside. He didn't want to go, so I let him stay in, and then I fed him his food. I'm doing this thing where I will whistle with my fingers when I give Wilson his food, and then he comes, so that if he is leaving, he will respond to it. I have done it for around one or two weeks so far. Then I picked up his poop, only one.

I had recapped that I had done my reading, because I had done it prior to today, and I had done my Khan Academy, so then I watched the second *Austin Powers* movie. This one is the best of the three. A little bit after that movie I asked Mom if she wanted to go on a drive, and we did at around eleven. We first went to Bed Bath & Beyond because Mom had to return an order and get something new. I stayed inside the car. Then we went to Fairhaven to get Mom some hair stuff that her friend wanted her to have, so she did that. Then we went to Tony's and got some pumpkin bread, and we shared a soup. It was really good. We also had one for Tay once we got home. We both kind of reflected that this was a really weird time, and in both her and her parent's lives, whether they have ever seen anything like this, masks and stuff, stores filing for bankruptcy, parks closed, not very many social interactions. Then we went to La Fiamma and got some pizza for dinner.

We came home, and Tay had his pumpkin bread, and we didn't do anything, really, for a bit. Then Mom saw something on Facebook, that one of her friends was making cupcakes, so we went all together and got four of them. Then we had dinner; we had pizza, our favorite salad, and after this we are going to have cupcakes. I really think that they are going to be good. We smelled them when we got home, and they smelled really fresh, so I think I'll like them.

Friday, June 10, 2020

Is it really Friday? Really, I didn't know, and I wouldn't have all day, but I did write, so I kind of have a knowledge of the day of the week. I love that feeling, when you really know that summer has arrived. Yay.

I woke up and was going to go downstairs but once again fell asleep and then woke up to it being almost seven, so then I finished my reading. I had already done half of it the day before, so that was nice to get it over with. After that I went downstairs, and Mom was on the phone. I went to the computer, but Tay got there just a little bit faster than me, and he did his KA, what I was going to do. So, I went on my school computer and signed into my account and got my phone to listen to music. I am getting better, and I started to continue on to geometry. What I was doing was figuring out missing angles for triangles and intersecting lines. I don't know it immediately, but after five minutes I have got it down, and then I move on to the next one.

After that I had both my reading and math done for the day, and then I waited a little before deciding to watch the final *Austin Powers*. Then Tay wanted to watch, and we watched it and that was great, and then we finished it. It was really funny, by the way. Then I went out to see where Mom was, and she was on her trainer for her bike. I saw my scooter and decided to just stroll around the driveway on it, and then Tay came out and did the same thing.

Then Mom and Tay went on a drive and went to the toy store, and Tay got some more juggling balls. I think he wanted to get to juggling five. I had originally wondered, if I could juggle that I could just use Tay's, but Tay didn't like that idea as much as I wanted to. So, I just decided to get a few to avoid arguments in the future (argument, in Taylor's case: where Tay doesn't like what you are doing and uses a raised, annoyed voice to express his anger). Just for you to know in the future.

They came home and a little bit later Mom and I took Wilson on a walk. We went to the main trail and then to a trail that we don't usually go to but went anyway, and then we turned back and went back the way that we came. Then I played some soccer. I haven't played in so long, but I am going to try to be the best I have ever been—not just get back to where I was, but I haven't completely lost my touch for the game.

Saturday, July 11, 2020

I woke up in the morning and kept waking up and then falling back asleep. It wasn't like I wasn't getting a good sleep, just that my brain couldn't decide to either wake up or fall asleep. So, then I was like, *Okay it's seven thirty. I have to wake up.* I went down and there was no one there. Not even Wilson. Then I realized that Mom had gone to work. She left a note that I needed to feed Wilson. So, I still didn't know where Wilson was, and then I went outside and saw Wilson was there, so Mom must have left him out right before she had left for work. So, I fed him. Then Taylor came down once I came in. I saw that it was an odd day, so I picked up poop. There actually wasn't any, so I just went back in and was going to do my Khan Academy, but Tay was going on the computer to do the same thing, so again, I just went on my own computer. I have gotten to 40 percent done with it, and that was in probably eleven days, so I will finish it by the end of the month. I think I will complete it on the twenty-seventh. That is my guess.

Then I started to do some YouTube on my phone and I heard Dad come in. We said hi to him, and Wilson was very happy to see him. Then I went downstairs to try a *Madden* NFL franchise mode, and then Tay came down and he wanted to play some *Minecraft*, and that was some fun.

Then we went to the football field and played and it was really fun. We haven't played for a while. And we also went to Hospice House to give Mom coffee. Instead of waiting around I did my stretching and warmed up there. The field is really close, and you could even see it if there weren't any trees in the way. We each made some good catches, but no one got any interceptions. After one of the touchdowns, I told Dad that I was going to get the first interception. So, we kept playing and I almost got an interception, but it kind of bobbled too much behind me. We kept playing, and then Tay wanted to get some water. He said he only wanted to do one more drive. Dad and I wanted to play more, but then he would get the ball for the last one. I really wanted to get an interception. No one had got one so far, and then on the first one Dad got, like, seven yards. I felt like if I tried harder, I could have gotten one on it. The next play he kind of only wanted a ten-yard pass or something, but he kept going downfield, and then the ball was in the air and stayed there for a while. Neither Tay nor I had to move because the ball was going right to us. I don't really know exactly how I got it, but I did, and I think I just had a good timing on the jump. I got the one and only interception.

Sunday, June 12, 2020

We got to sleep outside, and I slept on the mattress next to Dad, and next to Wilson, who was on the mattress next to Tay. I woke up right around when Dad woke up, and we went inside. I decided that because I had done KA for the day, I was going to finish my reading. So, I did that, and I am reading one of the new books that Mom and I got on Amazon. It seems good so far, and I am just starting it, so I don't know everything. I can't wait to find out the ending. Then Mom came up in my room and said that she had to go to work and that it would probably be for all day, so she said bye, and Tay was still asleep. Tay actually slept past eight, and while he was sleeping, I was doing even more Khan Academy. I am going to finish the next unit in the next two days. I think I could tomorrow if I do a little bit extra, maybe two hours and not one.

Then Tay and I did our screen time. First, he wanted to watch his show, so he did that for a little while. I watched YouTube and then asked if he wanted to do some *Minecraft*, and then we did some. In the middle of it,

272

Dad said that he was going to go on a bike ride, and when he was done, we heard, and then we came up a bit later.

We had lunch, and then we all were going to say hi to Mom. Dad had made bagels, and we got two of them for both Mom and one of the people who works there, that Mom wanted to give one to. So, two bagels for her, and then we got her some coffee at Starbucks. Across the street, we also got some food for her and then we went there. Wilson tagged along, and he had fun. When we were waiting, we played hot potato with this small ball, and that was beautifully fun instead of doing nothing.

On our way home, we got the mail. There was a package, and when we opened it, we saw that it was a volleyball that Mom had gotten on Amazon. Because Tay has that adjustable net that he got for his birthday, we were just thinking of things to use it with, and we used that. So, Dad and I tried to play a bit of that, but to be honest, it wasn't really a ton of fun. I think it could be if we played with all, Mom, Dad, Tay and I.

After that, I don't know how we thought of it, but Dad got his fly rod and we started for the first time to learn how to cast in the yard. It was fun, and after Tay and Dad went inside, I just did it for an hour by myself. It is fun, and I feel every ten minutes I get noticeably better.

Monday, July 13, 2020

I woke up early. This is the four-month marker since Friday, March 13, when we were going to school and in fifth period they announced on the loudspeaker that there wouldn't be school for six weeks due to the global (then) epidemic (turned pandemic), COVID. Later they announce that there will be no more school. That really seems like ten years ago. We have adjusted, but it is crazy that all spring we missed school. Then we missed the last day of school. When I started writing, I was assuming that I would be writing for, like, forty days or something, not more than 120. Now it kind of seems like we are looking down a tunnel that is too long to see the other side. What will it be when it is my birthday, in another four months, or when it is 2021?

I woke up and thought that it was, like, six thirty or something, from looking at the sky and how bright it was. But after rubbing my eyes and looking around, I went in and saw Dad, and then I gazed over to the clock that read five twenty. The next time I looked at the clock was ten minutes later when Dad and I left the house, with both Tay and Mom fast asleep. A fly rod between us and a bag with more flies than anyone could count at my feet.

We went to Whatcom Falls Park, and I had the flyrod in one hand, looking at the end, constantly avoiding outreaching branches and leaves. We went to a part that was a little pond that had little trees. I looked for spots where fish could be while Dad tied a fly. There weren't many fish in sight, but I kept casting. I didn't catch any in the hour that we were there. But I probably learned a lot, and I got to feel the way to cast with the tug of the water. Afterwards we walked back, and after getting in the car, Dad proposed getting a doughnut because it was the first time. So, I got one. We got home at almost exactly seven. We didn't go through the garage but went through the front door to be quiet.

Mom was in the living room. We said good morning and she asked how it was, and then we noticed that Tay was still asleep outside. We also saw that Wilson was at the door wanting to say good morning to everyone. Tay woke up about ten or fifteen minutes later, probably from Wilson getting up and the opening of the door.

We ate breakfast and then I did my reading for forty-five minutes, after doing my screen time, some of it with Tay. After my reading I said hi to Wilson, and Mom and Dad were going on an hour-and-a-half bike ride. Later I cast the fly rod a little in the yard. I put peanuts back into the squirrel feeder that I made. I hadn't checked on it for a while. Then I did weights after lunch and Mom went to work. She will be back at seven thirty. Dinner was good, and at seven, Tay and Dad are going to fish in the same spot that I went to.

Tuesday, July 14, 2020
I woke up and we slept outside. We all went outside, and even Mom came out, and I was where I slept outside the night before. So, I woke up around about seven and saw that only Taylor was out, and then I came inside. Mom was asleep in her own room, and Dad had gone fishing with Jason. So, Tay was asleep, and I left Wilson to be with him. Then Wilson started whining so I let him come in, and then he wanted to go outside, and then I tried to find his collar, and then after a bit I found it, and he went outside. I think that Tay is now sleeping in a lot more than I am. I am older, but as you know, sleeping is not something that I do a lot. So, he will probably end up sleeping until like ten or something in a few years. And I will continue to wake up at six thirty.

Then we did screen time and Tay and I played some *Minecraft*. We did one, but then Tay got stuck and we did a new one. All of them were really fun, so we played and then we came up. A little later I did have a hot dog. Then I left to lift weights and did what I usually did. I did five sets of twenty lunges, fifteen push-ups, ten triceps, and ten sit ups. Then I did another five sets of ten squats, ten military presses, ten curls, ten something else, five sit-ups, and then five pushups. So that was what I now usually do.

I went up and Mom and Dad went on a walk. So, I ate some Cheerios. Then Tay came up and had a bowl of cereal, and then he went back. Then I wondered where he was, after I was done. He was downstairs playing with Legos. We don't usually play Legos on a regular basis, but he was, so I decided to join him. I did that with him and made my own Lego thing. That was really fun. I also found a thing that we had got a bit ago. It is a robot-looking thing that you try to fold up into a cube. I haven't seen it in a few years, so I did that.

Mom and Dad came home just a little later. I went outside with them, and Wilson was all wet because Dad probably gave him a bath when he was done with the walk, because I can guess that Wilson was all dirty and he got completely wet. It was a really sunny day, and I did a lot of my reading and KA yesterday, so I had a lot of the day without doing reading or using my brain much. I think after this I will do my reading and then my KA so that I can do the same tomorrow. It is going to be a good day tomorrow.

Also, a football player just signed a four-year contract up to eighty-five million. I say this because he is on the Chiefs, which is the team that Mahomes is on. And the player Chris Jones plays defensive end, and that is a position that the Seahawks are weak on. So, I was wondering if the Seahawks could have traded for him. Also, the Washington Redskins are changing its name because it is offensive to Native Americans. I think that it was a good idea, and I was cheering for them to do it. Unfortunately, probably the only reason was because people that they got money from were wanting to cut ties if they didn't change the name. So, it is about money, not what is right or wrong.

Wednesday, July 15, 2020

I guess that we are now halfway into July, so that is kind of halfway into summer. We were going to sleep outside, but then Dad went in because his allergies were bad, and so were Mom's and mine. Tay doesn't have any allergies, but it seemed like he couldn't fall asleep, so at ten we just decided that for us to get a good sleep we should also go inside. So, we did that and then I had a really good sleep. I didn't wake up until maybe around six thirty or seven. I think Mom and Tay also had a good sleep after.

Tay was still asleep when I was going downstairs, and after a little while, Mom and Tay woke up. I did my Khan Academy. I also have been doing really well with Khan Academy, and I have done six out of the seven units. The last one is a really big one, but after that I will do some algebra. That will be good, and I think by the twentieth I will end eighth grade.

I took a shower and was going to go on a walk with Mom, but we decided not to do so. Tay and I both did some screen time separately, and then we did some screen time together. Dad had to go to the fire station today, but tomorrow he will be back. Then I think tomorrow I will go fishing with him in the afternoon, and I think that will be really fun. Tay and I played *Minecraft* and had a lot of fun. At the end, Tay went back and did some of his own screen time.

After that, Mom came back from a hike with a friend, and then she and I did some hill repeats in the back hill behind the yard. We were going to do twenty, but then at ten Mom wanted to cut it to fifteen. So, we did fifteen and then came home. Tay hadn't come like we thought he might have, but then he and I went on our bikes to the mailbox, and I brought a backpack and the key, so I got that and then we came back.

Then we had tacos for dinner, and it was really good, and I think we are going to have some dessert. I think that we are going to sleep inside instead of outside because Dad is at work, but maybe tomorrow we will.

Thursday, July 16, 2020

Well, instead of going to bed outside, because we were probably going to have some allergies, we decided to sleep inside. But we quickly realized that it was too hot upstairs to sleep, so we went to the basement, and we saw that we could sleep in the twin beds that Tay had put in the basement when he got the bed from down there. I slept in one and Mom slept on the other. Tay slept on the floor in between us. Even though he could have gotten one of the mattresses from the deck, he just put a blanket down and got another one to put on top of him. We slept well. Later in the day I saw that I had this nasty bite behind my right earlobe. It itches a little but doesn't hurt. I rinsed it and took a shower later, before I did my writing in the morning.

I woke and I saw that Tay was still there on the floor. I tiptoed on the outside of his outline from the blanket and then silently walked upstairs and saw that no one was awake. Mom had woken a little earlier and had put Wilson outside so that he wouldn't walk around for both Tay and me to wake from. I tiptoed to the computer and did my Khan Academy. I am making good progress toward finishing. I won't finish tomorrow or the next day. I think it will take one more day after that before I complete it. Then comes algebra.

Mom woke up when I was doing math, and then I finished and said good morning to her. Tay, once more, woke up at eight. Then we did our screen time, and it was fun. We played *Minecraft*, and then we came up and I ate a little and then went up to do my reading. In the middle of reading, I heard Dad come in, so I said good morning to him and went back up to read. After I finished, Tay and I did a little more screen time. Then I ate a hotdog for lunch and had some Cheerios.

We had a good afternoon, and for dinner Dad made some really good enchiladas. What he put in the middle was a yam, and that was good. After that Dad and I went off fishing. Dad told me to not put on socks, and I didn't. So, when we got to the river, the fish started biting, but we couldn't keep one in for a bit. Then we went through a time where we didn't see one. We went back up to the path and a little downstream, and then we saw that there was a fish or two there. Then we could start casting, and he was just getting the line out and then one snagged it and let go. Two or three casts later the same fish was there, and by that time I was close enough to have Dad hand the pole to me and reel. It was a nice one, and we let him go. Then we realized it was getting late, so we came back home.

Friday, July 17, 2020

I woke up downstairs once more and Tay was asleep. So I went upstairs and said good morning to Dad. Then I said good morning to Wilson, who was wagging his tail. Mom and Tay woke up a little later. I said good morning to them and then did my Khan Academy. I am getting closer to finishing it. I think by the twenty-first at most, nineteenth at the fastest amount of time. It is probably going to be a few more days than the nineteenth. I did a unit test, so now I just have to practice all that I got wrong, and then I can finish.

Tay and I played *Minecraft*, and I think for tomorrow I will do a new longer-term world instead of doing ones that are, like, twenty minutes long. I don't know if Tay will want to join or not, but I will be fine if he does join. Maybe we could be in the same house or something like that.

We had breakfast, and even though I usually have it for lunch, I had a hot dog so that I could fill up for fishing. We got our back packs from school and filled them with snacks for the ride home and the way back. I got Cheerios, cherries, crackers, and more fruit. I also got gum, but I ended up not having any of it. I would have, but I just forgot. Tay packed his bag and then he, Dad, and I went to the car and Dad put two bamboo fishing rods in. Then I took shotgun and Tay took the back. We decided that Tay could have the front on the way back. It took one hour to get there, and for the last fifteen minutes there was a dirt/gravel road and countless potholes, and then we finally got there.

While Dad was putting together Tay's fly rod, another car came from right behind us. There was someone else that was going to fish the same river. They went further downstream, so we didn't see them after we went on an undesignated path to the river, and we hopped over mossy rocks. We started close to the car, and in the spot that Tay was at he got a bite in the first minute and caught two in the first ten minutes. So, Dad got that fly and put it on mine and then I got one. We didn't change the fly the rest of the time, but we kept going up stream. It was slippery and there were no bites, so we came back down a half hour later. On our way down, one tried to get Tay's, and then I went to the same area but stayed out of his way, and I caught one of the two that were there. Tay wasn't very happy that I took his fish, but he didn't get one there. We went to where we started, and in one pool I found a fish, and it kept going at my fly. But I couldn't get him. I couldn't find him after he went after my fly fifteen times. Then I went to a bigger pool, and there was a fish there, and then I didn't find him for a while. Then I was going to dry my fly, and I thought it got caught on a rock by the line and started squirming, and I caught that fish! At the end of the day, we got a total of six or seven fish. We let them go, though; we never keep them.

Saturday, July 18, 2020

I woke up downstairs. I did my reading the night before and was reading until almost eleven. I really like the book that I am reading, and I hadn't done my reading for the day because we were fishing all day. Then when I was falling asleep Tay started to do the scariest snore. Now, I would also wonder, *How is a snore scary?* Well, I could tell that his nose was very congested, and I was worried that I would be falling asleep trying to keep the snoring out of my mind, and Tay, the possibility that Tay stops breathing and suffocates. I know it is pretty out there, but still, you didn't hear it.

I did my Khan Academy and then I learned later in the day that on the weekends we didn't have to do our KA. Well, I could have learned that, like, eight weeks ago. That means that I won't do it tomorrow. I also know that I will finish eighth in a few days, so I cannot worry that I will cut it close and not complete it on time. So, I did that, and then I was going to do my writing, but then Tay said that he wanted to do his writing, and it should have been fair. We did rock-paper-scissors or something, but he didn't think about that, and then he did his writing. I did my reading at that time and then my writing when he was done, and I finished my reading.

Then we played some *Minecraft*. Later we came back up and ate, and I had some Cheerios. Mom came back from the trails with her friend Ali, and Ali was going to buy my old bike for her son, Finn, for his birthday. It was too small for me, so I didn't need it or anything. But If I do go on the trail, I can use Mom's mountain bike.

Then I played with Wilson and I waved at Phil, who was driving by. He got out and opened the door and his new dog came out. I got Mom and Tay, and we talked, and the dogs played really well together. Then Phil left and went up to his house. We said hi to Wilson and went inside. I ate more Cheerios, and then we had dinner after having a water gun fight in the backyard. It was really fun, and then after dinner Tay and I did some chores and then watched a movie called *Jack and Jill*. Adam Sandler played both Jack and Jack's twin sister Jill. It was a funny movie, and we should have watched it earlier.

Sunday, July 19, 2020

I woke up in the basement, like yesterday. I looked next to me and saw that there was Tay, and he was on his side, clearly still asleep. I took a few minutes to get out of bed and then saw that Mom was in her room, just waking up. Wilson came up, so I petted him and then did my writing. That took an hour, and then Tay came up. I helped Mom make coffee. I filled up the thing to the level 4 and then I gave it to her, and she put two scoops of coffee grounds in and flicked the switch to *ON*, and then she had it later. I asked Tay if he had to do his writing, and if he didn't, if he wanted to play *Minecraft*. He reminded me that I had to pick up Wilson's poop, so I went and got two, I put it in the big garbage under the sink and put that in a bag into the garbage in the garage.

While I was finishing up *Minecraft*, Mom asked if I wanted to go with her to get some groceries. I said I would think about it and then I ended up saying yes. I stayed in the car while she went into Haggen. I saw a few people from the car. There was one person who had a small car. He was kind of overweight and had three really small dogs. I saw him pull up and leave, and one of the three dogs barked, but the others didn't. I saw another person that was smoking and then put a mask on and went in. I assumed that they were really young, twenty something, from the small bit that I could see, but she actually was sixty something, and I thought it was sad to see someone smoking. Wilson was also in the car with me, and he was a good boy. He just looked out the back window the whole time and looked at people walking by. Mom came and then we went home.

Dad came home right when we came, and we hugged and then we all put the food that Mom got into the fridge. Dad didn't though, because we told him that we had a surprise for him and that we were going to make dessert on Mom and Dad's anniversary, nineteen years. So, we did that, and then we just stayed around, and then Donnett came over and got our old scooters that we never use.

Later in the day we went to see Ru, Phil's new dog. Dad hadn't seen her before because he was at work the time before. We stayed up there for a while, and then Tay and I came to see how Wilson was doing. Tay came back quicker than me. I stayed for an extra ten minutes and I lay in the hammock. Then I we went back a little later. I think we are going to sleep outside tonight and maybe have ice cream.

Monday, July 20, 2020

We slept outside today, and that was really fun. After that, Tay and I played *Minecraft* for a while, but Tay also did watch his show. Then I did my reading and finished the book that was really good. I think it was called *A Better Man* or something, and it had a twist at the end of the book.

I took a bath after that, and then I brushed my teeth. Dad went fishing with a friend (Mike), and they were going to meet at around seven, but Mike forgot his shoes on the way there and had to go back, and then they met at nine. They stayed until three thirty, and then Dad came home and said that he caught zero fish, and all together they got zero. But Mike stayed later and ended up catching twenty-three.

We went on the trail before Dad came home, and we went on the main one. Then we got to the fire road and Mom saw a friend from work, and they talked for twenty minutes. By then Tay, who gets hot fast and way more than anyone else, didn't want to keep going. But we tried a little more on Papa Bear and then turned around. I got a good idea for where we could go, but Mom remembered that she had to go home for something about food that she was making. So, we just went home, but we made the plan that tomorrow we are going to go swimming. And I am going to do weights in the morning, and that day will be super fun. So then for dinner I had some really good enchiladas. I had three or four, and then we watched something on Disney+. The play *Hamilton* was on, so we got to watch that on Disney+ and it was only eight dollars or something.

Tuesday, July 21, 2020

Mom and I were going to sleep outside with Tay and Dad, but I started noticing that my allergies were coming, and I decided that I didn't want to deal with that. So, Mom and I went inside and to the basement, and we each slept in one of the two twins. (Mom calls them the Bert and Ernie beds; she remembers *Sesame Street* way better than either Tay or I do.) I slept great and then I woke up and went up, and I saw that Mom woke up and thought she was awake and then went back to bed in her room. Dad was awake.

Today was Mom and Dad's anniversary, so we said happy nineteen years. Then Tay woke up. Mom and I went with Dad and Wilson to the beach a few minutes away and went swimming. I did only two laps and Mom did nine or something. Wilson also got a good swim.

When we came back, I had brunch and then did weights. I did five of A day and five of B day. Later Dad got a call from Phil that he got a woodpecker inside his house, and we helped him get that. Then we celebrated Mom and Dad's anniversary, and they went and got a little food. We had some really good steak for dinner, and we had Mom's cake that she made for dessert. It was all really good. Then we played some volleyball, and then I took a shower. I think we are all going to sleep in the basement because it is so hot on the upper two floors. I think we may go fishing tomorrow at the place where we caught seven fish. If we do, it may be in the afternoon and Mom might come with us and she could learn soon. That would be fun, and I really hope that Mom will come. That would be great. Also, I think I am going to get a haircut soon.

Wednesday, July 22, 2020

I woke up downstairs, and Mom and Dad were both upstairs. So I went up there and saw that only Wilson was awake, so I just did my reading. I also did Khan Academy and got really close to finishing the whole thing. I can, by the twenty-fifth, and I could, by tomorrow. So, then Tay and I played *Minecraft* for a little, and then I took a bath and came back and helped Tay with *Minecraft*, and we had lunch, and then we packed our snacks for the afternoon. We were going fishing again, so I got the front again on the ride there, and then we got in the car and started going.

It took one hour to get there, and we saw that there were some people there already, so we just went on the other side of the river. I went to one pool and got a bite but nothing more. Then I moved the slightest bit up and got one. The other people left, and we went on their side, and I caught one there. In all, I got four fish. It was really fun being there, and we were there for, like, three hours. We went up and down the river, and I think we all really liked it, and it went by too fast. One fish was thick and one was really small. The others were average fish. On the way home I ate the snacks that we packed, and then we got home.

We had a good dinner. I had some leftover steak. Mom had a tough conversation at work about a nurse that said some racist things; that was brave, and she had to talk to her boss. Mom also took a COVID test because she had a cough over the weekend. Tomorrow she should get the results.

Thursday, July 23, 2020

I didn't know what day of the week it was until I did my writing. That was really cool, and now we are kind of on the second half of summer, so now I am going to just try to enjoy it a lot before it goes, because it won't be back for a whole nine months. I wonder what I will be like in nine, twelve months. I think we should have the cases going down in eight or nine months, and in twelve we will be able to go around like usual. I can't wait for that.

I woke up and went up and said hi to Wilson and then Mom. Dad was at work, so we called him that day but didn't see him. I did read, and I did some screen time with Tay. Mom and I went on a drive, and that was fun. We went to Whole Foods and Tony's, then we came home, and I got the mail for Mom. But when I was getting in the car, I hit my elbow on the way in and it hurt a ton, and it was kind of painful to do weights, so I didn't do them, but I will tomorrow. I am putting an ice pack on it now, not because it hurts all the time, but I wanted to make sure that it gets better fast.

I did my Khan Academy today and ended up finishing the grade. That means in five weeks I will have completed both seventh and eighth grades. Then I am going to do some pre-algebra, not the whole thing, and then I will do the most I can do for Algebra I. I will do a little, but I can't finish it by the middle of July.

Friday, July 24, 2020

I woke up in the morning and went upstairs and said good morning to everyone. Then I did my reading later in the day, and I am reading a book that I first got Dad for Christmas. I didn't have a book to read, so I am going to read this one, *Chicago* by Brian Doyle. It is a good book and is entertaining. Mom and I got the newspaper at eight, and Tay was asleep. We got it the day before, but Mom got it herself that time. We get the newspaper for four days while one of our neighbors doesn't need it, and this is the second day. We also will get the Sunday paper the next day.

For dinner I had some tacos. I put some ground beef, cheese, guacamole, and salsa on it. I had six. Mom and Dad had some tofu, and it was finished with some peanut sauce, so I didn't have to do dishes because I am allergic.

We got to sleep outside, and Wilson was really happy. Mom was thinking of sleeping outside, but then we realized Mom had to go to work at around six thirty. So, I slept next to Dad, and Wilson slept between Tay and me. We had to set up one half of the deck, but the other half was already there. It is also at the time that sundown is around ten thirty or so, meaning it was light when we fell asleep.

One last thing is that yesterday a Seattle team entered the NHL, what we've known for a while but haven't gotten a nickname until yesterday. Starting in the 2021 season the Seattle Kraken are going to be in the NHL. I don't watch hockey, but I am happy for Seattle, and it will be another team to keep an eye on. They will be in the Western Conference. The last new team that came to the NHL was the Las Vegas Knights. Now all we need is for the Supersonics to come back.

Saturday, July 25, 2020

We got to sleep outside, and that was really fun. Dad, Tay, Wilson, and I all did, and Mom decided not to because she had to go to work really early in the morning. So we all got a good night sleep (I think), and I woke up and saw Dad go inside, and then I came after and said good morning to Mom right before she went to work. I did my writing for the day before, Friday.

Then Tay and I did some *Minecraft* for a little while. Also, in one month *Madden 21* is going to come. I wonder what will happen in the next football month with trades and stuff. So, we played *Minecraft*, and then we came up and had some food, and at 10:40 we started driving to go get our own computers that we got for school. Then the freeway got closed because apparently someone drove their car into one of those big signs that are green and have white writing on it saying where the nearest cities are and how many miles away they are. So, we got there one hour later than we were aiming to get there. But we got them, and then we took Wilson for a small walk to get some bagels, and Tay also got a smoothie. We came back, and in total there were five hours of driving.

We also got some news at the end of the car ride. Mom told me that Uncle Steve sent her something and that the Seahawks traded for someone good. We didn't know yet, but when we pulled up, we got the news that we got Jamal Adams, who is a strong safety and no doubt a top three at his position, and by some the best. I am really excited and can't wait to see how he plays.

Sunday, July 26, 2020
So, Dad had to go to work at eight because there were projections that there would be protests.

For the computers we got, we set up the basics but then couldn't set up the Microsoft package for Home and Student, which includes OneNote, Word, Excel and PowerPoint. So, I kind of accidentally started setting it up, and then I decided to try and finish it, so I got all of that on the computer. Then I tried to help Tay do his, but something happened with the code. If I try a little, I think I could still do it, but I didn't feel like messing around with it because it wasn't as easy as mine was, and a detour could mess it up. In conclusion, my computer is all set up and I technically don't need to use the old family one ever again. I also took my writing that was on the other computer and emailed it onto this one. Tay's computer we will do tomorrow, probably when Dad gets home.

I did my reading and I'm going to read *Ready Player One*. I have read it twice before and it was really good. It also has the main character's name, Wade Watts, the same last name as mine, which is neat. Tay and I played *Minecraft*, and I did some YouTube. Mom went swimming and on a hike with her friends. For the hike, she brought Wilson, but he stayed home while they went swimming.

We stayed outside kind of the whole afternoon, and I played some basketball. Mom and I got the Sunday paper, and we all read that outside on the deck. For dinner I think we are having pasta, and we could possibly convince Mom to watch a movie.

Monday, July 27, 2020
I woke up downstairs, and then I took my book and just went straight upstairs because if I said hi to Wilson, I might wake Mom or Tay. So I did all of my reading, and I went downstairs one hour later. I continued reading *Ready Player One*, and he got the first key. I kind of remember how it goes, but actually, when I visualize it, I think of the movie, and it doesn't have the same things as the book, I was reminded. Maybe I should watch its movie when I finish it.

Then I played *Minecraft* with Tay. I think in the next few days I am going to do something different than *Minecraft*. I think I might watch a movie tomorrow. Mom went on a one-and-a-half-hour bike ride, and she said that it wasn't easy. It also got up to eighty degrees, so that was hot. I did some YouTube as well. Mom came home from the bike ride, and then at eleven Dad came home with some food from Fred Myers, and we helped him put it away.

Mom and I went on a drive, and when we came back, we had some lunch, and I had some soup and crackers. Then we started talking about going swimming and got all packed up and headed to Euclid Park. When we got there, the small parking lot was full. Overall, for a small beach, there were a dozen cars. So we went to Padden, and it was also really crowded there, but we got a parking spot. We went to this small part, and there was a lot of the tall grass, so we had to get through all of that with our three floaties. There is one watermelon-decorated doughnut shape, an avocado, and a normal looking yellow one. So, we were there for about an hour, and we came back another way and got our stuff from the place we started at.

After going home, we had a really good taco dinner. I think we may be able to sleep outside tonight, and maybe Mom will join us. It is really hot, and I just looked it up, and it is eighty degrees still, at seven fifteen.

Tuesday, July 28, 2020

We did get to sleep outside and that was great. I seemed like I was going to maybe have allergies, but instead, after talking for a while, I went straight to sleep and it worked. I was next to Dad, and on the other mattress was Mom and Tay. Wilson fell asleep at Tay's feet. Mom couldn't stay out the whole night, but it was cool that she tried. So, we slept great, and when I woke up, I saw that Wilson was on his back and all four of his paws were in the air. He was right where I saw him last.

I went inside and, instead of playing *Minecraft* with Tay, I played some *Madden* and made a new team. I am the Forty-Niners and I have Russell Wilson and a lot of good players. I hope I can play a few seasons with the team. But at the end of the day, before we had dinner, I had played a tiny bit of *Minecraft* with Tay.

Joey Bosa, whose brother also plays in the NFL, signed a record contract for his position. I think that is okay, but he isn't the best at his position, so he shouldn't get a record contract. The team that he signed his five-year contract with is the LA Chargers. They were good a few years ago, but overall, they have been kind of bad. Also J. Clowney is still unsigned. He did play for the Seahawks, and he was good. If the Seahawks gave him a contract, the whole off season would be a grand slam, between getting Jamal Adams and resigning a few other players. They didn't really have an amazing looking draft, but I think that it could still be an amazing one. Kind of like the Seahawks 2012 draft where they were graded as an F but ended up with three or four really good players, including Russell Wilson and Bobby Wagner.

Wednesday, July 29, 2020
So, we got to sleep outside again, and Mom had to go to work for a whole twelve-hour shift, from seven to seven, so she didn't sleep outside with us. In the morning, I saw her getting ready for work, but she didn't come out to say bye because Dad was still asleep, so she went out and then Dad woke up a little later. We went inside, and at seven we did some screen time. Instead of playing *Minecraft* I played *Madden*, and I am 9–0 so far. I am the best team in the NFL and I am the Niners, even though I don't like the Forty-Niners, hence the Seahawk rivalry, but I wanted to be a different team than I had been before.

After that I did my reading and some weights, and then I finished the rest of my screen time. I think I am going to stay with the team for a while. Then after that we had lunch and then we didn't know what to do. Dad went on a bike ride for a little while, and when he came home we decided what we should do.

We went to Mom while she was at work, but because we had an inner tube that was in the back, we didn't have Wilson. Mom didn't want a coffee, but we got goggles from her car and then went out to Padden and did some swimming. We also earned some screen time as a reward, so we did that later. We had pizza and I made some ice cream, and we may sleep outside.

Thursday, July 30, 2020
Now is the real day that I have reached one hundred pages of journaling! That is incredible, and of course no one thought that we would be writing that much. It has been four and a half months since we did write on the Monday after we were off of school. So much has happened, from dad's knee, to making homemade bread, to going on the trails. Also, all the stuff in world news, with coronavirus. Now, I think in the US there are 150,000 deaths. That is a lot of people, and it is so sad. To be honest, I wish that I wouldn't have to do my writing this long, because every day I write, more people get sick, and COVID isn't over.

We got to sleep outside again, and it was really fun. Then we got up and I did some screen time and Mom and I went swimming. We got to swim back and forth in this little public part of Lake Whatcom. So that was fun, and then Mom and I went on a drive. We went to get some Tony's, and

I had some soup and Mom got some sushi to eat. My soup was hot, so I only had a little and I had the rest on the way home.

Tay went swimming later and Dad went on a run. He was gone and we did some more screen time, and then Phil and Sue came over for a bonfire. Tay was really tired, and I know this because eventually he fell asleep on the chaise. It was funny to see him kind of wake up once they left.

Friday, July 31, 2020

I fell asleep quickly and I think so did Tay, so then I woke up and Tay was still asleep. I then went and did my writing for the day before. I looked at the time, and it was six fifteen. I did my writing and listened to music and did some Khan Academy. Mom and Dad said a few days ago that starting tomorrow all we have to do is our writing and thirty minutes of reading. We don't have to do our KA or anything else other than that. We were excited about that, so that starts tomorrow.

Mom woke up and saw that I was doing my writing, and she was surprised that I hadn't slept in for a longer amount of time. After I did my writing and KA, I hugged Wilson. Later we went and tried to let Wilson swim, but he was more interested in smelling the bushes around, so we just went home. Tay and Mom also went swimming, so they did that, and I did my screen time.

At one o'clock, we got in the car and went to Gavin and Carter's house. We were really excited, and when we got there, we went to a little beach a walking distance away. Then we went swimming to a floating dock and stayed there for a while, and then Carter texted Logan and Kaden, and they came over and we played some spout ball, and then we went back in the water. So that was two hours long, and then we came home. We watched a movie later in the day, after dinner.

Saturday, August 1, 2020

Tay and I both fell asleep downstairs, and I woke up a little and then tried to go back to bed, but I just went back upstairs and said good morning to Wilson. I petted him for ten minutes, and a little later I heard that Mom was awake, so I said good morning to her. She wanted to have coffee, but she just woke up and didn't want to get up to make it. So, I made her some coffee, four cups of water and half a cup of ground coffee. The coffee grounds smell amazing every time I smell it. I kind of grew up making it with Dad for Mom and him, and it is how I learned how to count, so it is the best smell in the world.

Then I did some screen time. I played some *Madden 20* and was playing in franchise mode and went 16–0, something I haven't done before ever. Then I got to the Super Bowl. It was 3–3 late in the fourth quarter, I think. And then my opponent, the Bills, got a long touchdown. Then it was 10–3. I ended up getting a touchdown, and then time expired a moment later. Then it was overtime, and I won the toss. I got to the red zone. I have gone and run for most of the time because it would be less risky than to throw. I got another first down and then I tried to run with Russell Wilson, but I couldn't cross the goal line. On fourth down I hiked the ball, shuttled to the right, and threw. It reflected on one player's hands and then fell to the ground, turnover on downs, three-yard line. On first and second down I stopped them on the run for a loss. On third down the quarterback stayed in the pocket and then I forced a fumble and then an offensive lineman picked it up. Another player tackled him to the ground, safety. I won the Super Bowl, 12–10.

Mom and I were outside when Dad said that he was going to mow the lawn. And I just said, "Hey, I should try to mow." So, I mowed, and it wasn't that hard. After that I took a shower. Then we had tacos for dinner and fondue for dessert. It was really good. We also watched a movie called *Groundhog Day*.

Sunday, August 2, 2020
We got to sleep outside again. When we were falling asleep the bugs were out, so that was kind of annoying, but I fell asleep fast enough. Mom went inside before any of us fell asleep, but we also had Dad tell us a story, just for old times' sake. So, he told us a story called "Willy Wonka, the Craziest Monkey to Ever Live" and that is the bedtime story he told us when we were little. Then we fell asleep, and I was asleep the whole night, and then I woke up. After Mom went in, I took the spot that she was in because it was more comfortable. Then I woke up, and I think Tay had woken up a little before me. I stayed out for a while. I bet that originally, I woke up at six, but for the next forty minutes I was thinking about writing a book, and what it would be about. I am not going to say what it will be about. I don't really know yet, but I am going to get pen to paper.

After waking up, Tay and I did our screen time. I played more *Madden*. And there is only a little more than three weeks left until *Madden 21* comes out. When it does, I think we are going to buy it. I hope that it is going to be good. I actually don't know if Tay will want to buy it, but if he doesn't, I don't know, I guess.

Then after that we played outside for most of the middle of the day. There are new neighbors that moved in, and they have three kids that are younger than us. The oldest is one year younger than Tay and is going to go into sixth grade. So, she was walking, and Mom said hello because she came by when she was watering her plants. I think the three names are Peyton, Graham and Shiloh, from oldest to youngest.

Then Dad made some homemade bagels, and they were really good. The time before, Dad didn't put all the seasoning on it, and it wasn't really good. This time he did, and it was way better.

We saw that the neighbors who live across the street, the Taylors, got a new puppy. The Taylors just have the same last name as Tay's first, so I hope that it isn't confusing. We also played Flyer's Up with Dad and it was fun. At the end I jammed my finger, and I iced it, and then we watched a *Little House on the Prairie* episode. I also started writing my book. I didn't give it a title because I think that would be a disaster if I did. It kind of sets the book in stone, and then I would give up after fifteen pages. I am also going to need to acknowledge that this book isn't going to take one month to write, but probably over a year. My deadline for the book though is that there have to be over 230 pages, because anything else is too short. For right now I named the word document Book Z, to symbolize the unknowingness of the future for the book.

Monday, August 3, 2020

So, we slept inside, and Dad went to the fire station. I am sad that he has to go to the fire station, but he will be home for four days after. In one week, we are going to go to Sandpoint for a week-long vacation. Sandpoint is where we had many memories, even though we are not going to the condo that we always went to, the one that Gammy and Paw-Paw had owned up until a few years ago.

So, we woke up, and I was the first one to be awake. Then Tay came up only a half hour later. Mom woke up later and I started to make the coffee for her, but she finished it.

Then the next thing that we did was screen time. I played some *Madden* and it is going well. Even though I am going to continue playing, and I hope that I will do it for five-plus seasons in *Madden*, I think I will watch a movie tomorrow just to relax. That would be fun. I have never watched *Pirates of the Caribbean*, so that might be something that I will do.

Mom and I decided to go swimming in Lake Whatcom, after she convinced me to. So we went, and it was cloudy before it got warmer in the afternoon. But we did that, and it was cold and also really choppy, so we still got in, but it wasn't very warm. I did only one lap. Even though I could have done more, I didn't feel the need. I did weights later, and I swept and mopped later. We spent much of the afternoon outside, and then we had a really good dinner. I had four enchiladas. I think one of my teeth is coming in, so I will see if it does, because I don't know for sure. Sometimes it happens to be a tortilla chip firmly in my gums, which honestly, is always disappointing.

Tuesday, August 4, 2020
Wow. A lot has happened and most of it starts right after I did my writing. So, I guess I will just go play by play. So, after I did my writing, Mom asked me if I wanted to go with her to give something called a BOSU ball to Susan. So, we went there, and we were laughing the whole way down. Then we got to her front door, and she wasn't there, and we were just planning to jump away and go home. Mom was holding the BOSU ball, which was pretty big. I put down a plant and Mom put a thank-you card under it so that it didn't blow away. Then we turned around and Mom fell. There are two stairs that are smaller than usual, which she wasn't expecting, and then we decided to walk away instead of staying there. She didn't get very scraped up, and then she started limping. Then she noticed that she unknowingly had to hold her wrist with her other hand, and that her arm was hurting a ton. So, we got home, and I got her an ice pack, and Mom was feeling dizzy, and she started sweating on the walk home because of the pain.

Mom called Dad, but he was on an alarm, I think, so then she called Katie, Dad's sister who is an ER doctor. She said that it might be broken. Then I called Donnett because she had had shoulder surgery, and we got a sling for Mom's arm. That night we all slept downstairs, and I slept on the floor. In the middle of the night, Mom went upstairs because she was in so much pain and she didn't want us to get a bad sleep hearing her moaning in pain and crying. She only slept a little and had a painful night. At around four she woke me up to help her open the Tylenol and Motrin. Then I checked on her around ten minutes later and ended up falling asleep on the couch in the living room. I had to help her with a few things but then slept to seven.

Mom called some people that she knew and ended up getting an X-ray once Dad came home at nine, because she couldn't drive. She said that it was too painful.

Later she got a call that she had fractured her bone. We don't know if she will need a cast or not, but it hasn't gone down in pain. Dad, Tay, and I went swimming at Padden, and we did some screen time.

Earlier in the day, before Dad came home, I helped Mom shampoo and conditioner her hair. We went upstairs and I got the water started and rinsed it with the water and then put on shampoo and then rinsed it quickly. Then I put the conditioner in and got a Gatorade water bottle and rinsed her hair and then got her a towel to let the hair dry.

Wednesday, August 5, 2020

Well, Tay and I slept downstairs while Dad and Mom slept in their room. I came up at around six and saw that Dad was asleep where I was asleep on the couch the day before. Mom said that she didn't get a very good sleep but that it was better than the day before. She said that on a scale of one to ten that it was a four, and last night was a one. So, then Tay woke up right at the same time as Mom. Dad and I were both awake for the last forty-five minutes. We did our screen time, and I won all three games and ended my second regular season with a perfect record. I am undefeated.

Then we were home alone for three hours while Mom had to go to the doctor to check out her arm. The doc said that it should heal and that she would only use the sling for a week or so before just testing and learning to move the arm more. But she is going to go back on the tenth to see if it got worse, and in that case, she would need surgery.

Mom and Dad came home with sushi, and we talked about how the new school will be mostly the same as Kulshan because they will both be online, but the new school will be less time online. They already have paid for the first semester of the new school. Kulshan is new to being online and doesn't know exactly how to do it yet.

Then Tay and I went swimming at Padden with Dad. We went to the fishing area and then went out on our floaties and swam some laps and earned some screen time. Around the end we treaded water for five minutes for more extra screen time.

We did our screen time after we went swimming, and I won the Super Bowl. I played in *Super Bowl 55*, and in the third quarter Russell Wilson, my starting quarterback, dislocated his shoulder and was out for the game. Then Matt Moore, my backup who is pretty bad, played. He got one touchdown, but it was my defense that saved the game after Russ got injured. I won the Super Bowl 21–3.

I played with Wilson and we played some chase with his toy, and that was really fun. For dinner we had pasta, and then we had ice cream with some magic shell. I also put some berries on top.

Thursday, August 6, 2020

We got to sleep outside, which was great. Then we went inside and I said good morning to Dad, and Mom woke up later, and then Tay and I played some *Madden*. I only played one game before I got up and took a shower and brushed my teeth.

Dad and I went in the car at 9:10 and left a minute later to go to the dentist. I have a tooth that is a baby, and its adult tooth is coming in, but it isn't budging. So we went there to see if they wanted to pull it later. They looked, but it took a while because the dentist had to give some little kids some cavity fillings. But after a while he came and said that it will indeed need to be pulled. So then they caught me off guard by saying that they could do it right away. In my mind I wasn't sure if I wanted to, but in the end I just thought that it would be nice to get it done in the same visit. After I went to Dad's car to make sure it was okay, because he had to wait outside, I went back in and they gave me laughing gas and a shot in my mouth. It got numb quickly and then they pulled it out. I heard a snap, and then I connected that they snapped the tooth and then got the second half out after. It didn't hurt much.

Then I went to Dad's car and I bumped into the wall because of the laughing gas. And then I tripped on the tire stop while getting into the car. That was funny.

We played some football later in the day. Because I got my tooth pulled, Tay and I got to do a little extra screen time. I explored the woods around, and then we had some dinner. I had a hot dog, but I didn't like it that much. I think that we are going to sleep outside tonight, and I am going to finish my writing right now because I really want to have some dessert, maybe some ice cream. Bye bye.

Friday, August 7, 2020

Today was quite busy. First we woke up outside, and then Tay and I came in a little after the garbage man came by and got the garbage. I woke up before he came, and I would have woken up later because the garbage truck is insanely loud and wakes us all up if we aren't already up.

Then we went inside and Dad was doing his writing. He had gotten up a little early and did a lot of writing. Also, we don't have to do our reading anymore, because summer is almost over. So, we just woke up a little and did our screen time. I went to take a shower and Mom put some stuff in my hair because she said that it was really dry. She said to take a shower a half hour later, and then I took a shower and used a new shampoo and conditioner that Mom got for herself a few weeks ago. For *Madden*, now it is going to be three weeks until the new game comes, and that is going to feel like two because we are going to be on vacation at Sandpoint. But in *Madden* right now, I am still undefeated. Soon I will get to a fifty-game milestone without losing, and I haven't gotten even close to that any time before.

I texted Gavin and Carter to make sure they could still come over today, and they could but said they were going to be a little later. So they came over at one thirty. First we played some hide-and-seek and that was really fun. One time I hid under a tree and Tay went right next to me and didn't see me. That was super fun, and then we had some snacks and it started to get cloudier. We played Ultimate for twenty minutes or so, and then we had a water fight including the hose and water guns. It was just starting to rain and we all got drenched, but I was the least wet. We had some pizza, and then they had to leave.

Saturday, August 8, 2020

Okay, so we slept inside today and in the basement. Dad had to go to the fire station, and I heard him get up in the morning. Then I went back to bed and woke up at 7:10. I was greeted by Wilson, and I saw that Mom and Tay were both awake. Tay and I did screen time in the morning. We are going on a trip, so we aren't going to play *Madden*, but then we will go and get *Madden 21* in twenty days. I can't wait to get the new one, and we will have to quit the teams that we are on so far. If you pay some more money, you can get it three days early, but I don't feel the need to do that.

After doing screen time I observed that it had rained and was continuing to rain. Then after it stopped raining, and it was still wet, I got a backpack and got on Tay's bike and went to the mail and got the newspaper. We got Donnett's again, because she is camping and allowed us to use it again. So, I got that and then biked up the hills and got home. We then proceeded to read the paper.

Mom took a nap later in the day because she felt that her arm hurt. Tay tucked her into bed, and we did some screen time because Tay said that we would do the dishes later in the day. So, we did that and then Mom woke up and we went outside for a little. There are some new neighbors, and one of the kids is a girl a few years younger than both of us, and she was walking their dog. The dog came onto the yard and Wilson decided to hump the dog. That left us all in an awkward situation. It isn't my choice to include this in my writing, but in the future I will laugh at this, and to that future self: stop it.

Then we got some dinner. We don't have much because we are going to go on vacation, so we got some Mexican food and ate that, and it was really good. After dinner we had ice cream, played Bananagrams, played some football outside, and googled how to stop a dog from humping.

Sunday, August 9, 2020

We slept inside because tomorrow we are going to finish packing and go on a trip. Tay and I also won't be writing, but we will probably include stuff about it after the trip. So, I woke up and went upstairs to see that Tay and Mom were already awake. Wilson was outside. I said good morning to them and then we did some screen time. I played three *Madden* games and I continued to be undefeated, and I finished the regular season.

Dad came home a little bit later and then went on a long bike ride. So Tay and I finished our screen time and then went outside with Mom. It was a nice day, and we played some football. Mom was out there on one of the chairs, so we got to be with her while we were playing. Then after Dad got home, I told him that it would be fun to go swimming at Padden, so we went.

We forgot our towels again, so we let the sun dry us off. We got out and went into the little section where there are a ton of reeds, and we just moved through them until we got out. Then we saw Dad, and we went over there and did some swimming. We each finished with six laps. It was a pretty warm day, but the last lap was really cold. Then we went to the shore on our innertubes. Tay got a smoothie afterward, but I didn't because I was so cold I think I would die if I had a cold smoothie.

Then Dad went with Wilson, and they went on a swim. They went to a little beach a fifteen-minute walk away. After Dad came back, we packed a lot. I got all of my clothes into one backpack, and I got another backpack to put everything else that I will need, like a hat, headphones, a football, sunglasses, etc. Mom was frustrated packing with one arm, so I decided to help her very much.

Then I did screen time that we earned from swimming. Mom also said that she doesn't like that a ton. But I went through the playoffs. The first game was against the Rams, who I played in the final game of the season. Then I played the Panthers and I won. And I played the Super Bowl. I won 17–6, and I'm still undefeated.

*September 2020

From August 9 to September 15, I stopped writing because of the excessive attention that was needed to get ready and to adapt to the new school,

Williamsburg Academy. The classes are all online on Zoom, a video conference app. All of the schoolwork was assigned and returned online. Understandably, setting up the laptops and the accounts for Williamsburg took a while, with distress on the side. We picked it up pretty quickly. In this month or so, a few things happened that weren't explained or talked about in the journal. The following are things that will make the future entries better understood.

Schedule: The schedule for Williamsburg, or specifically, when we Zoomed (the verb that I use meaning that I used Zoom), each class that we had we Zoomed twice a week. These classes included STEM (basically science), leadership (a class on becoming leaders), math (I started at eighth grade math and then switched to algebra a few weeks in), language arts, and humanities (social studies). I also had one class, photography, that had assignments assigned but no Zooms.

Fantasy Football: Dad's fire station has a Fantasy Football group that they do every year, and he was invited to join but doesn't know much about football, so instead Tay and I took his spot last year, and this year we each got our own team. There are some terms I use for football that may be unknown to people who don't watch football, like TFL (Thursday Night Football), sack, WR (wide receiver), OT (overtime), etc.

Football: I think I already have mentioned this, but we are Seahawks fans. The Seahawks' quarterback is Russell Wilson, their star wide receivers are Metcalf and Lockett. Jamal Adams plays defense and was recently acquired from a trade with the New York Jets.

Air Quality: The air quality measurement isn't written about, but the higher the number, the worse the air quality.

Ru University: Ru University, or Ru U is the book club that Phil created, where Tay, Dad, and I go to his house and talk about the book that we are reading together. He called it Ru U after his new dog Ru. He says that Ru is the mascot of the "university," which is fun. Ru has been at most of the meetings, and she's very chill and went around to each of us and sat with us.

Sandpoint Trip: On the trip to Sandpoint with Gammy and Paw-Paw, we stayed at a condo/hotel. We had to set up our intro meeting to Williamsburg. There was barely anyone at the place that we were staying at, so we had a lot of fun and enjoyed the beach and grass without many people there. Tay and I played football pass in the yard, and we also spent most of our time in the pool. We played fun games and raced in the pool as well.

There was an outlined area where there was a no boat zone and just for swimming so the people swimming could stay safe. We went around the area and looked for anything interesting that we could find. I found a My Little Pony toy. I think the toy was the best find.

There was also a ping pong table, and we played plenty of ping pong and even added consequences to some matches, like loser has to jump in the lake. Even though it was August, Pend Oreille was still mildly cold.

The hotel that we stayed at was a nice place, and no one was there (we think because of coronavirus). There was an awkwardness with masks because we were in Idaho where no one was wearing mask. We were more comfortable wearing a mask, but we eventually ditched that idea, but we decided to try to be safe by staying outside, not going on elevators with other people, etc. Gammy and Paw-Paw also didn't care for masks, so they didn't do anything about wearing a mask or staying safe. It was fun and weird to have a break from masks, but we still tried to stay safe.

Gammy and Paw-Paw were very generous on the trip, and they made sure that we had a lot of fun. It was great to spend time with them.

Tuesday, September 15, 2020

Well, it's been over a month since the last time that I wrote daily here. A lot of stuff happened but I will just cover that a little later. I think that there is a time where I am going to quickly cover all of the last month. One thing that happened is that the Seahawks and the NFL started on time, and I think that in itself is a great accomplishment. COVID is still a great factor, and I don't think that the numbers have gone down. The Seahawks won their game versus the Atlanta Falcons, and the score was 25–38, and Russell Wilson and company did amazing. Jamal Adams was a beast in his debut, gathering twelve tackles, a sack, and two or three TFLs. Tay and I also joined Fantasy Football with the fire fighters, like last year. I will say who I got tomorrow, but I got news today that my best player, Michael Tomas, will be out for a week or two.

Another thing that we did today is we went to the beach and into the water and swam for a little bit. All five of us went. A little bit before that, Wilson went with Mom and one of her friends for a walk, and they got a little lost, but not for a long time.

I had a Zoom in the morning, like usual. I started at eight and then continued for two hours. Today I did homework for leadership and math. Tomorrow, I have a lot of Zooms but I hope that I can get some language arts stuff done and finish STEM.

Tay and I did screen time, and as I said before, I found out that Michael Tomas will most likely not play against the Raiders. Next week the Seahawks play the Tom Brady–less Patriots with Cam Newton at the helm. The Seahawks are also again referred to as a top five team. A final note to think about, the Forty-Niners lost their first game to Arizona. I am happy that the Forty-Niners lost their first, but I also don't know if I should be scared about the Cardinals. The Rams won as well, but I am not too worried about them yet.

Wednesday, September 16, 2020
Well, it is Wednesday, and I woke up at six thirty. For the past month or so, Tay and I have been sleeping in the two twin beds that are in the basement, because both of us have our beds on the top floor and we are also on a big hill, so it is really hot. So, we have either been sleeping outside or sleeping downstairs. The two twins are actually the two parts of the bunk bed that Taylor had, but remember, he took them down.

We haven't been sleeping outside, because for the past week or so it has been really smoky and the air quality is unhealthy to breath a lot in, and sleeping outside you would get a lot of smoke. I think Wilson is the most bummed about this, but it is clearing up. Saturday was the worst— you couldn't even see the Hutchinson's house from my window. The smoke is definitely still there. Compared to other places, the air quality is okay. Ours is at 200 or so and there are some places that are under 800. The smoke comes from the fires in California, but there are also fires all along the coast, and Dad said that there are hundreds of fires just in Washington, but mostly on the east side.

I did Zoom for four hours straight, and that is a long time. After that Tay and I did screen time. Then we came up for lunch and I had a grilled cheese sandwich and tomato soup. I did weights after that. In a few minutes, at two o'clock, I am going to Ru University for book club. I will talk about it later, but later I think we are going to watch a movie, and I will do a little bit of homework. In the next few days, I will talk about some things that I haven't included yet in the journal that happened between August 10 and the middle of September.

Thursday, September 17, 2020
I forgot to do my writing until now, at eight. But I guess that I am going to just do it now. So, I woke up and came upstairs, I said hi to Wilson, and he kind of stayed where he was. I brushed my teeth and took a shower. Dad left for the fire station and Mom and Tay were still sleeping. I did my math and

language arts Zooms. Then I did some screen time and switched on and off between being productive and doing screen time and just relaxing.

Yesterday we watched a Netflix Documentary called *The Social Dilemma*, and it was really eye-opening. It talked about all of the negatives of social media. We were originally going to watch a movie, but we watched that instead. It was super eye-opening and somewhat scary to know that our every move is watched. The cool thing is that I have never been on social media; Mom and Dad strongly believe that we don't have social media.

Not much interesting happened today. There was one assignment for math that I redid, and I was really happy when I got nine out of ten right. Tomorrow I am going to make a day of only a small amount of schoolwork, and I am going to enjoy being outside more, so that is my goal for tomorrow. Also, there is a TNF game and the Bengals and the Browns are playing, two of the worst teams in the NFL, but I have a WR on the Browns that I am playing, so I will kind of pay attention throughout.

Friday, September 18, 2020

Well, it is Friday and that was really nice, because we don't have any Zooms on Friday, so that was a little bit of time that I had free. I woke up at 6:20 and I came up to say hi to Mom. She was going to work. I guess it was only documented a little, but after Mom broke her arm, she didn't go to work until today. So, this was her first day, and she worked twelve hours, and I am writing this right before she comes home, so I guess I don't know how it went. Her arm doesn't hurt at all, but she has this thing where her arm will pop, and it is really loud, and it hurts. So, she went to the doctor, and the doctor said that they have never heard about an arm broken like it is snapping, so she got an MRI or something, and it is still possible that she has to get surgery.

So, after Mom left, I was motivated to have this be an easy but productive day, so I did my reading and then took a shower and brushed my teeth, and Tay woke up around that time. I did weights in the middle of the day and Dad came home at ten. Then around noon I did some schoolwork, and I did a STEM lab that included hot and cold water and seeing how more air appears.

We then went swimming at Euclid Park. We were going to go to our main spot, but there were other people there. So, we swam a little and gave Wilson some exercise.

For dinner Dad made some pizza, and it was really good. One last thing that I wanted to say is that Tay and I started a survival world in *Minecraft*. It went really well, and we made a ton of progress. Taylor basically quit it a little in and will only join every once in a while.

Saturday, September 19, 2020

Okay, so today is Saturday, and we are really two-thirds done with September already, and that is pretty hard to believe. I find myself just going through ten seconds of awe that we aren't going back to school but going online for the fall. I really miss school in person, and it will be great once we do. Like yesterday, I woke up feeling very motivated to get my checklist done, so I woke up, did some screen time, brushed my teeth, and then did weights— five of B day, and three of A day.

After exercising, I took a bath and a shower and then regrouped and thought about what else I had to do. For chores, I swept the floors. Dad mopped, and Tay vacuumed the basement. Mom had to go to work again, but in the middle of the day we went to see her on her break, and we got some stuff for dinner from Joe's Garden. That is right next to Hospice House (where Mom works), and we got some corn. Dad was the only one that went in; Tay and I stayed in the car. Quickly after leaving Dad realized that he had forgotten his wallet, and he found it.

Then we came home, and I have been doing some schoolwork. Soon I have to do a military interview, and I am going to interview Paw-Paw (Dad's dad). I am looking forward to doing that and learning a bit more about what he did in the military.

Sunday, September 20, 2020

Sunday Football, that is what I was thinking about when I was waking up in the morning. I had no Zoom, no homework, and there was going to be football all day long. I woke up and then came upstairs to see Wilson and Mom. Taylor woke up a little later. Dad was at the fire station, so he didn't get to see the football games with us, but he got to see some of the games from the fire station because there were not many calls.

After everyone was awake (Mom and Taylor), we decided that we should go to Haggen and get some chips and Kit Kats, so that is exactly what happened. Well, we were going to just go to Haggen, but Mom wanted to go to the beach, and we saw some people there and they were going kayaking, and there was this one guy that got on this surfboard with a stick and a motor under that thingy. None of us had seen anything like that before. Then Mom and Tay went to Haggen and got some stuff, and then we drove home to watch some football.

The Seahawks game wasn't on until 5:20, so we had to figure out what games we were going to watch until then. We wanted to watch a Packers versus Lions game, but it wasn't on. So, we watched the Forty-Niners (the Seahawks' rival) versus the Jets. The Forty-Niners were really good, and they are in the same division as the Seahawks, so they are a natural rival. They made it to the Super Bowl but then fell to the Kansas City Chiefs. The Forty-Niners were really hit with injuries that game, with Nick Bosa (torn ACL), Solomon Tomas, Raheem Mostert (knee), and Tevin Colman all leaving the game, and all will likely miss one or more games. Nick Bosa is probably out for the season. They already had injuries with guys like Richard Sherman, George Kittle, and their best WR all missing the game. The Niners won the game. Then we watched the Chief's game, and they won on an OT field goal. Then we watched the Seahawks game at 5:20. It was against the Patriots, and once again it came to the goal line, where Cam Newton got stopped at the one-yard line.

Monday, September 21, 2020
So, it was Monday, and we had school, so I had to Zoom for four hours. After that I barely did any schoolwork for the rest of the day. The classes that I had were math, STEM, leadership, and humanities. Those classes are two days a week, Monday and Wednesday. On Tuesday and Thursday, I have math and language arts. On Monday and Wednesday I do so much Zoom that I don't do much actual schoolwork.

After school I did some screen time, and I did some *Minecraft*. For the longest time, Taylor and I have been playing *Minecraft* on the old version, but in the next few days I think I am going to play the new one. The thing is that the screen gets cut off when we play with two of us, so if I play, I will be the only one who does it. Tay could do it too, but we would only play it one at a time. It will take some time to get used to it, but once I do, it will be much more fun. I think if I do, Tay will also follow my lead.

Then after we did screen time, the whole family went into the car, including Wilson, and we went to a little beach and started to walk into the water. It was freezing and incredible how cold it was, but after we got in, it wasn't as cold as I thought it would be right after we got in. We swam and we treaded water. We have been doing this for a few weeks now, and it always is super cold but then warmer when you get in. Mom has also watched some Netflix things about this, that it is really healthy for you to jump into cold water.

Tuesday, September 22, 2020

So, after waking up, I said good morning to the family, including Wilson, who is definitely part of the family. I read the news, and Taylor and I both, before we did our Zooms, went to Fantasy to go to the Waiver Wire to get some new Fantasy players. I won't explain what it means exactly. But Taylor dropped some of his players, and he also realized that his top three players had some injury concerns. One or two of my players are injured, but they are more short term and will only miss a week or two, if that. I have won in the last two weeks and am only one of the two people in our ten-team league to do that. Again, we play with Dad's fire fighters, so it is fun to be in second place when there are eight other grown men who so far can't figure out a way to beat me. Tay is in fourth place, and he has won once and lost once. He kind of had an unlucky week, but hopefully he will bounce back. He is playing Mark Mellein, who is in first place and is the other person with two wins and no losses.

Then I did my two Zooms, some math homework, and a bit more, but then a little after that, Mom, Dad, and I all went on a walk on the trail, with Wilson. That was one hour long. After that Mom realized that her Seattle appointment was at a different time than she thought. Then she rescheduled for later in the day, and somehow the whole family decided to go with her on a field trip. It was fun to get out of Bellingham, and Mom did a lot of shopping after. We got some pizza at University Village, then Mom shopped more, and then we drove home and got there at 8:40.

Wednesday, September 23, 2020

It is the middle of the week, and what I did was I woke up and then saw Mom right before she left, and Dad was also awake, Wilson also. So, I got to say goodbye to her before she left. She doesn't need to work for a little while after today, so that is great. I said hi to Wilson and then also Dad. When I was going upstairs, I didn't even know that Mom was going to work, but I'm glad that I got to see her. Tay was asleep.

Then I did math and STEM videos. We get a ten-minute break in the middle of each of our Zooms. I think Tay had three Zooms on the day. So, after STEM I did my leadership class. It has already been a stormy day, but the last ten minutes the power was out, so Tay came up and said that the power was out. It flickered right before, but then it was off for good. Dad had gone to a neighbor's house and didn't bring his phone. It actually only lasted twenty minutes overall, and then we spent five minutes trying to find the Wi-Fi, and then we finally found it one minute before the next Zoom, humanities for me, was scheduled.

Then I did some screen time, schoolwork, on and off. Wilson was unhappy that it was such a rainy day, and he spent the day sleeping. Dad, for our exercise of the day, showed us one that was doing one push up / squat / sit up, and then doing it again every minute but increasing by one. So, we did that for our exercise. It was definitely surprising how difficult it gets after a little while. I started it thinking that I could do a lot more than I ended up doing.

Mom also came home early, so that was great. We had enchiladas for dinner, and I watched a new show called *The Office*, and it is constantly funny.

Thursday, September 24, 2020
I woke up in the morning and went upstairs to see Dad and Wilson. I heard them from downstairs and then twenty minutes later went up. Wilson was of course happy that another family member was awake, because Mom and Tay weren't yet.

Then I did two Zooms. Math and language arts were good. For math, the Tuesday and Thursday Zooms are just for homework, so I don't have to go out of my way just to do it. Then after the Zooms I played on the new *Minecraft* again. I am learning new things about it every day, and I am liking it more and more and more. I can't wait for a week or so when I have a more stable base and living routine in the world. After that I can explore freely.

Mom and Dad went to the store while I was doing my Zoom, and they came home with a new sink for the main bathroom. I admired that they were so fast in doing it. Dad spent the majority of the day taking the old sink off and putting the new sink in. After that he also painted the whole thing the color of Mom and Dad's bedroom.

Then for school I had to do two interviewing projects and I had decided to interview both Gammy and Paw-Paw. The one for Paw-Paw was about someone who was in the military. It didn't have to be a family member, but it was easier and was more fun, I think. For Gammy, in a different subject we have to do a family essay on an older family member. So, I decided to interview Gammy and Paw-Paw at the same time, a two-for-one phone call. I learned a lot about both of them that I didn't know before. It was really interesting and cool, even if it was for school.

Friday, September 25, 2020
Well, it was really nice to not have to do any Zooms today, so I had the whole morning without Zoom, when sometimes I would Zoom for the

entire morning and barely get a break. I do know that there are other schools that have six hours a day (or so) of Zoom and then homework after that. That would be even more brutal. So, in the morning, even when not doing Zoom, I did my homework, and that was good because it meant I didn't have to do much over the weekend.

It was really a rainy day until near the end, and it cleared up, but I think it started to rain after that. Tay made pie with Mom for a schoolwork project at school, and the pie was good, but I like the other pie that Mom made a week or two ago. The reason behind that is that this pie didn't have fresh blueberries, but canned or something.

Saturday, September 26, 2020
Well, the weekend was here. It was nice that I didn't have schoolwork to do, for the most part. I woke up at five and couldn't fall asleep, and I was kind of hungry. So, one hour later, after realizing that I wasn't going to fall back asleep, I went upstairs. I was the only one awake besides Wilson. Tay came up an hour later, and then Mom woke up about twenty minutes after that. I made Mom coffee. A little after that, when she was doing the dishes, she realized that I had made the coffee without a certain piece of it.

Dad came home a little after ten. Tay and I did screen time and added on to the *Minecraft* worlds. Mom went to do some stuff in town. I didn't do any schoolwork today, because there is such a small amount that I could do it tomorrow. Also, tomorrow is the Seahawks game. This week they play the Dallas Cowboys. The Cowboys are 1–1 while the Seahawks are 2–0. I think the Seahawks will pull out of this game with another victory. My guess for the score is 38–34, Seahawks stay undefeated and win!

It was rainy, but after lunch Mom and I went on a drive. We went to Joe's Garden. Mom had gone a little earlier in the day but then realized that it was the last day they were open for the year, so I went back with her, and we got some more stuff there. Mom went to a new boutique shop and got some things. I stayed in the car. When she came back, the bag smelled like poop. We saw a little brown thing smeared on the side of the bag, but we don't know if it was poop or not. My question is, how did the poop smear get there?

Sunday, September 27, 2020
So, it is Sunday! Football! But we do have some school tomorrow, so that's a bummer. But its Sunday! So, this was amazing. We got to sleep outside, and that was really cool. Because of the smoke and then some dilemmas with cleaning the sheets (because they smelled like smoke), it took a while.

But we got to sleep outside, and then I woke up and went inside at six thirty, and then everyone slowly woke up. Mom went inside in the middle of the night. She said that she had a rough night sleep. She slept until 8:40 or something like that. Dad, Tay, and I all went to the store and got some football food.

The Seahawks game was later, at one thirty, so it was a while. We watched some ten o'clock games on and off. Taylor and I played downstairs in the basement while the game was going. We did some of the regular stuff like reading, and I read one of Taylor's books for school. It is a really good one that I have read before. The book is called Wonder. I did other stuff like brushing my teeth, showering, and other stuff.

I took a bath, and then a half hour later the Seahawks game was on. The game was against the Cowboys. The Seahawks didn't get the first points of the game, but on the Cowboys' first drive they got a field goal and three points. The Seahawks then got a big touchdown for Locket and then kicked the ball off, and the Cowboys fumbled the ball and had it at the one-yard line, and the Seahawks got a safety, 9–3. The game stayed as a Seahawks game for most of the game, and the Cowboys' kicker missed an extra point, and another one was blocked. The one big play in the middle of the game is that DK Metcalf got a deep ball and was one yard away from a TD but casually walked after catching it, but a Cowboy player hit the ball out and no TD. Then the Cowboys were getting a comeback and were one point ahead. And then Metcalf redeemed himself and got a TD. The Cowboys didn't quite win, and Dak Prescott threw an interception to close out the game. The score was 38–31 and I predicted yesterday that the score was going to be a 38–34 Seahawks win. So, I was really close to predicting it. Also, Russell Wilson broke some records with the most TD passes in the first three games of a season! Also, the last time the Seahawks were 3–0 they won the Super Bowl. They are the only team in the NFC West that is undefeated.

Monday, September 28, 2020

Well, usually Mondays are more sleepy days than anything, but we got to sleep outside. The compromise was that we were going to have to wake up at four because Dad was going to work. And we did that and I fell back asleep. Mom had to also go to work at six thirty, and I woke up right after she left. Then I decided that this was going to be a productive day, so ten minutes after getting out of bed I started to do my reading. Fast forward a half hour and by then Tay had also woken up, and then I showered and brushed my teeth. I had about forty-five minutes until my Zoom, so I exercised for a half hour and did weights.

I Zoomed for the next four hours. Actually, I did three Zooms because that morning I was emailed that my last Zoom was canceled and that I had to watch the video for one of the earlier ones and take notes on that. Mom came back right after I finished my last Zoom.

We kind of just chilled the whole afternoon. It was fun to know that I got all of my stuff done early! I did some chores but that was kind of it. There is one last football game this week. It is going to be a good one because it is two of the best teams, the Ravens and the Chiefs. My Fantasy Football opponent for the week has a few guys playing, so I hope that I still win. Tay lost this week in Fantasy, so he is 1–2. Unless something crazy happens, I should still be one of the two undefeated teams.

Tuesday, September 29, 2020

Well, today I did practically the same thing that I did yesterday, as far as the morning goes. I did sleep in my bed for the first time in forever because the weather isn't hot anymore and signs of fall are popping up all over. So, I did that and then woke up at 6:18, precisely. Then I went downstairs and read for twenty minutes. Then Tay wanted his book back, and then Mom woke up a tiny bit later, and then I asked her to do Drill Sergeant with me. So, we went downstairs, and she told me what exercises to do, and we did that for a half hour. Then I took a shower in the basement, brushed my teeth after that, and went onto Zoom for two hours.

After the two Zooms, Mom and I went on a drive for two hours or so. We went to the Chuckanuts and to Larrabee Park. We haven't gone there in a long time, but we have videos of Tay and me going there when we were young. I learned that it is the first state park of Washington State. That was really interesting because, even though I had never thought about it, I would have thought the first park would be in the Seattle area or Olympia, but that was cool to learn. After that, Mom went to Haggen and we went home.

Dad was home when we came back, and it's great to see him because he's home for four days. I did some schoolwork around the day. Mom had an appointment. A little later, Tay had to go to an appointment as well, and Dad drove him, so I was home alone. I finished the schoolwork for today. For dinner we are going to have chicken enchiladas! Also, I hope that we get to sleep outside tonight. Tomorrow we are going to play football, and I am really excited because Tay and Dad and I haven't done that in forever.

Wednesday, September 30, 2020

Well, I didn't even think about this, but I just checked the calendar and today is the last day of September! It flew by so quickly. Next month is October, and that is the month that is my birthday. My birthday is on October twenty-first, so that means that tomorrow will be the three weeks leading up to my birthday. So, I woke up outside—we got to sleep out there, so that was so fun. At five or so, I woke up and realized forty-five minutes later that I wasn't going to go back to sleep, so I went outside. Mom was getting ready for work, so I got to see her before she left. Dad woke up before Tay did, and I did my reading and exercised for the third day in a row. I am kind of getting a rhythm going on how my morning works. Then I did four hours of Zoom. I didn't have to do schoolwork today, so that was another plus.

We are also still doing Fantasy Football, and now that I am undefeated, I am feeling very good about myself going forward. But Tay offered me a trade, and I had to get it before he thought about it again, so I took advantage of it. It is the second trade that we have done this season, but it is definitely the bigger one and probably the one that will have the biggest impact on the season. I traded Aaron Jones, who is a top five or top ten Fantasy running back, and CeeDee Lamb, who is a rookie, and pretty good, but more of a top thirty wide receiver in Fantasy. In return, I got the best player coming into Fantasy, but he got injured and will be out for three weeks or so. And I got Julio Jones, who is a top five wide receiver who was also injured for the last game. I won the trade, but time will tell. Tay had the short-term win because neither of the guys that I traded to him are injured, and he is 1–2, so he needs to start winning now.

Later in the day we went to play football, but first we said hi to Mom at Hospice House, and then we played football. It was really fun, and we haven't played in so long. We each got our share of touchdowns, but when it came to interceptions, I got three more than Tay (I got four and he got one), so that is kind of the thing I measure throughout and after the game. Tay had a fun time as well, so we will probably play that more as the temperatures go down and more NFL football is played.

Thursday, October 1, 2020

I woke up in the early morning and decided that because I had to do reading for schoolwork, I should do it later in the day after my two Zooms and just exercise in the morning. I was really sore from yesterday's exercising and playing football. But I still did it, and I felt good afterwards. I am still really sore, but it kind of feels good. I then did my math Zoom and worked on

STEM because it was a homework day and I had already done my math homework. Then I had language arts class and I was done with Zooms for the day. Until a few days ago, I would have done screen time, but we decided that we have to do screen time after dinner. Even though I probably would like to do screen time in the morning, it makes me more productive throughout the day.

So, I finished what I had to do with STEM and that was kind of easy, and after that the next homework that I did was my leadership homework. That was easy, and then I read because I had to read part of a book, and that actually took an hour to finish, so I am glad that I didn't do a half hour of reading on top of that. I have a good system going on, where on Monday I do no homework, on Tuesday I do two of my six subjects for homework, on Wednesday it is a long Zoom day like Monday, so no homework. Then finally I do two subjects of homework on Thursday and Friday.

We played football today, and the better field, the one at the high school, was open! So that was fun to play there. The actual gameplay wasn't as exciting to explain, with only one interception each. We had a lot of fun, but near the end Tay was grumpy. We then went to see Mom at her work. Tay said in the car that he was grumpy because his toe and his heel still hurt. His toe has hurt for, like, three years or something like that.

Friday, October 2, 2020

It was so nice to not have to do any Zooms today! So, I woke up and took it a little slower to get to exercise and do my reading. But at, like, nine or so, Mom and I went in the basement and did Drill Sergeant, and that was my exercise. That was for a half hour, and then I realized that I had to do one hundred pages of reading, so instead of reading for a half hour it was more like an hour and fifteen minutes. I was really excited when I finished my reading, so I relaxed for a little more. I forgot to say, but I also took a shower and brushed my teeth.

Dad did some yard work in the afternoon. Mom was tired from working the last few days, so she tried to take a nap, but then she said that I was walking too loudly, so she didn't get a nap today. Taylor did schoolwork and screen time. He has been watching *The Office* more and more. It is a really funny show, but I just don't feel like using my screen time on it. While everyone was doing that, I finished my schoolwork for the week. It felt so amazing when I was done with it all. I first did my humanities and that was why I had to read my hundred pages. So, I did that, and soon after that I did my language arts, and it was really fun after doing my schoolwork. Mom and Dad went to the beach and Wilson got a good swim in.

The last thing that was something, that kind of grew throughout the day, is that Donald Trump, the president, got coronavirus. That is ironic because during lockdown Trump has downplayed COVID. That was the news in the beginning of the day; later in the day there were reports that he was hospitalized, and that was crazy as well. Trump is seventy-four. As it comes with the job, he also has high levels of stress. None of this is good news for Trump, health wise.

Saturday, October 3, 2020
So, I woke up at the same time I usually do, and then I went downstairs. It felt good to know that there were no Zooms and no schoolwork to do, so I took it nice and slow in the morning. Dad had gone to the fire station, so he was gone for the day, but Wilson was awake as always. Mom and Tay woke up a little later.

For reading, I didn't have to read a book for school, but I still have to do thirty minutes at minimum every day, as a house rule. So, for my reading I finished reading *Wonder* and that was a really good book, and it was cool to reread it. There is also a movie that the family has watched before, for *Wonder*, and it has some good actors in it. The famous actors in the movie are Owen Wilson and Julia Roberts.

Mom made some beans in a crockpot, and I helped her make those. I didn't know that it was so easy to make them, but now I know. After that we went on a drive to Whole Foods to get some stuff for dinner. Mom got a card for our friend Ian, who helped Mom figure out what the MRI of her arm was about. After that we dropped off the gift at their house. Mom also went to Woods Coffee, because she had a gift card.

We didn't do anything that interesting this afternoon. As for Donald Trump, nothing eye popping happened, but there were people on the news that were wondering if he was downplaying how serious he is at risk, and that was what Mom had wondered earlier. For dinner we had enchiladas and the beans that I made earlier. It was also good because we got guacamole.

Sunday, October 4, 2020
Okey dokey, so I woke up and I took my time to get out of bed, but when I did, I saw Mom before she was leaving for work. So, I got to see her, and Wilson was upset that she was leaving, but then after that he was okay. I did my reading after Mom left. About 7:05 Tay came down. I had heard him upstairs, but I didn't actually see him. Five minutes later I fed Wilson, and he ate all of his food. Some days he doesn't, so that is the only reason that I am mentioning it, so that's all.

For the next three hours, Tay and I were mostly waiting for the 'Hawks game. We were home alone until the last ten minutes when Dad came home from work. I did my exercise for the day and then I took a shower twenty minutes before the game started. Again, Dad came home and we went downstairs. Dad also took a shower because he hadn't so far.

Stats to know: The Seahawks came into the game 3–0 and leading the NFC West, widely considered the toughest division in the NFL. Russell Wilson had just set the NFL record for most TDs thrown in the first three games of a season, with fourteen. DK Metcalf, in his second year in the NFL, had the third most receiving yards in the NFL and in each game had at least ninety-plus yards and a touchdown.

The game took a while to become entertaining. The Dolphins are one of the worst teams, and even though they were losing the whole game, they kept it close so that the Seahawks had to make sure that they didn't give up anything cheap. Then in the fourth quarter, the Seahawks pulled away to end up winning. The Dolphins actually only got one touchdown and kicked five field goals.

To end the game, Russell Wilson met the NFL record for the most TDs through four games, at sixteen, tied with Peyton Manning. The Seahawks are also 4–0 and the only one in the NFC, but if the Packers win, they will also be undefeated. DK Metcalf, as of the end of Sunday, is leading the NFL in receiving yards, and that is a big deal. Metcalf is on par to be an NFL top five wide receiver.

We played football in the afternoon. Dad went on the trail, Mom came home, and for dinner we had some really good pizza. It is an ice cream night, and I am pretty sure that we are going to sleep outside! So, all is good, and the Seahawks are undefeated. Last note: The Seahawks are 4–0 for the second time in franchise history. The only other time that they did, they won the Super Bowl, and the Seahawks have never been 5–0, but that could change next Sunday!

Monday, October 5, 2020

About two weeks until my birthday. That will be really fun. From the beginning of COVID we haven't had many birthdays, and the last one was Tay's in April, six months ago. After my birthday, Dad has his birthday on the first, the election takes place on the third, and then two weeks later Mom has her birthday. There isn't a ton to enjoy about having your birthday with coronavirus. Like, friends can't come over. But it will be fun to have cake and just a celebratory mindset, because no one has had that in a while.

It was amazing. We got to sleep outside, and then I woke up at 6:33, and then I actually didn't exercise in the morning, but I did do my reading for thirty minutes. It was some book that was written more than a hundred years ago. I didn't know about it, but it is called *Pollyanna*.

I did four Zooms, and that was a lot. We have something called midterms, and it counts for a big chunk of my grade, so the teachers in some of the classes are starting to prepare us for that. But besides that, I really like doing my big Zooms because I don't have to do actual school assignments. Next week we don't have any classes because of the midterms.

After that, Mom and I took Wilson on a walk, and we went on the trail for an hour. I wanted to go on the trail, but I was skeptical when Mom said that Wilson was coming, because I didn't feel like possibly dealing with Wilson and other dogs on the trail. I ended up asking myself what was the worst that could happen. We had a lot of fun on the trail, and we didn't see anyone.

Tay had a PT appointment, and Mom and I went on a drive. We didn't actually go on any errands, but we went around the lake (not the whole way around; lake Whatcom is large). I hadn't gone so far around before.

For dinner we are going to have tacos, and if you haven't realized yet, our whole family likes Mexican food a lot. Mom and I the most, I would say.

Tuesday, October 6, 2020

I woke up at 5:30 and felt tired, so instead of getting up I went back to bed. When I was going back to bed, I was hoping that I would wake up one hour later, but when I woke up, I saw that the time was 7:01, and that was kind of disappointing. Then I went downstairs and found that no one was awake, and when I was going downstairs, I forgot that this was Tuesday, as in Waiver Wire Tuesday. So, I got some players in Fantasy, and I was the first one to do so, I think. Tay woke up around a half hour after that. Before my two Zooms, I brushed my teeth and took a shower.

My first Zoom was math, and because it was either Tuesday or Thursday, it was a homework day, so I did two thirds of my math homework. That went by quickly, and after that I did my language arts class, and that also went by fast.

I finished the rest of my math homework. After that I felt that I needed to do another subject, but I didn't know what one to do. I settled on doing my leadership homework and I kind of did my schoolwork scattered around the day. I did my reading, as part of my leadership homework.

Later in the day Mom, Tay, and I all did Drill Sergeant in the backyard. That was about thirty minutes long. Then we went in the front yard, and Mom asked if I wanted to go get the mail with her, so I jumped in her car. There wasn't any exciting mail there. We also saw a UPS man going the other way, and we saw that there was a package at the steps. Again, nothing exciting in the package.

Final note: Now fourteen people connected to the White House have coronavirus.

Wednesday, October 7, 2020

We are in the middle of the week now. I can't believe that it is already the tenth month. Well, this is a fun day to think about numbers. I am fourteen days from becoming fourteen. I don't know, but I feel that I am less excited about my birthday compared to when I was around seven years old. I still like presents, but I am not obsessed with them. It will be great.

I got out of bed at the optimal time, six thirty. I did my reading quickly after getting up. I also got to see Mom before she went to work, and Wilson wasn't happy she was leaving. We were going to be home alone for another four or five hours because Dad was going to come home a little later than usual. I also exercised before doing my Zooms.

Four Zooms later I looked up from the computer. Dad was home—I saw him come home forty-five minutes or so earlier. So, I hugged him once I got off. Tay got off his Zooms faster than I did, so he was already upstairs.

I had to do schoolwork and review a little bit for midterms, mostly for STEM. When it comes to midterms, I am not too worried about humanities, because it isn't an actual test, or math, because that one should be easy. In leadership or photography there isn't anything midterms wise. For STEM I feel like I am prepared. The last one is language arts, and I don't know how I will fare, because it is word study and that probably means verbs and nouns, and I don't know about that one.

In the afternoon I also did screen time and I played *Minecraft* and my world is turning out good. I think soon it will make a big jump to being really good.

Thursday, October 8, 2020

We got to sleep outside! I woke up at seven or so, and I saw the lights were on inside. When I approached the door, I saw Mom and Dad were already awake. I said good morning to them, and a minute later we heard Wilson scratching on the door. We didn't let him in because we knew that Tay was going to want to keep him out there. Tay came inside momentarily, and we all said hi to Wilson, who was super excited that he had woken up, and that he had just slept outside. No one is going to work tomorrow, so I hope that we can sleep outside again tonight.

Because it was already past seven, I couldn't exercise and read, so I had to pick only one. I settled on reading and continued reading my assignment on George Washington. I am going to finish this week, and that is going to be amazing to be done with it, because I have been reading it the whole time that I have been at this school. I had my Zooms, and for homework I did about half of what there was for LA (language arts), and I did the little that there was for STEM, and then I did my photography for the week. So, in conclusion, tomorrow I will just do humanities and study for midterms, mostly for language arts, because that is the one that I am worried about. One assignment in STEM showed some videos on test stress, and I think I am going to do fine.

Later Mom and I went for a walk on the trails with Wilson. Wilson really enjoyed it, and it was nice. That was my exercise for the day. When we came home, I did my screen time. Tay turned on a game, and it was Tom Brady's Buccaneers versus the Bears. I hope that the Bears win, because that would be good for the Seahawks, because the Bucs are 3–1 and are most likely going to be a big threat. The Bears are also 3–1, but there is no way that they will keep it up for the whole season.

Friday, October 9, 2020
We slept outside again, and of course that was amazing. I woke up with no rush and then finally got up and went inside. Mom had to go to work an hour later or so, and she worked for three hours or so. Dad was awake, and Tay slipped in a little later, and Wilson followed.

For reading, which was one of the first things that I did in the morning, I read more than six hundred pages of my book for school. Six hundred pages! It was actually nearly a thousand pages, but for school we are only reading one part of it, and it is kind of more like two different parts, and they are written differently. I have been reading it for the whole time I have been in school, and it has taken a long time to complete. I had actually been reading it for the last few days, doing my weekly hundred pages. I am just really mentioning it because after around fifteen minutes I finished it! That was really an annoying book to read. I would reflect that it didn't have to be such an irritating book to read if I had spread out my reading between days, because sometimes I would read one hundred pages in one sitting, and I didn't like that.

After that I did my exercise. Today was the day that I did my weights. It was good that I did my exercise and my reading in the morning. I also pulled out the yoyo from the basement, and that was something that I hadn't used in a while.

I did my schoolwork after that. Going into the day I thought that I would study and finish my schoolwork. After reflecting, I didn't have to do all of that, and I had decided to do my humanities, and it took a lot less work compared to what I expected. So, I didn't study and revise my paper, but I have all day tomorrow to do that. I am getting less nervous about doing the LA test, because some of the videos I had to watch for an assignment made me feel like I can be prepared.

At eleven we got into the car and met Mom at the doctor's office. We were going to get our flu shots. I remember being really scared when I was little, but now I wasn't very scared. It was a nice surprise that we got to do it outside, because I didn't feel like waiting in a doctor's room to get a shot.

After that, Dad went to go run some errands, and Tay and I got in Mom's car, and Mom realized that we had an hour to kill. So, in that hour we went to the beach at Fairhaven, got some Fairhaven pizza and more stuff. Then after that I got a haircut. It would kind of be an understatement to say that I needed one, but I am glad that I got that done.

Later we watched another Netflix documentary on climate change and had dinner, and Tay and I did our screen time. That's it.

Saturday, October 10, 2020

Well, it was the weekend, so first off, that was great. Dad had to go to work today, and he has to work the whole weekend, so he won't get to watch the Seahawks game with us, but Mom will. I woke up at around seven and went downstairs. Because I got my shot yesterday, I didn't do weights in the morning, but I did do some reading.

Mom, Tay, and I went for a drive later in the day, and first Mom went to Trader Joe's and got us some really cool snacks for the game tomorrow and, I guess, for later. Something that we did after that is we went to Taylor Street. Yes, same name as my brother. It is a really steep hill that Mom used to run up to get exercise. So, we climbed up that and it was really fun to get a good walk/run. Well, I was the only one that ran because Mom and Tay are both kind of injured, so I was the only one to run. I feel really lucky that I don't have any type of injury.

Later in the day I did some studying for midterms. For language arts, I am not able to have any notes, and I am kind of off on verbs and nouns, so what I did is to memorize it if I said the meaning out loud. I think that is going to work really well.

Later Taylor and I were playing outside for an hour, and I won't go into detail, but we both clashed, and I can say that we both did stuff that we shouldn't have done. The thing that I did was, after Tay gave gum to me, I threw it, and then later I tried to put it back in his mouth. Tay then told Mom and Dad (on the phone) about it. I ended up getting in more trouble than Tay, and I feel that that is unfair. But I am actually not too mad about that, because I don't get in trouble much, and even though Tay slid by without getting a punishment, I feel that I will just let Tay be.

I feel that recently Tay is trying to say that he is a big kid and trying to impose male dominance. That's okay. It didn't happen with me, but maybe because I was the oldest. It's cute and actually really funny, so I like it because it makes me laugh. I think Mom and Dad knew that Tay would be a difficult teenager. I get to lie back and watch from afar. Maybe I should get some popcorn to go with the entertainment.

After that we had dinner and I ended up watching a Netflix movie (*Hubbie's Halloween*). It is really funny because it has Adam Sandler and a ton of actors from his movies. There were a lot of connections to his previous films, and that was fun to see as well.

Sunday, October 11, 2020
Ok, so I am doing my writing kind of late because of the Seahawks game. The Seahawks played the Vikings and the game started four hours ago. Another thing to note is that I am going to only write half of this now and the second half later, and I am going to start doing my writing in the morning so I have all day to do it.

I woke up slow because I can, I had no Zooms, little homework, and it's Sunday football. I also realized that my flu shot didn't hurt anymore. Tomorrow I am going to go back to doing weights. But I actually did my reading before even going downstairs, and come to think about it, I think I will again tomorrow.

I went downstairs and said hi to Mom and Taylor. They had already gotten up and by then it was kind of already eight. Mom got a good idea about an hour later, that we should all go on a hike on the trail. So that is exactly what we did, and I was kind of surprised that Taylor was really willing to go. For Tay, we have noticed it takes a long time to get ready to go anywhere, and he takes on average ten to fifteen minutes longer than any of us do. We went on the trail, and it was really a positive idea to go and do that. (This is where I have ended doing my first half of writing; in the second half I will talk about the afternoon and the amazingly crazy Seahawks versus Vikings game.)

Second half, ok. So, after we went on the trail we were in some good spirits. In Fantasy we were both feeling confident that we were going to win. The Seahawks' rivals, the Forty-Niners, were getting crushed by a bad team, the Dolphins, the same Dolphins that we beat last week.

Then I called Dad and he reminded me that I was going to go to Phil's to talk about our book and Ru U, our book club. I had gone with Dad every time, and this was the first time that I was going to go alone, because Dad was at the fire station.

So, I went over there at two, and it was raining a little, so I ran up his long gravel driveway and then knocked on the door. I saw that before I had knocked, he was watching the Cowboys versus Giants game. We talked about the book for a while, and after that we trailed into talking about the Seahawks. We discussed how the Seahawks game was on later in the day, Russell Wilson's great start, and DK Metcalf and his rise to becoming a star!

Then I went back home, and it was 3:35. The Seahawks would be playing the Vikings in just under two hours.

The game finally came, and it was brutal. The Seahawks were getting stopped on offense from Wilson throwing the ball deep because the Vikings were almost always playing with two safeties back, making it easier for the young cornerbacks. The Vikings' offense was demolishing the run game, with Dalvin Cook getting almost a hundred yards from scrimmage in the first half. The Seahawks seemed lucky to be behind 13–0. The second half, the 'Hawks got the ball and ran it three times and punted. Then on the next drive, Dalvin Cook got injured. You could tell right then that the Seahawks gained a significant amount of confidence. The Vikings punted and the Seahawks responded with a touchdown. Then they got the ball back off a punt (I think) and scored again. After that the Vikings threw it on the first play, they got the ball back, and right now it is 13–14. On that passing play, KJ Wright got an interception, the Seahawks scored on a Chris Carson thirty-one yard run, and the Seahawks were winning 21–13.

The Vikings managed a comeback and ended up getting twenty-six points, with the ball at the ten-yard line, with four minutes to go. It seemed like they would end up winning, but then the defense of the third down made a stop where the ball was a few inches from the first down; if they got the first down, they would almost certainly win the game. Then on fourth and inches, at the six-yard line, they had two options. The first was to kick a field goal and make it an eight-point game; the other was to go for it and be risky, but if they got a few inches they would win. They went for it . . . and didn't make it.

So, Russell Wilson has two minutes to win the game. He scrambles for a first down and they don't get an extra yard. Fourth down and ten, game on the line. Russell drops back, looks around. Then he throws the ball up into the air and finds DK Metcalf for a thirty-nine yard completion. They still have much to do, and Russell throws the ball to Metcalf again for a first down, first and goal. They throw it to Metcalf, and Metcalf can't catch it. Then another fourth down and goal, touchdown or lose. Russell finds Metcalf and does a roll and they win! The first time that the Seahawks, in their forty-four year history, have started 5–0!

Monday, October 12, 2020

Well, I guess that this is my first time doing my writing where I'm writing for the day before. One thing to say is that the power is out so right now, the next day, so I won't write a ton.

I woke up and tried to be productive, but it took more time than I thought that it would. But after I had got some stuff done, I was happy that I was done with my reading.

We went on the trail later in the day, and that was really nice as my exercise. Mom, Tay, and I all went, and we went in a little bit of a different direction, and that was fun.

I am not really writing a lot on the day, but this was probably a big part of the day. We had a family meeting to just kind of regroup ourselves after seven months of quarantine. It seemed good, and we got some good things through, like how we may do something like a family activity every day. Then we went for a break and Dad and Tay started talking and Mom and I got a snack. We came back downstairs, and Tay told us how he feels that he isn't treated fair in this family. There was so much that he said that I am just going to say that it was really big and will probably be significantly remembered with all of us later on.

I can say that while I feel that Taylor could have more respect in the family, his points didn't make sense and I didn't agree with all of them. He wanted me to be punished harder because he has had a negative experience, sometimes, with punishments. I feel that Taylor is trying to assert male dominance, and I feel that it might end with me having to stop it with a physical fight (not punches, but something where he really rethinks his point of view). But I am not going to go ahead and fight him one day, but if he asserts even a little bit, he may fight me, and you will hear about it in here.

We got La Fiamma pizza after that and it was super good.

Tuesday, October 13, 2020
This was a great day, and I guess I am here to write about it. I woke up in the morning and did my reading, went downstairs, and saw that Tay was on his phone. Dad was awake and Mom woke up a little later. It was super stormy, and it has kind of been the first time since spring that it was this windy.

"You know, because there is a game today you can't get players in the Waiver Wire," I said to Taylor because I assumed that he was on Fantasy, and because of coronavirus the NFL had to switch some games up, and one was on Tuesday. I think that it was the first time in sixty years that an NFL game has been played on a Tuesday.

After that I did weights. It was the first time in a little while, and Mom has been telling me for a while to do it only once every two days, and I am going to try it. I did that and it was great; I felt that I was ready for the day. I hadn't studied that much in the last two days, so I was going to try today.

I realized that Tay had all the leftovers from yesterday's pizza. That was probably large slices, and about three bowls of salad, the best salad in the world. I was okay because that means that I can go crazy in the future with leftovers, because I was pushing to just eat whatever you want, and this was the first time that Tay has the bulk of the leftovers.

Mom and I went on a drive, and we went to Dick's Sporting Goods to get some stuff. I needed a hoodie and a raincoat because I have been growing out of my hoodie and I don't have a raincoat that fits. I got some really great stuff there, and it was still windy. I got a sweatshirt, a shirt, and a beanie. Mom also got some shirts for herself and socks for both Tay and me. Then we got in the car, and Dad had texted Mom that the power was out, and we weren't too shocked. We didn't feel a rush to go home, though, because there wasn't much to do. We went to Fairhaven, and it was even windier there, and Mom realized that there were whitecaps on the water, and the wind was coming from the ocean. We took some pictures, and Mom got sushi.

When we came home, we went on a walk with Taylor, and Dad was getting some groceries. We played outside, and Mom got the mail. Dad texted and said that he got a message that the power would be back by two thirty. That didn't happen. We decided to go to Mambo's, and we wore masks, and it was weird. It was good though.

I like so much music, and I think that I am going to write a song of the week, where I say a song that I have liked listening to. Last week I will say that it was "Empire State of Mind" by Jay Z. The week before that it was "Leave Me Alone" by Michael Jackson. This week will be below.

Song of the Week:
"Mockingbird" by Eminem

Wednesday, October 14, 2020
Ok, I am going to have to get used to remembering what happened the day before, because it is going to take some time to get into a rhythm.

I woke up, and we haven't slept outside in a while, so that was something that I hope that we will be able to change today. I went downstairs and Mom and Tay were awake. I didn't rush to get some guys in Fantasy, because my team is doing quite well. Actually, I am in first place above nine other people. This week I am going to play Mark Mellein, who is in second. This may be a blessing or a curse, depending how it works out. This week I have all of my best players on a bye. That's my quarterback (QB) Russell Wilson, my best running back (RB) is injured for the game, my second best, Chris Carson, is on a bye. My best two wide receivers (WR) DK Metcalf and Michael Thomas are on a bye as well. So, I picked up a QB, I have my two other RBs and my three other WRs on my team, I have a new RB, and my Defense and Special Team (D/ST) and Kicker (K) are the same as last week.

So, to paint a picture, I only have one player playing this week that I had actually drafted three weeks ago. That's the reason that it could be a curse, because I am not prepared to stand my ground versus my toughest opponent. It is a blessing because not all of my best players will have scattered byes, and in the week that I am most likely to lose because of the players I am playing, it would be good to play the best other team this week. If you understand that. I am leaning on this being a good thing.

I did my exercise with Taylor and Mom. Dad was going to work, so he is going to come home tomorrow. After that I studied for my other two midterms. I was really hoping that I did well on these, which I had to take today.

I studied and reviewed math first, and I took notes and then signaled that I was going to do the test. The first two questions I was kind of confused on, but I saved those for later. I actually did really well and got 92/100, so I was excited.

Then I did my language arts one. I studied for that one too, but I couldn't take any notes for the test. That one I also got 92/100! That was good!

For the first test I had taken a few days ago, I was bummed that I only got 76/100. It was for STEM, and the reason that I am going to put that low of a score on is that I was scared that I had gotten the wrong due date and that I was going to get 0/100. I didn't, but that was something that I was stressing about when I was doing it.

That afternoon I don't think we did anything that was really highlight worthy. (I felt really glad that we had power, because I had to prepare for what I would have to do if we had no internet for midterms.)

Thursday, October 15, 2020

Yep, still not used to thinking about yesterday. Hopefully, it will be easier later. One thing that I can say is it is really cool listening to music while doing my writing. It kind of makes me write faster.

I woke up, and Dad came home a little later. Before he did, I did my reading and finished rereading *Ready Player One*. It was still as good as it was the other times that I read it, and I feel envious of my previous self who got to read that book and didn't know what the ending was. It is also a good movie; I should rewatch it later.

Dad came home. We hugged him and were happy to see him. He is home for four days, so hopefully we get to sleep outside for multiple days. He will be home for Sunday, and I guess it is a shame that on the day there would be football the Seahawks aren't playing. But there will be more games.

Dad went on a bike ride for two hours or so. He was a little grumpy when he came home, but when he came back from his bike ride, he was happy and grumpy-less! He did tell me that he took my phone away from me and he felt that so Tay was satisfied, he would take it this week for Fantasy because I don't usually go on my phone too much. I think that it will actually be a fun experience to not check Fantasy and have suspense the whole time.

We got Wilson in the car and went to Hospice House, got Mom some food and caught her on her break, so Wilson got to see her, and we got to check in. After that we thought that it would be a great idea to go to Padden and let Wilson go in the water for five minutes or so. I could tell that it was really cold. We saw a lot of ducks that Wilson also saw, but what was really cool was we saw one duck that was albino. I think that is really rare. Dad said that he had seen it yesterday when he went to Padden.

Friday, October 16, 2020

Friday, I woke up in the morning and did a little reading for *To Kill and Mockingbird*. I realize this now, but the song of the week is "Mockingbird," and the book I am reading was mentioned previously. The book was really good, and the part I read was the big part. I kind of realize that this is the part that makes the book such a good book, but it's not finished yet.

I did weights in the morning again. Today was the weights day and the next day will be the day that I do Drill Sergeant. But Mom will be at work so I will have to simulate it as well as I can. I didn't have any schoolwork, so that was really nice. I did some chores, and that was cleaning up around the house. We made a sheet to write what our chores are for each day, and that is working really well. Tomorrow I will mop. One thing we put there was to sweep/mop three times a week, because Wilson will be inside more.

I can't believe how much time has gone. In spring we realized that there was something called coronavirus that was new, and we got out of school, and we predicted that it would be for around six weeks and then we would be back for another six weeks.

In summer we were getting used to thinking that the coronavirus will be a part of our lives for longer than six weeks, but we enjoyed summer and kind of got used to it. We predicted that it would still be safe for everyone to go back to in-person school, without much thought about the coronavirus.

Now we are in fall, and we are hoping that this whole thing will be gone by February or so, but now a developed pattern is showing that even that won't happen, and there isn't really any end in sight.

Saturday, October 17, 2020

I am trying to remember . . . it takes a while . . . we slept inside, I woke up in the morning, and after that I realized I wasn't going to go back to sleep. Dad was downstairs on the computer, and I said good morning to him. Then I saw Wilson and he seemed happy to see us, but he was sad when Mom told him that she was going to go to work. Her shift was twelve hours, from seven to seven, the whole day.

I read and did weights in the morning, and I had gotten everything done at nine fifteen. I was really proud. I also swept. Tay was also done, and we were so happy that we were done. For social studies, or humanities, I had to watch a movie before Monday, and I decided that because I had so much time, I would watch it today. It was better than I was expecting. It is considered a classic, I think: *Mr. Smith Goes to Washington*. It is about this guy with no political experience that is appointed as a senator. I am not going to spoil it, just in case you, the reader, will watch the movie. Dad and Tay watched with me. I had to take a few notes, but it was still a great experience.

We were going to have Gavin and Carter over tomorrow, but then we saw that there was going to be some rain tomorrow and today was going to be a nice day. We told them and they were all for it.

At two, they came over and we had so much fun. We talked and then we played some hide-and-seek. Then we decided to get another version, where there is one hider, and the three seekers try to find the hider and hide with them, and the last one to find the hider loses. We had fun playing Ultimate Football, and we had pizza after that. We got cupcakes because you could connect it to my birthday—it's in four days!

Sunday, October 18, 2020

It isn't fun when you have to wait two weeks for another Seahawks game, but in one week they will play. Today, however, not so much. The Seahawks are on their bye, so they don't play this week. The good news is that they can't have anyone get injured, and they can't lose (even though at 5–0 they haven't been doing that at all), so that's good!

I woke up, and we got to sleep outside on the deck. Dad was already inside, and Mom was getting ready for work. I said good morning to both of them. Taylor was asleep outside with Wilson, still. Dad then talked to a friend on the phone for a little while, and I really didn't have much to do. When thinking about how I was going to organize the day, I was really sore from the day before, playing with Gavin and Carter. I asked Dad after he was off the phone if today could be my exercise break day, and he said that was okay.

I did screen time at eight for one hour. Because we had only done one hour yesterday, we got three hours today, to make up for the hour we missed.

Taylor watched some football. I wasn't too interested, because I was quite sure that my Fantasy team was going to lose this week, and the Seahawks weren't playing.

We didn't do anything exciting today. At one we went up to Phil's house to talk about *To Kill a Mockingbird*, and we decided that for the next reading we were going to finish a book and then the next time we meet we will pick a new book to read. I wonder if it will be as good as this book.

Monday, October 19, 2020

Today was the first time in around ten days that we went back to doing our Zooms. We had midterms and then we also had fall break, but we didn't do much. We have never had fall break before, and it was only for half of a week. I woke up, showered, and brushed my teeth. Before I did my Zoom, I also read and did my writing, to get prepared for the day.

After the four Zooms, I didn't have to do any schoolwork, because it is a long day. Mom and Tay went to the dentist for Taylor's teeth. Tay has a lot going on with his teeth. Let me tell you, in the briefest. He has braces on his top teeth, his two front teeth are small, his bottom four front teeth are chipped. He has a small jaw, an underbite. Because of the underbite his gums behind his top teeth are all disturbed tissue, and it hurts for him to have a full bite. Because of his underbite he also has headgear that he wears to bed, but it falls off at some point in the night, every night. He needs to have it on for thirteen hours or it doesn't work, and he wears it for probably seven or eight hours. This is in addition to his PT, acupuncture, and more. I am glad I don't have any of that.

Tuesday, October 20, 2020

Well, I guess that I have had a long time being thirteen, but tomorrow it will be time to move on to fourteen! Yes, you read that right, my birthday is tomorrow! I am super excited. I went downstairs and saw that I was the only one awake. I had two Zooms, and then I was going to do homework. My plan was to do math and leadership today. I did my reading and read more of *To Kill a Mockingbird*, and then I wrote about yesterday.

I had two Zooms. For math the type of Zoom is the Zoom where you just do your homework, so it is barely a Zoom. I got three fourths of my math done for the day, and I was excited that I got all of that squeezed in. I did my language arts Zoom, and that didn't require a ton of thinking. I am starting to realize that there are some classes that I could do without doing Zooms. Language arts and leadership are two of them. STEM is quite important, so that should still be an online Zoom. I learn from the humanities Zoom too.

Then I did the rest of my homework after my Zoom. Meanwhile, Tay was doing his two Zooms and started right after I ended. The leadership homework was a piece of cake.

Then in the afternoon Mom and Dad went on a hike. After that, Dad also went on a run with Wilson on the trail. Tay and I did screen time, and that was fun to do. My *Minecraft* world is now good, and there isn't really stuff that I need. It looks super great and finished. Now it will be even more fun to play in the world.

Then Mom told me that we were going to go to La Fiamma today! I thought that we were going to go on my birthday, but we were going to do that today and then go somewhere else tomorrow. I was more than fine with that because I got La Fiamma.

Wednesday, October 21, 2020
It is crazy that fourteen years ago, to the day, I was born. I feel that it is incredible how the time went, because it feels like it went fast but also slow at the same time.

We got to wake up on the deck. On the mirror, Mom had written, "Happy Birthday, Cody!" That was really cool of her. I had to do my reading, and one thing is that even though it is my birthday, I still have to do school.

Four hours later I did all of my Zooms. Then I did screen time and watched YouTube. After that hour I had some lunch. I had a grilled cheese sandwich, as good as ever. After that I played basketball outside with Taylor.

I came inside a little later, and at two thirty I opened most of the presents that I got. I was really grateful, and I got a basketball, a football, an exercise ball. I also got some clothes and a hundred-dollar check (!!) and that was all super cool. I had one last present that I was going to open later, from Gammy and Paw-Paw. (We were going to tonight, but we forgot).

After that we went to the place where Gammy and Paw-Paw were staying. We got some french fries before we went to Anthony's restaurant. I originally thought that I wouldn't want any, but then I had a few. There was this one dip, and it was so good, so I had a ton of french fries. Gammy and Paw-Paw got some cookies that they gave me. I loved that, and of course I will share with Taylor. We had an amazing dinner at Anthony's, and I got a really good steak, mashed potatoes, and bread. Then for dessert I had a slice of cheesecake, and I haven't gotten that from Anthony's before. Then we drove home and I called Mickey (my grandma on Mom's side), and then I ended up opening the present at home. It was AirPods, and I was really thankful for that. Right before I went to bed, Dad measured me on the wall where we have been recording our height when it is our birthday. I had grown a lot more than other years, so that was cool to see.

Thursday, October 22, 2020
Well, it was my first day waking up being fourteen, because technically I was born at seven in the afternoon or something like that. We didn't sleep outside, because Dad was at work. I came down and Mom was awake. Tay

could sleep in as much as he wants because he has a Zoom later today, at ten. I have a Zoom at eight, so I did my reading and my journaling for the day.

I had two Zooms. My first one was a homework one. Instead of doing math homework, because I had already finished it, I did language arts homework. Then I actually did the language arts after that, and that was fine.

Then I continued doing homework after the Zooms. For homework I did the rest of my language arts and then photography, which was incredibly easy. In hindsight, I wish I had done a little more homework, because I have a good amount of homework to do tomorrow.

Friday, October 23, 2020

It was so nice to not have to do Zooms in the morning. What I did do is this: I was one of the first to wake up, and I looked at my computer because I needed to figure out what book I had to read and how much of it for humanities. The book was called *Whatever Happened to Justice*, and I had to read a few chapters of that. It was simple enough to read. Then I read some other book for school, and I was done with my reading!

I did my writing and exercise after that. For my writing, well, that was what I wrote yesterday. Then I did my exercise. Today was the day for weights and I did that for a half hour.

Taylor then wanted us to do our first hour of screen time, so we did that, and I was on the Xbox. This world is so fun to play in, but I think what I am going to do tomorrow or a day after that is to make a new world. I know that it is a tragedy that I am going to stop using this world right when it gets good, but I have learned so much from this world and I feel that it would be cool to be in a new world, with a new start!

I did schoolwork after my hour of screen time. I did most of both of the last two classes, those being STEM and humanities. I have more to do tomorrow, but for now I think that is a good achievement.

Saturday, October 24, 2020

Well, tomorrow is football, but until then we just wait. I didn't have any Zooms again today (it's Saturday, so of course there isn't Zoom), but schoolwork was unavoidable.

The classes that I needed to do next were STEM and humanities. It wasn't too much work. I got it all done but then realized that I hadn't planted the beans for STEM. Oh well, I'll just do it tomorrow.

Not much really out of the ordinary happened after that. I can say that I am very excited and kind of worried about the game tomorrow. It is Sunday Night Football, but the Cardinals are a good team.

For this time, I don't really have any song of the week. I have a few songs that I am listening to more, but not one specific one.

We got to sleep outside and that was really cool to find out.

Song of the week:
I don't know, not one really big one.

Sunday, October 25, 2020

The election is so close! I am worried. Even though I know who I want to win, I don't think that they will. I am preparing myself for the disappointment, like the last time.

We went to sleep. I woke up in the morning, on the deck. Taylor had come inside because he was too cold. That meant that Dad and I were accompanied by Wilson outside. I woke up and Dad did too. I told him that it was five. I mentioned this because it totally looked like it was one in the morning, also known as the middle of the night. Wilson seemed uncomfortable, and we came to the conclusion that he wanted to go outside. He was happy to go, and we could hear the frost under his feet. We were pleasantly surprised when five minutes later he came back in. We fell back asleep and then woke up and went inside.

There were no games for a while, but we would have to wait.

Mom and I went on a drive. We went to the Chuckanuts and then to the bakery, because we wanted bagels but also because Bret Simmons was coming over and the plan was to give some to him.

Dad had started a fire when we came home, and we could see that Bret's car was there. I stayed out there for a little while. Taylor didn't come out, and then a little later Jason came over, and his two kids, Silas and Lucas. Tay still didn't come outside, but I was out there for most of the whole time. I had a s'more and it was really good.

Then the Seahawks game came on. The Seahawks started with a 10–0 lead. Then it got closer and went into overtime. Wilson threw three interceptions, and it was a winnable game, but we lost. If you are wondering, that is why I am not writing a ton. Because who would enjoy going into depth about their team's loss?

Maybe next week. But the Seahawks are still 5–1 and as good as anyone in the NFC.

Monday, October 26, 2020

So, I woke up in the morning and was thinking about how there is a really weird transition between the weekend of no school and then Monday. I don't think it will ever make much sense to me. After my four Zooms, I did screen time and then had some lunch. Not much happened after that.

I did think that now I am going to start a new phase of my writing and will put a little bit of emphasis on the daily stuff. Like I did just now, and that was the whole day. Now I will write about something that has much to do with stuff that I will want to remember in the future. Maybe we will write a book on our COVID experience—132 pages so far, so a good amount of material. We also played football.

One thing that I haven't talked about at all is Dad's Ironman and how that has kind of gone public. Somehow the *Seattle Times* (not Bellingham but Seattle) wanted to do a story on Dad's Ironman, and doing it alone, and how it can be a type of symbolism for resilience during a tough time. Dad didn't want anyone to know, because he feared that it actually wouldn't make it into the paper, and he didn't want to go around giving an explanation. It made it into the Sunday paper, and it was on the front of the sports section. There is one picture that is super massive of him. There is even a picture of us with him, and it was really cool to see that. This, Mom reminded me, will most likely never happen again for him, so it is big!

Tuesday, October 27, 2020

Wow. I can't believe that we are so far in the year. In a few days we will be five sixths of the way done. We are not at the end yet; we will have Halloween, the presidential election, Thanksgiving, and Christmas. Today was my short Zoom day, and after that I did two classes' worth of schoolwork. Dad was gone and at work today, and he will be home tomorrow. Mom works tomorrow.

Nothing big happened today to talk about, so I will discuss something that I will be talking about for the next week and that will impact the whole world, in some way, I guess. This is the presidential election. This is going to be the last election that I am not included in. I turned fourteen just a little bit ago, so I will kind of be observing how this works, this politics thing, I guess. It isn't that I was oblivious until now. I knew when Trump won last time, and unfortunately, I don't remember a ton about Obama's two terms. So, in a way Trump is the only president that I have analyzed. Mom and Dad try to say how this isn't how politics used to be, and I understand that. The one thing is that I don't think politics will ever be the same.

The polls are another part of United States politics. I have taught myself to give them zero thought. The first time that it seemed, to my knowledge, that the polls were so wrong was last time. They showed the Democratic nominee Hilary Clinton ahead. They were quite wrong. The problem with polls is that a person who is voting for one person could alter the polls by saying they are going to vote for who they are not. I would say it would be a pleasant surprise if Joe Biden won. I don't feel like talking about politics much. I don't want an overly strong opinion on the side that I am on. I am a kid, and talking doesn't do much. It is better to acknowledge the bad, but to not focus on it until you can't do otherwise.

Wednesday, October 28, 2020
We got to sleep outside again. It was great. It was my long Zoom, so no homework. We played football again, and that was amazing. We have been playing football more again, and I think that it might be that football season is definitely here. Tay seems like he can play too. Also, I did screen time, and that was fun. I am continuing to play *Madden 21*, and I realize that now Tay is also doing it. It was funny, I stopped playing *Minecraft* and not even one day later Tay started to play *Madden*.

The thing that I am doing for the bulk of my writing is focusing on one aspect of my life or something that happened on that day. For today I had humanities, and we did a simulation of the judicial branch. I was a supreme court justice along with eight other people, and the other people were lawyers discussing a case. This was a full-on sim and we got to ask questions to the lawyers on the case. It was really fun because there were times when one of the justices would dumbfound one of the lawyers, and it was always really funny to see. Then after that we justices went into a virtual room and had ten minutes to discuss it. I feel that I had convinced justices to change their mind. In the end I voted that the case was unconstitutional, and that side won the majority. It was super fun and I feel that I did a super good job!

Thursday, October 29, 2020
Ok, I had two Zooms today, but it was okay. Then I did a really big chunk of this week's homework. We played football today, and it was really cool and fun, but then Taylor and I ran into each other, and I bruised my elbow so I couldn't play anymore. It hasn't even been twenty-four hours yet, and I have iced three times. I took a Motrin, so I am going to try to turn it around as fast as I can. I am hoping by the election it is better. That is just my projection.

We watched the movie *To Kill a Mockingbird*, and it was really good. I was surprised how much they replicated the book to the movie. It was made in 1963, so maybe how they made book-based movies was different. In movies now, it could be a whole different story to someone, but I think the film producers change it so that it is better for the audience, and it makes it more entertaining and more likely that someone will recommend the movie, and they get money. It was really interesting that movies were made differently before.

My *Madden* team is also coming together really well. I have good players on my team, and the teams are all mixed up, and they call it a fantasy draft, even if it isn't Fantasy Football. My goal is to be undefeated for as long as possible. Tay made one too, and I think I am going to challenge him to see who could be undefeated longest.

Friday, October 30, 2020
Ok. So, it is the day before Halloween. Not that much is happening on Halloween. Anyway, tomorrow is Halloween, then the next day is going to be Dad's birthday, and the 'Hawks are playing. The next day is Monday, and it is a long Zoom day, so the day will go fast. Then it is election day, and then the next day will be the day where we will know for sure who the president will be for the next four years. That's a busy week, and there won't be anything like it for another four years.

Not much special happened today. We have Halloween tomorrow. Mom plans on going to the store to get some candy, but I don't think that needs to happen. I helped my elbow a little, and it is going in the right direction, but it isn't healed yet.

One thing I want to discuss today is 2020. The way it's going, I am not too excited about seeing the results of the election. It started off, and people were all like, "Guys, 2020 vision! This year is going to be great!" They made resolutions, and looking back, they will call COVID the reason that they couldn't complete it, but really, they forgot what it was three weeks into the year. Then in February we were kind of introduced to what the coronavirus was, but we thought that it was more of a problem that China would deal with. We went to Hawaii and that was really cool. On February 24 (2/24), Kobe Bryant and his daughter, among others, died in a helicopter crash. This was quite heartbreaking and kind of like September 11 (9/11) in the way that 24 was his number, and 2 was her number. Then as March rolled around, there was talk of schools closing down for a while until everything calmed down. On Friday the thirteenth, we were told that we wouldn't go to school until the second half of April. Then sometime in those six weeks, we were told we wouldn't go to school for the rest of the year. It is sad how we celebrated not being at school, in hindsight. I will finish the second half of this 2020 reflection tomorrow, possibly.

Saturday, October 31, 2020

HALLLOWWWEEEEEEENNNNN!! *Huh? Coronavirus? Halloween is canceled? Awww, come on, man.*

Well, it was Halloween, and actually we had a few things that were really fun. I woke up quite happy because tomorrow the Seahawks play. The Seahawks are playing the Forty-Niners, their nemesis. The last time we played them, it was the last game of the season. Whoever won also won the NFC West, now considered the best division in football. It came down to a throw that Russell Wilson threw, and it went to the one-yard line, but they stopped Jacob Hollister a few inches short of the TD. The time before that it went to overtime, and the Forty-Niners kicker missed the would-have-been-game-winning field goal. Then the Seahawks got the ball and kicked a field goal and won the game. The latter game was a lot like last week's game. It was crazy.

For Halloween there were a few neighbors who said that they had little bags at their door, and we went up to their houses and got a good amount of candy for a compromised Halloween. One neighbor had hidden Halloween rocks that she painted, and if you found one you could go to her house, and she would give you a bag of candy. Dad and Jason made a little treasure map thing, and at the end there was candy hidden up on Galbraith, and we found it. That was creative and exciting.

Sunday, November 1, 2020

Happy Birthday, Dad! It's Dad's birthday today, and I feel that it is always fun because Halloween and a birthday are back to back. We got to sleep outside, but Taylor thought that it was too cold, so he didn't sleep out there with us. Just Wilson, Dad, and I did. It was a football day also, so it just made things that much better. We went on a hike and got some Halloween decoration that Dad had placed for the scavenger hunt yesterday. We crossed paths with a neighbor, and she decided that she was quite scared when she saw a witch seemingly flying. At a closer look, it was attached to a tree branch. The Seahawks game also happened. I'll write about that in a few paragraphs.

Ok, back to a little recap of 2020, so far. Ok, school ended for the year. That is when we started to really stick with doing writing. So, we realized that this might be a little longer than a six-week vacation. We thought for sure that we would be able to go back to school in the fall. Well, look where we are now. Anyway, we had the optimism that maybe the end of the seventh month would result in the end of COVID. We definitely enjoyed summer. We did Khan Academy and more. Meanwhile, in August we started to get ready for online school—not that we wanted to, but because that is what COVID had in store for us. Then sometime in that period, the actor for *Black Panther* and other great movies died in his forties of colon cancer. Here we are, and the election is in less than a week. This is going to be another chapter of 2020.

The Seahawks game was at 1:25, but it felt like an hour later because today was also the daylight saving time change. The game started, and the Seahawks got the ball first, and they were not clicking, and they had a three and out. This happened a few times and then the Forty-Niners fumbled, and the Seahawks got the ball. Then the call was reversed, but in the next play we intercepted the Forty-Niners. The Seahawks got into a rhythm, and then Metcalf swerved around defenders for a forty-six-yard touchdown, and the Seahawks offense never stopped from there. The defense also played its best game of the season, and the Seahawks won 37–27. Most of the Forty-Niner's points were garbage points, and the game was kind of over at 30–14, but the Seahawks were leading at one point, 30–7. The Rams lost their game versus the Dolphins. Their rookie QB on the dolphins, Tua, is going to be a really good player in the future, I think. The Cardinals were on a bye, and the NFC west is the best division in the NFL, and the Seahawks are on top. Here are the standings. With the new playoff format, all of the teams can make the playoffs: Seattle 6–1, Arizona 5–2, Los Angeles 5–3, San Francisco 4–4.

Monday, November 2, 2020
Ok, today was the day that was sandwiched between Halloween/birthday and the election. It will end tomorrow, and that is incredible. Taylor didn't sleep outside again. Dad noticed it, and I don't disagree, but Taylor is being grumpy. Hopefully he will turn it around in the next few days. I had my long Zoom day, so I didn't do any schoolwork, and that was kind of good, but I didn't really like staring at the computer for four hours. When I was done, it was the afternoon, and we did screen time.

We tried to play football, and after a few drives I realized that it wasn't going to work for me to play football. I went inside, and Taylor and Dad played pass. I looked up to try to figure out what my elbow was. I know it will probably be vague, but I have a bone bruise. I have seen it in the NFL, and it isn't a fracture, but it is a few steps below it. There doesn't seem to be much to do, but I am going to ice two times every day, because it seems that will help. All of the symptoms of a bone bruise I hit, so I am confident that that is what it is.

I guess I should talk about Fantasy Football, now that we are deeper in the season. Right now, I am going to be in second place. In Fantasy, only this person Mark Mellein and I are consistently in the top three spots. I think I have been in the top three the whole time. I am 6–2, and Mark is 7–1. After that, there are, like, two people that are 5–3. This is also going to be the week that Taylor and I are playing each other. This is the first time we are going to play and probably the last of the season, if we meet in the playoffs. Meanwhile, as I am trying to be in first place and get a bye, Taylor is trying to get in the playoffs. He is in eighth place, and you need to be in the top six to get in the playoffs. So basically, if the regular season ended today, Tay wouldn't be in the playoffs. This is really ironic because last year we had the same team, and Taylor put blame on me for us not winning. It would be really funny, after we were in the playoffs last year, if he doesn't make it this year. That would be a funny reflection for him to think about.

Tuesday, November 3, 2020

Well, here we are. It is incredible how long it has taken, leading up for this, and now it is going to be over. I woke up with the realization of what day it is. It is Tuesday, so I did two Zooms and two homework things. The classes that I did were math and some other one, I don't know for sure, language arts, I think. Then I did screen time. Also, today Taylor made a trade with Mark Mellein, the person in first place for Fantasy. I don't think that Taylor won this trade, but that isn't good or bad, because they are both competitors.

Then the election started. I was nervous. Taylor set up the couches in a way that we could all see the election screen the best. We were all in the basement. Dad is going to work tomorrow, so he won't see tomorrow.

In the beginning it looked too early to get any impressions. The two states Biden thought he could flip, and it would be really good for him, are Texas and Florida. Florida was looking possibly democrat but then it pulled republican. Then Biden had, like, ninety one points or something, for a lot of votes on the coast. The swing states look like they are all going to Trump. By the end of the night, it seems like Donald Trump is going to win the election. There aren't any for sures.

Wednesday, November 4, 2020

I woke up at four in the morning and went to my computer and looked up the most recent election results. The stuff that I saw wasn't much of a change, I thought. The few states Joe Biden needed to win are Arizona, Nevada, Wisconsin, and Michigan. Pennsylvania is also one that would give him a big lead, but in some scenarios, he doesn't need it. He wasn't leading before, but he had a really good chance with it when I looked.

We watched the election before my Zooms, and to be honest, the amount of the election kind of took me off rhythm, because I haven't exercised recently. That is partly because it is rainy and my arm hurts. Most of the exercise I do uses my arm, so I will have to use some other stuff.

This was my long Zoom, so that was good that I didn't have to do schoolwork. I split-screened the election coverage and my schoolwork for a few of my classes. Some classes I am in I kind of don't need to do a Zoom. The first class, math, for today what they were talking about I already knew.

Now, at the end of the day, this is how the election is looking. Biden is in the lead, but it is going to go down to the wire. I think this is the longest time that it has taken for the United States election to decide a winner.

Thursday, November 5, 2020

Okay, well, I can say a few things happened today. I did my school and two of my other classes. Election wise, nothing major happened. I also had an assignment where I had to write a memoir of myself, so far. Here is what I wrote for my assignment:

> *I was born on October 21, 2006. I was born in the same place that I have lived for my whole life in Bellingham, Washington. Bellingham is a small but steadily growing town. Bellingham is a place where there are many mountain bikers, evergreen trees, and loyal Seahawks fans. Seattle is just two hours south, and where my dad works. My dad works as a Seattle firefighter, and he wakes up before the sun and drives to Seattle. He originated at the eastern side of Washington in Spokane, where there is a natural border of a mountain range separating it from the Pacific. He went to college here in Bellingham and found himself not finding anywhere else to live long term. As a triathlete he would go around the west coast to race, and one race he went to was in California. My mom was born and raised in California. Like her sister, she never had any intent after high school to stay in the Golden state. She pursued being a nurse. Mountain biking led her to*

triathlons. She saw my dad at one race. They didn't meet until friends of friends knew each other.

Fast forward a couple of years and they are married. Fast forward a few years after that and I was born. At the time I was born they found a few holes in my heart. They projected that they would all heal with time, and they all did, except for one.

When my brother was born, my parents realized that the condo they were living in was getting smaller as we got bigger. They then began to shop for houses and put up the condo. This is the same time that the stock market went down, and they couldn't sell the condo. My dad was always in Seattle working overtime, and my mom had to contain two children while keeping the condo clean for people to look at it. Finally, they sold it. They got a way lower price than they thought, but they also found a great house to live in for a really good price.

Only seven to nine months after we moved in, something was wrong. The walls were soggy and then, after some inspecting, there was mold in the house. Around this time, I also developed asthma. The mold was something that pointed to this. This resulted in a lawsuit, and it wasn't a short one. After we couldn't live in the house we moved back into another condo. That was for a little while, and then my family rented a basement from one of the other families at my preschool. Then after that, for around a year, we rented the whole house of another family friend, as they were going to Washington, DC, for a year. In total, the lawsuit was two years long. In the process, all of the clothes in the house had to be thrown away, another result of the mold. In the years since then we have made the house so much better.

Now our house is a place where all of my memories are. From learning how to ride a bike, and being introduced to soccer, it is also where my parents drove my brother and me to elementary school every day for five years.

School was really fun, and I was really lucky to have such an amazing experience. I was the new kid, because when the lawsuit was finished, I was going to enter first grade. I can remember for the first three months or so, I was kind of just finding out who everyone was. I only can remember one or two instances where I was bullied that year, and they were so short and happened such a few times that I don't know if it is really necessary to label it as such. I have not been bullied since. I have heard so many stories at Williamsburg where *people have had such a negative time at school, and it just makes me that much more grateful. I currently cannot wait to get back to in-person school, because my personality demands it.*

In third grade, I went to Seattle to a children's hospital for a checkup with my heart. They have done this probably once a year, and it is routine. This time, though, was different. The doctor talked with my mom about surgery. The surgery she was talking about is where they would go from a vein and travel to my heart and put a little piece in the hole that was not yet filled and plug it up. Eventually, this patch would be covered by tissue and would not even be visible from the heart. One month later, I went into a room for surgery.

It is weird how now, and kind of for my whole life, I have not let my surgery be any part of defining me. It almost never comes up in conversation and I could bet that 75 percent of my friends don't know that I had heart surgery. It went well, and I went back to school a little more than a week later. I had good timing, because it happened right before spring break, so I got an extra week to recover before school.

I should talk about the impact of the surgery. So, the hole was in the wall that divides old blood being renewed. The doctors realized that I was getting around 60 percent of the blood in my lungs that I was supposed to get, and now that is fixed. Prior to this surgery I was a small kid. I recall that I was around 12th percentile in height and 6th in weight. Now that it has almost been five years from the surgery, I am around the 50th percentile in height and 30th in weight.

A year after that I played in tryouts for a soccer select team. I was really excited when I got the news that I was on that team, and I was even more happy because this was the second time I had tried out. The first time was one month after my surgery. In hindsight I was in no position to try out for something like that, but I felt I could. I played on that team for one year, and the next year I forgot to try out again, so I played on a recreational team. Then the year after, I kind of decided that I didn't want to travel everywhere, and I did school soccer. I was planning to try out this year to prepare for possibly playing high school soccer, but like most things, that was canceled.

Oh yeah, and how the coronavirus hit the world. The good news is that my parents had good job security. I think I will always remember hearing on the loudspeaker at Kulshan Middle School that school would be over for six weeks, and then we would come back. Everyone didn't think that it could be more than six weeks, so there was cheering because there was no school! In hindsight, I think everyone would have reacted differently than they did then, had they known it would last this long.

Then we did school online, and then we got the news that we would finish the school year online. Summer was really fun, and we made the most of it. Then my parents talked about doing a different online school to start the year. I opposed this idea because I wanted to see my friends at school, even if it was on a computer. Not too much to anyone's surprise, I was overruled, and we went to Williamsburg. Now, after a while of getting to know what the school was about, I think my parents made a good decision for my academic life, and I will look back in hindsight realizing that this was a fun experiment. When I go back to public school, I will be really excited to be back, but I will leave knowing that I found this new community that I never would have known about otherwise.

I don't plan on slowing down;
my life is just getting started, and the best is still to come.

Friday, November 6, 2020

The election is still not over. Sorry, we have to wait longer. Hopefully when you are reading this all will be over. I woke up and I didn't have to do any school Zoom. I did schoolwork today and I also saved some for tomorrow. Besides that, when we woke up, both Pennsylvania and Georgia flipped to blue, so Biden is even closer to winning the election. Numbers came in throughout the day, and the thing is, all I can say is that all of the numbers that came just pushed the likelihood that Joe Biden becomes the forty-sixth president. The polls thought that he would win most undoubtedly, but I knew that this would be one of the closest races in the 244 years of the US.

Something really fun that we got to do is go to Sehome High School fields. My arm hurt for the first half of it, and then I just kind of got used to it. I didn't play very well, but the amount of fun was insurmountable. We did that for about two hours. I will go tomorrow but Dad is going to work, so we won't play football, but we could play soccer or something like that with Mom.

Dad got champagne for when Joe Biden is the president. He told us that this was the first time that he had ever bought it, in his whole life.

The Seahawks game is soon. The game is at ten, so we will be able to play football after that, and I would love to do that. I think I had the most fun there than I had ever.

Saturday, November 7, 2020

Biden is president. History was made today.

So, I woke up in the morning, I did my reading, and for that I read a book called *Whatever Happened to Justice*. I have to read it for humanities and after that I remembered I had other homework to do, and I did that later in the day. Mom went on a bike ride, and then I did some of the homework that I had to do. I looked at the news and nothing major had happened. I did read, however, that Joe Biden thought that this would be the day he was elected president.

I took a shower, and when I got out, I heard that Mom came inside. She said that Joe Biden had been elected president of the United States. This was crazy, because the one time that I didn't look at the news he got elected.

With Joe Biden being elected president, he will go to office on January 20. In the meantime, who knows what Donald Trump will do. Saturday Night Live was really funny, with their skits on the election. That was fun to watch.

There were celebrations everywhere in New York City, Atlanta, Pennsylvania, London, Paris, and Washington, DC. It was cool to see people come together in such a time where there is division.

I think that it is interesting that during this whole time there were people in my Zooms that had Trump flags, and some of them were very vocal about not wanting Biden to be president, and in a sort of denial when he was elected. I think they also made fun of him a few times.

I think that politics now have gone off the rails on both sides. I think that there's a point where politics should stay as politics was treated even just ten or twenty years ago. I didn't live to remember, but it seems like it was a lot more respectable with both parties, and they were respectful to each other. Everyone wants the best for America, and politics is just people debating how they want that done, what that looks like, and what that includes.

Sunday, November 8, 2020

Ok, so today was the day of the Seahawks game. We woke up and we were happy that it was an early game. We all went on a drive, Mom, Tay, Wilson, and I. We went to the Chuckanuts, and that was cool because the mountain goes to a farmland, and then there is a bakery that Mom said was really good, but we found out that it was closed for a few more hours. So, we left and got on the freeway and got home, and there were five minutes until the game.

The Seahawks lost the second game of the season, versus the Bills. The game didn't start well because they got the ball and got a return to the other side of the field. They scored quickly to make it all the way to 17–0. The Seahawks were horrible on passing defense. They did fix a problem, but they also found another. They fixed the pass rush and got seven sacks, a season high. The Seahawks offense was fine, but Russell Wilson, who is the lead for MVP, threw two interceptions and two fumbles. The Bills scored on all of those turnovers.

In Fantasy Football I was playing Taylor. It was actually really close and I was losing by twelve points or something, with only the Sunday night game left. All of Tay's players played, so he was stuck at 142 points, and I was at 129, but I had a kicker and a WR still playing. The game was the Bucs versus Saints. The Buccaneers were three-point favorites, but they lost. At half time it was 31–0 and the final was 38–3. That was good for the Seahawks, and my Fantasy team. I beat Taylor by around six points. I am 7–2 right now, and there are four games left in the regular season. Last year I got seven wins, and with more games left, I will exceed that, most likely.

Also, when looking out the window we saw Ashaan, and that was cool because we haven't seen him since COVID, except for one time. We played football and soccer; it was really cool to see him!

Monday, November 9, 2020
It is never fun to see the 'Hawks lose and then realize that the next day is Monday, but it happens sometimes, and the loss the Seahawks faced wasn't so bad for playoff positioning. The other teams that we will be competing with, most notably the Bucs and the Cardinals, lost also. Anyway, Monday means a long Zoom day. The first was math, the second was STEM, the third was leadership, and the fourth was going to be humanities. I got an email before the class started that humanities was canceled because the teacher was sick. I guess that it is interesting how they don't have substitute teachers for Zooms, but it worked out well for me anyway. She said in the email that instead of Zoom we should work on our homework for the week. I did a lot of the homework that I would have to do that week, so that was great. In other classes it was an interesting dynamic to see people's reaction to the political activity over the weekend.

Then after that Taylor did his chores and an hour of screen time. I took a bath while he did that, and the thing is, Tay's chore was to sweep and mine was to mop. The mopper in this situation is very vulnerable because his job requires the sweeper to do a good job. Tay did a poor job and that was not very nice of him. It was okay, and this happens a lot, but it is one of those things that needs to be highlighted.

Then Mom and I went to Mambo's and got some food for dinner. We went home, and when I ended up eating, it was really yummy. The plumber, David, came over, and we had something that needed to be fixed in Mom's bathroom. I don't really know why, but we haven't used the toilet for a while because I think a part was broken.

In *Madden* I am actually still in my first year, and I am 13–1 or something, and this is a team that I can tell I am going to stay with for a while. I have never been with a team for more than five years, and I am going to try to really stay with this team for ten years! I think just to stay with it for ten would be great, but my goal is to get ten Super Bowls.

Tuesday, November 10, 2020
Today was the day that I officially won Fantasy for the week, versus Taylor. Now I have bumped to a 7–2 record with Taylor at 3–6. This is hilarious because last year Taylor criticized that our team wasn't *really* good because I had the final say in all of the decisions, so he was eager to have separate

teams. Of course, this is an accusation that wasn't true at all, and the way he accused me was also eager for separate teams. Now the best that Taylor can do is tie the record that we got as a team last year, 7–6, and if he doesn't, he could seriously not make the playoffs. I want him to make the playoffs though. I am going to make the playoffs, and the only thing I am worrying about is getting a bye. In that sense, I am in second place with a one game lead, and there is only one person in third, and I am playing him this week. If I win, then I can almost say for sure I will get a bye, and if I lose, I just have to win as much as possible. Tay is in eighth place, and the top six teams make the playoffs.

This was our short Zoom day, and after my two hours of school, I did homework for two subjects, math and leadership. I am in a good position for homework this week. I can't wait to go back to public school, and it will be weird because most likely I will be going into high school, so that will be an experience anyway.

Wednesday, November 11, 2020
This was a long Zoom, but that's okay. I had math and I did schoolwork while in class, because the things that were being taught, I had already learned. I got some good things out of the way in that hour. This followed the last three Zooms, with not much to be said about them. After this I remember that we had to go to the doctor. I was kind of expecting a shot, and I got one! Lucky me! Then we went to the doctor and got some of the regular measurements. This was just a checkup, with the shot, an interesting one. It didn't hurt at all at the beginning, and as the fluid came in, I realized that it was going to be sore. Writing around twenty-four hours after it, I almost didn't realize that I had any.

Some news came in today, for the Super Bowl. News came in that the Weeknd would be performing the halftime show. I watched a video a few months ago, and it was actually Michael Jackson that made the halftime show something to look forward to. Before that, it was not common knowledge and there was almost never anyone famous that performed. There have been some good and bad halftime shows. I remember that the two Seahawks Super Bowls were good, one with Bruno Mars. I also remember that Super Bowl LIII was a boring one, with Adam Levine and Maroon 5.

Thursday, November 12, 2020
Ok, so this is the day that I had to do schoolwork, and I had a short Zoom day. The first I did was schoolwork again for math. The next was language

arts. We went to the Sharpe's house, and we were going to take care of Ru for a day. Taylor went up once when I was doing my Zoom, and then Mom and I went after that. Ru is always so happy to see anyone, but the problem is that she is too happy, and when I take her out to go to the bathroom, she won't go, because she wants to be pet instead.

Friday, November 13, 2020
The last time that it was Friday the thirteenth, we went out of school and haven't come back since. Nothing big happened today though, like that. There were no Zooms today, just schoolwork. Looking back, I could have done more schoolwork that day, but no problem, because I will be doing it tomorrow.

I did my journaling and looked over my schoolwork. Then I took a shower and brushed my teeth.

I went back to doing weights today. I hurt my arm—and that still hurts a teeny tiny bit—and then on my other arm, I got a shot, but now I am ready to do weights again. I think I just haven't done it in a few weeks, so I wasn't really warmed up, and I was a little stiffer.

I tried oatmeal, and that was not great, but it was still good, and I am going to have it more and more. I had honey and frozen fruit on it, also cinnamon and apples. Some of it was not very good on oatmeal, but the frozen fruit was really good on it. I will see if there are other things that I could use on it, maybe brown sugar.

Saturday, November 14, 2020
I feel that the days are just becoming more and more routine. I don't like it. I woke up, like always. Like always, I did my reading, did my journaling, showered, and brushed my teeth, all in that order. When going to in-person school, there wasn't that much routine.

For my schoolwork today, I had to do a photography assignment. I had to take five photos of different foreground, middle ground, or background in the photos. I took some photos of the creek and the pond. In the back yard there are some big rocks, and when pointing it up to the sky, that was a good photo.

Also, my phone and I have an issue. The problem is that my phone doesn't want to live. This isn't what I want, so I charge it when it is dead. The dilemma is that it will die on its own, without even using it. A regular phone would just die when you use it, and the battery goes down. Mine will just drain its battery on its own, without me using it. This is a mystery.

I got some *Calvin and Hobbes* books, and I read them. Also, Taylor and I were playing a game in the basement, and it includes a lot of half tackling. In *Calvin and Hobbes*, they also play a game that includes a lot of tackling and made-up rules; it is called Calvinball. So, we decided to call this game Calvinball. This game is really good, and it will probably end one day with someone getting hurt.

Also, we all kind of cleaned out the house and got a *lot* of books out, and Dad took everything out of the garage because in the next few days the garage is going to be painted or something. I don't know if it is paint, but the color is going to change.

Note: In the future someone eventually does get hurt from Calvinball.

Sunday, November 15, 2020

Okay, so I woke up in the morning and was excited that I didn't have any Zooms and only had a tiny bit of schoolwork left.

I read and then also did my writing for yesterday. Mom went somewhere, and the Seahawks game was going to be at 1:25, so we would have to wait a little before that came on.

Well, not much happened except the 'Hawks game, so I will just talk about that. The game started, and the Seahawks stopped them to a field goal and then they scored, so they were leading 7–3. Then a little bit after that they got a touchdown, and a little bit after that the ball was knocked out of Jared Goff's hand, and we got it.

This was exciting because we needed it right there, and we started twenty-five yards to the touchdown. Then Russell Wilson made a horrible decision and, instead of running, threw across his body and it got intercepted in the endzone. If he had run, he could have gotten the touchdown.

We ended up losing the game to the Rams, and after this the Cardinals won on a last second Hail Mary. So, in the NFC West, the Seahawks are in third place with tiebreakers. The top three teams are 6–3, and then after that the Forty-Niners, who have been really hit by injuries, are 4–6 or something like that. The Seahawks game really made expectations drop. The Seahawks are going to play the Cardinals again, the team we lost to in OT a few weeks ago. This game is going to be the most important game of the regular season for the Seahawks, so we need to win this one to have realistic odds at getting the number one seed. I also lost in Fantasy and so did Tay, so Tay probably needs to win all of the rest of the games for him to get in the playoffs, meaning his chance for five hundred dollars is narrowing.

Monday, November 16, 2020

It is never fun to wake up on a Monday, and it is a lot worse when your football team has lost. Tay and I know for sure that we had both lost this week in Fantasy, but this doesn't matter for me as much as for Taylor. I looked at the next few weeks of the Fantasy regular season, and Taylor would probably need to win all of his games. He is also playing Mellein the week after this, and he is so good that I could predict that Taylor won't make the playoffs. I have already talked about the irony of this, because of last year. I really am excited for the fact that I could win Fantasy Football!

I had my Zooms, and I had already done homework for math, partially because I didn't have anything to do after the Seahawks lost.

Mom's birthday is tomorrow, so she wanted to watch a movie. We were going to watch one movie, and then we changed it to a movie that seemed popular and was actually really sad. It was called *The Fault in Our Stars*. I liked it. Then I went to bed.

Tuesday, November 17, 2020

Okay, Tuesday. I woke up and Dad was the only one awake at the time. Then Taylor came down, and guess what—this was a special day. It was Mom's birthday! So, when we heard that she was waking up, we went and said good morning. I went up to my room and got the slippers that I got her. As I did, I forgot that I hadn't made a card, so I set down the slippers and went and made a card. Mom got coffee in bed, and when she got out of bed, she got to put on the slippers. Mom already knew that I got her slippers, and that was really something that I liked. Also I didn't have to wrap it.

I did my Zoom upstairs for the first time. I figured that it was too loud downstairs and I could listen and talk better during that time. Those two Zooms happened, and the two classes that I did were STEM and leadership. I had already done math earlier, and I could, for my schedule, do just one more class. I didn't because I would be thankful in the future.

Mom opened more presents, and she got stuff like chocolate and also Dad got her a weighted blanket. I have never heard of it, but I can assume that I am going to like it a ton. Mom's friends came over at eight and went into the garage. In *Madden* I won the Super Bowl, the second of hopefully ten.

Wednesday, November 18, 2020

We woke up in the morning, and when going downstairs, Taylor reminded me that the Seahawks game is tomorrow. This is great, and we are playing a team that we lost to the time before. It is weird to lose three of four games after winning five in a row. The Seahawks really need this game, because if they win then they will be ahead of the other teams at 7–3. The Seahawks, after this, play four games that are extremely winnable. They have the easiest teams to play for the rest of the season. The Seahawks at best case are 13–3, and at worst they miss the playoffs. They will be 12–4 or 11–5, and that could win the NFC West. They haven't won the NFC West in three or four years, but this seems like the year.

I did my Zooms and it was four, so I didn't do any schoolwork. That was fun. Tomorrow I will be doing schoolwork, and that might be good to get something done. Tomorrow I am going to do my language arts and photography, and that shouldn't be hard, but it just takes time.

We watched another movie, and it was okay but not as good as the last one. We haven't watched a comedy movie as a family in a while, so I am going to make sure that is what we do watch next.

Thursday, November 19, 2020

Okay, today was a fun day, and it started with me not wanting to get out of bed. I was tired but I had a Zoom to do. So, I got up and went downstairs. Taylor was still asleep, but Dad was awake. Mom had gone to work earlier, so I didn't get to say good morning to her. I am noticing that after Tay is getting his head gear off, he is sleeping in a little more, and on Tuesday and Thursday he doesn't have Zoom until ten, so he can afford to do that. On the other hand, I have a Zoom starting at eight on Monday, Tuesday, Wednesday, and Thursday.

While I was doing my Zoom, Dad said that he was going to go on a bike ride. So, I was done with my Zooms and Tay was doing his Zooms, so I did homework. I did (almost) all of my language arts, and I had about four other assignments that were things that I just needed to finish up. I only have humanities and photography left, and both of those should be easy enough.

After that, there were a few hours where our minds were seeing when the time would hit 5:20, because that is when the Seahawks game is. This was going to be the hardest game left in the season. All of the other teams we are favored in, and the LA Rams are a team that defeated us, but also the Cardinals beat us. Let me tell you how that went.

The game started with the Seahawks getting the ball, and they marched down the field and ended with a twenty-five-yard touchdown to DK Metcalf. He then was tied for the most receiving touchdowns in the NFL. This was a good start because DK hasn't done well with the Cardinals before. He ended the game with three receptions, forty-six yards, and a touchdown. He almost had another one, but the ball hit him in the facemask. He had another that could have been big, but it fell behind him. Russell Wilson did well and had two touchdowns, but more importantly, he didn't turn over the ball, and he made great decisions. The game ended with a fourth and ten and the cardinals were twenty-five yards from the end zone. The ball was snapped, and Murry could have moved up in the pocket, but he didn't, and that resulted in him getting sacked by Carlos Dunlap, the longtime Bengal who was traded to the Seahawks three games ago, and he already has three sacks in three games.

Friday, November 20, 2020
I found myself eating Mambo's Italian food in the pool table room, using a small chair and a big chair as a table. I asked myself, *How does one get in this situation?* Well, here is what happened:

I woke up and I didn't Zoom, but what I did do was everything that is usual, reading, writing, shower, and brush. There was going to be a painter, and he was going to paint the garage; he was late, and Mom didn't know when he would come.

The painter, he finally came. Mom said that he said that the paint wouldn't smell good at all. At this point I am doing a writing assignment for school. Around twenty minutes after he came, I smelled it, and it smelled toxic, so I moved to the basement with Mom. Tay was already there doing screen time. In the basement, it was not bad with the smell.

This changed when the heater came on. It circulated all the smells, and then the basement was as bad as any other room. So, I did my writing outside, and I realized it was too cold. We decided to leave, and we went to Fairhaven with Wilson. Mom opened all of the windows in the house to get the smell out while we were gone.

Mom got a coffee from Starbucks, and she met one of her friends. Her friend gave something back to Mom that she borrowed. We didn't know how bad the smell would be when we came home, so we decided that it would be better if we got dinner. So, we got Mambo's, and drove home.

When we came back, Taylor noticed that there were little gnats around the house. We didn't think much of it, and we came in fast. Then we saw some in the house.

What most likely happened was bad luck. There must have been a hatch near our house, and the bugs were so small that they could go through the screens. Mom FaceTimed her sister, and she did some research and found a solution to put in cups that attracted the bugs into the water, and then they would drown.

It wasn't as bad in the basement, and when I ate my food, I warmed it up in the microwave and then went downstairs in the basement. I decided to go in the pool table room because it is the farthest away from any windows, where the bugs came from. This is how I was eating a fancy meal, alone, in the basement, with a makeshift table.

Saturday, November 21, 2020

Okay, so, it's the weekend. One thing with COVID and this new school is that the weekend isn't celebrated, because, at least for me, I will have schoolwork. What I can celebrate about on weekends is football, but this week the Seahawks have already played. Okay, well, I got most of my schoolwork done already, so that is something to be excited about. Actually, with the Seahawks playing early (and winning), it is really easy to root for other teams without worrying that we could lose.

Dad came home and the bugs were almost all gone. The concentrate that we made really worked to attract and drown the bugs. Looking to tomorrow, it won't be a problem. We are going to do a second coat on the garage, so we will probably end up leaving again.

Tomorrow is Sunday football, so I am excited for that!

Sunday, November 22, 2020

Sunday football! I know, I actually didn't use my screen time on it, but on Fantasy—that is when all of my players are playing. I knew that it was going to be a close game between me and the person I was playing in Fantasy. As said before: the Seahawks had already played so there wasn't any stress in that. The Seahawks have a mini bye week with not playing until Monday.

I did my reading, and I was determined to get everything done fast. I brushed my teeth and I took a shower; I did my writing and everything else.

Seahawks wise, the Saints won, and that wasn't great for the Seahawks with the playoff picture. Joe Borrow, the number one overall pick in the draft, tore his ACL in an injury that didn't look good at all. He got carted off and is over for the season.

The Green Bay Packers were playing the Colts, and this was a game that seemed like it would be a Packers victory. At half they were leading by fourteen points, and then the Colts forced it to overtime, and the Packers got the ball. The Packers had already marched down the field to get the field goal to make it overtime, so everyone thought they would do it again. But, after catching the ball, a Packer fumbled and the Colts won.

The Chiefs and Raiders game didn't affect the Seahawks, but I was playing Mahomes in Fantasy, and if he got a touchdown, then I would lose; otherwise I would win. He had to do a game winning drive and I lost in Fantasy. It isn't too bad because Fields lost, and he is who I am competing with for a bye.

Monday, November 23, 2020

Okay, Monday. Not much happens on Monday and this isn't much different, so let's see. Umm . . . well, after taking a shower I did my writing, and you just read that writing, probably. I did my Zoom. I am trying to find a good place to do my Zoom and to organize all of my stuff, but Taylor won't give up the desk without a fight. I looked at the homework, and for most of my classes I have less than usual, because Thanksgiving is coming up.

Actually, the statement above isn't true. Today the guys did another coat of paint, so we left that day and went for a walk. We were mostly in one room for the day, because it stunk from the fumes of the paint.

Thanksgiving is really a cool time because you can think about everything that you are thankful for. I really enjoy being thankful for the small things. Of course, I like thinking about the big things like a happy family, a house, and health. But I have a joy in the small things, because even fewer people can be thankful for them, so they are not mentioned.

In football, the Monday Night Football game was the Rams and the Buccaneers, and we wanted the Rams to lose. But either way, it would be good. The Rams won on a field goal, and the Bucs could be in a bad position if they lose to the Chiefs, something that is probable.

Tuesday, November 24, 2020

I did my Zooms. I only had two today, and then for Thanksgiving I won't for the rest of the week. I am excited about that. And I also said this yesterday, but there isn't much schoolwork. So, I did the Zooms.

After that I did the usual things. I did screen time and played in the playoffs in *Madden* and won my third Super Bowl. To refresh you, my goal is to get to ten Super Bowl wins, and part of that is to rebuild and not keep every player. So, my QB in *Madden* is 99 overall, and he will be asking for a ton of money next year. Instead of paying him so much, what I did is I drafted a QB in the first round. He played a good first game and he is the future of the Chargers' franchise.

Okay, first, to the thing that I just found out before writing this. Another great died. First it was Kobe, after that it was the *Black Panther* actor, and now it is a soccer great, Diego Maradona. He was considered just as good as Pele. Soon it will be so sad to have Pele die; he is actually twenty years older than Diego's sixty years.

Taylor and I were playing Calvinball in the basement, and the goal of the game was to hit the football out of the other player's hand. On the first time that we did it, I got the ball and Tay missed the ball and it hit my hand. I knew I jammed it, and then I lifted it up to my face and it was all crooked. Tay saw it, and I got lightheaded, and then we were headed for the ER. It wasn't crowded. I became a lot calmer quickly after Dad and I got in the car. They took X-rays and they said that it was dislocated—that was pretty obvious to me. They splinted it and it hurt, but they did pop it back in place. The pain didn't decrease a ton. Before they popped it, they gave two numbing shots, and because it was in a joint, it hurt a bit.

Wednesday, November 25, 2020

I fell asleep pretty well, considering that I hurt my finger the day before. The great thing is that there are no Zooms on Wednesday or Thursday and we don't have any on Friday either way. I did finish some things up with school. If I had had school, I wouldn't have done schoolwork, because it was a long day. I was planning on taking a shower, but I didn't, because there were no ziplock bags. The doc said that I couldn't get my hand wet because of the stuff holding the stick together.

Okay, here is my assessment for the thumb. Daily things depend on how it goes. I can say that writing is easy, because I am a lefty and I hurt my right. I can also eat. The thing that is really the worst is typing. It is super hard to type because my thumb can only be in one spot, and it gets in the way, and I am finding myself typing the Equal button a lot instead of Delete. I feel that my writing will be slower and less because I don't want to type much. It's quite annoying.

Thursday, November 26, 2020

Thanksgiving!

Well, I'll say that I love eating good food, so Thanksgiving is pretty much handmade for someone like me. I woke up in the morning and it was, like, seven thirty, and I guess that I kind of slept in. I still despise typing with a hand in the condition that it's in. Maybe I should show you how much I mistype with my thumb. *Maybe I s hould s. how you hpw musch*

347

I miss type with thtis thing. There,vtats my average sentence. (It was fun to do that. Hopefully, it wasn't too hard to read. I won't do that again.)

So, for Thanksgiving there were supposed to be three games, but one game was canceled because players on the Ravens got COVID, so they pushed it back. I had one player playing today, and the other guy I was playing against was playing two guys. They both did really good, and my guy only got four points. Outlook's getting grim for me to get a bye, but a good one for the moment because that is the spot that I am in currently.

We also got the Christmas stuff out, and that was fun. We got the stockings up and decorated a little bit. We are going to get a tree tomorrow, and I can't wait.

For dinner, Mom and Dad made amazing food. It included the best mashed potatoes that I have ever had, ham, veggies, and Dad's baby breads.

Friday, November 27, 2020
Look at that! It's Friday, and that means that it is officially Christmastime! We got the Christmas stuff from the basement, there were a lot of lights, and Dad had also bought a ton of other white lights.

There were our stockings. Mine is bright blue one and all of the others are some shades of red. Last year we got Wilson his own because he deserved to have it. One year we got Wilson ten tennis balls, and then the year after that we got him a combination of chew toys, tennis balls, stuffed toys, and peanut butter treats. We also had Tommy the Elf on the Shelf. Even though we had figured out the whole Santa thing, we still hid Tommy every day.

No Christmas is complete without a tree. We went to Stoney Ridge to get our tree. We went there two years ago, and last year we cut down a tree in our yard. That was a tragic mistake, and it looked like Wilson had taken a bite out of it. The tree we got this year was perfect, and the cool thing is I didn't carry the tree with Tay and Dad because of my thumb. I wouldn't get a good grip on things with that hand. I also read a headline that the original people, like the Neanderthals, used their opposable thumbs differently than we do now. I will try to look for that article again.

Mom came home from work at seven and we had apple pie that was really good, but by the time we were done, we couldn't set up the tree tonight. We will put the lights on later.

You could also call this day the revenge of the little gnats. They came back. Dad found where they were coming in through a gap under the door, so he put tape there, and I think that closed them out. He also made some of that solution.

Saturday, November 28, 2020

Now that it was the weekend and Dad was gone, I realized that I didn't need to do schoolwork, so I took advantage of that. I had my checklist, and as I didn't have to do Zooms, I could sleep in a little.

I didn't do my reading until later, but at midday Mom and I went on a hike with Wilson. Wilson had a lot of fun and he smelled everything. We were on the trail for an hour, and then we went for a drive.

Mom and I decided that we should get Mambo's food, and we got takeout. She forgot to order it in time, so we went to the parking lot to order. While she was ordering, I was looking at the new building that PeaceHealth was building. It is massive. Then the person on the phone said that it would be ten or twenty minutes before it was done, so we went to the beach. We saw a lot of people out and about, and we thought that the beach wouldn't be any different.

When we got home, we had our food. We couldn't decorate the tree today, because Dad was at work, so we are going to do it tomorrow.

We did, however, decorate the basement with lights. We also arranged the room so everyone could watch the movie. We watched *Christmas Vacation*, and that was a good movie, as always. Then I had pie, and tomorrow is football! The Seahawks aren't playing until Monday, but there are some good games tomorrow.

Sunday, November 29, 2020

The Seahawks are not playing today, but tomorrow they will be playing the Eagles. The Eagles' quarterback has been playing poorly, so they may have their rookie backup get a few drives of playing.

Meanwhile, the Sunday games have some really interesting playoff impacts. One game, the Saints versus Broncos game, is interesting because the Broncos don't have a quarterback. One of their wide receivers that played quarterback for two snaps played. He only completed one pass. The Saints won and that wasn't what the Seahawks wanted, but who thought the game would be different. The Bucs got demolished by the Chiefs, and the score makes it feel closer.

One game that was probably the most important for the Seahawks was the Cardinals versus the Patriots. The Cardinals were going to win this game and had a 10–0 start ahead. They lost on a last second field goal. The same thing happened to the Rams versus the Forty-Niners. We are not usually Niners fans, but we are for that game.

The Packers won, but that was expected. Today was a slow day and tomorrow we have school, but the dread is compromised because the

Seahawks are playing. Tomorrow there is also a 100 percent chance of rain. Tomorrow will probably be like today. The whole morning we will be inside doing Zoom, the afternoon I have a teeth appointment, and then there is the Seahawks. Dad got the Sunday newspaper for me too, because I will need it for a school assignment soon.

Monday, November 30, 2020

My chances of getting a bye week are getting worse, and it may basically be out of the question, if one was to go that far. I lost this week and Dynamite and Fields both won. Next week if either of them wins, I can't get a bye, and even if they both lose and I win, it isn't a gimmie.

I woke up and checked the news and also the schoolwork I had to do. The only thing left of my schoolwork was a photography assignment. I did that assignment, and that was just five types of photographs. Midterms are in two weeks or so. That is something that I am training myself not to worry about. The finals only count for a part of my grade, and I continue what grades I have. I will have mostly A's and nothing worse than a B even if I didn't do the midterms.

The Seahawks game. According to a graph by ESPN, Russell Wilson has the best record in prime time, TNF, SNF, or MNF, ever. The last time the Seahawks played the Eagles was in the playoffs where Metcalf had 160 yards, which set the NFL record by the most yards by a rookie in a playoff game. The Eagles famously passed on Metcalf for another wide receiver who has 214 career yards. Metcalf got 177 yards and set some franchise records, one for the fastest Seahawks to reach a season of a thousand yards, and Metcalf is leading the NFL in receiving yards. Only Tyreek Hill also has a thousand-plus yards. The Seahawks' defense played amazing and for the first time this year carried the team. The offensive line was attacked, and they couldn't get any consistency running the ball.

Tuesday, December 1, 2020

We are in the final stretch. There is only a little bit left in the year. We are now in December. Tomorrow I am going to go to the doctor for my hand, and that will be good to get an insight on how I am going to get this back to normal.

Yesterday Taylor and I got a game that we thought was on PS4 but is on Xbox. We decided that we would play it after we each did our two Zooms.

I did my Zooms first, and those lasted two hours. Tay had that whole time to do his chores and what not. So, those Zooms were good, and nothing really happened. After that I did my schoolwork. I didn't do the hard parts for this one, but I will possibly do things tomorrow that are harder. I did most of math and photography,

Tay did his Zooms; I was doing my homework at that point.

Mom retaped my hand because we were using the same thing after redoing it earlier, and it doesn't stick as well. It is still more loose than usual, but I am just going to go to the doctor tomorrow.

Tay and I played *Gang Beasts*, and it is a really silly game. It is one of the easiest games for me to play with my thumb. I'm looking forward to playing it with Tay tomorrow. After we did that, we went on a walk with Mom and Wilson.

Wednesday, December 2, 2020

Okay, so I woke up. Now, at the end of the day, some things have changed. I did my Zoom, and this was my first of the Zooms. Math was good and it didn't take too long. After that I did fifteen minutes of STEM and then left my Zoom because Mom and I had to go to the hand surgeon guy to see what is going on with my thumb. I emailed all my teachers the day before, and I missed the rest of STEM and all of leadership. I can watch a recording for these classes later.

So, I did that earlier. We got in and it was actually kind of sad because the doctor is also a plastic surgeon. It seemed sad because all the posters for surgery had slogans, like, "Everyone will notice; no one will know." It seemed sad that people would take the route of surgery for their looks and losing weight.

The doctor said that he wanted to put a cast on for three weeks so that it would be still. I went with it, but it was not what I was thinking coming into the office. I kind of thought it would have been a better option to not put a cast on, and it might hinder how much fun I can have in the snow, if it snows.

So, after that I watched the recordings of the classes, which is cool because you couldn't do that with in-person school. For some parts that I didn't think were important I used the option to make it 1.5x speed, or sometimes 2x speed. That made it so that everything that they were saying I could hear, but faster!

The cast is okay because I can use my other fingers without worrying about my thumb. I can still play with my cast on, and that was fun for Taylor and I to play more *Gang Beasts*. It's funny because the name makes the game seem violent when it is really silly.

Thursday, December 3, 2020

Thursday. So, this was my first full day having a cast on, and it is actually easier to type than with the splint. I don't need to worry about my thumb, and I have my four fingers to type with full ease.

I woke up and had already done my reading the night before, so I did my writing. I didn't take a shower yet, because I am going to wait until Mom gets a plastic thing to protect the cast. The ziplock bag is okay, but water will get inside it most of the time, and I don't want any water.

I did my two Zooms, and I did schoolwork for my first one and got a few things done. For schoolwork, what I was going to do is finish up things and do all the language arts homework. I didn't get to do all my homework, because one assignment wasn't working and another I was going to do a different day.

I looked over my grades again and saw that now I will get A's or A- in all my classes if I don't do any finals. I am going to study for all of it, and I am going to take the tests, but I am not going to worry about it, and I will not overstudy. I feel it is kind of unhealthy to worry and try so hard on my tests.

Tay got his braces off, and he said that they hurt a lot. When I got mine off, they didn't hurt. He also took a before and after picture. I'll be honest, I can't see a major difference between before and after his braces came off, and that's sad because he has had a lot of pain. The one thing I can see is his front two teeth are kind of straighter, but all of his teeth are chipped or small. It makes me feel really lucky that I don't have chipped teeth. I may need braces again later, but for the most part they are all good.

Friday, December 4, 2020

So, we have actually had everyone's birthday since COVID. Tay's was on April 25, near the NFL draft. All summer we had no birthdays. We went to school in August, and in October it was my birthday. Then it was Dad's on the first and Mom's on the seventeenth of November. Now, that will leave one buddy, Wilson. Wilson, who was named after Russell Wilson, was born on a great day for a Seahawks dog. He was born on the twelfth-man day. December twelfth (12/12) is his birthday, and it is eight days away.

I had no Zooms, like usual, and I celebrated that. I did have schoolwork, and I didn't do as much as I could have. I did all my assignments for humanities, except for one. I finished my last language arts assignment. Tomorrow I will complete the STEM I need to do, and I will do my leadership assignments.

Tay and I did screen time and we played *Gang Beasts*. Mom and I went on a walk through the neighborhood. We didn't see anyone. Dad was going to go to work tomorrow, and we did play Clue, but I didn't win any of them.

Saturday, December 5, 2020
The days to Christmas are going one by one, without much attention. Next week is finals week, and then we will also have a break, and that starts on the twentieth, so that means that there are fifteen days left in school. This is also nine months of writing. More like eight because we kind of took that first month of school off.

For Christmas I have everyone's present set up. It was nice to get it done early, and I got Taylor something really cool. It's a beanie, but it has Bluetooth music in it so Tay can listen to music with it! I haven't always given Taylor good presents. Once when I was little, I gave Taylor just a calendar for Christmas. I got Dad a book written by former president Barack Obama, and Mom earmuffs. She picked them out for me to buy her, so she knows what I got her.

I did schoolwork, and I did what I had to do to make sure I would be okay for the next day. I also wanted to get enough work done so I could have an easy day tomorrow, when the Seahawks play the Giants. I really just have to do schoolwork tomorrow, because I read the night before, tomorrow is our chores and PE day off, I am doing my writing right now, and after this I take a shower and brush my teeth. For homework I have to write a comic and then submit that, and I have to interview a parent for twenty minutes, and that should be it.

Tay and I played *Gang Beasts*, and that was fun, and we are getting better and better. Tay also started a *Madden* team, and he is doing really well with that. We went on a walk through the neighborhood, and Tay came this time. Wilson got a short walk with Mom after that, and he enjoyed that.

Sunday, December 6, 2020
So, in the morning I woke up and Mom was awake, but not Taylor. I didn't mention this yesterday, but in the morning we saw a coyote and Wilson was outside without his electric collar, and he was barking at the wild animal. We got him inside and he stayed there for a half hour, to be safe.

The Seahawks game was on at 1:05, but I did my schoolwork before that, and I had to do a comic strip on civil disobedience for humanities. At first, I did it smaller. That didn't work, because the camera couldn't catch the words. So, I did it in bigger letters, and it was fine. After that, there was an hour before the game was over, and Mom and Dad and the whole family went on a hike. We went all the way to the end of Not Sure (yes, the name of the trail) and back.

The Seahawks game started well. The Seahawks were moving the ball, and then they were stopped in the red zone and settled for a field goal. Before halftime, the Seahawks blocked a punt and got a safety from that. At halftime, 5–0. And then the Seahawks couldn't do anything on offense, and on defense they did their part, but the Giants got the running game going. The Seahawks had the chance for a game winning drive, but it went to fourth and long, and they batted down the pass.

I interviewed Mom later for a class assignment. It was a dessert night, meaning I had ice cream.

Monday, December 7, 2020
So, Monday. This is going to be an interesting two weeks. School wise, we have classes all week, and this is kind of the last week of classes. Next week there is class on Monday and Tuesday, and those are our last classes of the semester. Then we take our midterm tests. Well, actually, the photography one and maybe the STEM one will be due on Sunday. After that, we have two weeks off, and then we come back on the fourth, I think. I am kind of unsatisfied with the length of winter break, but then again, I won't be sledding during the time I have a cast.

I did my four classes, and math was just like all of the math classes. STEM class was actually really fun. We had time to debate about who should deal with cleaning up the world. This was set up by our teacher, and he gave us a day to research and gain opinion and facts to back it up. In leadership, we shared a thing about an interview. In humanities, we did a simulation.

I did my chores, and they have changed now. For my cast, I can't do the dishes and some other things without help. So, Dad said that I would just unload the clean dishes every day. That was cool and it works well.

For screen time I did a combo of *Gang Beasts* with Tay, and I watched the second *Hunger Games* movie with my second hour.

There really is nothing else. The weather is getting colder and the ground is frosty and slippery.

Tuesday, December 8, 2020
Well, I can say one thing that I learned earlier today, and I will because it is possible that I will forget it when I am writing tomorrow. For STEM, the midterm counts for the most of any class, 15 percent. Last time I didn't do well on the quiz, but I learned that there won't be a quiz for the final.

Instead, presenting the challenge project to the class is what midterms is. This is great news because that is something that I was prepared to do anyway.

We woke up and I had two Zooms. On the first Zoom, I finished my math homework and now I only have the finals for that class. Also, for each class there is a study guide that helps us go over what we have learned and what will be on the quiz. I looked at this, and I am doing it. I'm doing a good job with my goal to not be stressed with midterms.

Mom and I exercised, and I am still trying to find ways to exercise with my cast. I think I want to do some, but I can't do weights, so that is a real bummer. But I will be going on more walks.

Wednesday, December 9, 2020

The middle of the week. It was my long Zoom, and I guess that this is going to be the second-to-last long Zoom of the semester. When it comes to finals it doesn't matter anymore about STEM, and that was the one that was the largest part of a grade in my class. So, I am not worried. I think that I want to do well on my finals anyway, just because I don't want to do poorly.

For my first class, not much really happened. I did math class and after that I did my STEM class and we continued to do our debate. It was fun and funny because in that class I don't talk a ton besides when I have to. And talking a lot even when it wasn't required was funny because, like yesterday, they weren't expecting that. Not only that, I did well. It's not like I did well because this is the only person I am, and I would generally think I am better. I knew I did well, and the main reason was no one could rebut my points, but also more than that.

Then I did leadership and humanities, without doing much. In humanities we finished our simulation, and it was my least favorite of the semester because there wasn't much group talking.

The *Gang Beasts* update came, and it was so fun to see. That was really the main thing that we did the rest of the day. Mom made a good dinner, and when I fell asleep, I woke up to the fire alarm, and it was beeping because it was in low battery. I didn't like this, however, because it was in my room. Taylor set up a bed to sleep with Wilson, but in the end, he just slept somewhere else, meaning that was my plan B.

Thursday, December 10, 2020

Wilson's birthday is in two days, and this is going to be a fun weekend. But first, tomorrow is going to be a chill day. Saturday is Wilson's birthday and the MLS cup, where the Sounders could win back-to-back MLS cups. That would be cool if a Seattle team won the championship while I was doing my writing, so that it would be experienced. On Sunday, the Seahawks are going to play the 0–12 Jets, who haven't won a game. This should be easy, but after the Giants' game, I am not going to underestimate anyone. But if the Seahawks lose this one, you can forget about them being a Super Bowl team.

Mom went to work, and I was downstairs because of the fire alarm that needed a new battery. I didn't get a great sleep, but I still had Zooms to do. So, I woke up, did my writing, and took the mattress downstairs. My two Zooms zoomed by, and then I did schoolwork throughout the day. I think I did a good amount of schoolwork.

Tay had his Zooms, and I did some screen time then, and I also did my chores, the dishes. I tried to play *Madden* by myself, and it worked really well. I went back to my old *Madden* team, the one I was using just two and a half weeks ago, before I hurt my thumb. I am not as good without my thumb, and it is easier to miss tackles, but I still am doing good. I have won three Super Bowls. To get you caught up, I drafted a new quarterback and traded my old one, who was a Superstar 99 Overall, but I was paying him a lot and needed someone new.

Friday, December 11, 2020

Friday! So, this is Wilson's last day being two, and soon he will be three years old. Wilson was born on December twelfth (12/12) and we got him on the day of the Super Bowl, so he's a Seahawks dog. The Seahawks don't play tomorrow, but the Sounders are playing in the MLS Cup final. I read an article in the *Seattle Times* that a victory could make it official that the Sounders are a dynasty. That would be really cool if the Seahawks win the Super Bowl, or if the Sounders win tomorrow.

There were no classes today, but finals are coming up, so that means that we have to study. The only one that I could get an 89 percent on is photography, if I don't do it at all. So, in one class, it is an assignment to study for an hour, and this makes sense normally, but I don't need to worry about it. I will study so that I get an A, but for that class, I think I get an A either way.

I didn't get a great amount of schoolwork done, but I got my Capstone project done, and all I have to do is study for two classes and do one final, because it is due earlier than the other ones.

Mom and Dad went on a date, and they said that we could have extra screen time, so we got to play *Madden* and *Gang Beasts* together.

Saturday, December 12, 2020

Wilson's B-day! Okay, so Wilson is now three. Mom had to go to work until four, so that meant that Wilson would be spending the day with us for a while. We all wished him a happy birthday. Taylor had slept downstairs with him, and he brought the mattress up. Tay has definitely been sleeping in, and he probably will have a growth spurt.

For schoolwork, I had one big thing that I would have to do. I was prepared for a midterm. For photography, the due date was earlier than the other ones.

I did some studying for the midterms, and I also played with Taylor on the Xbox. I am getting used to playing *Madden*, and Taylor and I play, and I am winning most of the time. I wonder if I would play like this after I got my cast off, just out of how familiar I would be.

I took the test. I had fifty multiple choice questions to answer, and there was a maximum of ninety minutes to take the test. I could use the reading articles as a reference during the test, and that helped a lot. Tay and I are in the same class for photography, and he also would take the midterms. I got forty-eight out of fifty questions right, and my final grade for that class is a 99%, or an A. Tay took the test and got forty out of fifty. I think he still gets an A.

We also cleaned up the house for Mom. To celebrate Wilson's birthday, we went to the dog store Mud Bay and got him treats, stuffed animal toys, and bones. Then we went to the beach so that he could go swimming. Even Wilson was less enthusiastic, but he still went into the lake in December.

Tay and I watched the Sounders' game, in the finals. They couldn't do much in the first half, and in the second they couldn't score but they played better. They fell short of another MLS Cup, and Columbus won 3–0.

Sunday, December 13, 2020

Woooooo! Today was a great day, and I am here to tell you about it. There was barely anything I had to do in school. I went downstairs.

Now that I am in the playoffs for Fantasy Football, there is one rule. Win, or don't get the cash. Last year, when Taylor and I were playing, we got into the playoffs with the fifth seed, and we lost that game in the first round. This year, I got the fourth seed. Playing the fifth, Taylor is out of the playoffs. I had played the Rams' defense, and that was really important to start off this week. I was not playing anyone in the ten o'clock window. My dudes, Russell Wilson, DK Metcalf, and Chris Carson were playing the Jets.

The game started off by having the Seahawks let the Jets get three points on the first drive. Then Russell Wilson and the Seahawks got a nineteen-yard touchdown and marched down the field. On that drive, DK Metcalf tweaked his foot and was out for the drive. He came back good as ever and got a touchdown next. For his TD celebration, he went up to the camera man and used the camera. On his way to the sidelines, he got a piece of paper from his teammates with this message: "DK, Happy Birthday!!!! 4 Day All Expenses Trip from the WR's." This was really funny; his birthday was actually the next day, and two days after Wilson's.

This continued. By the third quarter, the score was 37–3, Russell Wilson had four TD passes, and he probably would have gotten more if he played more. They let all of the backups play on both sides of the ball, and the final score was 40–3. Their kicker missed three field goals, and that was really funny to see throughout the game. DK had sixty-one yards, including a five-yard touchdown. Chris Carson had seventy-four yards and a rushing TD. The seventy-four yards included an explosive twenty-eight-yard run.

I won this week in Fantasy! That was really great, and I will either play Dynamite or Mellein, both really good, and it will be tough if I want to win.

Monday, December 14, 2020

Monday, the second-to-last day that I would be doing the Zooms. Also, more things happened today, so I will give you a little news recap. I should do this more often. First, Donald Trump, who lost the presidential race, is desperately trying to overturn it. He has gone to court fifty-six times for this, and he has lost over fifty. Today was the day that the electoral vote became "officially official" that Joe Biden is the president. Also, the vaccines are being shipped out. The Pfizer is the first one that is coming out, but right now they don't have one that they have tested to see if kids can use it, so far. Mom and Dad will get it first because they are first responders.

I did my Zooms. Some of them were celebrations because it would be the last one for the semester.

Tay and I did screen time, and I watched *Napoleon Dynamite*. It really to me wasn't that funny of a movie, compared to how popular it is, but I think it's fun to quote the movie.

My phone, for at least six months, has had a horrible battery. It got really bad, where, after charging it at 100 percent, it would die in two hours. Mom was going to get a new battery for it, but after talking to the guy at the store, he said that it would just be better to get a new phone. So, I got Mom's phone and Mom got an SE 2020, which is basically the brains of the newest phones while looking like one of the old ones. The new ones are kind of ugly and have four cameras, so that worked well with Mom. Also, it was only four hundred dollars, because it doesn't have any of the crazy features.

So, I set up the phone by myself. Mom told me if I had any questions she had the Verizon store phone number, so I called the guy at Verizon twice so that he could help me set it up. Usually, they would do this at the store, but COVID-19 changes that. It took a little, but I completed it!

Tuesday, December 15, 2020

Last day of school! Besides finals, for me, Tay has completed everything. This was the last day of Zooms. I have three finals left to do, but there wasn't really anything that I needed to do for the Zooms. They were more like Christmas parties, and that was fun. We played a few games.

The finals that I have to complete are my math, language arts, and humanities. I'll break down each one for you. I want to get a good score on them, but most likely it won't matter, because I will get an A regardless. The one that I am most excited and confident to do is my math. I am really prepared for that. The one that doesn't matter if I complete it or not is the humanities one. I already have a 99+ percent on that one, and the quiz is worth 5 percent of my grade, so even if I get a 0, I am at 94+, meaning I still have an A. The language arts one, I will still get an A, but I want to do good on it.

We played board games later in the day and I won a game of Clue. Then we played Sorry and Dad won a game of that.

Wednesday, December 16, 2020

I woke up with a goal. My goal is to do some finals today. I was planning on doing two today, but I decided that one would be fine, and that I would do two tomorrow. I think that I am going to do the language arts one first, because I won't get the score of that one. If I had gotten a poor score, then I would probably not have done the other, humanities. I will get humanities after. I will get an A either way, but I don't want to do nothing on my finals.

The day started by getting ready, and I did my chores, the dishes. I did my writing and made sure that I was full and ready to do the finals for math. Math, because it is a high school class, has to be proctored so that they make sure they don't cheat. I used ProctorU, an online proctor that is a computer brain. ProctorU is a Google extension that watches you take the test to make sure you don't cheat. I was more worried that I would mess something up setting up the recording for ProctorU and I would get a zero on the quiz. The quiz was not as easy as I had predicted.

Thursday, December 17, 2020

Okay, so I was going into today thinking that I should do the last two of my finals. I did one but not the other.

I did the first one and that was the language arts one. That one is worth 5 percent of my grade. It is quite weird when you click the "start test" button; I got a big rush of thinking *Let's do this.* More than half of the quiz is worth a written assignment, so I didn't get any of that back yet, but I only got two wrong for multiple choice, and I think I will be getting all of my written responses right.

Then I did the dishes, which is my chores every day, because of my cast. I am going to get my cast off soon. I think that I will get it off on the twenty-first or the twenty-third. Up to six days left. I can say that it hasn't itched at all like people said that it would. Either I am lucky or everyone else overreacted.

Then we all went on a walk on the trail. This was fun, and we went on Not Sure. They newly named the trail we had called Todd's Trail. Then we went up the road to Baby Bear and down the road all the way back to the exit of Not Sure, and we went home. Since yesterday, when we exercised in the basement, my quads hurt, because I can only do core squats, lunges, and planks.

For screen time, Tay and I did a combination of *Madden, Rocket League* and *Gang Beasts.* I also did YouTube.

Friday, December 18, 2020

Seven days, one week until Christmas. We have the top of the garage decorated with lights, we decorated the tree a while ago, we also put Christmas lights up in the basement, and we put it on when we watch a Christmas movie.

I woke up, and for school I had one last thing to do, my humanities final. That was the last thing, and I was done for the semester. It didn't matter if I had got a 100 or a 0, because I would get an A either way, because the class only has the midterms and finals worth 5 percent each.

I got a 90 on the quiz, and it was easier than I thought that it would have been.

Three of my guys on Fantasy are out with injuries, so it is really looking grim for my team and in the playoffs. This isn't good. I am only two games from winning five hundred, so we will have to see how it plays out.

Saturday, December 19, 2020

Tomorrow is the day that the Seahawks are playing, but for the first time in a two-week stretch the NFL has two games playing today. The Bills beat the Broncos, and that didn't matter for Fantasy, or the Seahawks. So, then the Panthers lost to the Green Bay Packers, who the Seahawks wanted to lose, and I was playing against Davante Adams, one of the best wide receivers in the NFL, and he underperformed, and that is really positive for my chance at beating Mellein.

So, now that the vaccines are approved and they are being distributed, Mom volunteered to help give the vaccine to doctors and nurses and firefighters because they get it first. She did a training yesterday, and today she went to work all day to give them. She wasn't planning on getting one today, because she didn't think it was her turn, because she wasn't directly dealing with COVID patients. But she got the vaccine! This was a fun surprise, and now she will get the follow up one three weeks from now.

Before Mom went to work, she wanted to go on a hike, so at eight we went up on the trail. It was really fun, and it started the day off right.

Mom and Dad FaceTimed Gammy and Paw-Paw and I said hi.

Also, I am done with schoolwork, so my days are a lot freer. Hopefully, that doesn't become boredom, but I don't think it will.

Sunday, December 20, 2020

Today was football Sunday. I felt like I wanted to wait until the game.

The Seahawks are playing the Washington Commanders, and they are a below .500 team, and we should win, but they have a top five defense. I predicted the Seahawks to win 23–17, and the Seahawks I thought would still be harassed by their defensive line, and the team's defense was great. The Seahawks offensive line isn't amazing.

The game started with a three-and-out for the Commanders, and their backup quarterback was playing because Alex Smith injured his leg. The Seahawks led at half time, 13–3, and Russell Wilson at that point was not sacked by the team, and that was eye opening.

The second half included an increase in the run game. Chris Carson was rushing for eleven, twelve, and eight yards. Then they put Carlos Hyde in as running back, and he got a fifty-yard run to the touchdown. This was great, and then the Washington team attempted to make a comeback, and they got down to the red zone, 20–15, and then the Seahawks' defense came up big with back-to-back sacks, and the Seahawks survived.

But my Fantasy team didn't survive. They lost and now it is over. I will be working to get on the podium for a third-place matchup, and that would be a fun end.

We also went on the trail with Wilson today, and as usual he loved it. We looked at the forecast for tomorrow, and it is going to snow, it says. I don't think it will, but we will see.

Monday, December 21, 2020

Well, it snowed. It didn't snow until midday, so we didn't get to play in the snow for the day, but we will be doing that tomorrow. It was a great sight to see when the snow came down. I was skeptical because of the seemingly too high temperatures, but look what happened.

So, Mom went to work. Dad was going to get his COVID shot, and he was on a phone call for an hour trying to schedule the appointment. It is at UW, so he had to take a while to drive there, and the snow started to fall when he was gone. So, that left Taylor and me home alone for that whole time, and Mom and Dad said that we could do extra screen time, and we did. We also played a lot of Sorry, as we couldn't play Clue with two people.

They also announced the Pro Bowl for this year. Due to the coronavirus, they said that they wouldn't be doing the Pro Bowl like usual, but somehow connected to *Madden*. They still wanted to award the honor of having that label. The Seahawks tied three other teams for the most Pro Bowl players on their rosters, at seven. The Seahawks' Russell Wilson got in, as did DK Metcalf for offense. It seemed like Metcalf would get in, but to assure it is amazing. On defense Jamal Adams got one; he has gotten one every year in the NFL, excluding his rookie year. Diggs got in, leading the Seahawks with four interceptions. Bobby Wagner, who is still the best linebacker in the NFL, got his again. Tyler Ott and Nick Bellore, two special team players, got in too, and that was a pleasant surprise. I would also say that they kind of snubbed our punter, Dickson.

There was a game tonight, and the Steelers, after winning their first eleven, have lost three in a row, and they aren't really good teams. They don't look like they can win the Super Bowl, like they disguised the first eleven weeks.

I am getting my cast off two days from now, and the next Seahawks game is against the Rams, and if they win this one, they win the NFC West!

Tuesday, December 22, 2020

The snow stayed through the night. We were planning on a little more snow, because the forecast said that it was possible there was more, but three inches was what we got. I am excited that there is snow so early, because that means that there is probably some more snow soon.

Also, when Dad came home from the store today, he brought a puzzle home, and it is a thousand pieces! We started it, and we have been doing it and adding on a lot. Dad said that we should start by getting the border and all the side pieces. Taylor and I worked on the edge pieces while Dad was separating the other pieces into colors.

I am going to get my cast off tomorrow, and that will be something that I will be experimenting with. I wonder if I have to do PT.

Then we played in the snow. Tay had everything set out a few days earlier. I didn't have anything, so we went into the basement and I found everything I needed. I still have my cast, so Dad helped me put a hat over it and used a lot of tape. I can't wait for Christmas, and the Seahawks game.

Wednesday, December 23, 2020

Today was the day. Today was the day that I got my cast off, and there are a few things I want to say about my early Christmas surprise. The first is that the cast didn't itch like I was expecting it to. This was a pleasant surprise. Also, it enabled me to not think about my thumb, and if it had to be hit by something.

They had this saw thing that was loud, and it actually didn't rotate, but vibrated and took the cast off. I will say that I was very jumpy when they were doing it, and I was trying to not move, even though it tickled.

After I got it off, the doctor said that I needed a brace to wear during the day, to make sure for two weeks that I didn't re-dislocate it. Mom called three stores, and they didn't have it, so we ordered one on Amazon. I didn't go outside and play in the snow, because I was going to be careful with my hand.

There weren't any crazy new things that happened today. Tomorrow is Christmas Eve, and that will be really exciting—and then, Christmas!

Thursday, December 24, 2020

Well, it has been a while since last Christmas Eve. A lot has happened. Here we are again, and I wonder what the next year will bring. Hopefully, nothing as overwhelming as the last 365 days.

I woke up and I realized that there are less than twenty-four hours until Christmas. We worked on our puzzle and made a ton of progress today.

Aubrey (Gavin and Carter's mom) said that they were going to drop off some cookies, and it was really cool to briefly see them.

There is a Saints game that will be on tomorrow. As a Seahawks fan, it would go a long way toward them losing, but the Vikings aren't great. Step one for the Seahawks is to win the next game, and if we do that, it is still possible to get the number one seed, but it is a real longshot to get there. The Seahawks, I predict, will win, 29–24, and we will get the NFC West for the first time since 2016, I think.

This is quite a brief journal entry, but tomorrow is Christmas, so a longer one is in store.

Friday, December 25, 2020
Christmas!

I was really excited for Christmas, but the good thing is I was able to get a good sleep. Sometimes you can't sleep because you are so excited, but I did wake up at two or so, went to the bathroom, and Tay woke me up at five. That was the arrangement that we had, and then we went upstairs and organized our presents. At five fifteen Tay went into Mom and Dad's room, and I came with him, and they thought that the time was six that everyone was going to wake up.

An hour went by, and Mom and Dad got their sleep. Tay and I worked on the puzzle. I also went on the couch for a half hour and got a nice nap. Mom had a hard time getting out of bed, as she woke up early yesterday and was tired. Then, after rallying the troops, we got to giving presents.

I gave Mom earmuffs and a scarf. They were super soft, and Mom picked them out for me to get her. For Dad, I got him a book that Barack Obama wrote, on kind of his life. I got Taylor a beanie that can play music in the ears. One thing that I got was a new Xbox controller, and so did Tay. I also got a new Stanford University sweatshirt.

There was one thing, a big thing, that was kind of for the whole family. So, when Mom and Dad bought this house, it was, like, twelve years old. So, they kept the TV that was in the house, because the old TV was, like, permanent on the wall and we still have it now. We think that it is probably as old as the house, and that would mean it is around twenty years old. Well, we are going to get a new TV! It will be so fun to get one, and the TV we had started dying and had problems.

We spent the rest of the day just relaxing, not doing much. The snow is still here, but it is going to melt soon.

Saturday, December 26, 2020
Huh, weird how that happens. December twenty-sixth is one of the oddest days of the year. The Christmas preparation and celebration ends so suddenly, and the twenty-sixth is the symbol of the end. The twenty-sixth is looking forward to the new year, and this year more than ever, people are looking forward to seeing a glimmer of light at the end of the tunnel.

I woke up, and Taylor and I did screen time, and that was really fun. I found that I have transitioned from *Madden* to mostly *Minecraft*. I kept my *Madden* team, and when I go back to *Madden*, I will have a great team to continue. Playing *Minecraft*, I have a base in between two mountains, and I have developed bridges that go across. Taylor came up with the idea a week ago to get *FIFA*, and we haven't gotten *FIFA* since *FIFA 18*. Tay and I split the cost.

Another thing that happened is that the snow melted. This happened overnight. There are piles of it on the sides of the street, because when the snowplow came the snow must have been really compact, because those clumps were the extent of the snow.

The Seahawks are playing tomorrow against the Rams and there are stakes for both teams. If the Rams win then they can assure themselves a playoff berth. If the Seahawks win, they win the NFC West and can assure at least one homefield playoff game.

Sunday, December 27, 2020
Hey, it's Sunday. What does that mean? The Seahawks are playing! They didn't play in the early game window, so we had to wait a while. Also, I kind of didn't pay attention to Fantasy Football, and I felt that I didn't need to try to get in the top three.

No really meaningful games were being played, so that meant that we didn't need to look too much at the early game. Mom was at work, and she had a fifty-fifty chance of coming in time for the Seahawks game at 1:25.

Our big thing that we did while Mom was gone was to put all the Christmas stuff away. We took the ornaments off the tree, and then we took off the lights. The lights were more difficult than I would have thought. The tree is outside, and the game is going to be on soon.

Mom got home fifteen minutes before the game began! This would be the last game before the new TV is up. The Seahawks game started, and the first half was really interesting. It was 6–6, and the Seahawks' defense was playing well. The Rams' defense was good, but that was not surprising because they are the number one defense in the NFL. In the second half, the Seahawks took control and the Rams' quarterback Goff dislocated his thumb, the right one just like me, and popped it in on the field, and played the rest of the game! The Seahawks' defense didn't give up a touchdown the whole game. It was the second time in three weeks. DK Metcalf is six yards away from Steve Largent's record. He hasn't had a hundred-yard game in a few games, but that is because Russell Wilson isn't throwing it as much, and the other teams figured out how to take away the deep ball. Seahawks win, 20–9.

Monday, December 28, 2020
Okay, so today is the day. Mom said that the guy who was going to come and put in the new TV would be here at nine. So, Tay and I did some screen time on the old one, and we also did a before and after picture of the TVs to see the difference.

The guy came on time, and he was really nice. Mom wanted us to go and see how he put the TV together so we could know how to do everything. Mom helped him get the old TV down and she said that it must have been a thousand pounds. Even though she was joking, it was definitely heavy. Compared to the new one, it was so bulky.

After a little bit of trouble shooting, they got the TV up. We all thought that it was too small. We weren't being snobs or anything, but with our TV set, there is a hole in the wall because that is where most of the Xfinity stuff is. The set clearly needed a big TV. Our old one worked because there was a two-inch border around the whole screen, and with this one there is no border. This is because our TV was so old.

The guy said that we should just go back and get a 65-inch instead of the 55-inch we have. So, Mom and I went to Costco and returned it and got a new one. While we were there the guy said that he had ordered the wrong speakers and needed to order the new ones, and that could be a couple of days.

The new "new" TV was perfect, and Taylor and I love it. Also, he rebooted the controller to make it easier for Mom to get music while she works out in the basement. We didn't have 4K resolution, as the TV was twenty years old, and now the screen is a lot clearer and cleaner.

Tuesday, December 29, 2020
Well, these are the final days of the year. It's incredible that we have made it. It isn't over yet. I swear, I can't deal with another 2020 in 2021.

There is a story that I read today, and the story was that at some point in the next few years Messi is going to go to America and play in the MLS. Specifically, he is going to play in Miami, where David Beckham owns a team, Inter Miami CF. It's a new team, and it would be so fun to go to a Sounders game against Miami and see Messi. It said that it won't happen for a few years, because of contracts, but at some point.

We all went on a flat trail along the road, and I was encouraging them to run with me, but they wanted to walk. So, I would run for parts and then run back to them.

Taylor and I played on the big TV, and then after dinner we watched a movie. It was based on a book that I had just read. I had read the book before, and I had watched the movie before also. *Wonder*, I would say that it is a great book that reflects a good movie, with great actors.

Wednesday, December 30, 2020

I woke up in the morning and was greeted by a happy Wilson. Today was a day of more things that were small, and they were projects that we did. Tay and I did screen time and we played *Madden, Minecraft*, and more.

I went with Mom to Trader Joe's. I stayed in the car when Mom went in, and I people-watched, and Mom got groceries and stuff to make granola. The granola I don't really like, and the smell while it is made is bad, but my dad and everyone else loves it.

The Seahawks game is on Sunday, and we are at the number three seed, and no matter what, we will be at least the three seed, win or lose. But there is an opportunity to get the two or even the one seed. If we win, and the Saints or the Packers lose, then we get the number two seed. If we win and both of them lose, then we get the one seed and the only bye. As the three seed, we would play the winner of the Cardinals versus Rams game. I would rather play the Rams, so *Go Rams!*

Mom made granola and homemade marshmallows! These she makes once a year, and they are so good!

Dad and I went in the hot tub, and Mom came in a little after we came in. Not much else to say, but Wilson is still the best dog in the world!

Thursday, December 31, 2020

Okay, today is day 365. The last of an unforgettable year, 2020.

So, I woke up and was greeted by Wilson, who was very excited as always. I had done my reading before, so that wasn't something that I have had to worry about. School starts soon again, and my mentality for this semester is to crank it out and look towards summer. Mom and I looked at the school's calendar, and school ends in the middle of May. I may try to get a lot of things done in photography early, because that is a self-paced class that I could do whenever, and that would be cool to get it done fast.

Dad came up with the idea that we should go to Mount Baker and go sledding. This was a great idea, so we had a big breakfast with biscuits, sausage, and eggs. Then we got our snow stuff and sleds that we got for Christmas. It would be a one-hour drive, so I brought my air pods and my phone to listen to music and podcasts.

We were stopped when we were almost at our destination, because there was an avalanche and they had to clean it up. Dad said that they said that it would be a half hour. Wilson was in the car, and dogs were running around, and Wilson's whining clearly showed that he was envious. None of us were going to deal with Wilson with all those dogs, and Wilson isn't neutered, so that could be another thing not fun. After fifteen minutes there were two or three big booms and Dad said it was the dynamite they use to clear out all the snow. After what felt like an hour, we started driving again, and it was crowded everywhere. It was really surprising, and we struggled to find a parking spot.

We figured out soon enough that we couldn't sled on the snow because it was too deep, so we made a snowman. Wilson had fun, and Tay then tackled the snowman, and the snow was so deep!

Friday, January 1, 2021
Well, it's quite odd that I write 2021 on the date above. It is a new year, and the start of this year is not how I would have envisioned it a year ago. But here we are, and now we are going to forget 2020 and push forward in 2021.

I woke up and went downstairs at seven thirty, after staying up until midnight for New Year's. It was unfortunate that there wasn't anyone there with me but the show that they did, with brand new technology called sky mapping.

I wasn't tired at all today, and that was something that I felt was odd because Mom and Dad had expected me to.

Today we wanted to play a board game, and we came up with Monopoly. This game we haven't played for a few months, and what I can say, it is still fun. The first game, I collected all the railroads, and that proved to be a good idea. I ended up winning that game easily, and I got everyone's money.

We did start a second game, but Dad has to go to work tomorrow, and Mom will take over the game. So far it is even; I have got all the railroads again.

Saturday, January 2, 2021

So, not a ton happened today. I think I will keep this short. A day is twenty-four hours long, and I'm doing a lot for all of those twenty-four hours.

We played some Monopoly today again, and Dad went to work, so Mom took over for him. Dad wasn't in a great spot when he left, and the game ended with Tay winning. Tay got a few houses that were more expensive, and that went well for him.

We also watched *Shark Tank* late in the day, and that was really something that was fun for us to do. We watched some good ones, and all but one got a deal.

Before I talk about the *Shark Tank* episodes, I will mention that we started learning the guitar. This was something that was Mom's idea, because she has been on and off about having us learn a musical instrument. So, we watched a YouTube video that did a little bit of introduction and got us learning the basics.

Shark Tank. So, the few that were good: One had glasses that would protect your eyes from getting a lot of damage looking at screens, like iPhone and computers. Another was cat boxes, and another was a healthy snack alternative, and it was oatmeal that was already prepared, and you didn't have to put water in it, or heat it up. It was called MUSH.

Sunday, January 3, 2021

This is the last regular season game in the 2020 season, and then comes the postseason. The Seahawks had a low chance of getting the one seed and a bye, but that was a low chance where two very good teams had to lose.

The Seahawks game started a lot like how the Ram's game went, low scoring until the second half. The Seahawks were stopped twice by the Forty-Niners in the red zone and settled for three each of those times. The Forty-Niners had one or two chunk plays and it was 6–6, and then 6–9, Forty-Niners winning. At times like this you worry about the Seahawks' offense, and their lack of going downfield if they don't have the perfect game plan.

Then the Forty-Niners got a touchdown, and now they are leading by ten. The other games that the Seahawks needed for teams to lose had pretty much been decided, and the Seahawks were going to be the three seed. Then the Seahawks got multiple Tyler Lockett touchdowns in the fourth quarter, and the Seahawks got a come-from-behind win. The Rams versus Cardinals game was whoever won got in and faced the Seahawks. The Cardinals' quarterback got injured and they didn't score after that.

The Seahawks will be playing the LA Rams again, at Lumen field. The Seahawks are early favorites. The Rams played their backup quarterback today, and they may next week too, if Jared Goff isn't ready.

Monday, January 4, 2021

Today was the first day back to online school, and this is the second semester. The first went by so quickly, so I am hoping for more of the same. After this, hopefully we will be back at real-life school. I will be in high school, and I know it's a long wait, but I will see everyone again.

All of my classes were the same, mostly the same kids, with some new ones. The new kids were a bulk of kids from California. Taylor had one or two class changes, where he is going to Zoom on Tuesdays and Thursdays at seven. I had a class that early before, but that changed later. That was a math class. Tay sleeps in more than me, so he is going to have a tougher time than I did.

Mom gave vaccines again today. Some days she is in recovery, and that is easy for her, and sometimes she gives them, and that is stressful. She did that today.

I am starting to listen to this new music that I like. These include the likes of R.E.M., the Dave Matthews Band, the Wallflowers, Red Hot Chili Peppers, Counting Crows, and Matchbox Twenty.

It's been raining every day, and tomorrow is the day that the speakers are coming for the TV. These days are going to be the same, every day, and we are going to find things that are small and will lead to the end of COVID

Tuesday, January 5, 2021

So, I was done with the first day of school, but there is still more to do. For today, I had two classes, and the first one was math. I had already done class yesterday, so I wasn't seeing anyone new for that. This was also a homework day, so I didn't really interact, but I was just doing my schoolwork for math. My next class was language arts, and I hadn't done that class before, so I got to see the new kids that were in that class.

Mom went to Seattle just for a day off. She had an appointment, but she also was going to spend the Christmas money that she had gotten, and the gift cards to Macy's and stuff. So, she was gone for most of the day, and she came home around four.

Mom came back, and somehow she brought up that there is a segment that was on the radio, where people talked about secrets that they had, but they stayed anonymous and didn't give their name. Because Mom was driving, she was listening to the radio, and one person came on and said that she had worked at the Pentagon and the government was going to release to the news what they know about aliens. Now this was far out there, but just to research things, I looked, and a bill was passed recently that said they would have to say what they know. I want a record of this in case something happens, but I am quite skeptical.

Later we watched a Disney movie called *Mulan*. It was good and I liked watching it.

Wednesday, January 6, 2021

Today was a really crazy day on the news. But my day, at first, started normally. Today was a long Zoom day, and this, to be honest, was the first real day of school because the first long Zoom day on Monday was barely about what we were going to learn but more of setting up class to learn. So, nothing crazy happened, and then I did my math, STEM, leadership, and my humanities. Then as I was coming out of the room, I was doing my Zoom in. Mom was downstairs turning on the TV, and something crazy was on the news, she said.

On the news, what I saw was surreal. There were hundreds and maybe even thousands of Trump supporters chanting at the US Capitol Building, where the House and the Senate were finalizing Biden's victory. It was crazy to see, and this just got worse and worse, and the senators and representees were told to hide behind their desks and put gas masks on in case the police had to use gas.

The people started breaking into the Capitol. People were smashing through the windows, and you could see people in the Senate chamber. Someone sat in the vice president's chair, and people were still being very violent outside. There was thrashing between the police and the violent supporters of the incumbent who lost the election.

Later that day. we went on a hike. Tay couldn't, because he needs new shoes really bad. When we came back, the national guard had gotten everything under control, and in the end four people died. One was shot and three had unrelated health emergencies. This was a shock to most old people, who have seen enough history to say that this doesn't usually happen. I cannot, however, because I haven't experienced much history.

Thursday, January 7, 2021

Well, today was a more uneventful day than yesterday. The first thing that I did was my two Zooms, the last of my first week. I got some good homework done and finished my math homework when I was doing the math homework Zoom. Then I had language arts, and I did not do schoolwork for LA today, as I am going to do it tomorrow.

I did homework for humanities and also leadership. Leadership was easy, and as it is the first day, I didn't expect much. The same could be said about humanities. Instead of doing the reading assignment then, I waited until I would usually do my reading, which is before I go to bed.

Mom had to go to work and Dad was already at the fire station, so we were home alone until two thirty. I don't really have anything that I am really doing much of for screen time, and it is possible that it is still going to be *Minecraft*, but I am just not sure what I will be doing.

Mom got her booster vaccine! Mom said that they said that for this one she could get flu symptoms because of the body getting used to the vaccine. She said this morning that she had a bad night's sleep, and she has been really tired, almost like she is sick. It should only last two or three days.

The Seahawks play soon, and I am super excited.

Friday, January 8, 2021

Today was also uneventful. There were no Zooms today, and I feel that it was really fun to start the day not getting up needing to think about school.

The schoolwork that I did was language arts. I cranked it out in the morning, and it wasn't that hard. It just took time. Tomorrow I will have photography to do, and then I will be done. I did leave one assignment from LA to do on Sunday.

The Seahawks play tomorrow. I am excited to see what they can do, but I am also worried that by the end of the day the season could be over.

Mom was still recovering from the shot and was really having a tough time doing much. She was tired and had some of the symptoms that they said she could get. She said that her back was burning. That was something that wasn't on the list, and that confuses me a bit.

Saturday, January 9, 2021

Well. I was excited to see the Seahawks play, but it is over now (*sigh*). The Seahawks lost and now it will be a while until we see them again. When being a playoff team, there are a lot of upsides, but unless you win the Super Bowl, you end your season with a loss, no matter what.

The Seahawks didn't score first, and the offense really only got thirteen points, even though DK Metcalf had a late touchdown.

The Rams were playing Wolford (the backup quarterback) instead of Goff, but Wolford got a neck injury, so they went to Goff early. Neither team had a good offense. Russell Wilson gave up a pick six on a wide receiver screen to DK Metcalf. That was the only WR screen to be a pick six that year. DK had a good game, but no game is good unless you win. Now there are other games on, and I am going to be rooting for the Saints, because this is probably the last season Drew Brees plays, and he could win a Super Bowl this year, only his second. On the AFC I am rooting for the Chiefs, and if they don't make it, the Bills. Rooting in the playoffs is hard because you root for a team to lose, but when they win and your team loses, sometimes you end up rooting for them because of who they are playing. So, if the Chiefs play the Bills, and I am rooting for the Chiefs, but the Bills win and go to the Super Bowl, then I could be rooting for them the next week if they play someone like the LA Rams. It's difficult, but this Super Bowl will be amazing, with all great offenses left in the playoffs.

Sunday, January 10, 2021

Well, today was the first day that the Seahawks weren't in contention for the Super Bowl in a while. The football world still goes on. The first game that will be on will be the Ravens versus Titans. There is some rivalry there. Then the Bears and the Saints play. The Bears are massive underdogs and shouldn't win. Then the Browns and the Steelers play, and there is division rivalry there.

I finished my schoolwork. I had to do a prompt for language arts. I think that this semester for LA is fairy-tale-type writing. I do remember when in third grade we did a unit like this, and it is going to be fun, I bet.

The Ravens game ended with the Titans throwing an interception. When they had met last time in the regular season, the Titans had danced on the Raven logo after winning. After the interception was thrown, the Ravens danced on the Titans' logo. That was cool to see.

The Saints versus Bears game was on Nickelodeon. This was the first time that Nickelodeon had done something like this, and they did really well. The Bears kept it close for a half but couldn't finish, and the Saints won 21–9, and it should have been 28–9.

The Browns haven't made the playoffs in so long, it would be just a celebration if they got there. But they scored 28 in the first part of the game. They held on after the Steelers got a comeback going, and that was really nice to see them win.

Next week the Saints play the Buccaneers, the Packers play the Rams, the Bills play the Ravens, and the Chiefs play the Browns. I am rooting for the Packers, Saints, Bills, and Chiefs. If they all win, I am rooting for the Chiefs in the AFC and the Saints in the NFC.

Even when the Seahawks are out, the playoffs are here!

Monday, January 11, 2021

Okey dokey. So, today is the second week of school. There is something to be said, that school is going to go by really fast, and to just pay attention to it so that later you can focus on summer. Summer vacation is a way better subject to study, if anyone was wondering.

I had all of my Zooms, and I brushed my teeth, and I have been making more smoothies. Tay has made a *lot* of smoothies, and I am mostly having them once a day, as a breakfast before my Zooms. I also have changed now; I am not taking showers before my Zoom. I don't like being soaking wet while doing my Zooms, so I am just using a beanie instead. My new desk is so much better. There is peace and quiet, and I don't have to use wired headphones. I use my Apple Airpods instead, and I hadn't used them as much. One thing about the AirPods is that it reminds me when I need to clean my ears.

Today was my exercise day off, and I really can't say that there is much that happened today. Today was Monday, so I didn't need to do schoolwork. I am going to do a longer entry tomorrow, so this will be justifiably short.

Tuesday, January 12, 2021

Days are blending together, looking the same as every other. Sometimes people are gone for work, but the day is just the same. This is a reality that will be lived through for the next few months. Never shocked by COVID numbers, death numbers have the same weight in mind for five or five hundred thousand people. The world seems that it is only in this three-story house. Barely going out of the neighborhood. Day A and Day B may as well be the same. Events are forgotten, because the tunnel vision is on the sameness that is brought each day. The only thing that could separate days are worldwide news events.

Mom went to work today, and she was giving vaccines at the hospital. This is something that, when looking at the nations, the quantity of vaccines is not the problem; it is that people can't give out the vaccine fast enough. Mom is seeing everyone she used to work with at the hospital but hasn't seen since she started working at Hospice House.

I have started to learn this new thing that uses nothing special, and it would seem easy. This is flipping a pen or a pencil around your thumb. It took me about forty minutes to do it the first time. I am getting it on an average of 13 percent success rate. I want to get to full consistency and get it nine out of ten times.

For homework today, what I did was math and leadership. I figured out a schedule on what subject to do on what days, as it was an assignment for leadership.

Dad made pizza today, and it was really yummy. We pulled out a game that we haven't played in a while, Chameleon. We are doing a lot of board games, and it is quite fun.

Wednesday, January 13, 2021

This was my next time doing a long Zoom day this week. Not much happened. Taylor has an appointment tomorrow.

For exercise today, I did weights for the second day. Taylor was playing *Madden* while I was doing that, and it is nice that my thumb is getting better. I was kind of conservative with this thumb, and in the long term that is a good thing.

Taylor and I are now playing *Madden* instead of *Minecraft*. *Madden* is so fun too. I am continuing my strive for a dynasty and my goal is to get to ten Super Bowls. I have three or four right now, and my team kind of dropped off when I hurt my thumb. By doing that, I couldn't play *Madden* with a cast, and I waited for when I would be good. It's been six weeks, and to give a recap: I have a rookie quarterback after trading Deshawn Watson. I have DK Metcalf, who is the highest rated he could be. I have a running back who has set records, and I drafted him earlier.

There isn't much that is happening these days. It is disappointing because I don't have a lot to write about.

Thursday, January 14, 2021

Not much happened today, like always.

I did have class, and that was good, and I got to doing schoolwork. I did LA homework for today; I also did one of the two STEM assignments. Martin Luther King Jr. Day is soon, so that means that we won't have school on Monday, also meaning that I can spread out what homework I do. I have, like, one assignment for each class left, and I can do that some other time.

For my exercise today we went on the trail. Taylor still didn't come on this one because he hurts afterwards.

I am finding that while there are still other small things that happened today, they don't really matter to me, and therefore, why put them in here if their only purpose is to fill up space. My day, and what matters to me, doesn't change that much.

Friday, January 15, 2021

Well, interestingly enough, I don't really consider Friday a weekend day, because it isn't usually, and I do a bunch of schoolwork, so that means it isn't really a weekend day. My photography class is on hold because there are some tech difficulties. Well, less homework for me this week. I did my humanities class homework, and so far what I can say is, this semester is connected to how we see the work.

I was taking a bath and Tay said that *Madden* had disappeared. This was really weird. When I got out, the game had gotten uninstalled. So, we had to install it again. The good thing is that all of our progress wasn't lost, and I had a team going and I want to get to ten Super Bowls and around a dozen seasons. So, all was saved.

In *Madden*, speaking of that, I did my playoff run. The conference championship was not as difficult as the divisional. The Super Bowl, however, was an easy win. I pulled away quickly and then I had to sign my players during the off season. I didn't have a good draft, and I think that I didn't get the value I wanted for the draft.

Mom FaceTimed with a firefighter's wife who is her friend, and we said hi to them and her kids. It was fun to talk to people.

Dinner was good.

Saturday, January 16, 2021

Okay. So, the day started like always, with me waking up. Today was football. I didn't get to watch much of the football. The games that were on were the Bills versus Ravens game, where Taylor in Fantasy got forty-eight points on a double with his defense, and he generally doesn't get a lot of points.

The other game that was on was Green Bay versus the Rams. The Rams had the number one defense and GB had the number one offense. The Seahawks had lost to the Rams the week before. I wanted GB to win well and good either way. But, with the Rams playing them, it was nice to see them lose. They lost, and it seemed like GB wanted to get ahead and put the game away but couldn't do it, until the end and they won. I praise Goff for playing with his thumb like it was, as I know how it would hurt.

In Fantasy this means that all of the guys that I played will be getting two or three times their points next week for winning.

Mom pushed us to go outside, and we also were talking earlier about playing more soccer, so we played outside. This was really fun to play again, and I still think that I got it. We played for a half hour, and then, for Taylor, everything was hurting, so he stopped.

Sunday, January 17, 2021

Well, interestingly enough, today was a day the news said that Trump supporters might go to the US Capitol again. That didn't happen though, and I bet that it is because of all of the reports saying that there were way more people defending the Capitol. This was good, and I kind of forgot that this was a possibility. Well, that is really nice, and a good outlook ahead to the inauguration.

Speaking about that, I want to get a few things about this straight. One thing is that Trump is not going to attend the inauguration. Vice President Pence should make an appearance, but this is the first time in a hundred and fifty years that the president prior to their election didn't come to the inauguration. Instead, Donald Trump has ordered that he will get a red-carpet exit, which is really unusual.

The first game that happened was the Chiefs against the Browns game. The Browns had the worst playoff drought leading up to this season, and the Chiefs won the Super Bowl last year, so there was some contrast there. The game was close, but the big thing was that the League's best quarterback, Patrick Mahomes, who is on the Chiefs, got hit in the head and was dizzy. It was a horrible sight to see. He couldn't stand up right away, and he was out for the game. The backup won the game. Patrick will have to go through concussion protocol for next week's game, and that is unlikely.

The other game was the Saints versus the Bucs and Tom Brady. The Saints lost and it was most likely the last game of future Hall of Famer Drew Brees. He was emotional at the end, and it was unfortunate, because I was rooting for him to go to the Super Bowl. Well, next week I will be rooting for Aaron Rogers and Green Bay versus the Bucs. And I will be rooting for the Chiefs versus the Bills. Overall, I will probably be rooting for the Packers to win the Super Bowl, and rooting against the Bucs and Tom Brady at all costs.

Monday, January 18, 2021

Today is Martin Luther King Jr. Day. I feel that this day matters more than it has before because of all that has happened with race in the last year. I think that it is really crazy to think that this was only sixty or seventy years ago, and that there are people who still remember when this was happening. I wonder if I could ask one of my grandparents.

Dad was working today, and that means that he will be working on a holiday and getting time and a half.

Mom and Tay had an appointment and they almost missed it. It was for Tay's eye, and it was just for a scratch. Mom thinks they made a mistake, because they dilated his eyes, which gave him a headache and didn't seem necessary.

Not much happened again today. So, these entries are shorter.

Tuesday, January 19, 2021

Well, today is the last day of the Trump presidency. That is something that is crazy, and there is so much that I could review from it. Something that really sums it up is that he is only the third president to be impeached. He is the first president to be impeached twice. This is also in one four-year time frame, compared to what some presidents have in two terms. He almost did it in a one-year span, about totally different things.

This morning I was very productive, and I did my exercise and chores. Today I had two of my classes. My first class was math, instead of what was usually a homework day. Because I had not had class the day before, it was a learning class. Then after that I had my language arts class.

In *Madden* I went to the Super Bowl and won my fifth. I played Atlanta, which was also hosting it. I didn't have a great draft, but there were a lot of people who will evolve and be very big in the future of the Super Bowl runs.

Tomorrow is a big day, and it will be interesting to record it.

Wednesday, January 20, 2021

Woke up in the morning. Hey, it's Inauguration Day.

Well, the thing is, the inauguration happens at noon Eastern time, but because we are in the Pacific time zone, it happens at nine. I do Zooms at that point, but during my ten-minute breaks I got to peek at what was happening.

This Inauguration has been celebrated so thoroughly that they had a big ninety-minute special at the end of the day, and I will talk about that later.

There were a lot of famous people there. Trump did not attend the inauguration like most presidents do. He boarded Marine One and went to his house. At the inauguration everyone was wearing masks, even the Republicans, who were told by Trump that they were a sign of weakness.

It was really cool to see all of the former living presidents together. Jimmy Carter couldn't come, but he is really old at ninety-six years. I am reading Barack Obama's book on his presidency, and it was cool to see him. They said on the TV that it was apparent that he was the leader of the former presidents. Biden was his vice president, so it was also probably really special for him to see that.

Lady Gaga and Jennifer Lopez both performed at the inauguration, one doing the "Star Spangled Banner" and the other doing the Pledge of Allegiance (I think, don't know for sure). I was doing Zoom during this.

After my Zoom I did screen time, and Taylor said that for the moment he didn't know what to do for screen time, but as of the time of writing this, I think he has a *Madden* team he will stick with.

The big thing at the end of the day was all of these people coming together to celebrate the election. This doesn't happen, Dad said, but with such a relief that they have a president like Biden again, it was due.

The TV special host was Tom Hanks. People that performed that I can remember are Katy Perry, Foo Fighters, Justin Timberlake, a few famous country singers (I don't listen to country), and other people that I know of but can't think about right now.

At the end there were a lot of fireworks, and it was a cool shot to see the president looking at them. This was probably a historic day, and it will be cool that I was able to record my witnessing of it.

Thursday, January 21, 2021
Just now, I accidentally wrote 2020 instead of 2021 when writing the date. This made me look back at the last three weeks of journal entries and I realized around 5 or so of them had the same mistake, getting used to 2020 when it is 2021.

Today not a ton happened that I can really say was big. I had my two Zooms and I did my homework. Tomorrow is also a homework day, but I feel that I will be doing more of the remaining homework on the weekend.

Friday, January 22, 2021
Ok. Well, time to say what's going on. Not much, to be honest. There were no classes and I did barely any schoolwork, kind of to just take a break, and that was something that I really enjoyed.

Dad, Tay, and I all played a lot of Chameleon. Mom played with us some, but we play in a way that is a little different to her standards of how we should play. Sometimes we do really random things from our words and letters. Well, sometimes Mom thinks that this isn't the right way to play, so she doesn't play with us all of the time.

For exercise I did weights in the basement. I think that now is a good time for me to start playing football again with Taylor, like when we did at Sehome. The one thing is, it is still very difficult for Taylor to play football. He doesn't go on walks with us much anymore on the trail because of injuries, and that makes it seem that it wouldn't be a good idea for us to move at top speed. Everything in his lower body seems to have a problem with tightness, and it is all connected. He went to a doctor a little while ago who said most likely it will continue to hurt until he stops growing.

We went to Ru U for the first time in a while. We kind of forgot and were just not very connected with Phil on arranging it. Another thing, Ru wasn't there. The deal with Phil and Ru's previous owner is that she would be pregnant one final time to have a litter. Well, she is going to have a C-section soon and she is really pregnant. So, we brought Wilson as a substitute teacher, and I feel that he did a good job. The book we are reading, *Carry On, Mr. Bowditch*, is a good one. We talked about the Revolutionary War that was happening in the book.

Saturday, January 23, 2021
I almost wrote 2020 again. It is difficult to remember. My theory on why this is also very difficult is that this is a new decade, and for each time that we write this instead of 2019 is 2020, meaning that the third digit is the same, and it is hard to change two digits without confusion from before.

Not much has happened. Well, the two big games are happening tomorrow. I'll give my predictions for now. I think that the Packers are going to beat Tampa Bay. My one problem is that I struggle to envision a south or east coast team going into Lambeau, in cold, probably snowy weather, and winning. I think the score will be 38–20. I am rooting for the Packers with this game.

For the Chiefs, I think that they will win this game, but it won't be as high scoring as people would think. The thing is this is in Kansas City and the Bills are also used to the cold, as it usually is in this place. So, this game is going to be a closer one at 25–14, and the Chiefs win. I am rooting for the Chiefs to win this game. If the game is how I predict it would be, I will be rooting for the Chiefs. The order where I would root for a team would be Kansas City, then Green Bay, then Buffalo, and last (Tom Brady and) Tampa Bay.

Sunday, January 24, 2021
Hey, we are two weeks from the Super Bowl. That's cool, and after today we will know who will be there. Today I didn't need to do much schoolwork, and that's—never mind, I'm not going to talk about that, let's get to the games!

The first game was the Packers versus the Tampa Bucs. I was confident that the Packers were going to win this one, out of the two games. I was wrong. Isn't that funny? The Bucs seemed to know how to play a football game. And the Packers were losing in the first quarter. The second quarter wasn't much better. The Packers let a forty-yard touchdown end the half. The second half was a different story, and the Packers got really close to winning. They couldn't finish it, even with all the opportunities to do so. This means that Tom Brady is going to the Super Bowl, and in his first year with a new team.

The other game ended how I predicted. The Chiefs are just so hard to stop, and it seemed going into the playoffs that the Bills were the only ones that could. Mahomes will be playing Tom Brady. This is like a young goat versus a big goat.

Monday, January 25, 2021

Okay, well this was Monday, not much. There are precisely around fifty-two or fifty-three Mondays in the year. Take the twelve Mondays that are in the summer, where everything doesn't matter, and Monday has the same meaning as Tuesday, Wednesday, or the weekend. These months are great. So, when you take into account holidays and breaks, that will leave us with three dozen or so Mondays, all seeming to blend into a sync that's similar.

Concluding from the previous paragraph, look for the Monday entry with the most words, that doesn't align with summer or a holiday, and you will get how today was.

In *Madden* I retired my coach. I was at a point where it started to become routine and I knew I needed to stop. I didn't complete my goal of ten Super Bowls, but I did get to six, a personal best. This was a thing that I was proud of, that if I continued with it, I would get to ten, unlike before. But I didn't see the desire to march to the goal anymore. For screen time, Taylor and I played a *Madden* game of Tampa against Kansas City. This concluded with Taylor (KC) winning. Not fun, but if it is an outlook of what's to come, I can justify.

I changed my computer background to a funny cartoon of a kid with two options, money and fame or cool waterslides. And he was walking to the waterslides. I want to be like this kid, and I found it so funny every time that I opened my computer.

***

Note: After this day, I decided not to write anymore. The reasons for this were that there was nothing going on, so each journal entry was pointlessly bland and empty. This was also combined with me not having any motivation to continue the writing going forward, because I thought that COVID would be over quickly and things would go back to normal after this final journal entry.

But it wasn't, so on May 29, 2021, I restarted my journal, only four months after I thought that I was done. Even though I restarted my journaling, Taylor didn't. I restarted my journal because I felt that there was more of this story that I didn't want lost or unrecorded. So, my journaling continues.

Note: Even though my journaling restarted in May, there are still many things that I remember between the journal entries. They are all part of my life in between this time, and they are all things that I remember and want to write about. So, here are basically the highlights of what happened in these four months. All of which were memorable parts of my life and are important to the story of COVID's continuous presence. I don't have specific dates for any of these events, so I will group them into two different categories of when they appeared in my life, February–April 2021 and May 2021.

February–April 2021

Watching *Stanley Tucci: Searching for Italy*:

Every Sunday, there was a show that we all watched as a family, where a guy, Stanley Tucci, goes around different areas of Italy and learns about the food in that area, and its history. I think we all really liked it and looked forward to it because it was so interesting.

Mom's side of the family is mainly Italian. Her grandma or great grandma spoke little English and mostly Italian, so I think it was really interesting for her because she kind of got to learn more about the food and culture of where her family was from. Mickey and Papa (Mom's parents, my grandparents), and Michelle and Steve (Mom's siblings) also watched it every Sunday. On their family group text, they would talk about it as it was happening.

Mom got a lot of inspiration from watching the show and started making homemade Italian food. My favorite thing she made was homemade marinara. This was also what she made the most. She focused on it and made adjustments, and each time it got better and better.

The Super Bowl: Chiefs versus Buccaneers:

The Super Bowl this year was played in Raymond James Stadium, which is the first time that a team (the Buccaneers) hosted and played in the Super Bowl. This was Tom Brady's first year playing with his team, and the Chiefs were looking to win a second Super Bowl in a row. They won last year when they beat the Forty-Niners.

COVID was still very much in effect, and for the event they only had twenty-five thousand fans allowed at the stadium, to be safe and to not make the Super Bowl a super spreader event like some holidays have been. With the Super Bowl hosted in Florida, there still wasn't that much care put into preventing COVID.

The Buccaneers dominated the whole game, and Tom Brady won his seventh, and his first with the Buccaneers. The Chiefs really played badly compared to the standards that I put them to. I was rooting for the Chiefs, but I'm happy that the Buccaneer players got a ring. The final score was 9–31. The Chiefs didn't score a single touchdown, and that was the first time ever under Mahomes that that happened.

The halftime show was really good, with The Weeknd playing all of his best songs. It was a good halftime show, not the best ever, but it was pretty good. I liked it.

Russell Wilson was at the Super Bowl, and he was sitting next to the commissioner of the NFL, Roger Goodell. Russell really didn't look happy when the cameras showed him, and later Russell went on the Dan Patrick Show (a football podcast) and he kind of threw the Seahawks team and offensive line under the bus. This fueled a lot of trade speculation and eventually it was all that was talked about in the NFL news.

NFL Draft:

The NFL Draft also happened. It was hosted in Cleveland, where they relaxed the rules for COVID, which was accompanied by declining numbers of people who had COVID. This year, unlike last year, teams could return to the draft rooms, so they could all be together, instead of having to Zoom like they did last year. Last year when they Zoomed, there were also some technical difficulties, so I don't think the NFL wanted that again.

Even though I didn't journal for the NFL draft, I did write down predictions for each of the top selections:

QB Trevor Lawrence: Will be great, but not as good as Mahomes or Brady

QB Zach Wilson: Won't do well with the Jets, but may be better with a second team later

QB Trey Lance: Will constantly get better with Kyle Shanahan
TE Kyle Pitts: Will be a top three TE every year for a long time
WR Chase: Will be good, will be in a few Pro Bowls
WR Waddle: Will make multiple All Pro teams, will be better than Chase
OL Sewell: Will be okay, but Detroit will have wished they got someone else

The Seahawks only got three people in the entire draft, which I think ties an NFL record for least number of draft picks drafted in a year. They got wide receiver D'Wayne Eskridge, cornerback Tre Brown, and offensive lineman Stone Forsythe. I don't know what to think of any of them. Mostly I was just surprised that they only stuck with getting three picks. I don't know how any of these guys will end up, but I think Eskridge is going to be the best out of all of them, because he is really fast, and Wilson will be able to throw him big throws that he can quickly run to. I think he may be as good as Lockett at one point.

May 2021
Williamsburg Finals:
It's weird for me having the school year end so early. But the semester is coming to a close. I haven't had any finals tests for any classes before this year, and going into finals with all A's, I only had something to lose. Each class approached finals differently, and the final test weighed different amounts. I had to study for these finals, and in some classes, there were no finals. This was really nice, when there was either a project or nothing for finals, because a test is more stressful and requires you to use everything you learned in one sitting.

One class that I had finals for, math, caused serious stress, and I think it is really interesting how I reacted. So, I talked about last semester for math, because it's a high school class and they can't take any chances that anyone is cheating. So, they use ProctorU to make sure that no one cheats on the test. Well, everything seemed like it was going well. But then, without going into a lot of detail, the test and ProctorU weren't working perfectly and there were technical difficulties which kicked me out of the test, with ProctorU still running. I was out of the test before I answered any questions. I could definitely feel my heartbeat go fast. There was only one chance to take the test and the teacher specifically told us that she couldn't really help us get a second chance if the power went out or something like that happened.

I decided that I should keep the ProctorU running, because if I shut it down that might just cause more problems, so I ran to get my phone and call the Williamsburg helpline that the math teacher gave us in case we had any questions or problems. My phone was dead, so I got Mom's phone and told her I couldn't really explain much. So, I called them, and they transferred me to someone else, and I had to be really careful. After the person on the phone told me that they fixed it for me, I took a big sigh of relief.

I ended up getting an almost perfect score on the quiz, and I ended the year with an A in the class!

My other finals went well, and I ended the year with all A's. Taylor also ended his year with all A's, and one A-minus. We both got an email a little later that we both were on the Williamsburg Honor Roll.

Final Thoughts of Williamsburg:
Then, just like that, the Williamsburg experience ended, hopefully. I do have to say, it was a very interesting experience learning there, and I really haven't recorded my opinions of the school or said that much about my experience at all. Now that the year is over, it's time to reflect.

First off, like many kids during COVID, online school was very much a unique experience. From what I have heard from Gavin and Carter, many people at public school, when online, take it as a free pass from school. They didn't learn or pay attention. At Williamsburg, that wasn't the case, and for us, that wasn't what Tay or I were thinking of doing.

I found that many of the kids in my classes were part of the Church of Jesus Christ of Latter-day Saints (or Mormon Church). And, I hadn't seen a religion so incorporated into a school before, and I don't know if the executives of the school did this on purpose. Anyone is totally entitled to their religion, but it was sort of awkward for me to be a part of it. It was new for me to experience so many people incorporating religion into conversation. I don't know why so many Mormons were in the class. But my best guess is that what the church teaches isn't perfectly in line with what the public schools teach.

With religion being a big part in almost all the students' lives, the teachers were very open about different topics that may conflict with the church. For example, science class.

Williamsburg is a school that was based in Utah, and the majority of people in the school were from Utah. The school seemed to be a Republican-leaning school. Just small things that the teachers said, and some of the books that were given to us to read gave me this impression.

I do feel bad for another big population of students, who said that they had gone to public school but had gotten bullied, and then it got so bad that they had to leave the school, and that landed them at Williamsburg. No one deserves to get bullied, and it's crazy that it could be so bad that someone would have to leave. I'm glad to say that I have never experienced real bullying in my life.

The only problem that I did have with the teachers and students that talked about getting bullied, however, is the picture that they painted of public school. They described it as always being a fiery hellhole where they brainwash you, bully you, and make you feel left out because of cliques. Weird. And not true. Saying that all public schools are like this is a pretty powerful statement, and from my experience, it's false.

Even with the school being the way it was. I learned a great amount and the teaching was really good and geared well towards learning at a pace where it didn't waste time. It also put responsibility onto the students that I didn't see in public middle school. The schoolwork made it so that your time and effort was required. I don't think that anyone in any of the classes didn't take the work sort of seriously.

The school also allowed students to be themselves. Which may have been something that the bullied students, or the Mormon students, couldn't achieve with public school. Though it was borderline impossible for friendships to be bonded because of Zoom, it seemed like there was a good community that was made with all of the students.

It was a good experience, and I really learned a lot from the teachings, and from my understanding of the school.

Looking Forward to Summer:
Hello Summer!

I am planning on having a great summer and really living it up. Because, once summer is over, it's high school next. Which will probably be more schoolwork than I've ever had, even more than Williamsburg. I don't know what I'm going to do all summer, but in Bellingham there aren't that many months that have great weather.

This summer we're going to go to Priest Lake, in Idaho, for a few weeks. Tay, Mom, and I have never been. Dad grew up going to Priest in the summer and renting a cabin there for a week or two. Dad was at the fire station when he heard another firefighter talking about his parents rented out an A-frame at Priest Lake. So, Dad asked a little more about it, and now we'll go there in the middle of summer for a whole month. It's nice to have something to look forward to for summer, and something to shake up the middle of summer, because summer can get routine.

Summer Rules:
Each summer, for our whole lives, we print a summer rules checklist and put it on the fridge. We come up with the rules together, and this year it looked something like this:

- Art is not a daily checklist job; it is very much recommended that you do it most days or multiple times in the calendar week.
- Workout, though it is required every day, is not to appear on the checklist that you have to check off. Every day you should get out of breath.
- Reading is required an hour a day no matter the circumstances or the day of the week (seven days a week, sixty minutes a day). On the rare occasion that you are not able to complete those sixty minutes a day, you will have to make up for it the next day before screen time is done.
- Schoolwork, even if it is stated that it is optional, you must do it if it offers academic learning or otherwise helps you catch up on something that you may have done at school for that class.
- Writing is required to be done once a day. The amount that you write may vary but you should do a page or around thirty lines of writing. The format that you use may vary as well (paragraphs, poems, recalling quotes from day, book, TV, etc.) You should in some way be writing about your day and your thoughts and feelings on the outside world and news/numbers on (possibly) the coronavirus (COVID-19).

Daily Checklist:
- Reading
- Writing
- School

Also, these are requirements to help you complete daily tasks:
- Brush teeth 2x
- Shower/ Wash face 2x
- PT 2x

Also: Pick up Wilson's poop (every other day, my job one day and Taylor's job one day)

Finally, any complaints of being bored or having nothing to do results in no screen time the next day. So, we also print up a whole list of fun things we can do at home, like games and projects. If we need ideas of something to do, we can just look at the list.

Light at the End of the Tunnel:
COVID numbers, starting around the middle of January, started sliding down. And it kept sliding, then it hit a middle point and plateaued, and then it went down. COVID vaccines for kids twelve and older became available. So, the end is near. Which, after so long, remains very relieving.

COVID-19 Vaccine:
Children twelve and over were able to get the vaccine on May 10, and we were planning to get it as soon as possible because we wanted to be fully vaccinated by the time we leave for Priest Lake.

We changed our minds about the vaccine because of the possible harsh side effects and we had finals coming up, so we decided that we would wait until the finals were over to get the vaccine.

The vaccine place that we went to was close to the hospital where Mom works, before she decided to work at Hospice House. So, we got out of the car and followed the signs. I got the vaccine first, and then Tay was next. It didn't hurt that bad.

We didn't have any side effects with the vaccine, like there may have been. The main side effects for the vaccine were almost COVID-like symptoms, and they didn't last more than a day or two usually. The one thing that did hurt really bad was my arm. I tried to move it around right after getting the vaccine because usually that helps with the soreness that comes with getting a shot. It feels great to be vaccinated, but really, if being honest, it doesn't feel very important until I get the second dose, because then I'll be fully vaccinated.

The thing with the COVID vaccine is that not everyone is completely sold on the idea of getting it. Which honestly is very annoying. The vaccine rates are now plateauing at 50 percent. Most of the people who aren't getting the vaccine are suspicious of the government or the companies of the vaccine; they think the vaccine is really going to negatively affect them, kill them, or something else. I don't really know, but until they do get vaccinated, they sort of hinder some of the excitement and relief that it's over.

Another thing that is worth mentioning about vaccines is that while the US vaccine rate is going up quickly, other countries around the world aren't able to get vaccines as easily, and the countries can't afford it. This sucks for any idea that COVID will be over worldwide. That probably won't happen for a very long time.

There are seven or eight billion people in the world, which makes it understandable how vaccine production can't quickly cover everyone in the world. I'm glad that I live in the United States. Sometimes we don't realize how lucky we all are.

Taylor and FC Rangers Soccer:
One night while we were falling asleep on the deck, and figuring out who will sleep where and where Wilson will be, Taylor and I were talking about his injuries and how he is becoming a lot better with his toe and everything. Then he asked when the Rangers tryouts happen, and I told him it's usually in April or May, so before we went to bed, he looked online and the Rangers tryouts hadn't happened yet.

Then Tay asked Mom if we had enough money to do Rangers, because the amount of money is intense. She said yeah, but they needed to talk about all the aspects of Rangers before committing, and if he was thinking of trying out, he needed to make it first.

Rangers is the main premier soccer team in Bellingham. The practice field is twenty-five minutes away, but the Rangers are good. They have two or three team levels for each age: Gold, Blue and (sometimes) White. Gold is the best team. Not everyone makes it in, obviously. Because Tay and I have played soccer for so long we know and have been around Rangers. I never played Rangers, but when I was in fourth or fifth grade, I made their Ranger Development Program (RDP). This also required a tryout, and I made it the second year I tried out. RDP was basically Rangers for younger kids that weren't old enough to try out for real Rangers.

Tay made Rangers a year or two ago and played, but then got injured and didn't finish the season. By then I think we were all tired of traveling around, even though it was fun watching Tay play. So, he didn't do it last year either. (COVID was also new and around, which made it even less appealing.) Personally, I like watching Taylor play, but the traveling is time consuming, considering that I didn't like going around just to watch.

Mom and Dad eventually agreed that Tay could try out, because he seemed really passionate about it. Tay came home each of the practices believing that he did really well, and he scored a few goals over the three days of tryouts.

Eventually, Tay got an email that he got into Rangers G08 Gold (2008 is the year Taylor was born). We were all really excited for him. It was even more impressive because he didn't do much soccer the last two years compared to other kids at the practice. Tay also said that there weren't that many people at the tryouts, which I think may be because of COVID and less people are interested. Usually there are a lot of people at the tryouts.

Then Tay went to the practices. He said that one of the things that the coach was really focused on was running, and that is something Taylor is really good at. So, eventually Taylor came back from practice and said that he was lapping the other players. That's pretty impressive. So, he's doing good with Rangers and holding up with everyone else so far. All of this is while wearing masks, which makes it harder.

Papa is Sick:
So, recently, Papa (Mom's dad) lost a lot of weight without trying. And he wasn't feeling great either, so Mom was thinking that he was probably sick. This all started happening near Papa and Mickey's forty-ninth wedding anniversary.

Tay and I haven't seen Papa in two or so years, but we were also worried about him. Mom, as a nurse, really helped out Papa and the family and talked on the phone with Mickey and Papa a lot.

High School:
With Williamsburg over, it's impossible not to think about ninth grade. Honestly, I am most excited to see all of my friends again. Williamsburg was so annoying not to have any friends or any in-person people. Also, grades really count in high school, so that means that studying will have a real effect, because it'll now be on our transcript.

I also am excited to do sports. I know that I am going to do soccer, which is either in the spring or fall, and I might do cross country and maybe swimming.

We also signed up for classes. Dad said that he was surprised how many options there were. He said that it looked like a college course list. So we got that all set up, and I'm planning on taking Spanish for a language, an engineering class, and drawing and art. This is also with math (geometry), English 101, PE, etc.

Steve is Getting Married:
Mom's brother, Steve, proposed to his girlfriend. Mom's brother is, like, eleven years younger than Mom, and he has been with Amy for a little

while. Recently Mom heard that he was planning on proposing. So, that happened recently and now there is going to be a wedding.

The wedding is right when we are planning on driving to the lake, so Mom is going to go by herself, and the boys are all going to drive to Priest. Tay and I were invited, but after talking about it with the family and wondering what we should do, we decided that it would be best if Mom went by herself. Mom is going to have so much fun, and I think that she is going to have a ton of fun seeing all of her family and celebrating. I think it would have been fun if we all went, but honestly, I didn't have a very big opinion one way or the other. That will also be a good time for Mom to see Papa.

I think that Steve and Amy, from what I have heard, are going to be really happy together. I'm happy for them.

Reading *Mindset* Again:
Another thing that I did is reread *Mindset*, the book about a growth mindset versus a fixed mindset. With a fixed mindset, you're less likely to succeed and will have a negative mindset compared to a growth mindset, where you have an open mind when it comes to challenges and everything else, and with this mindset you're more likely to succeed. I learned even more by rereading the book, and there were parts which I related to much more than earlier and understood other parts differently.

I'm almost sure that I have a growth mindset, but it isn't difficult to see how easy it would be to have a fixed mindset.

Taylor Breaking Stuff:
Tay was doing a challenge in the backyard, and his goal was to juggle the soccer ball up the stairs that goes from the backyard patio to the front yard. Mom has solar lights along the side of the stairs, and one of the first things Mom said was to make sure that he didn't break the lights with the soccer ball. Well, he did break one of them while attempting it. Mom wasn't too mad, but I think Tay gave Mom money to buy a new one. Taylor also, a little later, reached his goal and juggled all the way up the stairs, which is impressive to me.

My Writing:
I guess this is pretty candid, considering if anyone is really reading this.

So, as all of this writing piles up into a pretty big amount, I feel motivated to share and do something with it. I think it's pretty cool just for myself if nothing else, but it would be so cool to share this. It wouldn't be easy and at some points not fun at all. But, I'm up for it.

I don't like to talk about politics much. A sort of hatred and panic of any kind is the opposite of what I have tried to put into this writing project. I have talked about political views in this work, but I would say very minimally, which reflects how I think. I don't talk or think much about politics; neither do I want to. The only time that I really remember caring a lot was when Trump was freshly elected, but I can say that it isn't any more something in my life. And, especially post-Trump, reading political opinions would be like eating a moldy banana. The banana had a time when it was edible, but I think now it would have a poor taste.

Ashaan and High School Soccer:
One Sunday Ashaan came over and we played soccer. He also talked about how he has been doing school soccer, that it was really competitive because you're playing with the upperclassmen at tryouts, and that unlike the Rangers, you aren't just with your age. There could be juniors that you're playing against. This means that if I want to do good with soccer next year, I'm probably going to want to practice and think about how to get better.

I am definitely going to play high school soccer in the spring, and I also have to find sports for the fall and winter.

I'm excited for high school. It's going to be fun and different. Honestly, I think I'm more excited about seeing my friends again than going to a high school.

Taylor's Physical Therapy:
Even though it hasn't been very well documented, I have talked multiple times about Taylor's long list of injuries and things that hurt him often. Recently Tay and Mom would FaceTime a friend who is a physical therapist who lives in Oregon, so the only way to get an appointment is through FaceTime. He is doing it free of charge. For Taylor, this is sort of his last-ditch effort. It seems like he has gone to everyone.

The PT is Jay Dicharry and he sent Taylor a thing that he invented called a MOBO board, which is basically a wobbly board to balance on, with a hole where the toes are, which helps with something. I don't really know, because I'm not listening in on FaceTimes. I think it's working though, from what Taylor is saying. That's great.

I guess it helps with arches of feet, too. Which is interesting because Taylor has very high arches and I have flat feet, or barely any arch in my feet. So, maybe I'll try using the MOBO board and it might help my feet. That would be cool. Dad also says that it might get me faster.

∗∗∗

Note: That is everything that I feel is necessary from the end of my original journaling to the reboot of the journal. So, my journaling continues ahead, starting from May 29, 2021. This journaling was more brief than the original but still an important piece to contribute to the project of recording my experience during COVID.

Saturday, May 29, 2021

It's weird writing again. I haven't done this in a while. I definitely needed a long break from writing. And when I was writing, I thought that the last entry was the end. I wasn't planning on writing any more. I felt that I was finished. But nope. I'm excited to continue. It definitely has benefits. Also, I'm motivated to write again. I had stopped writing because 1) I assumed I didn't need to anymore, and 2) I had lost all motivation at that point.

Today I started a new book by John Steinbeck. It's called *Travels with Charley*. In the book, Steinbeck drives across the country with his dog, Charley. I like it so much right from the little I have read so far. It is also fun to read when writing. I think it's very inspirational and important to writing and the process of writing.

Today Mom talked to her friends from high school. Mom grew up in California, and now living in Washington, she never sees her friends. Most of her closest friends from California stayed there. Every few years or so she goes down to California to see them, and also sometimes we go to California on Tay's or my birthday to see Mickey and Papa.

I wonder what it's going to be like once everyone disperses after high school. I assume it will feel like restarting from zero friends. Most of the people I know from school I won't see after school ends. I'll probably forget all of them, except a select few, which I think I will stay in touch with.

I also don't know if I'll come back to Bellingham after college (unless I go to WWU). I really have no clue right now. Bellingham feels perfect, but I think a lot of other places will feel perfect. I do have a strong feeling that I will stay on the west coast, living in California, Oregon, or Washington. I don't have any interest in being landlocked in the middle of the United States. I also don't know about the eastern part of the United States. I guess I will just have to figure it out by myself. I think the best way to do this is to travel the country, like in *Travels with Charley*. I think the idea of going around with your dog in the passenger seat seems like the perfect road trip. I would love to do the same thing at some point in my life.

I guess it's also possible that I will go out of the country and live in Canada or someplace in Europe. It would be fun to live somewhere in Europe for, like, six months or a year. I'll have to remember that.

We played frisbee golf around the yard today. How that works is each of us has a frisbee (usually Dad, Tay, and I play) and we come up with a target like a tree, the firepit, or the basketball hoop. We also came up with a rule that if someone hits the house, they lose fifteen minutes of screen time, and the other two people get fifteen minutes of screen time.

Dad doesn't have screen time but if he does hit the house, Taylor and I earn fifteen.

I also tried the MOBO board for myself today. Dad said that it would help me increase my arches. I'm definitely flat footed. Dad and Tay said this could make me faster, which would be cool.

I am wondering if I am going to possibly do cross country in the fall. I haven't looked into how to sign up or anything, but it would be a great way to get to know people that I wouldn't know otherwise right as school starts. So, I'll have to think about it. Dad also says that it would be a good idea to get in running shape before it happens.

Taylor's coach for Rangers has given the kids different workouts for running and body weight exercises. So, today for the running workout we went to the track. It's obvious that Tay just wants to sprint because he has found something that he really excels at. It's pretty cool he's super fast.

Sunday, May 30, 2021

Gavin and Carter came over today, which was fun. They said that they got the first vaccine, like we did. Also, Carter got his driver's license. Carter has already been sixteen for a while, but he wasn't in a rush to get his license. He finally did after eleven months of being able to. I wonder if I'll wait to get my license or if I'll get my driver's license the day I can. I imagine myself not waiting. I think it would be better to get the tests over with instead of procrastinating.

Ashaan didn't come over this Sunday, which is notable because he usually comes every Sunday now. I also thought about this: When we are with Ashaan, we all wear masks, even though after getting the vaccine we have been more loose putting them on. But, with Gavin and Carter, we haven't worn masks for a long time. I wonder why. I don't think we care much anymore about masks outside. Maybe it's that we want to be respectful of who we are with, and we cater to what they want.

Another thing that's pretty interesting is that for the most part we haven't hung out with that many friends besides Ashaan, Gavin, and Carter. We could hang out with other friends, but I think that those three are the ones that we have the most fun with and are very comfortable being with. I think other people hang out with a lot of friends, but Tay and I are so great just hanging out together. I don't think any of us feel the need to invite other people over. It would be fun, but it's also so much fun with Tay and me. I bet other siblings aren't as close as Taylor and I are.

Monday, May 31, 2021

Today Mom and I went on a drive, which was fun, and I thought it was going to be a relaxing ride, to just talk. Mom had other plans. She wanted to walk up Taylor Hill. (Taylor Hill just happens to be the street. It doesn't have any connection to my brother.) The hill is notoriously steep. At first, I was pretty resistant because I just wanted to chill and relax. But she convinced me to walk the hill. We had fun and laughed a little. I also felt motivated to walk past her and stop at the end of the stop sign. More laughing. And when we were done with the walk, we were at the top of the hill and could see the bay, which was a really amazing sight to see.

Ashaan came over today, and he's also going to be here tomorrow. We decided to not wear masks, which is ironic because I just wrote about it yesterday. We're all halfway vaccinated, so we're going to be fine.

Tay and I also measured our height for fun today. We are the exact same height! When Taylor is eighteen months older, it's probable that he's going to be the taller one. It will be weird if he's taller than me later, because he's always been my little brother, but soon he'll be my big little brother. I think it'll be fun sometimes.

I also was, for one of the only times ever, annoyed today. I don't know why, but it happened, and I'm very aware when it does happen. Today I felt that every conversation that we were having was pointless and recycled. The repetitive conversations were too much for me, so I did a good job of diagnosing it and not letting it affect anyone.

Tuesday, June 1, 2021

Today we went down to the lake, and we jumped in. Even though it's June now, it is still very, very cold. It took Taylor the longest to get in the lake.

While we were in the water there were multiple times where cottonwood tree sticks hit me in the face. I don't think the trees are cottonwood, but they look a lot like it. The flying snow-looking cotton or whatever kept the sky interesting, instead of nothing. Like, the fall has leaves that fall and fill the sky, and in the winter there's snow. Not so much with spring or summer, until today, I guess.

Before we went to bed tonight, we heard raccoons (at least I'm almost sure that's what it was), and it kept Wilson very intrigued. I don't know what he would do if he was face to face with a raccoon, but I would like to think that he wouldn't just bark constantly like most dogs would.

Wednesday, June 2, 2021

Today Mom and I swam laps at the Sudden Valley pool for the first time. When we got there, it was crowded with elementary school kids. Later we thought the elementary students probably had just gotten out of school. This wasn't ideal, because if we wanted to swim laps, we would need space.

We met a nice, older guy at the pool, Fred. Fred was swimming laps when we first got there. There were only two lap lanes, and Fred saw that they were full and that we were trying to swim on the edge of the kids' section of the pool. He gave Mom and I his lane for fifteen minutes. He said that circle swimming doesn't really work with all the chaos and such a diverse level of swimming experience. We had a lot of fun swimming, even though sometimes when we were swimming laps little kids would cross over the lanes and we would almost hit them. The pool is an outdoor pool, and it was nice to be outside.

Thursday, June 3, 2021 – Sunday, June 6, 2021

I crammed these couple of days into one because I didn't get time to write down what happened. With Gammy and Paw-Paw here, I didn't feel like writing everything down in between. I guess I can just do an overview of it.

So, we are going to see Gammy and Paw-Paw on our way to Priest Lake, but Gammy and Paw-Paw were already planning on coming over, so we'll see them two separate times in two to three weeks.

When they were here, we had a lot of fun with them. They didn't stay at the house, because it's difficult for Paw-Paw to go up and down the stairs. Paw-Paw has an autoimmune disease which slowly gets worse over time. It seems like he has gotten worse recently, which is worrying, but we still had fun talking to them and spending time with them. We haven't seen them in a bit.

We also played soccer with Ashaan and practiced knuckleballing, which is a technique where you kick the soccer ball and it barely spins, which makes it wobble back and forth. It's certainly difficult to do a knuckleball, but Tay and I are getting better at it.

While they were here, we got some bad news. Papa (Mom's dad) has cancer. Mom has been pretty sure that it's cancer, with the symptoms that she knew about like rapid weight loss. The type of cancer that he has is pancreatic cancer, which Mom knows and told us is a quick and very lethal cancer. I don't know if we are going to go over to California and see him, and if so, when. Mom's thinking of going over there soon.

Tay and I haven't witnessed anyone that we're closely related to die, ever. I don't know how I'm going to react when he passes. I don't even know at all if I'm going to cry, or what. I also don't know how Taylor's going to react either.

Monday, June 7, 2021
Today we got new soccer cleats. I looked at a few different types of cleats because I wanted one that was snug on the back of my heel, which was more difficult than I thought it would be. Then we went to Western's soccer field and played, and after that I went and swam for an hour.

Also, a few days ago Taylor got a Fitbit, and he likes it. I tried mine on for the first time in a really long time. I haven't worn it barely at all since COVID.

Friday, June 11, 2021 — Saturday, June 12, 2021
We got our second vaccine. It's so cool to have both done. They say that you aren't fully vaccinated right when you get the vaccine, but you have to wait a few weeks to be considered fully vaccinated and not have to wear masks in (most) places.

This vaccine hasn't hurt as much as the first one did. I got this shot on my left; my first vaccine I got on the right. Taylor got his second vaccine before me, so he can technically say that he was fully vaccinated before me. I guess we're still very competitive. But I did get my first vaccine before him. So, I still have that.

Monday, June 14, 2021
Not much to report today. There is one thing that happened that I could think about a little more, I guess. So, when Dad and I were watching Taylor play soccer, we saw a bald eagle on a branch high up on a tree, and there were other birds attacking the eagle. But the eagle didn't do much, he was calm. He wasn't in distress and didn't really fight back. The birds eventually left. Maybe this is something that can be used as good advice or a lesson to learn for things that happen later in my life.

Tuesday, June 15, 2021
Today Tay and I talked about people from Kulshan Middle School. I believe many people will be different when we finally see them after COVID, for better or worse, compared to how we remember them. I think this is sort of an unfortunate conclusion for me to reach, but it's true.

Wednesday, June 16, 2021

Mom decided that for Father's Day she is going to surprise her dad and visit him. Papa loved (and frequently wore) Hawaiian shirts, so she is also going to get one to wear when she visits him. She got a men's one at first, but it didn't fit, so she gave it to Tay and me. So, Mom is going to fly over there soon.

Friday, June 18, 2021

Today I got a haircut, and I think it was a bad haircut. It was too short. Honestly, it's annoying, but my hair grows so fast it probably won't matter because in a few weeks it will be great.

With us going to Priest Lake for three weeks, we aren't going to get a haircut there. Priest is a very remote place, so this was the last chance to get a haircut, or else it would be long. Which would be fun, I guess, but it would also not, because of the heat, which is likely going to be even hotter than here.

Also mom left for California for one week to visit Papa and for Steve's wedding, so it is just the boys home. We are going to pick mom up at the airport in Spokane on our drive to Idaho.

***

Note: At Priest Lake there is no reliable WIFI, and it didn't make sense for me to bring my computer just to journal. However, I did remember that I had leftover pages in my notebook from Williamsburg. So, my language arts and photography notebook became my journaling notebook for Priest. So I will write it out and, when I get back home, type it up on my laptop.

Friday, June 25, 2021

Tomorrow we will start driving to Idaho. We will be at Priest Lake for three weeks, and we will be spending some time in Sandpoint after Priest Lake. And we are going to stop in Spokane and stay the night. Then, all five of us (Wilson included) will head to the lake. Mom's flight out of California goes to Spokane. Basically, we will be gone a month total. Also, there is a heat wave in the Pacific Northwest, but the heat wave also includes Idaho and Priest.

We are going to be spending our time at Priest Lake in an A frame cabin. With no WIFI, no laundry (there is a laundromat there, though), no big town nearby (there are a few small stores and a gas station farther away). The town is where the laundromat is.

It is also Steve and Amy's wedding today. Even though we didn't go, they had a live video stream starting at six, and we will watch that. Mom is going to the wedding but Papa, because he is very sick, has to stay back at the hotel, and family came to visit him there. Mom made a video of him doing a speech for Steve and Amy to share at the ceremony.

Also, we are packing for the trip, and Tay and I will be in the very back of the car. Wilson will be in the second row, and Dad will drive. We will meet Mom at the Davenport. The Davenport is the Spokane hotel we will stay at for a day.

Finally, I'm not used to writing this much down on paper. My hand hurts so much!

Sunday, June 27, 2021

We got to the lake!

Mom's flight was late last night, and she was very tired. In the middle of the night, she got to the hotel by a taxi and went to sleep. She said that she wanted to hug us but we were already asleep and had locked the door (Tay and I had our own room).

When we got to the Davenport, Wilson was very scared to go up the elevators. I don't think that he has gone on one many times, maybe never, before yesterday. It's cool that Wilson can stay in the hotel with us.

It is still very, very hot outside. So, when we went to Starbucks while driving over here, Dad brought Wilson inside. The car said it was 104 degrees! The people that worked there said that only service dogs were allowed. Dad said yes, he is a service dog, even though it's not true. I was surprised, but for Wilson's sake Dad didn't want him to stay in the car. I guess Tay and I could have kept him, and we could trade him off to Dad after Dad went to the bathroom, and then we could go inside.

We jumped in the lake quickly after getting here at the cabin. It is a hundred degrees outside right now. There were some spots where we took a rest outside where it was borderline unbearable to even stand outside.

Last thing today: When we were driving, we saw a bear! On the first day of the trip, it's been a while since I have seen a bear. It got on its hind legs when we went back to see it! Also, when we got to the cabin, we saw a jackrabbit. Which is basically a normal bunny, but the species is a lot more athletic and definitely looks bigger than regular bunnies.

Monday, June 28, 2021

Tay apparently was sleepwalking last night. I was asleep. Today I took a nap, which I never do. I guess the hot weather wiped me out. Taking a nap was the best thing. I am going to take more soon if I get tired.

After I took a nap, I woke up and Taylor had a heat rash from the heat. He has gotten heat rashes before, and frequently gets heat exhaustion when he plays at soccer competitions, which happened two years in a row. Taylor had also gotten hurt in two other ways in the span of my nap. He ripped his toenail and something else, I can't remember now.

Also, today I threw up twice. Which wasn't very fun. For dinner we went to a restaurant, Cavanaugh's, and I threw up because I accidently had pesto, I think. I think I was allergic to something that they put in the pesto. I threw up right when we came back to the A frame.

Our neighbor next to us is Bob, who owns his own cabin to the left of the A frame, and he also owns the A frame. On the right, there is also a cabin is owned by a nice couple named the Shusters.

Tuesday, June 29, 2021

Today Mom and Dad are making plans to possibly see his family for the Fourth of July.

Dad and I went to the store today. We needed to get a type of shirt for Taylor, which didn't work out because the store didn't have long sleeve shirts with heat/sun protection.

I also started reading a new book today that Gammy and Paw-Paw gave Dad and me. It's called *On Writing,* by Stephen King.

In between Bob's cabin and the A frame there is a small shed with different canoes and stand-up paddle boards. There is also more stuff, but Bob said that we could use anything in there, and today I went stand-up paddleboarding. It has been a while.

Also, on the edge of the dock there is a basketball hoop which is connected to the bottom of the lake, which is only a few feet deep at that point. Where we are, the lake is shallow and sandy. Like, Tay and I can probably stand up and breathe for fifty yards or so. So, it makes playing there so much fun. Basically, the whole day we spend in the water or on the dock and playing water basketball, mostly the basketball game Bump.

Wednesday, June 30, 2021

Today we went to Hill's Resort for dinner, which is the resort on the other side of the lake. This is where Dad spent time every summer until he was eleven. Dad showed us the cabin that his family spent time in. He also told us that this is where he had his first kiss. Then, we had dinner there and I had a great steak and ice cream. Also, at the resort I got a yellow Priest Lake sweatshirt.

Today Mom, Dad, and I talked with the Shusters' (the neighbors on the right of the A frame.) They knew a lot about strategizing for high school and college, so they shared some valuable and interesting knowledge that we all wouldn't know otherwise.

With all of the college talk, I realized that I'm not sold on Stanford being the goal college that I want to go to. I need to think about this more, but even though my goal has been Stanford, I think it isn't one of my prioritized goals anymore.

I haven't mentioned this yet, but because of the trip, Gammy and Paw-Paw gave us multiple gift cards to different restaurants in Priest Lake, which was so nice of them!

Thursday, July 1, 2021

So, today I was reading a lot of *On Writing* by King. I feel this is a good time to describe my surroundings, because it is quite remarkable.

On the north side, there are layers of mountains, and as the mountains get farther and farther away, the mountains appear to be a lighter blue.

When I am looking across the lake, facing the west side, I can see turquoise covers for boats that protect the boats at Hill's Resort. But I can also barely see civilization across the lake, and the only reminder of outside life is the cabins near us, and the small town that is a few miles to the south of the lake. The town, Coolin, includes a post office, a small store, and a coffee shop.

In the sky, the clouds vary from dotted splashes of white to swipes and clumps of cloud. And I am covered right now by an umbrella with a faded color.

Under me there are planks that make up the dock, which swerves back and forth as I read. After a jet ski or a boat goes by, the waves are more dramatic and cause the dock to turn back and forth more violently. The bottom of the lake is covered in sun bleached sand and there are footprints from all the basketball yesterday. Because of the remoteness and lack of use, the lake water is one of the cleanest I have seen for a lake.

Taylor and Dad went fishing today. They told us that they saw a bear. They were pretty surprised. Then Dad had the bright idea to get closer to the bear. Then they realized that they made a mistake. It wasn't a bear—it was a massive golden eagle! They only found out once the eagle flew away, and for a second, they were confused why the bear could fly.

They didn't catch any fish, and with the heat wave, all of the fish were dead. Tay counted fifty-five dead fish that were on the banks of the river, and they didn't find one living fish. This is one example of global warming. It was sad to hear the unfortunate news. They took a video of it and sent it to the ranger station.

They did see two geese, and a baby goose following the two other geese. They said that the water was surprisingly warm.

Today, as a family, we all watched the sunset. If I haven't already mentioned in the journal, Wilson loves sunsets. A lot. He always watches them on the lawn at home. The blue hills turned gold with the bright sunset. Mom pointed over there and said that's where heaven is. I wholeheartedly agree.

The A frame's design allows it to withhold heavy snow by sliding it down. The A frame that we lived in had an entrance facing the unpaved road. The entrance opens up to the kitchen, and to the left there was the one and only bathroom. The bathroom has a toilet and the smallest shower I have ever seen.

The kitchen leads to the main room, which has an L-shaped couch, a few rugs, a four-chair table to eat at, with a light blue tablecloth. There was an old TV, which only had DVDs. There are three windows looking out to the lake, so we always had a view of the lake, even when we were inside. On the ceiling there are two fans, which are vital with the heat wave. They keep us from melting. There's a tight spiral staircase that leads to the second floor loft with a bed. Tay almost never slept upstairs after sleepwalking. None of us wanted him to sleepwalk to a ten-foot drop, so he sleeps on the couch. The A frame is a really cozy place. There are things about the A frame that I have to get used to, but I thoroughly enjoy the naps in the middle of the day.

Friday, July 2, 2021

Mom and Dad and I swam to the buoy and back today. They are both faster than I am, but today I think I did a good job keeping up with them.

Today we went hiking and saw a waterfall and trees that are apparently at least two thousand years old. Going hiking was the first time in a week that I wore shoes. I have only been barefoot or wearing flip flops all week.

Again, it was very hot, which made hiking unenjoyable in some parts. Especially when there was no shade to be under. That's when I was thinking this hike wasn't worth it. So, the hike had its ups and downs. On the hike we didn't see any bears or moose.

Finally, at six today the smoke alarm was beeping because its batteries were dead. Wilson was scared when he heard the beeping.

Saturday, July 3, 2021

Tomorrow is the Fourth of July. I don't know what we are going to do to celebrate.

The heat wave is practically over. It got over a hundred degrees for five days in a row. Apparently, most of the records in Washington, Idaho, and Oregon for hot temperatures were broken with this heat wave.

The Coeur d'Alene Ironman happened only a few days ago. And Dad found out, or heard from someone, that one third of the people who raced didn't finish, because of the heat wave. It would be miserable to do any race. I'm not surprised that so many people couldn't make it the whole race.

Sunday, July 4, 2021

Today is the 245th birthday of the United States of America. An interesting thing is that Dad was born in 1976, so he was born on year two hundred. This makes it very easy to remember how old the US is.

I haven't yet talked about the planes. I believe that there are two or three planes that are constantly flying around. Across from Cavanaugh's, there is an open field where planes land and take off. Also, I think one or more of the planes are float planes. The planes are always flying over the A frame. Dad told the story of when he went in a float plane here. I bet flying a plane is fun. It defies the rules that humans were given, and instead of staying on the ground, flying changes what was previously impossible.

Mom, Dad, and I went swimming in the morning, from the buoy and back. Mom and Dad did a lot more swimming than I did today. But I have found that I don't have to swim long before I feel awake and alive. More than Dad and me, Mom swims a lot. She swims basically every morning.

We all stayed up to eleven at night watching the fireworks. Only one or two people were lighting fireworks. This is because with the heat wave, and everything around us being so dry, the town said to not light fireworks this year. The small board outside the small fire station said there is a *very high* fire risk.

We were thinking that we were going to go to Sandpoint and celebrate Independence Day with Dad's family. But Dad got a phone call from his sister and from his mom, and it fell through because of an argument about politics.

I'd like to think that I will never fight with anyone ever. This probably won't happen, but I feel that caring about things like politics and religion so much that it affects your relationship with friends and family, is too much.

As for us five, I think we're good.

This Fourth of July taught me a lot, and it was a great celebration.

Monday, July 5, 2021

I woke up at eight thirty. This is pretty late for me. A little while after getting out of bed, Dad and I went in the car to do laundry and go to the dump. We listened to Death Cab for Cutie on the drive there. Good driving music. At the dump there was a free section of things that people had brought to the dump, but they put it in the free section because someone else might want what they were planning on throwing away. The free section has a bookshelf with books, DVDs, and other things like darts and water cups, etc. On the bookshelf there was a sign that called the free section the "Priest Lake Mall," which I thought was funny.

We got six books from the mall. Some of the books that we got were *Chicken Soup for the Soul* and *Moby Dick*. The books were old and worn, like books at the dump should be expected to be, but they were great, and I am planning on reading them on the trip.

Then Dad and I went to two stores to ask where the laundromat was. Once we found it, we put in four garbage bags of clothes and towels. I didn't think that we would have to stay at the laundromat for over an hour. Never being at a laundromat, I didn't think of the possibility that the clothes could be taken. Dad and I stayed at a bench near the entrance of the laundromat and read our new, dump worthy books. I thoroughly enjoyed one of the books, but after a half hour we went to the store and each got a hot dog and chips (I got Doritos). We don't usually eat like this, because the food isn't very healthy. But the treat was enjoyed.

On the way back, Dad and I went to a small Coolin store where a neighbor said that there was a writing workshop flier. We found the flier, but at that point we decided that it wasn't worth the time. I had recently read the part in On Writing where Stephen King hilariously rants about how pointless and stupid writing workshops are. So, that was good timing.

Mom said that she feels like cutting the trip down by one week. She says that she is overwhelmed with taking care of Papa (over the phone) and her family. She misses her bed at home and wants to see her friends too. It's undoubtedly difficult for her to go through what she is going through.

I don't know if going home early will make that much of a difference, but I think Mom and Dad will have to talk about it more.

We went kayaking and paddleboarding. I kayaked the whole time, and there was a spider on my kayak. I named him Henry. We went to the river and around a small island. Mom says it's best to kayak at sunset because it's calmer water and more beautiful. Halfway through the kayaking, I lost Henry.

I haven't talked about Chippy yet. Chippy is a squirrel that has been in the trees above the cabin for a while. He taunts Wilson, and Wilson always has his head up, looking in the trees, looking for Chippy. Chippy barks (or whatever noise squirrels make) at Wilson. For the most part Wilson just watches Chippy. They do this all day.

For dinner we went to Hill's Resort. I had a big pretzel and then got full. They had a movie projected on the beach, with big sheet as a screen. I guess they have one up for the kids every Monday. Today they were playing *Sandlot*. So we watched it.

Tuesday, July 6, 2021

Chippy and Wilson had a staring contest today. I didn't pay enough attention to figure out who won.

Today we went to an old goldmine. Dad went there thirty-five years ago, and he said there was a big shaft that he remembers being at the mine, but we couldn't find it. Maybe someone had it filled up or it collapsed, because I think that would be dangerous to have a giant shaft where someone could fall to their death. The gold mine was a gold mine for a short while until it was discovered that the gold they thought they were finding was actually fool's gold. We went there to explore and find fool's gold, copper, and other stuff. We found a lot, and I ended up swimming in my shoes and diving for treasure.

Wednesday, July 7, 2021

Today is Papa's birthday. Happy Birthday, Papa.

Mom wanted to go somewhere today. So, we went to Coeur d'Alene. Mom's sister lives there, but because Mom just saw her a week ago, she didn't seem to want to visit her. On the drive there Tay and I were eating Lifesavers candy. Each candy was individually packaged. I found one of the Lifesaver packages that was sealed but didn't have any candy in it. "What a rip off!" I said. I found this way too funny.

We went swimming in Coeur d'Alene, we got ice cream, and we went to the park near the hotel. Once Mom and Dad did a Half Ironman in

Coeur d' Alene for their fifteenth wedding anniversary. Also, today we went to the store, and they had a movie renting section, and we rented three movies: *Hobbes and Shaw, Mall Cop 2* and *Solo*. They are supposed to be returned in three days. Today we watched *Mall Cop 2.*

Thursday, July 8, 2021
Today I tried, and failed, to take a nap. I was tired today, so it was a bummer when I couldn't fall asleep. I guess I wasn't tired enough.

We went to Cavanaugh's for lunch. I got pizza sticks. I had a better time eating here for a second time.

Next to the restaurant there's a big grass runway for personal planes. When we were eating, we saw a few come and go. We were really close to the landings, and they went right by the restaurant and were very close to the ground.

After, we decided to go look at the runway, and we saw another plane leave. There were also parachuters that we saw floating down and landing on the runway.

In the afternoon Dad, Tay, and I all went out in the water. Tay and Dad went on a stand-up paddleboard and I went in a kayak. We were just going to see how far out we could stand up, and we went way out from shore, but we found something random. It was very mysterious to us, and we had no clue what it was. Tay found it, like, ten feet deep. Tay pulled a cinderblock and the two water bottles up from the bottom of the lake and we opened the bottles. One water bottle had small things, like small prizes. The other had a notebook to keep track who had found the treasure. The objects in the first water bottle were two plastic coins, a plastic army guy, solar lights notebook and pen. We uncovered the treasure more once we went back to shore. We brought the whole thing on the paddle board, cinder block included. The only way that we saw it was the two water bottles were bright orange and yellow.

Friday, July 9, 2021
Today it was only eighty-four degrees outside. We went to the local elementary school to play. Dad and Tay ran laps, Mom did Pilates, and I juggled my soccer ball. After leaving the school, Mom and I went swimming in the lake and then came in for lunch. Then we went to the rock waterslides that Dad told us about before we came to Priest. We drove up a dirt road for five miles. There were about a dozen really bumpy parts in the road. Dad says it's made to stop masses of snow from damaging the road. When we

were hiking up there, the parts that were in the sun were miserable, even though it was colder than it has been recently.

Finally, we got to the area where the water pool and slides were. We got lost for a while, and then we retraced our steps. I should also mention, Mom's toe is probably broken. Someone at Steve's wedding was dancing and accidentally stepped on her toe. She doesn't know if it's broken, technically, but she's basically sure. She has been really tough and hasn't talked about it that much or complained, but all the hiking was killing her toe. She kept saying that this is the last hike she is going on this trip. The slides were crowded, more than we thought it might be. Dad brought garbage bags for us to slide down the rocks on. There was a rope at the end of the slope to catch anyone from going too fast and flying and getting hurt. Most of the kids riding down were younger than Tay and me. Only Dad and I went down. Tay didn't go because he thought it was too dangerous, and by that point we had hiked so much there was no way Mom wanted to go, with her toe.

The water from the rocks was way colder than the lake water. It felt like four degrees. When we were all done sliding, we went to a lower, small water pool. Dad and I found a spot to get in, where the cold water was rushing down. The water was still extremely cold. Meanwhile Mom elevated her foot. Tay was acting like he wasn't having fun.

Leaving the place was a lot quicker than going up to the waterslide. Mom said that the hike felt like more than one and a half miles, which is what she was promised it was by Dad.

John and Dawn Shuster are back at their cabin. He says that he is the one that organized the treasure we found way out in the lake. He said that it was a geocache. Geocaching apparently is a thing where people have coordinates or directions to the treasure, and they try to find it with those clues. Then they write their name in the notebook. For some people, it's a hobby. It's funny that we found it by accident.

Saturday, July 10, 2021
We put the geocache back today so other people can find it too. Looking back, we're lucky that we brought the cinder block with us because it would be so difficult to find the cinderblock to reattach the two water bottles.

Today we started hobo fishing! So, with the idea of fishing in the river dead (like all of the fish in it) we have to fish on the dock if we want to fish at all. So, we are hobo fishing. Dad got two sticks, one for me and one for Tay. They were branches about six feet long he broke off the tree by the cabin. He attached a string to the end of each one, and then Dad went to the

Coolin store for worms. At first, we tried corn on the hook, but that was an epic fail. We had never used worms for fishing, until now, because we only fly fish. But now is the time for hobo fishing!

Eventually, the two fish that we found under the dock tried to get the worms, but the hooks were too small, and didn't get the fish. So, Dad is planning on getting bigger hooks later tomorrow at the Coolin store.

I took a nap today. Also, tonight we are going to watch a movie.

Sunday, July 11, 2021

Today we had success with hobo fishing, which I'll talk about in a second.

So, we spent two weeks at the lake, as of yesterday. There are definitely some things that I am missing from home, like a better bathroom, and a yard to play soccer. But I am really enjoying being here, and I am super excited for the last week here. But also, I'll be happy to go back home soon.

Hobo fishing: While I was reading, Tay caught two fish, and one more once I came outside. The fish was flopping around on the dock. Then, we found a really, really big fish. I started calling it the megalodon. It was massive! I lost my hobo stick, somehow, so Dad helped me make a new one. The megalodon ate three hooks and worms. After dinner, Dad is going to get a stronger line for the hobo sticks. It seems like this fish can eat anything. Once we ran out of worms, we tried corn again until we got more worms. It was the first fish we saw go for the corn, which must not be a fish's favorite food.

Monday, July 12, 2021

Now that I have been here for two weeks, I have been able to compare and contrast how Priest Lake is different from home, so today I made a list of observations on Priest:

- Fewer birds
- More bugs
- Weekends are busy, and weekdays are quiet. (A good measurement of how crowded it is: how many boats are around. During the week the water is calm, but the weekend isn't.)
- Strangers aren't as friendly. They avoid eye contact and don't talk much.
- It is hotter and dryer here. I haven't seen rain yet.
- Prettier sunsets
- More American flags

- More dead squirrels on the side of the road
- I haven't seen any banks, parks, food chains, etc.
- Almost every grocery store, restaurant, and business has a sign saying, "Workers needed," or that the business is short staffed.

Today I got an idea to write a short story. Maybe it's the Stephen King book, but I am more motivated to write now. My idea is about a fish that wants to be caught. Another thing that happened today is Tay finished his four-hundred-piece puzzle. Except, one piece is missing. We couldn't find it after looking around. Taylor, with his heat rash, had to stay inside a lot and started the puzzle quickly after we came to Priest. I think it's almost poetic to put so much effort into something just for it to never be complete.

Tuesday, July 13, 2021
This morning we smelled smoke. It's been so dry, with the fire risk at "extreme" for a week. It isn't surprising that there is a fire. We don't know where the fire is. Hopefully the A frame doesn't catch fire.

Today we were going to go to Cavanaugh's, but they are closed on Tuesday and Wednesday because they have a lack of staff and probably customers too.

At least the fire smoke makes for really cool and pretty sunsets.

Thursday, July 15, 2021
Today we went to another restaurant, Elkins. We came up with a game, guessing how many people would come up and say hi to Wilson. Elkins is in my top two restaurants that we have gone to on this trip. Number one for me is Hill's Resort.

After we went to Elkins we came back and went flashlight fishing at night. Which, Dad says, is cheating for fishing. But we weren't really fishing, we were hobo fishing! I bet a real hobo who fishes with a stick and string probably doesn't care about the rules or etiquette of fishing. I can see why it is considered cheating, because it is very effective. Tay and I each caught one fish. They were each about eighteen inches long! This is megalodon size! Now we need to try to catch the megalodon without a flashlight.

Friday, July 16, 2021
Dad and I went to the store and got a waterproof phone case. When we were there, we talked about the post office and how it works. I found it interesting.

Today we planned on going to Cavanaugh's. When we were driving over, we saw an ambulance, and a few other medical vehicles. There were also two helicopters. Two people got into stretchers that we could see from afar, and another came out of the helicopter. Then we saw another ambulance come to the scene. All of this was happening on the other side of Cavanaugh's, where the landing field is. This is also where the helicopters were.

Dinner was nice. The whole time we were eating we shared ideas of what the whole medical emergency was. Our best guesses were that there was a boating accident or a jet ski accident, or maybe a jet ski hit a boat.

Mom has been thinking of interviewing Papa, and she needs to do it soon, she says, before he gets worse. She wants to know some more things about Papa and his life. Mom is figuring out how to do the interview. I am planning on having some stories from the interview written in the journal, to remember. I might also add Marty-isms, and explain what a Marty-ism is. Marty is Papa's name.

Tay caught a toad today. Mom and I wanted to show Wilson the toad, to see how he would react. I don't think he has seen a toad before, maybe not a frog, either. Tay and Dad didn't like that idea, so we didn't show Wilson the toad. Since we have recently been naming the animals we see around here, we called this one Hoppy. Which is directly related to his hopping ability.

Hoppy has prompted me to make a list of all of the animals that we have seen on this trip. Many of the animals we have never seen before in person, like the jackrabbit.

- Squirrel (Chippy)
- Bear
- Moose (Dad saw the moose earlier)
- Horse (Tay thought it was a bear at first)
- Cow
- Jackrabbit
- Toad (Hoppy, specifically, is a western toad)
- Bald eagle
- Osprey
- Deer
- Golden eagle
- Smallmouth bass
- Lake Trout
- Great Dane (Winston is the Shuster's Great Dane)

411

- Wasps
- Fire ants
- Bugs and spiders
- Bat

A few of these animals I haven't written about. Like the lake trout. These are the massive fish, the megalodons. John says that the fish are invasive, and they aren't good. He also said that if we catch them again, we shouldn't throw them back in the water because the lake trout are bad for the other fish.

I also can't believe that I haven't talked about Winston. Winston is John and Dawn's dog. Wilson loves being with Winston. Winston is a big dog, being a Great Dane. He's nice. He and Wilson get along well. It's awesome that Wilson made a friend on the trip.

Saturday, July 17, 2021

The upstairs, where I sleep, is a mess of clothes. I need to clean that up soon. Tomorrow we are leaving the lake and driving to Sandpoint to visit Gammy and Paw-Paw.

Sunday, July 18, 2021 – Wednesday, July 21, 2021

These three days we spent in Sandpoint. We stayed at a place called Dover. We swam in Lake Pend Oreille, and we were caught off guard when we found out it got deep quickly. We were so used to Priest Lake that it was bizarre for us.

There was a pool and a hot tub, but we didn't go because it was a maize to get to and it was difficult to get out of the pool. There was a very specific way to get in and out, which was confusing why they made it so difficult to get in.

We went to Dub's for ice cream again. We went there the last time we went to Sandpoint, but this time we didn't wear masks, which was obviously very nice.

Speaking of masks, COVID cases are now going up again! The reason that the cases are going up is because there is a more dangerous variant to the original COVID variant. The Delta variant is stronger against the vaccine, which is also scary. While the Delta variant is now around, almost all of the deaths are reported as unvaccinated people.

Going to Dover was a great transition from the A frame. The plumbing was better, we actually had a TV, and the place didn't have cobwebs on the roof.

412

Tay and I looked forward to the drive home. We both like long drives because we try to take a nap and just listen to music. And there is plenty of candy. We drove back to Bellingham on the twenty-first. That was Mom and Dad's twentieth wedding anniversary! On the drive home, I counted that there were three different places that we stopped where there was a Starbucks next to a Taco Del Mar restaurant.

When we got home, the grass was dead because of all the sun. It was alive when we left, but the heat just killed it that quickly. Mom's plants were all alive. A neighbor watered them for Mom while she was gone.

When we got home, the most surprising thing was at the front door. The front door was actually what was surprising. It was shattered but still intact! Almost all of the front door is glass, and the main section was shattered, but not broken. The glass was shattered but still all connected, which is probably because a thin layer of plastic protecting it held it together. Nothing was stolen, and we aren't even sure that it was a person that caused it. It's possible the reason was the heat wave was too much for the door to handle, which also doesn't make sense because none of the other windows or other doors were broken. It's a mystery!

Thursday, July 22, 2021
Today we went to Western's track. I ran three miles, or twelve laps around the track. I am trying to get in shape for cross country in the fall. I am planning on doing cross country when the school year starts. For eleven of the twelve laps, I had a cramp from running. So, eleven out of twelve laps weren't enjoyable. Dad says that it gets better once I run on a regular basis. So, I am planning on running more. I'm motivated to get prepared for XC in the fall!

Friday, July 23, 2021
Today Dad taped the door and wrote a note on the front door that says, "Broken glass: please don't knock." Which I think is funny because the glass is pretty noticeable and it would take a pretty unintelligent person to knock on the door. Tomorrow the Olympics start. Which is great. Remember, the Olympics were postponed earlier because of COVID, but now.

Today we got Taylor soccer stuff and we also got new clothes because school is coming up soon. I can't wait for school; it will be eighteen months since I have seen my friends. We also went to Millwork Supply to find a new door because the old door is beyond repair. The funny thing about getting a new door is Mom has talked about wanting a new front door for years. So, we joked that Mom paid someone to break the door.

Saturday, July 24, 2021
Not much happened today. Something I haven't written about is that there is a new house being built across the street from the pond. The builders are loud. I am very impressed with the progress that they have made in such little time. The builders have already cleared out all of the woods where the house is going to be built.

Tuesday, July 27, 2021
We were *so* close, so close to finishing the pandemic. The numbers have gone back up, and the Delta variant is pushing the pandemic cases back up, 81,000 in the US today. The unvaccinated make up 99 percent of the cases. The CDC is now saying wear masks again in "high risk" indoor areas, no matter if you are vaccinated. This means that if this guideline still stands by the time school starts, we will have to wear masks at school.

Today Tay went to soccer practice, and Dad and I went to the co-op and got lemonade, apples, and a bag of chips. When Dad was driving, we saw a homeless person walking down the street, and one of his arms was gone. I thought of all the things that I have driven past.

Wednesday, July 28, 2021
Today Mom and Dad's family friends, the Nymans, came over for a bonfire. Leo, who is going to be a senior this year, also came over. We explored around with Leo and found this really bright orange feather. I looked it up but couldn't find out what type of bird it was. I don't remember ever seeing a bird that was so bright orange around the house before.

The Nymans' know the Bellingham High School swim coach, and they said that he's a great coach and that I should swim this year. I have already been thinking about it, after swimming with Mom at Sudden Valley and at Priest Lake. Leo has been a swimmer for Sehome, another high school. He said that he had a lot of fun being on the swim team.

Friday, July 30, 2021 – Saturday, July 31, 2021
Taylor had an out-of-town soccer tournament today. We all came to watch him, and the tournament takes more than one day to complete. So far, Taylor's team has won every game that they have played. It looks like they are going to go to the championship game!

Watching Taylor play soccer is fun, but it also makes me miss playing soccer, it's been so long. Soccer for the high school is in the spring, so I'm going to wait a little before playing soccer again. I think that other sports like XC or swimming will be fun too. Mostly, being on a sports team again will be fun.

Sunday, August 1, 2021
Taylor and his soccer team made it to the finals of the tournament. The game was close the whole time, and by the end of the game the two teams were tied. So, they went into a penalty shootout. They lost. The shootout was close too, but the other team did a little bit better.

Monday, August 2, 2021
With the Delta variant on the rise, and masks coming back on, it is easy to dismiss a big milestone that has been considered really important since the vaccines were given to the public. Fauci said that once 70 or 80 percent of America got vaccinated, things would go back to normal. Well, today it got to 70 percent, and even though it seems like things are getting worse with a lot of people vaccinated, it looks like COVID will end eventually. Right now, it seems like COVID is here to stay for a while. I had never thought that there could be variants of COVID and that the virus could mutate to become more resistant to the vaccine. With variants of COVID now around, all of this seems scarier.

Tuesday, August 3, 2021 — Wednesday, August 4, 2021
Taylor found out that one of the players on his team is going to change teams. I guess the player was already planning on switching before the tournament but wanted to do the last tournament with them. The player was really good. At first when I heard the news, I thought it may have been because they lost the tournament, but it wasn't.

Tay and I remembered that Fantasy Football is coming up soon! So, we went on the ESPN website and did mock Fantasy Football drafts, where you can plan and think about Fantasy Football and what players might get chosen and when. I think this year I might actually win. I am coming up with good strategies for drafting.

Tay, Dad, and I all went to Clearwater Creek to go fly fishing. The fish were alive here, and we each caught one fish. When I was walking on one of the rocks to get to a new section to try fishing there, I slipped and fell into the creek, which at first was shocking, but then I really enjoyed it. Dad also jumped in after I said how great and refreshing it was.

Thursday, August 5, 2021

Tay and I have continued planning for Fantasy Football. I have a good plan for what I want to do with the draft. Today there was a thunderstorm, and there was also a sunset. Wilson doesn't get nervous when it comes to thunderstorms, because when he was little the breeders would bang pans on purpose to get the puppies used to loud noises, like thunderstorms or fireworks.

The sunset was even more beautiful than the smoky one at Priest Lake. From our house there is barely much sunset that we can see, because of the trees. The best spot to see the sunset is from my room. It was wonderful that there was both a thunderstorm and a great sunset on the same day.

Today I went running again, and I beat my previous time. Getting a personal record (PR) is an amazing feeling every time, for anything in life. Today was hot, so the running felt very difficult, and worse than last time I ran.

I also had an orthotics appointment today, and I got new orthotics because I grew out of the old ones. I don't wear my orthotics for running, but for walking and just being in my shoes. I also don't use orthotics when playing soccer because there is no way that the orthotics can fit in the soccer shoes, which are very tight and small shoes.

Friday, August 6, 2021 – Saturday, August 14, 2021

I started getting back into juggling with a soccer ball. At the beginning of the summer my record was 32 or 34, and now I beat my PR and I got 198! My goal is to get to 200 by the end of the summer. Taylor has had a better juggling record than mine for the longest time. Now that I beat his record, he has started doing a lot of juggling. I don't think that he thought I would beat his record. His record is in the 180s.

On Monday we went to the All Comers Track & Field Meet. We have never gone to the All Comers Track & Field Meet, but basically, it's fun events for all ages, from elementary schoolers to grandparents. Taylor wanted to race, but I just went to cheer him on. Taylor got second place in one of his track events. I left with Mom a little later, and then when Tay and Dad got home, they told us that they couldn't find one of Taylor's events, out of the three he signed up for.

While Taylor was running, I was in the Civic Field stands reading a new book, *Slaughterhouse-Five*. When I started reading it, I wasn't very into it, but it has gotten better as I read it more. Dad says that it's a classic. One of the books that we got at the Priest Lake Mall was a collection of the author's commencement speeches. I liked that book. "So it goes." That might be one of my favorite book quotes. I like how it's simple but really is a true quote. So it goes, life goes on, stuff happens. I should use that quote more.

The first preseason Seahawks game happened. They played the Raiders, who is Papa's all-time favorite team. Papa was looking forward to the game. He loves the Raiders; his garage has many flags and posters of the Raiders. But he is from Seattle, so he has said that the Seahawks are his second favorite team. Mom thinks that Papa only has a few weeks left to live. Now he has a hospital bed in his house. The Raiders won, but the Seahawks defensive line looks much better.

Sunday, August 15, 2021

Today Mom and I went lap swimming at the Sudden Valley pool. At the end of the lap swimming, we decided to do a race. Just one length of the pool. I think we tied, and Mom said she was going her hardest. Mom thinks that I won. I think eventually I will beat her in a race, but right now I'm pretty sure we're tied. If we did a long-distance race though, Mom would definitely beat me.

Also, today we washed Mom's car. There is another heat wave here, and even though it isn't as hot as it was in Idaho, we stay inside in the middle of the day, when it's the hottest.

Recently I watched *Old School* and *Step Brothers*. Mom said that I could watch a few R rated movies a few days ago, so I have. I think both of these movies are way funnier than almost all PG-13 movies. I don't know why.

Jamal Adams, the safety that the Seahawks got in a trade with the Jets, is holding out for a new contract now. It's really important that the Seahawks sign him to a new contract because they traded so much draft capital to the Jets for him, and if they don't sign him, it wouldn't have been worth the trade. A news report came out that the Seahawks are not going to sign him and are planning on using a franchise tag on him for two years. I don't know how reliable the news report is, but I hope it isn't true.

Monday, August 16, 2021 – Tuesday, August 17, 2021

Mom had to go to work today. Later in the day she texted Dad that the hospice nurse that is taking care of Papa thinks he only has a few hours. It was difficult for Mom to get out of her shift at Hospice House, but she got out of work early. When Mom came home, she was thinking about what she should do, and the next day she got a flight out of Bellingham to San Jose.

Mom, as a hospice nurse, has tried to help her mom and dad a ton, but I think it is also putting a lot of stress and frustration on her, because some things are difficult. I feel so bad for Mickey. I don't know what she is going to do when he dies. She's been with him for so long.

Tuesday, August 24, 2021

Mom came home from California after a week because she couldn't stay down there forever. She spent time being with Papa and with her family. It turned out that he wasn't hours from passing when the hospice nurse called her, but before Mom left, she said her goodbyes to Papa because she won't see him again.

Dad and Mom went on a bike ride early in the morning. They went for a while, and Mom was planning on going back earlier than Dad. She came back before Dad did. She talked about how the hill to get home after the bike ride is difficult, and when she was living in Fairhaven it was all flat, making it easy to go for a while without dreading the end of the ride.

Mom and I went swimming. We did the same thing that we usually did. Mom said that before we got in, we could just relax and pretend we were in Hawaii. It kind of worked. When we were done swimming, we got a pack of gum.

After that we had lunch, and Dad and I went up on the trails on a three-mile run. Dad said we went faster than the last time, which is always awesome. At the turn-around point, I tied my shoes back up, partially so that I didn't trip on my laces, partially because I wanted a breather.

When we got back, Wilson greeted us, grabbing one of his toys. When I was getting a glass of water, I saw Mom on the back patio. I wanted to tell her about my new time. Mom seemed like usual, but as we went inside, she told me that Papa just passed. She said that everything went right, and someone was there when he died. Amy, Steve's wife, was by his side when he passed away.

Mom must have been thankful that it was going to be okay, and that nothing bad had happened. I gave her a hug, and all four of us sat in the basement. We remembered, asked questions, and wanted to be there for Mom. When we were in the basement, Mom revisited the past. I listened to her. Tay talked more. Dad wanted to be there for her.

The next few days we looked at old pictures and got to know more about Papa's life, who he was. Mom cried, I could tell, but not when Tay and I were around.

Thursday, August 26, 2021

Bellingham High School is farther away than Geneva Elementary and Kulshan Middle School. Geneva is just down the street, and Kulshan is less than five minutes away. Bellingham High is more like a ten-minute drive. We haven't timed the drive yet, which we are planning on doing on the first day of school, and I'll organize my time to get ready for school based on how long it takes to get there.

Mom was convinced that I should bring a backpack and a lunch box to the freshman orientation, which I wasn't going to do. There was really nothing saying that we needed to bring either, but I did tell her I would drink plenty of water before we went, to stay hydrated. I was planning on having a big breakfast, but I wasn't craving food. I knew I didn't feel nervous, but my mind, unconsciously, was tense.

When I got out of the car, my mind was scanning for my friends. It had been so long since I had seen so many. Wendy saw us and pointed out where my friend Logan was. I caught up with him. The last time I saw him was last summer. More and more people came out of cars, waiting outside. Everyone was looking around for their friends, like I had.

When the time came to go inside, the principal asked for us to go into the gym and for the parents to move to a different room, where the parent meeting would be. Before they were all set, we just stood at the entrance, waiting. Now I was seeing more and more people I knew. Everyone appeared similar to their pre-COVID selves, which was a relief. I was expecting people to be different.

When we went toward the doors to the gym, there was a line of older students who would be touring us around the school. They cheered at us, like we had accomplished something great.

There were tables with letters for our last name, and we were told to go pick our name tag up and go into the bleachers. The new name for the mascot, to be more politically correct, is the Bayhawks. Except all of the decorations on the walls still sported the old "Red Raider" logo.

All of the familiar friends that I had flocked to sat in the same area of the bleachers. We laughed and re-remembered each other. The teachers said things, nothing new or useful to anyone in the bleachers. They had us do team building exercises and split us into groups where we would go into a classroom and do more team building, in an attempt to meet new people. We got a tour of the place, then we went back into the gym. The High School people said old things we had already heard, and then released us for lunch. Lunch was cheese pizza. I'm thankful it was from a pizza place instead of school food.

After orientation, I went with some other people exploring the building and outside, and then it was time to go home. Mom, Dad, and Tay wanted to know more about what had happened while I was at orientation, but so much was filled with teachers saying nothing new, that I didn't have much to report.

Conclusion

My last journal entry was in August 2021. The collection of journal entries spanned over a year and a half. In between the first and last journal entry, I had grown so much and gained a tremendous amount of knowledge and learning experiences, as well as fun times. I can easily say that the pandemic changed me forever.

Even though the journaling mostly ended in November, COVID did not. In November 2021 alone, there was an additional two and a half million cases of COVID. There were also new variants of the virus that emerged. The Delta variant became the dominate variant of coronavirus in summer 2021 (WebMD) and was written about briefly in journal entries. The Delta variant was more contagious than other variants of COVID. It traveled quicker and became a concern. Also, variants were nicknamed by the World Health Organization as a different Greek letter. There were other variants of coronavirus like Alpha, Beta, Gamma. Delta was first discovered in India before it invaded the United States.

Then the Omicron variant became the dominate variant. In December 2021, Omicron caused the biggest number of cases per day in the United States. The Omicron variant was both very contagious and less severe. So, while Omicron skyrocketed to unpreceded cases per day, there wasn't much panic about it, already being vaccinated. With boosters available and more mild symptoms, there was still an indoor mask mandate, but Omicron wasn't terrifying for me. Omicron changed how COVID was thought about. At least, that's what I believe.

Booster COVID shots were administered to protect people even more, as it became evident that the effectiveness of the vaccines decreased over time. Boosters became officially available for adults in November. Mom and Dad both got boosted soon after. Boosters also became available for kids twelve and over on January 5, 2022. Tay and I got boosted.

On March 12, 2022, Washington State ended its mask mandate, which allowed people to not wear masks in indoor places like schools, stores, and restaurants. Masks were only still required in public transit and healthcare facilities. So, starting on Monday, March 14, 2022, Tay and I went to school not wearing a mask for the first time! I feel that it's ironic that masks came off almost exactly two years after in person school ended on March 13, 2020.

To conclude, I consider the journaling project complete. I journaled through most of the pandemic, I learned a lot, and I recorded most of it. The journaling will forever be kept in memory. Even when I forget what happened in 2020 and 2021, I'll be able to look back at my past.

I also hope that this journaling will provide information for generations that either were too young to remember what they lived through or the future generations that were born after the pandemic. What I believe will truly mark this assignment successful is the memory that will forever be stored in these pages. This journal is a tribute to the unique years that the virus presented to the entire world, and its memory that will be protected forever.

Cody Watts

Appendix
Covid Graphing

Graphs on daily cases and daily deaths for the United States (March 2020–June 28, 2022)

Source: John Hopkins University School of Medicine

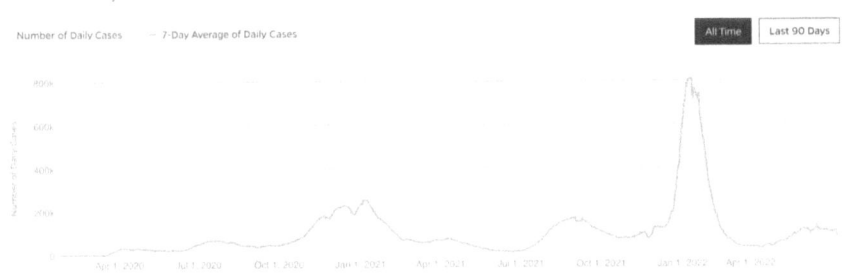

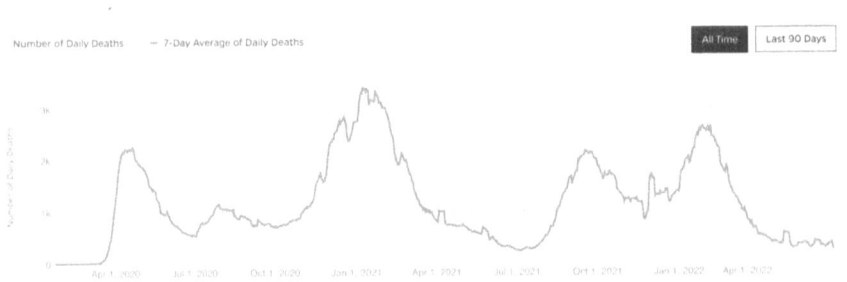